"One hell of a story!"

> — *Sir Sean Connery*
> *Actor*

"This is Europe's secret story."

> — *Vaclav Havel*
> *President of the Czech Republic*

"That villain haunts me yet."

> — *Miroslav Hermann*
> *Consul-General Czech Republic*

"Now you know what really happened."

> — *Alexander Kerensky*
> *Last Prime Minister of Monarchical Russia*

"The characters are believable and, God knows, the events covered are of terrific historical importance. The dialogue rings true, and I found that the plotting, with its swings of triumph and disaster, kept me turning the pages."

> — *Douglas Gibson*
> *President, McClelland & Stewart Publishing*

"Through the tumultuous times of war and the Russian Revolution, follow the heroes and their uncertain paths from war to peace. A great read."

> — *Sue Carscallen*
> *Author of* A Countess in Limbo

"It is impossible to read *In the Company of Heroes* without *Dr. Zhivago* coming to mind. As with Boris Pasternak's novel, or the classic movie from the 1960s, Hunt's book is also a grand and sweeping tale of war, revolution, love, ambition and betrayal played out from the luxury of St. Petersburg to the great steppes and snowy wastes of Imperial Russia. Hunt's book is no mere clone of the better-known tale; it is based on two true, fascinating, romantic and exciting stories. An enjoyable read."

— ForeWord Reviews

"An adventurous historical novel set in Central Europe during World War I, *In the Company of Heroes* by Canadian author Ted Hunt is the result of meticulous research from a private collection of War Department memorabilia at the University of Washington. The novel tells the incredible — and true — story of several individuals whose lives were wrapped up in the tumultuous events of the war and how they were altered forever as a result. *In the Company of Heroes* has been recommended personally by Vaclav Havel, among others. It is certainly one of the most fascinating accounts of 20th century Czech history written in recent memory."

— The Prague Post

In the Company of Heroes

In the Company of Heroes

Ted Hunt

GRANVILLE ISLAND
PUBLISHING
www.granvilleislandpublishing.com

Library and Archives Canada Cataloguing in Publication

Hunt, Ted, author
    In the company of heroes / Ted Hunt.

Originally published in 2011.
ISBN 978-1-926991-18-4 (pbk.)

    1. World War, 1914–1918—Fiction. 2. Russia (Federation)—History—Revolution, 1917–1921—Fiction. I. Title.

PS8615.U684I6 2013   C813'.6   C2013-902758-0

Editor: Renate Preuss
Book designer: Omar Gallegos
Cover artwork: Sandy Wang

Granville Island Publishing Ltd.
212 – 1656 Duranleau St. Granville Island
Vancouver, BC, Canada V6H 3S4

604-688-0320 / 1-877-688-0320
info@granvilleislandpublishing.com
www.granvilleislandpublishing.com

Printed in Canada on recycled paper

This book is dedicated to brave men and women from every nation who have been, over the centuries, forced by the failure of politicians and the greed of governments into the madness of war.

CONTENTS

PREFACE

While studying for a PhD in history at the University of Washington, I was offered the first opportunity to view a collection of World War I memorabilia that had been sequestered for fifty years. Searching through this historical treasure chest, I was privy to diaries, war memoranda, secret orders, letters and eyewitness accounts from 1914 to 1920 — the turbulent years encompassing WWI, Lenin's Revolution, the Red and White Civil War, and the little-known War of the Interventionists wherein USA, Britain and France secretly invaded Russia to thwart Bolshevism.

This factual story of love and escape is complex, and at times challenging to popular views, but every situation is accurately framed within well-researched historiography. Personal anecdotes, as incredible as they may seem, have been authenticated.

The novel has been reviewed by Czech authorities, including President Vaclav Havel, Consul-General Miroslav Hermann and author Jan Drabek, as well as Dr. Stephan Payne and Dr. James McNaughton, both US Military historians from the Monterey Language Institute.

This new printing of *In the Company of Heroes* has been expanded from the first edition by the addition of the compelling story of Major Markus Adler, the fictitious name of the very real young German officer who helped Grand Duchess Marie escape Lenin's purge of the Romanov family.

The only fiction in this novel lies with the three main characters, who are composites. All others are presented accurately: Masaryk, Lenin, Trotsky, Kerensky, Churchill, President Wilson, Grand Duchess Marie, Czar Nicholas, Generals Gaida, Syrovy, Kechek and Graves, and Admiral Kolchak. The repercussions of their actions still resonate in the twenty-first century.

More details of this long-suppressed story came to light from interviews with Alexander Kerensky, the last elected prime minister of Czarist Russia; Vaclav Havel, president of the Czech Republic;

Miroslav Hermann, consul-general; Jan Drabek, Czech author; Dr. Lister Rogers, from Stanford University; Dr. Stephan Payne and Dr. James McNaughton, US Military historians from the Monterey Presidio and Defense Language Institute.

Constant encouragement over twenty-five years of research came from Jack Hodgins, distinguished author; Douglas Gibson, president of McClelland & Stewart; Ray Hall, University of British Columbia; Tom Locke, advisor; publisher Jo Blackmore and her professional team at Granville Island Publishing; Sandy Wang, who painted the cover scene; and Helen Stewart Hunt, long-suffering wife and friend.

SAN FRANCISCO
AUTUMN 1988

Katherine Kazakova walked carefully across her penthouse patio to look out over San Francisco Bay shimmering in the morning sun. Just a bit unsteady, she took a firm grip on the railing; since her last birthday, the height from the nineteenth floor made her nervous. No matter, the view was worth it. Out to sea past the Golden Gate Bridge, wind from the endless rows of white-capped waves filled her lungs with fresh salt air and ruffled her favorite robe. It was cut from black silk and a thick line of gold embroidery tracked every edge.

"I know you've got pull, but how'd you get the jeweler to deliver on Sunday morning?" Natasha asked while placing three black velvet cases on the glass-topped table. "He wanted you to know . . . he's cleaned them all, and checked the clasps."

Thank you, dear . . . just an old friend," was all Katherine would say. She watched Natasha go back into the kitchen before sitting down to open each slender case and checking the name inside. From the first case, she removed a necklace with a coin dangling from a sturdy gold chain. She smiled to see the glint of the sharply etched Russian eagle on the back of this perfect twenty-five ruble gold piece. Then, with a practiced move, she slipped the chain over her stylishly cut white hair. Taking the coin in her hand, she began to stare contentedly at the solemn visage of Nicholas Romanov, the last czar of Imperial Russia.

"Babushka, breakfast," Natasha called, carrying a tray across the patio.

Katherine came out of her reverie to sit tall while Natasha poured tea. She took the coin in her palm again. "This will be yours one day," Katherine said with a matter-of-fact tone.

"Baba, don't talk like that. You know it upsets me."

"I only wanted you to know about the necklaces. They are priceless, after all."

Natasha finished pouring the tea before answering. "But you've never told me anything about them. Where'd they come from?"

The grandmother smoothed imagined wrinkles from her robe before asking, "How are things at the restaurant?"

Natasha smiled at the obvious dodge, but instead of arguing, merely answered. "Great as always. Regulars are afraid to miss their daily fix of news from the old country. The Balalaika's a gold mine."

"Good. See that it stays that way . . . the best on Russian Hill."

Natasha nodded as she put scrambled eggs on a gilt-edged forest-green plate. "You didn't answer my question about the necklaces. What's the matter . . . you didn't steal them, did you?"

The old woman looked away before answering. "Not really."

Natasha stopped serving and turned with wide eyes. "Not really? Oh my God . . . Babushka. What does that mean — not really?"

Just then a middle-aged woman in a terry-towel robe came out onto the patio with a mug of coffee and a cigarette. "Go ahead, Mama. Tell her about old Russia. Perhaps then she'll understand why Russians hate Americans, and why we don't trust Gorbachev, or Yeltsin, or Putin, or any of their Glasnost overtures — even if they are getting their troops out of Afghanistan."

Katherine's lips went tight. "Irena, I do not wish to–"

Natasha broke in. "Not now, Mother."

"Well, if she told you . . . you could tell me. She's never spilled the beans to anyone. One would expect her to tell her own daughter."

Natasha watched her mother retreat to the kitchen. She saw the grandmother's agitation, and sat down to take her hand gently. "Baba, if you don't tell me about you and Grandad, . . . who will?"

Irena's voice called from the kitchen. "There are things Natasha should know, Mama. You'll have to tell her sometime."

Katherine looked out to sea, still clutching the necklace. After a pause she whispered, "It would take too long. Your uncle and grandfather will be here any minute."

"Golfing at Olympic Club? They won't be back 'til after lunch." Natasha gently stroked her grandmother's fingers whispering, "What was it like back then?"

Katherine hunched her shoulders, but her eyes shone. "Wonderful," she answered slowly, "and terrifying. When I was your age, my life was filled with heroes . . . like your grandfather . . . and there were remarkable men on both sides of the barbed wire."

CHAPTER 1

KIEV
JULY 1914

Just a few days after her twenty-first birthday, Katherine Kazakova rode in a closed carriage down Shevchenko Boulevard toward the railroad station. There was a glow on her face as she looked out across the gardens and flowering chestnut trees sweeping down to the Dnieper River. She realized that there could be no city more beautiful than Kiev.

For a while she was content with this summer scene and the clattering hooves, but then the domed roof of the station came into view, and with sudden clarity she understood that by getting on the train to St. Petersburg, she could be making a terrible mistake: leaving friends, leaving home, leaving her father. She sat back to think it through, but hardly a moment had passed before she reminded herself that a Royal Appointment was the opportunity of a lifetime, and not something one could defer.

She watched her father check his vest pocket watch before reaching up to rap on the roof. "There's plenty of time, Papa," she said, staying his hand. "Let's enjoy it. Do you like my new suit?"

"Perfect," he said with a quiet smile. "Navy blue, almost obligatory for business, and it shows off golden hair so well."

Katya held his hand until the carriage pulled up to the main entrance. A porter opened the door and Papa stepped out quickly. "I must get a paper, Katya. Meet me at the gate."

Katya watched him hurry toward a kiosk while the porter took her bags. She frowned at the headlines: ASSASSINATION IN SARAJEVO! FANATIC SHOOTS ARCHDUKE FERDINAND AND WIFE.

Recent tensions had taken a nasty turn. She knew that Archduchess Sophia was with child. Tragic! Nevertheless, she tightened her lips determinedly and followed the porter into a waiting-room busy with soldiers carrying kit bags toward the gate for the far platform. A clock high on the wall showed five minutes past eight as she worked her way toward the marble counter. With a nod she accepted her ticket, then pushed back through the crowd to the first-class entrance.

There was her father waiting beside a chalkboard bearing the message: EXPRESS TO ST. PETERSBURG. FRIDAY, JULY 29, 1914. 8:15 A.M. He looked wonderful in his smartly tailored clothes she thought, but she could also see his anguish. His eyes squinted with worry as he broke the silence, "I wish you would reconsider, Katya. War is very close."

With a shake of her head, Katya presented her ticket to the attendant then moved through the gate to the platform and the waiting train. "We've planned this for too long, Papa. I won't let a career slip away just because Germany and Austria rattle sabers at the rest of Europe."

It was cooler as they walked under the platform's arched roof. High above them, windows stained with soot diminished the power of the sun, which speckled down onto flat-bed cars loaded with artillery pieces.

"What a marvel that you arranged the appointment . . . and to have Grand Duchess Marie as my confidante — unbelievable."

A flicker of pleasure crossed his face. "Never forget the power of connections," he advised while watching the porter stow the luggage.

"They'll see what I can do by myself."

He nodded. "I wish your mother were here."

"I know. I miss her too," Katya said as she slipped the porter some money.

"I would prefer you to leave the gratuity to me," he complained.

She brushed his lapels. "Sometimes bankers don't give enough," she said softly. "When will I see you again? We're both alone now."

Her father's emotions welled up as a whistle blew. "In God's good time," he managed to say. "Young men will crowd your day."

"Not until I establish myself."

"Your mother would be so proud . . . the first woman to serve in the Czar's Treasury. What a singular honor." His eyes shone with tears.

Not wanting to see him break down in public, Katya kissed him quickly, then stepped into the compartment just as doors up and down the platform began to slam shut. When the whistle blew again, and the train crept slowly away, she waved until her father was out of sight, then she pulled on the leather strap to close the window.

Looking out through her reflection she watched a tear thread its way down her cheek. "I'll get you to Petersburg, Papa," she whispered. "It's where we both belong."

. . .

Two long days later, Katya entered a richly carpeted office in the Treasury Building. A portrait of Czar Nicholas dominated the wall. Mr. Ordinov, Chairman of the National Treasury Board, was formally dressed in pinstriped pants and a swallow-tailed coat. He removed a pince-nez before striding around from behind the desk to offer his hand. "Ah, Miss Kazakova, this is a pleasure. So, this is the little girl who haunted her father's bank."

Katya smiled while accepting his handshake.

"I greatly admire your father. He taught you well . . . Just arrived?"

"Yes, sir. I found my room in the staff apartments then hurried over. I've been looking forward to this. Please call me Katya."

Ordinov frowned uncomfortably. "Hmm. We would best keep this professional. Not a whisper of favoritism."

"Of course," Katya replied, stepping back and looking at the floor.

Ordinov took a key from a vest pocket and walked to his private elevator. "I should show you the vault and the scope of your task before I get back to some rather urgent budget items. You will meet your colleagues during our regular Monday meeting."

"Thank you, sir."

Katya entered the brass elevator and stood beside Ordinov while he secured the folding door. A steady hum began as they descended.

With a slight turn of his head, he glanced in her direction. "How did you ever manage to secure the Grand Duchess as your mentor?"

"Father is a distant cousin," Katya said self-consciously, "and I am close to her age."

Ordinov nodded. "But you, like me . . . not to the manor born?"

Katya shook her head, feeling her face flush.

At the bottom floor they stepped out into a massive room with a floor of polished cement. The air was cool under the high ceiling. Ordinov nodded toward a castle-like door of oaken planks wrapped with iron straps which formed the far wall. "We have our own train tunnel beyond that door. Sentries are on duty around the clock." Ordinov gestured to the side. "The vaults are over here."

With a key, Ordinov entered a steel cage containing work tables. Two carpenters in coveralls looked up. "This is Miss Kazakova, our new actuary and member of the Accounting Board," he said. "Georgi here has been with me for twenty-five years. Boris, eighteen."

"Good morning," Katya said, as she shook each weathered hand. The men removed caps, bowing low.

As Ordinov swung open one of the barred doors and stepped into the first vault, Katya was immediately overwhelmed by the size of the depository. Golden ingots were stacked in rows, chest high and the width of a double-arm reach. They ran the length of the cavernous storehouse like miniature Walls of China. She stared, shaking her head.

Ordinov broke her reverie. "Beautiful, is it not? Two hundred and thirty tonnes."

"Breathtaking. And those?" she asked, pointing to the nut-brown cases on sturdy shelves at each wall.

"I'll show you. Georgi and Boris make them. Can you feel the dowel under the edge? Pull it toward you."

Katya reached up and pulled. The side turned down flat to reveal two columns of gold ingots stacked five high.

Ordinov looked pleased. "Clever, is it not? The other side is the same, so it is very easy to check the twenty ingots before seals are applied. Silver is over here."

Ordinov took her into a second vault where a similar arrangement for one hundred and seventy tonnes of silver ingots sat stacked in walls across the cave-like room. "It's going to take a lot of cases to store the ingots on shelves," Katya said. "Why not leave them here on the cement floor?"

"Just a cautionary measure . . ." Ordinov became slightly more formal, Katya thought, as he began again. "In the unlikely case we are ever forced to withdraw . . . of course the public must never hear about our precautions . . . and I certainly don't have to remind you of the need for secrecy — nor of your oath to the Czar. It's just that

I believe it would be prudent for us to admit that we are close to the sea . . . and Germany's navy."

Katya felt him watching her closely as they moved on to the next vault, a much smaller room where mahogany boxes covered a central table. Ordinov raised a lid to reveal squares of light yellow metal. "Seventy thousand wafers of pure platinum. The veiled treasure of the Urals, we call it. You are to take responsibility for this department."

Katya looked up quickly.

"I know, I know. Your specialty is foreign currency, but platinum's role could be very significant one day. Just be thankful that it is much lighter than gold to move."

Katya followed Ordinov into the last vault where the crown jewels were kept in glass cabinets. Leather pouches, each one tagged and numbered, filled the shelves in the room. Ordinov gestured with a sweep of his hand. "Incalculable wealth in gems."

Katya silently drank in the sight which few would ever be so privileged to see.

As they walked back to the elevator, she could feel Ordinov watching her again. He wanted to say something, she was sure. Finally he cleared his throat. "It is a great honor, I believe, to be entrusted with the tangible wealth of one's nation. However, it goes without saying that we must never discuss our work."

Katya looked him in the eye and nodded solemnly.

Back in his office, Ordinov held open the door to the anteroom with a slight bow. "And now, Miss Kazakova, my secretary has an office ready for you. Tomorrow there is church and a day of rest. Staff meeting, Monday at eight. Good day."

*   *   *

On Sunday morning Katya sat by her second floor window looking down on the courtyard between staff residences and the Winter Palace as she waited for Grand Duchess Marie to call. Katya could scarcely believe it: the Grand Duchess as her guide — certainly an indication that a lifetime career had been launched. At least that's the way it seemed on such a promising morning. Soon she would find a way to bring Papa to St. Petersburg; that would be wonderful.

Now here was the twenty-five-year-old Grand Duchess hurrying across the courtyard, balancing a large brimmed hat with one hand

and throwing a plait of black hair over her shoulder with the other. Katya smiled to recall that the Grand Duchess had just recently been fined twenty-five rubles for smoking a cigarette in public; she had also been criticized in the newspapers for wearing men's pants while skiing.

There was a sharp rapping on the door.

"Katherine Kazakova! Hurry, Katya. We'll be late."

Katya ran down the stairs and out into the sunshine. "Here I am, Your Highness." She had dressed with care in a frock the color of a yellow rose, a color so delicate that when the sun touched it, it seemed almost white, like the platinum in the vault. "Grand Duchess Marie," she said with a curtsy.

"It's Marie. You may call me Marie in private," the Duchess instructed. "Katya, in that dress you are the very personification of summer."

"Thank you . . . Marie," she replied, feeling a blush.

Marie stepped back to display her own dress, which had rows of pearls embedded from shoulder to shoulder across the bodice. These descending loops formed an opalescent triangle from neck to mid-torso. "It's a bit much, don't you think?" the Grand Duchess asked as she started toward the far side of the courtyard. A uniformed guard waited beside an iron gate set solidly into a brick wall twice his height.

Falling into step, Katya smiled. "Not for a Sunday . . . Marie."

She accepted Marie's outstretched hand, a friendly squeeze made her laugh, and together they ran through the courtyard gate past the starched guard and out into the square in front of the Palace. There she stopped, amazed at the size of the crowd standing patiently in the massive square concentrating their attention on the central balcony.

It was then that she noticed people at the edge of the crowd stepping aside to make way when they recognized the Grand Duchess. Men removed their hats and women curtsied. Katya saw that this politeness was acknowledged by the Duchess with an occasional unsmiling nod, but it must have been clear to everyone that politeness was the least Marie expected.

An elderly man with snow-white hair bowed with a sweep of his arm while Katya was led into the space provided. "Close enough," Marie said.

Katya scanned the gaily colored banners hanging limp from every gas lamp against the cloudless sky. She could feel the tension of place and time. The Admiralty and the War Ministry Offices stood solidly by, just across the square — monuments to authority which seemed to be hovering close to the ultimate source of power: the Winter Palace.

Not being familiar with procedure on such occasions, Katya was confused when the crowd suddenly, as if by command, fell to its knees. She looked up to see Czar Nicholas Romanov and Czarina Alexandra on the balcony and searched their grave faces before stooping to her knees beside Marie. Then she, like the rest, clasped her hands in a position of prayer.

Trying not to appear too provincial, she watched Czar Nicholas with hidden glances, her knees feeling the granite paving stones hard beneath her summer dress. He wore a white military cap and jacket with a sky-blue sash across his chest. There were medals and gold epaulettes too, but Katya could not take her eyes from his sad face, and when he looked in her direction she felt a sudden chill.

"Beloved citizens, pray for Russia. Pray for us," she heard him say in a composed voice. "Pray for our brave soldiers." He paused to survey the huge throng as his plea echoed out toward the River Neva. "Your Czarina and I have just come from church, where we have decided, with great reluctance, that war with Germany, Austria and Hungary . . . is inevitable. We must prepare."

Katya pressed a fist against her mouth when a low moan arose from the crowd and some began to cry. She was impressed that Marie could remain so composed. For herself, she was fighting panic, fearful that her new life could disappear as magically as it had arrived. She looked up at the Czarina, who also gave the appearance of great calm. Katya now understood the title: Her Serene Majesty. Like Marie, the Czarina was confident in God, and confident in her Czar.

"Do not be afraid," Katya heard the Czar say. "God will see us through." She thought that she could feel his joyless gaze examining her face. "France and Britain stand with Russia. Together, we shall sweep this evil Teutonic Alliance from the field."

Pausing now, he seemed to struggle with words, but eventually he placed both hands on the railing and in a troubled voice began again. "We call on all our subjects, all our citizens to help. Workers. Unionists. We urge you to pull together. Russians must put aside their political differences and personal ambitions to work for the greater glory. God bless you all. God bless Russia!" He stood quite still, looking down for a while. Then solemnly he turned to offer his arm to the Czarina.

The gentleman with the white hair took this departure as a signal to rise, and begin singing "God Save The Czar." The crowd surged to its feet and Katya was quick to join the strong voices singing so fervently that the royal pair stopped and returned to the railing. Here they stood to smile lovingly down on their subjects. The Czar seemed quietly happy again, like a child calmed by a steadfast friend. The Czarina's face reflected his new composure.

Katya turned to Marie. "We can help. There must be something for us to do."

Marie looked up at the balcony where high-ranking military men had stepped in behind the royal pair. "Russia needs warriors, not those sycophants surrounding the Czar. Where shall we find men like that?"

Katya took Marie's hand and started back. "Perhaps they'll find us."

CHAPTER 2

PRAGUE
OCTOBER 1914

Prague at dawn. Alex Branda entered a park on the West Bank of the Vltava River walking beside his father with their usual energetic stride. He could feel the chill of winter in the air as patches of white mist drifted downstream. Up ahead to his right, where the sharply pointed spires of Old Town

rose darkly against an orange sky, the mist suddenly burst into a golden haze. It looked to be the start of a perfect day.

Alex enjoyed these daily treks together; his father on the way to work in the glass shop near Old Town Square, and he to Falcon House Gymnasium before classes at the university. He may have been the only son in the capital city who, despite being twenty-two years old and a little taller, was proud to be seen walking with his own father every morning. And why not? Not everyone was the son of a man the caliber of Anton Branda, president of the Falcon Athletic Association, and a man of ardent political passion who was revered throughout Prague — even throughout Bohemia. Still, Alex was confident that no one's admiration exceeded his own.

Alex had always loved the peaceful dignity of the park with its regimented rows of precisely trimmed holly hedges set in patterns designed centuries before, now bristling with frost and giving clear direction to their way. Here there was a sense of permanence that made him feel part of some great plan.

"Are you ready for that clever little center of theirs?" his father asked, as pebbles crunched on the pathway curving beneath a long line of poplars. "He'll be dangerous."

Alex forced himself to breathe normally as he thought about the man he would mark tomorrow for the National Football Cup. He nodded. "I believe I am."

"Good. Then you can win."

Alex returned his look with a smile, hoping to reduce the worry he could see pulling at small folds near his father's eyes.

Their path opened out onto Na Kampe Street one hundred metres or so from the Charles Bridge. From here, Alex could see life-sized statues looming above the river's drifting mist, standing high on pedestals built into the sturdy stone walls and framing each side of the broad walkway. This was the ancient road from Prague Castle on the West Side, winding down the hill and across the river to Old Town Square, its gas lamps still showing the way at dawn with splashes of yellow on the dark cobblestones.

Thirty Gothic ghosts stood above the walls of this bridge, black against the morning sky in eternal martyrdom against the various tyrannies that had taken their lives. Bohemian saints and Czech heroes watching the river, watching the years, watching the citizens of Prague trudge by. Alex knew that his father walked beneath their stern gaze every day, alert to the presence of these silent guardians and well aware of the special atmosphere on this bridge where the conscience of the country was preserved as a permanent vigil for the path to freedom. For himself, Alex always felt an overwhelming sense of deference as he passed beneath their frozen stare. Knowing their determination, their strength and their sacrifice, could anyone feel less?

He glanced up at the statue of Jan Nepomuk and shuddered. How could a man summon that much courage? Condemned to the stake for his love of freedom . . . burned alive by his enemies, but still shouting defiance even as he choked on the flames. Alex frowned at the thought. As a student, he had not yet earned the right to cross this bridge with pride. Perhaps though, with the cup . . .

To the west lay the graceful park near the university he loved, and to his right the river gliding by the twisted medieval streets of Old Town, but he knew it was the bridge that was his preoccupation. It was, somehow, the key to his purpose, and he hoped that one day he might be able to walk across knowing that he deserved the privilege. But even as he formed this thought, he began to shake his head. To die for one's beliefs . . . I never want to face a test like that.

At the high arched gate on the town side, red and white Austrian flags fluttered near the Empire's black eagle as a reminder to all Czechs that freedom was nothing more than a dream. That flag does not belong here, Alex thought, not near this bridge. But of course, this was part of the usual Habsburg insensitivity.

It was here on the bridge, Alex supposed, that his father daily fueled his unshakable determination to excel, and perhaps it was the nearness to these martyrs now that prompted Anton to grip Alex's arm. He waited while his father searched for words, raking fingers through a head of wiry gray hair. Staring down the two lines of statues, Anton said in a troubled voice, "Be careful today."

"I will," Alex promised, feeling awkward with his father's intensity, and unsure of the source of concern. He changed the subject. "You didn't forget your lunch, did you?" He watched Anton jerk a thumb to the packsack slung from his shoulder. "Good. I've given you some rye bread with smoked ham with lots of mustard."

"Stop, don't tell me," his father said. "I won't be able to wait." They both laughed. "You feed me too well." Anton patted Alex's arm, his voice becoming serious again. "Be careful. Just be careful."

This sober caution wasn't like his father. He invariably kept Alex focused on school and football. That was enough. "I'll look after the politics," he'd say. Perhaps it was the lunch-hall rumors that had everyone uneasy, or the radio bulletins posted around town that lately seemed more ominous. Just before the game was not a time for distractions, so why was his father so troubled?

"Here comes your shadow," Anton said.

Alex turned to watch his closest friend lope toward them. Peter's Viking hair bounced with each stride, his warm breath streaming in plumes over each shoulder.

"Hey, Alex. Morning, Coach," Peter panted happily, his face bright with anticipation. "Tomorrow beckons."

Alex noted his father's frown at the examination of rust-colored hair curling over the collar of Peter's jacket. "Your hair's too long. Get to the barber," Anton said, starting away. He turned back. "I'll see you both at supper. No horseplay."

While they watched Anton stride toward the bridge, Peter echoed the coach's words: "No horseplay, but after the game we go to the Rathskeller. There are these two girls, just dying to meet us, and they like my hair the way it is."

"Oh, sure. You're just like Samson, and he lost more than his hair, remember."

Peter waved him off with a laugh.

Alex was cautious about Peter's wild schemes and a little uncomfortable, he had to admit, at the thought of meeting girls he didn't know. "The girls you find never last," he said, starting toward the gymnasium.

"These will. They're forever."

"Is that so? Wh-who . . ." Alex shook his head, trying to shed the annoying stammer that plagued him occasionally. "Who are they this time?"

"Well, I don't know just yet, but I'm sure they'll tell us after we find them."

Laughing, Alex chased after Peter, who sprinted across the lawn toward the broad staircase to the gymnasium. "Wait up, Romeo," he said pumping his knees high for the chase. "I'll cut your hair for you."

It was then he caught sight of a military sedan driving up to the main entrance of Falcon House; tires buzzed over the cobbled road pushing wisps of fog aside. The hood ornament perched above the grill was the ubiquitous black eagle of the Austro-Hungarian Empire.

Alex stopped, putting hands on hips, breathing deeply, and trying to control a growing sense of dread. He watched his friend run back toward him, the happy face now drawn and serious.

"Shit," Peter said, slowly shaking his head. "It's starting."

"Damn them," Alex growled between breaths. "God damn them all."

● ● ●

Oberleutnant Manfred Schumann stepped out of the rear door of his staff car while pulling on black leather gloves. Cathedral bells echoed around the great central square as he narrowed his eyes to examine classic pillars reaching high above the gardens and doorways. Seven o'clock.

Schumann watched two young men, Alex and Peter, move out of his way as they hurried to class. He was aware of the effect his presence evoked, in that they chose to avoid his eyes, already partially hidden by the steep-angled brim of his cap. Too bad they didn't take time to consider the good he could do for the university. He planned to make it famous, and they could play a part. But whatever they thought, it made little difference. He had a job to do and this would be accomplished with his usual dispatch. Their future was in his hands anyway.

Despite the full-length coat worn over his dress uniform, Schumann shrugged in the chilly autumn air and snapped up his collar. Then he marched quickly around the car with the metal heels of his boots ringing against the cold pavement. He opened the door for his unwanted colleague, Major Markus Adler. This young German officer, barely twenty-five, had made what Schumann took to have been a lucky decision at Tannenberg; when, despite a shattered collarbone, he successfully completed a sweeping move to surround the Russian Second Army. He was awarded the Knight's Cross of Bavaria, with the non-hereditary title of nobility and a pension. Then they made him a senior officer.

Schumann watched disapprovingly as Major Adler eased out of the rear seat. He wore a light gray German greatcoat, with the injured left arm bound tightly against his chest. Then, this far-too-young major took time to examine the students and the buildings.

As they climbed the stairs to the entrance, windows reflecting the slanting sun burst into orange fire. Schumann swung open the main door, hesitating just long enough to scan a row of offices in the foyer of the Falcon Association before walking abruptly to the one marked Dr. Joseph Scheiner. He pushed through the door, and waited while Scheiner rose from behind his desk.

"Well, Doctor," Schumann said, removing a glove. "I imagine you know why we're here. May I present Major Adler of the Bavarian Alpenkorps?"

He pulled off the other glove, dropping both on the desk between them. "Let's get on with it. I have a wonderful proposal for your young athletes."

The little doctor tugged at the vest of his suit, blinking rapidly behind his spectacles, apparently unable to find words. "Could you . . . is there any way we might, perhaps, delay this?"

Schumann looked up puzzled. "For whatever possible reason?"

The professor's eyes would not rise higher than Schumann's chest. "The boys . . . they graduate this spring."

Schumann might have predicted this response, and he allowed himself a clipped laugh. It seemed that it was he who inevitably had to take the role of the disciplinarian. "Nonsense! We have other plans. Don't you follow the news? Believe me; these fellows will have little use for university training. That's their delusion. They'll be told what to do."

He was about to continue when the major interrupted. "Excuse me, Professor. I would like to meet your students . . . Oberleutnant, kindly help me off with this coat."

Schumann frowned at this insult, but he hung up the major's coat. He felt a slow burn as they followed Professor Scheiner into the crowded gymnasium where young men worked on gymnastics apparatus. He was shocked when the young major actually looked interested in the activities. Adler — barely out of class himself — was captivated when a gymnast on the parallel bars swung to a handstand, then pirouetted to a graceful dismount. Schumann was further annoyed when Adler, continuing his lack of military composure, grinned and nodded to the Czech student. Schumann was seething.

The professor clapped his hands. "Attention please. Attention. We have visitors. Major Markus Adler wishes to speak to you."

Adler, his left forearm bound to his chest with a black strap, wore a gray dress-uniform with the Knight's Cross at his throat.

"Good morning," he began. "It is a great privilege to meet the athletes of Charles University . . . I have an invitation for you from General Helmuth von Moltke himself, Commander-in-Chief of Germany's First Army. He invites you Czechs . . . as Austrian subjects . . . to join us in an elite grouping — the Falcon Regiment. This is, of course, a great honor."

The athletes showed no sign of interest, and Schumann saw that Adler scanned their faces carefully before he continued. "With Germany, you will be part of a Teutonic Alliance building an empire from Hamburg to Baghdad. The economic implications are gargantuan. And, as Austrian subjects, you will play an important part."

Again, the Czechs kept their eyes to the floor.

Schumann wanted to speak but held back. Let this shooting star get out of the tight spot himself, he thought with an inward smile as Adler went on.

"As a favor to your professor, I will keep all two hundred of you together. Present yourselves tomorrow at the armory 7:00 a.m. Questions?"

Schumann watched, but no one moved. Then several young men turned toward the fellow whose performance on the parallel bars had caught Adler's eye.

Like the others, he wore a sleeveless singlet, gymnastic slippers and white pants pulled tight by elastic stirrups under each foot. His thick black hair and muscular shoulders were damp. Strong hands hung relaxed at his sides, with chalk from the parallel bars covering callused palms and coating the inside of slightly flexed biceps.

Schumann noted every detail: flat abdomen, lean hard lines on the face; and yet, despite his look of determination, this student had an air of sensitivity about him. He looked younger than the listed age, with . . . what was it? Boyish innocence . . . or was it arrogance? Schumann expected to enjoy this.

The student raised a muscular arm. Adler nodded. "Your name?"

"Alex Branda, sir . . . Excuse me, but is it possible to extend that time? We play for the University Football Cup tomorrow."

Schumann's jaw clenched in anger. "A football game?" he blurted out. "You're going to war!"

Before he could continue, he felt Adler's hand on his arm and stopped. The major said calmly to the students, "I'm sorry to be the one to tell you this, but your match has been cancelled. We need your help against Russia."

Then Schumann watched stunned with the rest of them as Adler stepped to the floor mats near the hanging rings and slipped off his shoes. Springing up, he grasped a ring with his right hand and hung still for a moment before performing a slow 'muscle up' with one arm until he was balanced, at attention, with the ring and hand at his hip. Then Adler made a controlled return to the floor.

Every eye was on the major as he slipped his shoes back on. He turned to the crowd, making eye-contact with Alex before addressing the group. "Together we are strong. An unbeatable force . . . as time will tell. Be at the armory tomorrow. 7:00 a.m." With this directive, he turned and marched quickly out of the gymnasium.

On the front porch, Schumann was astonished to be confronted by the serious but still calm Adler. "Oberleutnant. You are senior to me in age . . . and I respect that because we work together for the same cause. Nevertheless, see that you never interrupt me again."

Schumann felt compelled to respond. "Of course, but–"

"The Czechs don't like us," Adler said, breaking in. "Don't try to bully them into cooperation. They can be useful only if we handle them properly. Act as a professional soldier. There are codes to follow, and manners to match those codes."

Schumann stumbled, "They, they must conform to our rules, surely."

Adler remained firm. "If forced, they won't. Don't try that again. I've warned you."

Schumann felt his face flush with anger, but he saluted and walked back to the car to open the door for Major Adler.

● ● ●

Standing at the stove in his father's kitchen, Alex tended to a pan of spitting sausages. He ladled them out onto plates beside shelled boiled eggs and took them over to the kitchen nook where his father sat. "This is crazy," Alex said, hanging his apron on a hook by the sink. He searched his father's face, now red-eyed and worn. Anton usually slept well, but not last night.

"My fault," his father said. "They've been following me. Now you're under suspicion. Schumann knows things. He'll be on you hard to keep us both in line."

"So I go to war. You know . . . I'm not sure I could shoot anyone. What an incredible decision."

"Would you kill if I convinced you how important it was?" Anton asked quietly, as he fidgeted with the handle on his cup.

"You're probably the only one who could."

"Well then, your country is that important. What do you think I've been training you boys for all these years? The drills and the matches. The championships. What were they all for?"

Alex was surprised. "For sport? For us?"

Anton lowered his voice. "Nothing so prosaic. It was for the moment you'd rise against Austria."

Alex sipped his tea slowly. There was an ache behind his eyes. He needed time to examine this unexpected revelation. He needed time to think ahead. "So I'm supposed to lead Czech-Slavs against Russian-Slavs, to repair Austria's economy?"

"Never against Russia," Anton said quickly. "If you value freedom, then you know that Slavs must stand together. Our moment is coming. You and your friends can help."

"What can we possibly do on the Polish Front?"

His father's voice rose in intensity. "Watch for your chance. Get to Russia, and with the Czar's army, throw these bastards out! We've laid the foundation politically. Now you boys have to do the work."

Alex was startled. "I had no idea you were in so deep."

"Of course not. I tried to keep you out of it."

He watched his father. "But this is treason. Is the Falcon Association part of it?"

Anton nodded, looking straight into his eyes. "Up to the hilt. Every man. Every woman."

In the silence, Alex became aware of the tap-click tap-click of a pendulum's ratchet wheel. He watched Anton gave a quick look toward the clock above the kitchen sink before pulling at the gold chain slung across his vest. Alex caught his father staring for a moment at the round picture on the inside cover. Alex knew what was there — a smiling young woman holding a baby in a white christening gown. He had secretly studied that picture as a boy, trying to memorize her image whenever his father had left the watch unattended. Now he wanted to ask about that young woman, although perhaps this was not the right time.

Anton snapped the cover closed, then picked up a battered suitcase. With a sad look on his face he opened the front door. "Come on, son. Mustn't be late."

A horse and cart clattered by.

Out on the cobbled road Alex hesitated. He turned to his father. "You never told me where M-mother went."

There was pain in Anton's gaze. He looked uncertain about answering at all, but finally said, "Back to Bratislava."

"Why?"

Anton looked down. "I'm not sure."

"Because of m-me?" Alex asked, inwardly tensing at the sound of his own wavering voice.

"Good Lord, no!" Anton said, coming out of his slouch. "You were five. What can you remember at that age?"

Now Alex looked down the twisting road. "Not much. Sh-she kissed me. Told me to be a good boy. I- I thought I was, but she left."

Anton worked hard to formulate an answer, but before he could respond, a voice echoed up the road between the gray stone cottages. "Recruits! Parade!"

Two young men carrying packsacks hurried down the narrow road. When they glanced over, Alex started after them, but Anton grasped his arm by the elbow, speaking urgently, his voice suddenly hard. "Don't dwell on your mother. It's your weakness. Women are capable of spoiling resolve. Dismiss her."

Alex said nothing. He felt a twinge of resentment. How could he ever dismiss his mother? But he was too drained to protest the advice. He kissed his father's cheek as they embraced, and when his lips brushed the tanned skin he could smell the strong clean scent of shaving soap. It was then he heard the fierce whisper: "Your country needs patriots. Do this for me."

Alex gave a thin smile in agreement. "You have my promise," he said, shaking his father's hand and trying to squeeze away any doubt. He was angry that he should feel so vulnerable, and was reluctant to pick up his suitcase. But when the military voice called out the second time, he hurried with his father down the road to the granite fortress at the bottom of the hill.

The passageway into the building was narrow. Alex joined a group of friends waiting their turn to pass slowly through the gate. We might make it through the war, he thought, as he shuffled forward with the rest. But when he came to the last archway over the main gate with its stout metal straps and flanking guard stations, he realized with a shock that he was alone, despite the numbers of recruits in the subdued crowd and the faces of friends all around him. His throat tightened as he looked up at the wintry clouds, charcoal gray and heavy with snow, then he turned back toward his father and stretched his hand above the crowd for one last wave.

● ● ●

As Katya entered the Treasury Building she checked the lobby clock. Fifteen minutes early, she noted. Good. She smiled at the guard and walked up the staircase to the mezzanine floor.

In a small office she hung up her coat and took a moment to check her image in the glass. Blonde hair was pulled tightly to the back of her head in a style that accentuated two commanding blue eyes; occasionally she remembered, with a smile, the youth who had compared them to the color of the Caspian Sea. She knew they attracted, even startled, some men but this she did not mind. She was happy to return their gaze because she wanted to speak to men directly, the way they spoke to each other.

She walked down a long carpet to the conference room. Just outside, she paused and took a breath, straightened her back and then twisted the brass handle to open the door.

A few heads turned as she entered the room, but the majority of the eleven men on the Accounting Board continued chatting, smoking their cigars, making it apparent that they were going to ignore the new woman proposing to enter their ranks. Katya recognized the atmosphere immediately and was tempted to turn away, but she quickly corrected herself by walking over to the nearest colleague and offering her hand. "My name is Katya. You must be Anatoly. Chairman Ordinov has told me of your work."

Anatoly was taken aback, stumbling with his answer. "Um. Very good . . . Miss. Um, yes. I believe you sit over there."

Katya started across to where he pointed, noticing that other men turned away at her approach. One man stood apart from the others. His dress was fashionable. His hair was sleek with pomade. He watched her with disinterest, or was it boredom? Nevertheless, Katya approached with a smile. "Gospodin Rovskoy. What a pleasure. I must say, your new Treasury bill is remarkable."

Rovskoy turned with a half sneer, pulling on his cigar. "Which one?"

"I was thinking of the 5,000 ruble note."

"So, the art work impresses you, Miss?"

Katya took her time, noting that everyone was listening now. "The art work is fine, Mr. Rovskoy, but I was referring to the boldness of the concept. Five percent return on 5,000 rubles in one year — daring. I'm sure it caused debate."

Rovskoy looked at Katya over his glasses as if studying her. "So, as an actuary, what is your prediction? Do you think it will succeed?"

Katya smiled privately — so he has heard of my work, she thought. "How could any businessman refuse a large profit backed by the Czar himself? I thought it brilliant."

Katya looked around the room. They were all watching her now. "Where should a newcomer sit?"

Anatoly hurried over and pulled out a chair for her.

CHAPTER 3

STANFORD UNIVERSITY
JANUARY 1915

Leaving the Engineering Quad, Victor Lindal swung onto his bicycle for a ride across the Stanford campus. He felt a private satisfaction in wearing his athletic award sweater — not that he could remember ever being shy about his accomplishments. He had to admit though, that this award was an honor which stirred his pride. It was much better than the good looks he was grateful to have inherited from his mother. The sweater had been earned.

He pedaled slowly, taking time to admire two new buildings painted white and glistening in the sun. Clubhouses for men and women had been built replete with arcades to complement the larger Stanford Union. The French doors looked smart, and there was a new dance floor in the Women's Clubhouse where a broad balcony wrapped around the second level. He waved in a good-natured way to two coeds looking down at him.

"Hey, Vic," one called while striking an elaborate pose: hand on hip, and a finger pointing to the dimple on her cheek. "Save me a dance Saturday?"

Victor laughed at her bravura. "You bet," he called back before pedaling on. He was tempted to stop and talk. He liked girls, maybe too much for his own good, he knew. There was something about them; an anticipation in their watchfulness perhaps. Whatever it was, he imagined he could sense the expectation of joy in their searching eyes, or at least a hidden question, and invariably he felt moved to answer it — or to try.

If he stopped now, though, he would most likely be late for rugby practice. Besides, there was business to look after. He needed a summer source of income since he had just been accepted into the Graduate Languages Department, and the quickest, sure-fire deal he'd heard of was advertised over at the Men's Clubhouse. It was something to look at.

Victor slowed the bicycle by scraping his feet on the gravel in front of a porch with wide white pillars which invited the breeze. Red tiles on a slanting roof deadened the heat from the lunch-hour sun. On the lawn stood a notice-board. He sat on the bicycle seat reading the latest poster:

He read the poster a second time to contemplate the art work, designed, he supposed, to emphasize the urgency for preparation. A fierce-looking soldier wearing a spiked German helmet stood in a threatening pose with bayonet pointed and a wild-eyed stare. Victor grunted at this exaggeration and dismounted to guide the bike's front wheel into the wooden frame of a bicycle rack.

He strolled through an entrance archway to the Student Union Building, then turned down a Mexican-tile staircase into the cool basement. He kept walking through the long arcade, past the billiard room, the shoe repair stand and the barbershop, until his eye caught a sign which read: **JOIN THE PLATTSBURG PREPAREDNESS MOVEMENT.** Here, he turned in.

A thin man with a bristling military haircut rose from a chair tilted back against the wall and came to the counter. "What can I do ya for?" the clerk asked, grinning at his own humor.

"I might sign up for a Plattsburg camp with the National Guard," Victor offered, not wanting to be rushed.

"You're kidding," the clerk said, opening a cabinet drawer for some forms. "My first customer. Name and subject?"

"Victor Lindal, and I've just been accepted into the Department of Foreign Languages. So, I'd be pretty interested in anything to do with the Intelligence Service and the War Department."

"OK. Fill these out. You report to the gym Tuesday at 1800 hours."

Victor began filling out the forms, aware that he was being watched with interest by the bored clerk. "Say, Vic, I don't want to seem nosy or anything, but with your looks you must have an easy time with the fillies, so why would a rich guy even think about the National Guard?"

"Rich. Ha, that's good," he said with a private smile. His family never had much money, although there had been rich moments. He found himself remembering the day when as a schoolboy, he had brought pussy willows to his mother in their small home outside San Jose. She had been standing bare-armed beside the wood stove in the hot, scrubbed kitchen. She almost always had a soft calmness on her face, but when she saw the pussy willows tears welled up in her eyes — making Victor wish with all his heart that he had brought her something better than branches cut with his pocket knife from a bush down by the railroad tracks. He promised himself that one day he would try to make her a little happier, not that she ever complained. She seemed content enough with her life near the railroad, although to Victor there did not appear to be much gaiety. His father was a hard worker but always kind of quiet, and most commonly away. Victor wanted her to laugh more, as she did when accepting his spring blossoms. A natural blonde, she had stroked back his nut-red hair pretending to search for an explanation for the deep color. "My chestnut," she said, enveloping him with a hug to her soft chest. He could smell fresh bread and orange peel on her apron, and he was content to submit to her examination as an acceptable form of affection.

"I wouldn't be anywhere near this school if my dad didn't run the Southern Pacific train to Los Angeles three times a week." Victor clasped his hands in the prayer position and raised his eyes toward the ceiling. "Thank the Lord for Leland Stanford's generosity. May God rest his soul." He winked at the clerk but knew in his heart that his situation was no joke. It was fact. "Just a poor, old-fashioned immigrant family trying to get by." He then went back to filling out the form.

The clerk nodded. "Oh yeah? Where you from?"

"Before we moved out here? Chicago, the largest city in Bohemia, all the Czech immigrants there say." Victor looked up from the counter. "Is there money for this?"

"That's the deal. You go to summer training camp. Six weeks down at Monterey Presidio. Cavalry. Weaponry. Physical jerks. That kind of stuff. Used to be at your own expense, but now you get paid for the summer."

"Kind of a dumb name, Plattsburg Preparedness," Victor said, looking at the sparse furniture in this antiseptic room. The counter-top still had a shine of newness to it, and the stars and stripes on a wooden staff in one corner was the only attempt at decoration.

"If the good citizens from the great state of New York shell out the bucks, it's their name. So, how come you're joining up?"

"Need some pesos for grad school. Plus, I've always wanted to see Europe or maybe Russia . . . and we'll be in the war sooner or later."

The clerk shook his head in disbelief. "Boy, are you backing the wrong horse. You ever hear of the Monroe Doctrine? 'Don't tread on me, pal. And we ain't never goin' over there to let you try.' There's no way the US Army will ever get to Russia! You can make book on that."

Victor smiled easily, handing over the completed papers. He carefully screwed on the top of his fountain pen. "You might be right, but one never knows. See you Tuesday at 1800 hours . . . whatever that means," he laughed. "I'm in no hurry. As long as there are girls on the beach at Monterey I'd be reluctant to trade California for Russia."

Outside again, Victor walked across the stadium practice field toward the team changing-rooms beneath Stanford Stadium. The sun was hot, and he conceded that he'd be spitting cotton during their wind-sprints, so he thought only of the motionless air inside the change-room and the constant coolness from its unpainted cement walls stretching up into high dark corners behind the grandstand seats outside. It was a private place, like a cave, where sound was muffled and the heavy air remained cool for the privileged members of this chosen clan.

Inside, he folded his sweater, placing it carefully on the top shelf of his wooden cubicle. On the facing board at eye-level in bold print on a piece of adhesive tape was his name: **Mercury**. He smiled at this irreverent yet personal form of humor and kicked his shoes under a seat bolted to the rough cement wall. He hung his pants on a nail hammered into one of the slats running down the side of his space and tossed his undershorts onto another.

Walking naked in the still air felt good, with his feet padding across the cold concrete floor toward the weigh-in machine. He breathed in the fresh scent of wintergreen from the rub-down table as he rattled the weights across the scale, which balanced at one hundred and seventy lean pounds. A pinch of the skin produced nothing but skin, and the chromium bar reaffirmed his height at six foot, even. The results of this ritual he recorded in the captain's log.

Four players shuffled into the quiet room while he sat tightening the laces to his boots. He could feel a wash of warm air through the open door and felt a twinge of annoyance at being disturbed.

Lefty Rogers, the team captain, casually tossed his kit bag into a cubicle. "Hey there, Merc," he said with a smile. "Glad you're early. Heard you're joining the army."

Victor shook his head with a wry smile. "Only the summer camp. Ya know . . . news sure travels fast around here. And the thing is, you're always in on it."

"Ahh. I saw you go in," Lefty said. "I just don't want you doing something dumb that could screw up a good thing. There's no need joining the army. We'll get to Europe as a team."

Lefty Rogers was the largest man on the Stanford rugby squad. A pre-med student, he walked peacefully in that aura of polite self-assurance that big men seemed to enjoy, but Victor knew that Lefty could turn tough when it came to getting what he wanted. His special place was in the line-out where he could use his height and his strength; where at times he showed a willingness to use his fists — even though his first instinct was to persuade through logic.

It was Lefty who had spotted Victor as a candidate for the team, watching him in a football scrimmage. Victor had played well that day, but was both astonished and complimented when Lefty Rogers, a campus man-of-distinction, approached him to say: "You, sir, have Mercury's speed, and God intended you to play rugby."

Well, there wasn't much else he could do after that but work out with the squad, discovering that he liked the game, liked the travel and liked the players. They were full of life, and dedicated to the peculiar appeal of this new game. So they all worked hard to play it well. Almost every one of his new teammates had come from the regimentation of gridiron football, and they welcomed the spontaneity of rugby. He was pleasantly surprised to find that somewhere along the way he had become a valued member of the team. The nickname signified his acceptance.

"Good news," Lefty announced. "The I.O.C. put rugby up as a medal sport for the next Olympics in Antwerp — when they get that stupid war over with. I figure if we train hard, work on the set pieces, we could be in the running. Nobody, not even the New Zealand All Blacks can get around American tackling. Besides, I think a tour of Europe will do us all good."

Victor laughed with the rest who were changing into their shorts and cleats. The dream was a long way off, but there should always be a dream. And when Lefty Rogers spoke about it, there was a ring of credibility with which few could argue. At least Lefty wasn't urging his team into war. Besides, Victor thought, as he had pointed out to the Army clerk: California is much nicer than Europe in January.

* * *

The morning after her first Treasury Board meeting, Katya met Rovskoy in the hallway of the Treasury Building. "Miss Kazakova. A minute. You may be correct about my Treasury bill. They're selling like Dutch hot-cakes. I should take you to dinner tonight to celebrate."

"A nice gesture, Gospodin Rovskoy, but not necessary. Just so the war effort moves forward." She walked down the long stairs to the main business floor where crowds of well-dressed customers lined up at the counter for war bonds and Treasury bills. Six clerks were very busy. One looked at Katya, raising a hand. "Miss Kazakova, this gentleman has some questions."

"Of course, right away." Katya smiled at a well-dressed man with a top hat. "Won't you step into the office, please?"

The gentleman took off his hat, smiling softly. "You wouldn't be a woman to gull the uninitiated, would you?"

"Show me a woman who isn't," Katya laughed. "Are you trying to pass yourself off as uninitiated, sir?"

His smile widened. "Quite so. Have you heard the news from the front?"

"Yes indeed. Dramatic advances. It's wonderful."

"Perhaps it is time for me to invest in Russia's future."

"Of course. We appear to be on the threshold of a new era." Katya smiled, gesturing to a padded leather chair for the gentleman.

CHAPTER 4

THE PINSK MARSHES
JANUARY 1915

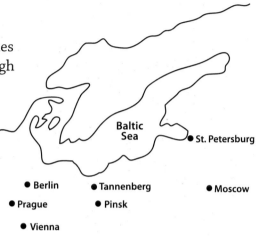

Leaving the Austrian trenches behind, Alex tramped through knee-deep snow out of the forest and down a hill onto the Pinsk Marshes which opened before him like a dead, white hand. He stopped in the buffeting wind to check the long column of men following him. They looked a ragged lot, wrapped against the cold in winter hats with fur flaps covering their ears and much of their faces. But he could still see the worry in their eyes as he led them toward the other side of no-man's-land where Russian fortifications waited. Neither side wanted the marshes.

Numbing bursts of wind hissed down their path and spirals of snow whirled along the icy ruts. Leaden skies pressed in, choking every horizon with a thick mask of gray.

Aching with cold, Alex winced and leaned his shoulder into the gusting wind. His action was more protective than aggressive because his legs trembled with the threat of cramps and he worried about a creeping pain in his toes. He stopped to flex his feet inside the brittle boots, but then continued to lift tired thighs through each new clutching drift, resigned to continue a slow passage down the longest trek of his life.

He was stopped just then by a shout distorted in the storm: "Sergeant Branda!" He turned to watch Oberleutnant Schumann gallop toward him on a struggling horse. The blowing snow provoked fits of coughing from the beast as it came to a halt in front of Alex. He felt a stab of sympathy for the horse, although he quickly realized this to be a strange response when his friends were just as badly off.

Horses don't know the rules, he had once explained to himself. Men do.

"Yes, Oberleutnant," he called back through the wind.

"Stop here," Schumann demanded. "These men sleep-walk. Can't you damned Czechs understand we're close to Russian lines? You're useless in this state. Fall out. Half an hour."

Alex turned dumbly to obey but was stopped by another order. "Sergeant," Schumann said in a warning voice. "Tell those idiots to stay off the trail. Russians do have patrols, you know. I'll tell you once. Keep out of sight!"

The troops sank gratefully into deep snow at the side of the road. The holes they made formed pale blue splotches on a monotonous field of white. Peter joined Alex, and they pressed their backs into a bank of snow to create a shelter against the wind.

"How're the legs?" Peter asked, his worried eyes peering from behind a frost-ringed balaclava. "You've been breaking trail for two days now."

"Not too bad."

"Here, I'll give 'em a rub." With both hands he began to shake the stiffened snow from the heavy material of winter pants.

"They're all right," Alex said in a tired voice. "I need sleep. How are the boys?"

"They're wondering what Schumann's got against you. Why doesn't he lead the way?"

"Get some rest," Alex said, pulling knees to his chest, leaning against the snow-wall with closed eyes. "You know damned well we're sacrificial lambs."

Peter said nothing, shaking his head from side to side. "I know," he said finally, "but I can't believe that you, of all people, would give in. Schumann'll kill you."

Alex half-opened one eyelid. "I'm not giving in," he said, drifting toward sleep.

"What then?" Peter persisted.

"I'm going to get us out. I just don't know how, yet."

Even as he dozed, Alex knew that he should not make rash promises like that. In all their years together he had never broken his word to Peter, and he knew he was trusted because of that. So he felt a twinge, remembering their predicament, but he had to get them out.

He woke with someone shaking his shoulder. "It's Stefan," Peter said.

Alex moved on his knees to peer into the whirling snow. "Damn," he said, waving his arm at his ever-keen friend Stefan striding across the trail toward their snow-pit. "Get back!"

The young soldier smiled as he crossed the forbidden path and crouched down in their cave. "I saw you talking," he said in a low but urgent voice. "Any plans yet? We're all ready. Whenever you give the word."

Alex and Peter exchanged looks but before either could answer, Schumann galloped up. "Sergeant! Who is that fool? I told you to stay out of sight."

Alex clambered from the pit and called into the wind, "Private Stefan, sir. I'll discipline him tomorrow, you can be sure."

"You'll do it now," he ordered. "Take him to that tree."

Alex looked toward the higher ground where a lone tree shook in the storm. He grasped the horse's bridle, speaking in a private way. "Could it wait, sir? There'll be too much unnecessary damage in this weather."

Schumann snarled, jerking the horse's head, which turned the animal in a half circle, knocking Alex to the ground. "Do as I say!"

Stiffly, Alex pushed himself up from the pathway as Peter approached with Stefan. Alex saw the fear in Stefan's face as the full impact of his situation became clear, and Alex felt his outrage grow as he reluctantly began to lead Stefan to the tree. Under its gaunt branches waited a youthful lieutenant, the youngest of the four Austrian officers supporting Schumann. Alex could see the lieutenant's feet shifting self-consciously in the loose snow as he waited to take charge of the punishment.

At least some Austrians disapproved of Schumann's disciplinary methods, Alex thought when he saw the lieutenant's mouth pull tight in displeasure while he turned Stefan's arms behind his back. His wrists were snared by a hemp rope, then the end pulled tight around a branch, until Stefan stood on tiptoes with his hands stretched high behind his back to head level.

Schumann watched from his horse.

Alex moved close to Stefan as if checking the rope, while trying to think of a solution. "Hold on!" he whispered.

"Stand back!" Schumann ordered.

Alex turned, ready to confront the Austrian commander, but Peter pulled him by the arm toward their shelter, whispering in a strained voice, "Wait."

From their snow-pit, Alex watched with the rest of the Czech company as Stefan hung from the tree, swaying with the wind, silent in his private agony.

Ten minutes passed and Alex slid a shell into the chamber of his rifle, then snapped the bolt firmly into place. I can't let this go on, he thought. Perhaps now is not the time, but there are only five officers. And when is the correct time to mutiny?

Peter interrupted his thoughts. "You've made a decision," he said.

Alex looked up wearily. "Not necessarily, but I'm ready to."

He got to his feet and trudged to the officer in command, with Peter following at a distance. Schumann smoked a cigarette standing beside his horse, which sheltered him from the gale. His four Austrian officers huddled near a fire, more interested in protecting a fluttering flame to heat beef jerky than in any plea Alex might extend.

"Oberleutnant Schumann, shall we let him loose now? He's had enough."

"I'll be the judge of that."

"His arms will freeze."

Schumann turned on Alex angrily. "It would only mean one more useless, armless Czech. Would you care to join him, Sergeant?"

Alex felt a sudden rush of energy. He stood tall, his eyes now wide and alert as he said in a low voice, "You've seen this before, haven't you? You know the damage . . . and you ask us to serve your bloody dictatorship."

He watched Schumann's face pinch tight as the Austrian reacted to the treason. Schumann raised his hand to strike, but Alex held his composure without flinching. He could see that Schumann stopped his hand, perhaps aware of the dark shapes rising from their snowy beds on both sides of the road. Every shadowed eye was fixed on Schumann. Cold, tired men waited for a signal from Alex, a sign, something to lead them through this nightmare, something to release their anger and hate. The wind's low whine was the only sound, and Alex thought he saw the moment when Schumann realized he had gone too far, just as Schumann's face tightened before groping for the holster at his side. Woolen gloves slipped on the shiny leather as he fumbled with the flap concealing his weapon. "I'll have you shot!"

In one smooth motion Alex pushed his rifle's muzzle under Schumann's chin. "You'll have to do it with a bullet through your hat."

Schumann raised his hands in surrender. The horse whinnied and shied away.

Unexpectedly, Alex heard a shot behind him. Holding the rifle's barrel in the notch of Schumann's throat with one hand, he stepped back in a half-turn to look. The junior Austrian officer lay face down in the snow. His arm was outstretched, in his hand a pistol still pointed at Alex. A steaming red puddle seeped from under the young man's chest.

Peter stood nearby with his rifle held at waist level in both hands. Blue smoke curled from its barrel while he turned the body over with the toe of his boot.

Alex called loudly to his men, "Arrest the officers!" Then he turned to Peter with a grateful look, blowing a silent whistle through a long breath.

"Watch him," Alex said, tossing his head in Schumann's direction as he hurried toward Stefan. "Cut him down!" Alex called. "Carefully."

"Disarm the officers," he ordered, moving energetically down the lines of men as the Czech soldiers left their snow shelters in the marsh to scramble back onto the path.

"Horses for supplies!" he called out again, watching with satisfaction the vitality surging through the company. "Well done, boys."

Alex came over to Schumann, who stared in disbelief. Alex avoided the man's eyes, not wanting to risk the emotion of a discourse. "I'm taking the horses. You didn't use them well anyway. Crawl back to Vienna for all I care." Alex then turned away with a shout, "Fall in, boys. . . . We're off to Russia."

It seemed that the wind died along with the young Austrian lieutenant left stiffening in the snow, as one by one the remaining Austrian officers turned away to trudge back toward their line on the western edge of the swamp.

Alex tramped along beside Peter who turned excitedly to ask, "Why didn't you shoot the bastard?"

Alex thought about that for a while. It was perhaps a mistake to have left him alive. Perhaps all the officers should have been killed. He prayed to God that he'd guessed correctly. How was he supposed to know such things? After a while he simply shook his head. "We're not butchers. Not yet. And I won't be forced into it."

Clouds the color of gun-metal muffled what little light the winter sun had to offer, but the white snow helped, so Alex pressed ahead over the wide frozen swamp, directing their march between the encroaching lines of dark trees on their flanks. He felt somehow on a private schedule, looking for the Russian lines which he calculated must be somewhere at the eastern edge of the marshes, while at the same time being painfully aware that there was no turning back. Not now. Not ever.

All but the snow-covered marsh was black when he finally stopped, listening, trying to define a faraway swish of air. "Take cover!" he bellowed. "Flare!" Almost instantly, a brash orange light broke above them, and guns flashed from the shadows. "Don't shoot!" he shouted. "Hold your fire! Jan, hoist a flag of surrender!"

Alex scrambled through the powdery snow over to Peter who was lying beside Stefan. "Spread the word. No shooting! Wait it out!"

"We're trapped!" Peter growled. "What can we do?"

The flare drifted closer and closer to the snowy field, sending sparks of orange bouncing from every angled crystal and highlighting the tension on their faces.

"Keep your poise," Alex replied firmly. "Tell the men to hold fire."

Peter aimed his rifle at the shadows, but after a few seconds crawled quickly away. Minutes later there were only occasional shots; and finally, none.

Jan had a white flag of truce hoisted on his rifle. Now he was on his knees, waving it from side to side as high as he could reach.

A rough voice called in Russian from a dark line of trees: "Identify yourselves."

"Czecho-Slovak brothers," Alex answered in the same language while trying to determine the Russian position.

"Prove that!" the voice echoed again.

Alex lay in the snow trying to think this through, then heard a chilling command in Russian: "Fix bayonets." And with the harsh sound of metal on metal he saw the dread on the faces of the friends lying around him.

Stefan groaned, "My arms . . . so cold."

"All right. We'll fix that," said Alex standing. He heaved Stefan to his feet, then scooped him up in his arms.

Peter lay in the snow watching anxiously. "Alex, stay down, for God's sake." But he was already moving forward, carrying Stefan.

Another flare popped in the gloom, lighting the way to reveal a line of infantry soldiers marching toward Alex, bayonets at the ready.

"Sing with me, Stefan," Alex invited. "Show our Russian brothers who we are," and in a strong voice sang:

> *The Slavonic soul is burning;*
> *It shall see no aging.*

Stefan and others nearby joined in, and there was at once a new strength and power to the sound of their national hymn:

> *Hell and thunder, all in vain;*
> *Is your unfriendly raging . . .*

A Russian voice barked another sharp command, and the line of infantry broke into a dog-trot across creaking snow, their bayonets lowered to the attack position. Czech faces watched in doubt as the line came closer. Jan was on his feet now, waving the flag of surrender from side to side, the cloth flapping with each swing.

Alex shouted as he marched on, "Sing!"

He prayed that the Russian commander would respond. Sweat froze on his eyebrows. It's almost too late, he realized.

At last he heard the rough voice shout, "Hold!" and he allowed himself to exhale.

"They're coming, old friend," he said.

Stefan smiled, thumping Alex on the chest. "Good man, Alex. Well done."

Alex could see a man stand up from a shallow Russian trench fifty metres away. In his white hooded smock he remained virtually invisible against the snowy marshland. Field glasses hung against his chest as he walked through the line of troops with bayonets held at the ready. "Will you look at this?" Alex heard him say to a major following close behind. "They're all coming now, following that one carrying his comrade. It's genuine. Give the order to stand down."

The major hesitated, but following a stern look shouted: "At ease."

Then the hymn's rich sound grew stronger as more and more Czechs rose from the snow to sling rifles over their shoulders and join in. Alex saw the Russian colonel smile. There could be no mistaking the joy on each face and the sincerity in their voices as they stacked their rifles in neat cones in front of the Russian line, before taking up a parade-for-inspection position in three ranks, as directed by the vigorous arm signals of a bustling Russian sergeant.

"What are we going to do with them?" Alex heard the major ask incredulously.

"Send them to Petersburg," the colonel replied. "Ask them to stand with Russia. That is, no doubt, why they've come over."

Alex felt a stab of doubt when he heard the major's response. "We won't need strangers to defeat Germany. You can't depend on them."

"Don't you think we could use men like that fellow?" the colonel countered, pointing to Alex, still striding forward the last few paces with Stefan in his arms. "He carried his comrade more than a hundred metres. Arms of steel. Will of iron. We can use these men. They have nerve. And they're Slavs. Besides, who knows what the future holds for any of us?"

Hearing this exchange, Alex shifted Stefan's weight, and with a smile called out in Russian: "Good evening, gentlemen. May we join you?"

CHAPTER 5

PETROGRAD
WINTER 1915

Katya carried a silver tray down the staircase of a prestigious home now used as the place of welcome for Czech soldiers new to the capital. Stacked teacups rattled as she stepped carefully on the Persian carpeting, its rich blue and toffee design as elegant as the old house itself. On the main floor, where carpets had been removed to protect them from increased traffic, she stopped in front of a worried-looking woman in a starched white apron.

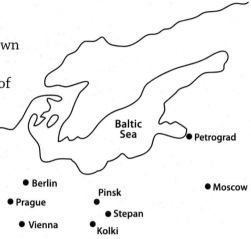

"Katya, I wish you wouldn't load the tray so," the older woman said. "You're always in such a rush."

"No worry, Mrs. Koslov. I haven't dropped one yet, have I? They'll be coming from their training soon, so I made it all in one trip."

The older women sighed as she took the tray. "Better get upstairs then, and keep a sharp eye out. I wish I knew how many are coming . . . we need more napkins from the linen closet. No lace."

Katya ran happily up the broad staircase. "Of course no lace." On the landing halfway up, she opened a door hidden by perfectly matched teak panels on the wall, and took her time selecting napkins to fold over her arm. She looked out the window down onto Sadovaya Street. No one yet. Just snowy pavement and the darkened towers of Kazan Cathedral outlined against the lights of the Winter Palace. A troika came swaying by, the three horses stepping lightly in perfect cadence.

The elegance of this old house reminded her of last July when she had first arrived at the Czar's court, and what pride she had felt to have befriended the worldly Grand Duchess, Marie Romanov.

Marie had taken over her social life, and so, within days, Marie had arranged for Katya to act as a volunteer hostess during evenings here at the Social Center where she welcomed men from Czechoslovakia who had survived their flight across no-man's-land in the gamble that Russia would free them from Austrian rule. It was comforting to know that such men existed. She hoped they could help sustain the monarchy — as well as, she blushed to admit, her career.

Katya was startled out of her reverie by a figure cutting across the snowy street outside. From the window, she saw an officer from the newly formed Czech Rifle Corps approach the Social Center. She heard the creak of the stranger's boots on the hard-packed snow and smiled when he stopped to read the sign hanging under the porch light. She admired his officer's greatcoat; obviously new issue, the handsome garment hung, perfectly tailored, to mid-shin. When the officer started up the steps she skipped down the broad staircase. "I'll get it," she called, even before the bell-chain had been pulled.

Madame Koslov and her friend, both in stiff aprons, looked up from their arrangement of refreshments on a long buffet table as Katya ran by. "Another neophyte," she told them.

"Well, don't frighten this one," the older woman scolded.

"You can't frighten these men," Katya laughed. "They're heroes!"

The doorbell chimed again as she crossed the anteroom to swing the door open. "There is no need to ring the bell here, my friend," she said in an energetic voice. "This is to be your home in Russia."

Alex stood rooted to the top step as he studied her face carefully.

"Do you like standing out in the cold?" she asked with a smile.

She saw that he was taken aback, but he recovered quickly, stepping inside to remove his cap. "Sorry. Didn't mean to stare. You are very kind, Mademoiselle."

Katya noticed that he had chosen the French appellation in a natural way, recognizing her as one of the educated class. This courtesy pleased her. She closed the front door and indicated the closet with a swing of her hand.

"Please come in," she said, turning a smile on his watchful face. When the officer had put away his cap and coat, she led him into the living room toward the two women at their refreshment table. "Would you like some tea and sandwiches?"

The young officer looked over the table at the two servers who lowered their eyes shyly. "Perhaps some clear tea," he said before walking to the fireplace to admire the brass staff and carved Russian eagle above the mantelpiece that held a new flag.

Katya saw that he expected one of the ladies to fetch his tea. He seemed a little formal but she made no comment. He was new, although his Russian was very good and virtually without accent. He must have had a meticulous teacher, perhaps a parent.

She decided he would be worth observing, so she merely poured a cup and took it to him where he stood facing the fire and studying the new Czech flag. "It's a bit ornate, don't you think?" she said as a tease.

"It's all we have," he answered sharply. The emotion was unnecessary, and he must have realized this himself, because while accepting the tea, he attempted a grin. Perhaps it was just tension. He needs a little more time, she decided.

"I find I must thank you once more, Mademoiselle."

"You may stop calling me that. My name is Katherine Kazakova, friends call me Katya. And you are?"

"Lieutenant Alexander Branda of the Czech Rifle Company, . . . at your service," he said with a bow. "But I warn you, a very new lieutenant."

Katya made note of his symbolic apology but still wondered why he remained so standoffish.

"Well, Lieutenant, you really are very early. Why not help me in the kitchen while you wait for the others?"

Katya watched him carefully, expecting a refusal, and she waited to see how he would couch his excuse. The serving ladies had seen this game before and Madame Koslov intruded to say, "There is really no need, sir."

But Alex surprised her and the two serving women as well, it seemed. His guarded expression suddenly brightened and the dark eyes grew warm. He immediately put down his tea to say with some enthusiasm: "Good idea."

The serving ladies watched Katya lead him to the kitchen, shaking their heads disapprovingly when he asked: "What can I do?"

Katya began loading bread and butter and cooked herring onto an island table in the center of the spacious kitchen. "Perhaps you could prepare the fish paste, I'll make sandwiches."

"All right," he said, removing his jacket to hang on a hook by the doorway. Then he rolled up his sleeves and began to strip away skin and bone from the cooked fish before skillfully breaking the meat into an oversized bowl.

Katya mixed egg yolks and oil for the mayonnaise while Alex chopped gherkins and capers and parsley. When she had measured out the lemon juice and vinegar, he picked up a wooden spoon and began whipping the mix with a practiced ease. There was a special power in his arms and shoulders.

"Where did you learn all this?"

Alex just laughed. "The kitchen was my job at home."

"Your mother?"

"My-my mother left us when I was five."

Katya heard the stammer and saw his embarrassment. She watched him casually as she cut bread slices for buttering. After a period of working in silence she asked, "Where's home?"

"Prague," he said in a voice she thought less strained.

"In Kiev we had many Czech friends. Papa was even thinking of sending me to the university in Prague."

"But he didn't?"

"No," Katya answered, suddenly serious. She worked without speaking, turning the response over in her mind. Perhaps it was the lieutenant's offering of openness that prompted her to confide in him so soon after meeting, or perhaps it was just her way of presenting another test, as she so often did with men. This man, she admitted, seemed trustworthy, and so she felt like continuing. "My mother was just a country girl. She became ill in the city. Tuberculosis. I wasn't allowed to kiss her, or hold her . . . for over a year. She died young — like Keats, we always said."

Katya looked away, deciding not to revisit those memories. In a few moments she began to work vigorously again. "I said to hell with the germs. I kissed my mother in her coffin."

She was sure she had shocked her visitor, but was impressed that Lieutenant Branda, with serious eyes as black as his rough shock of hair, showed no sign of being uncomfortable. He spread fish paste on bread with a wide knife, glancing up every once in a while to watch her with what seemed to be interest. She could count at least two scars on this young soldier's face: one on his upper lip and a thin white slash across the black eyebrow to her left.

It was an awkward moment, so Katya finished putting the food away, wondering if he would say more. When she determined he would not, she picked up one of the sandwich trays and turned brightly. "Well, we were both raised by zealous fathers then. They seem to have done all right."

Lieutenant Branda smiled at that, backing through the kitchen door with the other tray to hold the door for her before placing the sandwiches on the buffet table.

No one else had arrived yet, and she noticed a satisfied look on his face as he retrieved his teacup and strolled over to a large portrait above the fireplace. It featured a white-haired man in a black suit pointing to the horizon, perhaps to a new future for Czechoslovakia, she thought, looking at the portrait for really the first time. Although the subject was an elderly man, the artist had portrayed him as solidly built, with a defiant demeanor. She was surprised when Alex continued the conversation: "If you had come to Prague we might have met sooner. I studied under that man," he said, gesturing to the painting. "Professor Masaryk, a great political philosopher. I wonder where he is now."

"Hiding in Switzerland," Katya answered matter-of-factly. "Masaryk is trying to convince France and England that Czechs should have their independence. He lobbies for a Czech army to fight beside Britain on the western front."

When Alex raised his cup in salute, Katya laughed: "I must be having tea with a spy." She enjoyed this exchange, so was slightly annoyed to notice Lieutenant Rad Gaida, a regular visitor, watching from the anteroom. This confident-looking Czech officer with a soft brown moustache and trim gymnast's build stood beside the cloakroom door studying Alex carefully.

Katya smiled a greeting, then heard him say: "I hope that's enough sentimentality for one evening. I must interrupt."

Before she could recover, the officer had turned to Alex saying, "You'll excuse us, I'm sure." Gaida's lips were smiling but his eyes were not, and Katya was offended when he immediately turned his back on the lieutenant, a fellow Czech.

There was a searching look from Alex but she was relieved that he said nothing, taking a sip of the cold tea instead.

Gaida turned to Katya with a confident grin and took her hand. "Good evening, Katherine, how beautiful you look tonight."

The condescension in his voice caused her to bristle, but Katya fought it down, trying to summon her usual enthusiasm for the introduction of two new comrades. "Lieutenant Gaida, perhaps you should meet Lieutenant Branda who—"

Gaida broke in with: "Yes, yes. Of course," and folded her arm under his, turning away to lead her out into the anteroom.

Katya was annoyed. She had met Lieutenant Gaida before, several times. Still, there was nothing in their relationship to permit him to act in such a possessive way. She looked back over her shoulder to Alex, ready to apologize, but Gaida spoke first: "No need for that right now, my dear Katherine. I'm leaving for Poland tonight and have only a few minutes." With this said, his face appeared less serious and he advanced a half-smile before speaking in confident tones. "We'll drive the Germans back across the Vistula, march on Berlin and join the French and British as equals. Then," he added, trying to make his bravado sound more jovial, she supposed, "I'll come back for you as a general."

Watching from the fireplace Alex considered his first instinct to make an issue of Gaida's rudeness but decided against it. Gaida was a stranger. He was also a comrade-in-arms and would soon be on his way. No use starting something that had no beginning and no end. I'm not in competition with him, he thought, so he shouldn't worry that I'm invading the ram's pasture.

Alex had to admit, though, that he had been pleasantly at ease in Katya's presence. She was the most fascinating young woman he had ever met. Still, he did not understand why he should feel so attracted to this complete stranger, especially when she herself was so forward. He needed time to get used to forceful women, he supposed, and time to gain the poise necessary to hide his occasional stammer. The truth was, he admired independent thinkers of any age, men or women. Rarely had he been tolerant of people who were without thought — or worse, without courage to express them. It was just that he needed a little time. Besides, this aristocratic lady must have a thousand suitors.

While studying Gaida, he was distracted by the commotion of new arrivals clattering over the hardwood floor and into the room. As the crowd of soldiers swirled deeper into the house Alex was grateful to recognize many of the friends he had led across the border one month earlier. A familiar voice called "Alex!" and Peter Kechek pushed his way through, his Viking hair trimmed short in the military style. Alex met him with an embrace. "Hey, Petya. Good to see you again."

He shook his head in embarrassment when Peter wrapped an arm over his shoulder, calling to a group of soldiers, many of whom Alex did not recognize. "Brothers! Meet Alex Branda, the hardest working center-half ever to grace a football field. He has a pass softer than a maiden's caress." There was laughter then, as men stepped forward to shake Alex's hand.

"Your father's president of Falcon Athletics?" one asked. When Alex nodded there was a murmur of recognition and respect. Now even more soldiers approached. Most wore Russian-issue cavalry pants with tunics open at the neck. Their polished boots had comfortable-looking folds at the ankle, with soft leather rising to the knee.

He saw Katya watching from the hallway as Gaida continued to talk to her, his back to Alex.

"Where in hell have you been for the past month?" Peter demanded.

"Officer's training in Moscow . . . once we got Stefan fit again."

"So where is he? The rest of us were brought here for training by a Russian cavalry unit."

Alex hesitated. "Stefan is with Colonel Trojanov helping others."

Peter looked impressed. "More are coming?"

"Oh yes," Alex said, serious now. "That's what I want to talk to you about." He had been thinking about a bold, perhaps insane, plan for some time now, wondering when the time would come to test it in public. He had to find the right men, men he could trust, like the friends he had led out of Poland.

His voice grew louder, "Could I have your attention?" and the men in the room turned toward him, crowding closer to listen. Some drank tea. Others smoked Turkish cigarettes. All were serious and attentive.

As the large room grew quiet, Alex announced, "There are now fifteen hundred Czechs in St. Petersburg ready to fight for Russia." He paused, waiting as the men reacted to this new information with smiles and applause. "Thousands more wait across the lines, desperate to join us."

Again he waited, cataloging the reaction of the audience as they nodded in agreement. "With a Czech army, Russia will defeat Germany. Then we'll have earned our independence. That's the agreement with the Western Allies."

Now the men smiled, becoming more animated in their approval as Alex continued. "Gentlemen. That's why we, the first of the free Czechs, must help our conscripted brothers escape."

He scanned their faces, noting the looks of bewilderment. Peter frowned. "What could we possibly do?"

Alex shifted uncomfortably, not happy with the answer he was about to give. Nevertheless, he looked at Peter directly. "We go back in and get them."

Shocked disbelief gave way to a noisy reaction, causing Katya to look anxiously across the room. Even Gaida turned, suddenly interested in what was being said.

"Go back? That's suicide!" someone called out.

"Impossible!" shouted another.

"Branda!" It was Gaida, waving for attention.

Peter raised both his hands high for quiet. "Order, brothers. Order!"

As the noise diminished, Gaida spoke. "The Brno Eighty-Eighth tried to surrender to the Russians. They were cut down. Survivors ran back into Austrian machine guns. Every man, slaughtered!"

The faces in the crowd grew angry. There were dark curses, which made the serving ladies retreat to the kitchen. Katya stayed, Alex noticed. He stood motionless with arms folded across his chest until there was quiet again. Then, trying to keep his voice steady, asked, "How can we ignore them?"

Alex paced before the men, watching. "Will you shoot at Czechs across no-man's-land? Who will you shoot at? Your next door neighbor? Your uncle? You'll have to make that choice. And you'll have to make it next week on the Polish front."

The men stood silently, the glow from the fire accentuating the concern on each face. Finally Peter asked, almost in resignation, "What's your plan?"

Alex was now the only voice. "We form a special unit. The Falcon Company. All athletes." He looked hard into each face. "I want men who take chances. Total discipline, . . . top fitness, . . . unmarried."

Thoughtful eyes followed him uncertainly.

"You know who you are," he continued. "The Russian High Command has given us written approval. They'll warn their troops before our raids. We go back across the lines and our Russian comrades listen for the hymn as we come out."

Gaida's incredulous voice asked, more in derision than curiosity: "Trust a Russian peasant? Madness."

Alex nodded.

"It's a lot to ask," Peter said, stating the common thought.

"That's the price. Think it over."

The men turned to their neighbors in small groups, but before the voices could drown him out, Alex added loudly, "If you want to join the Falcons, see Peter, or me."

Alex saw the look on Peter's face. He followed Alex to an open part of the room, shaking his head. "You bastard," he said with a resigned smile. Grinning, Alex merely gave his friend a shrug.

"We've got to get our bunch together." Then he turned to watch Gaida put on scarf and coat. Holding his cap, Gaida kissed Katya's hand before leaving by the front door.

Alex was impressed by how serious Gaida was. If looks counted, he could be a good soldier.

"How soon before we get into it?" Peter asked, also tracking his friend's gaze to watch Gaida's departure.

Without taking his eyes from Katya as she held the door open for Gaida, Alex stated casually, "Matter of days. He's away tonight."

"Lieutenant Rad Gaida, a very ambitious fellow. The medical corps was too pedestrian for him. Rad wants to command," Peter said. "Leaving Miss Kazakova for you, perhaps?"

Alex watched Katya return to the refreshment table. She glanced his way, and he looked down at the floor with a grin. "No, no," he answered Peter. "A common soldier doesn't have time for a lady like that. She's an aristocrat and like opium. Maybe worse."

He looked back at Katya for another moment. "Maybe better."

* * *

From a second-story balcony at the Stanford University Women's Club, Victor watched angry clouds collect around the moon, but he still maintained a smile for the adoring eyes of the young woman sipping ginger ale at his side. He wore a new cricket jacket with long vertical stripes of green and purple on a cream background. She flaunted a tennis tan in her bare-shouldered silk dress. No bag of bones, he noticed. Miriam was an attention getter, and even a storm could not detract from his good mood tonight. He had completed a

Bachelor of Science degree in engineering — an accomplishment of which his mother was very proud — and this knowledge filled him with comfort. It seemed as if a great weight had somehow fallen away.

He felt in control. So much so, that when Miriam flinched, startled by the rumble of far-off thunder, he rolled his eyes to make her laugh. "It's all done with mirrors," he said. "Like Houdini."

Offering his arm, he led her back onto the dance floor where she blended lightly into his expert grasp. He took care to leave a breathing space between his left palm and her hand so that no embarrassment from perspiration was possible. He was also aware of the presence of four ancient but vigilant faculty women acting as chaperones to make certain that there was an appropriate space between the dancers' bodies as well.

Holding the arch of his wrist lightly on her back, he allowed the set of his shoulders to indicate his direction while the nasal wail of saxophones sighed out his favorite waltz: The Sweetheart of Sigma Chi. He was amazed at how easily she followed — or was it anticipation? She seemed to flow instinctively, so that he was mildly startled when there was a light touching during a normal hesitation step. He had held her still for a fraction of a second before signaling her to move toward him by taking his own step back. It was then that he felt her stride between his legs, pushing lightly for a moment against his flexed forward knee.

He paused on his back foot, dwelling on the brief sensation of her inner thigh because the touch had inflamed him instantly. Had he taken too long? They were turning again. Had she noticed? Her face gave him no indication when she glanced up briefly with an innocent expression.

"It's raining," he heard her say. "I hope you're walking me home."

"Oh good. Yes of course. I have an umbrella," he murmured, trying to keep his voice low, and trying to maintain a satisfactory deportment for the expressionless but practiced stare of the chaperones. Any sort of shoddy behavior at a university dance, even at year's end, would be grounds for dismissal for sons of immigrant workers on Leland Stanford's railroad; this thought immediately calmed his ardor.

As they walked back to the residences in the drumming rain he hunched under the wide umbrella, trying to think of something appropriate to say. He had found, when he first came to this campus four years ago, that he was better off keeping his mouth shut. He resolved to let the girl speak first; more often than not, she was the one who gave him an indication of what might lie ahead. Victor decided that this form of patience saved him a great deal of time by simply waiting for that which had already been schemed out by his consort of the moment.

They stopped under a wide oak at the side of the women's dormitory. He leaned forward under the noisy umbrella, brushing her cheek with his lips.

"You're a good dancer," she responded in a matter-of-fact voice. Then he felt her move forward, lightly straddling his leg again, just above the knee.

So she had known, back on the dance floor, and he smiled with the knowledge of having guessed correctly, but before he could speak, she turned her face up to his and kissed him with lips smelling softly of rose-scented gloss. Mesmerized, Victor listened to her whisper: "I have to go now . . . did you know that I live at the top of this tree?"

Victor looked up to see a soft light from a single window pane blurred by rain and leaves.

He watched her run up the path, disappearing as she turned the corner to the front of the building. In the drumming rain, he stood under the umbrella looking thoughtfully up at the window nearest the last sturdy branch. He continued to savor the delicious tingle from her kiss until another light came on spreading a yellow glow.

This is crazy, he thought, coming to his senses again. I could be expelled for just standing here! Madness. I'll be kicked out if caught. Then what would I do?

He started away but stopped. There's no one around, he reminded himself. And it's dark as it can get, with the tree a perfect cover. Still, to be expelled . . . His mind was racing. An open-and-shut invitation, made with a reminder that she would be up until the eleven o'clock lights-out. "Don't give up the ship," she had said. He grinned. It was an unbelievable invitation — more like an appointment. How can I miss that?

With a jump, he hung from the first branch before pulling himself up to a foothold; the gum rubber deck shoes borrowed from a yachting friend were solid on the rough bark. He looked around again — still no one in sight.

Climbing steadily without a sound, Victor came level with the window where he could see Miriam brushing her hair in front of a full-length mirror. He checked the strength of the branch before creeping toward the open window.

Now he could see her silk nightgown, clinging and pink. He pulled back instantly when he heard the sound of approaching footsteps on the path below. Holding his breath, he pressed against the trunk while looking down. Good God, he thought, swallowing hard, it's the Dean of Women.

His eyes followed while the Dean walked under the tree toward the main sidewalk. When for no apparent reason she stopped, his heart thumped wildly. He peered down through the leaves until she continued toward the lit street. After she turned the corner, he listened while her footsteps faded away.

I've got to get out of here, he thought, fighting panic as he stretched his foot carefully toward a lower branch. Unexpectedly the window opened and a voice whispered, "Vic."

In her arms moments later, he forgot everything except the push of her breathing and the touch of her hair. Through the fog he heard her say, "No, we mustn't."

"What? Mustn't what, for God's sake?"

"You know," she said haltingly. "I, I might get pregnant . . . I just can't."

Victor stared, puzzled. "But . . . then why?"

"Look," she said, putting her hands lightly on his chest through the open buttons of his shirt.

He watched her eyes glance to his briefly, then lower again before flitting back. He could not tell whether she was embarrassed or plotting, so he waited.

"Have you read of . . . how the French . . . avoid . . . pregnancy," she whispered before looking away, "while seeking pleasure?"

He smiled, deciding that it had been embarrassment after all. "Of course," he said reassuringly, starting to kiss her neck gently. He noticed how still she lay when he pulled undone the loose knot at her waist, and he heard no protestations as he began to kiss her bare ankles. He focused on her shallow breathing, listening to it as if in a dream remembering the metronomic sigh of the ocean, wave upon wave onto the beach at Monterey Bay. From somewhere far-off he heard the squeak of a bedspring.

There was an insistent rap-rap on the door. "Miriam," a woman's voice hissed. "Open this door at once!"

Victor grabbed his shoes in a bound for the window.

• • •

The next morning Victor sat nervously drinking coffee at a stained cafeteria table. His headache thumped between his eyes but he stood up as Miriam approached to sit across from him with a drawn white face.

"What happened?" he demanded in a sharp whisper.

"Nothing."

"Nothing? What do you mean nothing? What did you tell the Dean?"

He watched as she formed her words carefully. "Well, nothing to you," she admitted in a low voice. "After she'd searched the room, and even under the bed, she concluded that I was indulging in something she called 'shameless self-abuse' and that I should report to confession. Further than that, I'm forbidden to attend dances next term."

"Sorry," he said, somewhat relieved.

"No you're not. You're just glad you didn't get caught."

Vic nodded. "You're right. I thought it was the end." He felt his chest relax a little. His confidence was coming back.

"Well, I'm glad it wasn't . . . but it's not over. She found your award sweater."

The sweater! Cold fear pumped back into his empty chest. "My name's on the tag."

"I know," she said. "I told her I'd borrowed it."

She looked unsure of her decision, he thought, judging from the worry lines across her forehead. "Well done," he said as calmly as he could. "That was a good idea. We'll stay with it."

Although he did not think that particular excuse would stand up to scrutiny, he was relieved to see her face brighten up a bit while she nodded vigorously, and he tried to regain his composure.

I might have a chance, he thought hopefully, until he spotted Lefty Rogers making his way through the crowd. Victor felt his hopes drain away once more. He could tell by the look on the big man's face that he carried the burden of bad news.

"The Dean wants to see you," Rogers said.

Victor turned to Miriam who looked close to tears. "Don't worry," he said. "Shh. It's my problem. All my fault. My problem." He filled his lungs, then exhaled every last wisp. "Well," he said more for himself than the others, "I have an engineering degree from Stanford University at least. Maybe a turn with the army would be instructive. That would make a suspension unnecessary and an investigation redundant."

He didn't think he could manage any sort of a convincing smile so he just shrugged and shook hands with Lefty. "So long then. Maybe see you sometime."

● ● ●

Katya was content while the Czechs waited for military assignment on the Polish front. Alex visited the Social Center every day and she invariably found herself alone with him as he helped in the kitchen. It was difficult to tell whether he arranged their meetings or whether they just happened. Certainly he did not try to avoid them. Their conversations were long and seemed to center on their childhood, as if they were studying each other. She was now confident that he enjoyed her conversation, even the challenge of her abrupt insights which sometimes seemed to catch him off guard. She had made a mental note that there were times when his speech stuttered, but she was also happy to discover that the stammer occurred less and less in her company. He seemed intent upon her questions, so she assumed that he was becoming used to her.

She had to admit to being impressed by this quiet Czech who removed his jacket so readily to help, working with an ease few could pretend.

"I might remind you of someone," she said to him one evening as they prepared refreshments around the good salty smell of boiled fish. She had noticed Alex's searching gaze but was not offended by it. Since coming to St. Petersburg she had grown aware of the way men observed her. It was not the same as her playful student friends in Kiev. Some watched timidly as if in awe, some with a brutish hunger. And yet this young Czech, she thought, seems completely comfortable with me here at the table making sandwiches. He makes me feel unique. Yes, Alex was different. There was admiration in his watchfulness, yet there was also a trace of sadness it seemed.

Nevertheless, in his eyes she could see the aplomb of a man who knew his purpose. She could also see the determination to secure it; so determined, in fact, that apparently nothing, including an opportunity for romance, interfered with this burden.

Alex coughed uncomfortably. "Perhaps you do remind me of someone," he said, "but the image fades before I see it clearly." Then he busied himself spreading fish paste on the crusty bread.

From their daily association of now more than a week while waiting for the Russian High Command to decide where to assign the Czechs, Katya felt herself drawn closer to Alex. They were comfortable in each other's company. He began to walk her home after hours.

Strolling down Nevsky Prospect bundled in furs against the cold, she hooked his arm and watched the passing sleighs and automobiles glide through the circles of light under each street lamp. She felt quite small on this wide boulevard so busy with all the traffic for the National Library and the Kazan Cathedral. Although dwarfed by the somber buildings of state, she was proud to be so close to the center of power in the capital city and to be sharing this atmosphere with Alex.

One evening as they walked through the echoing fore-court of the Winter Palace where she had first heard the Czar's call to war, Katya realized that Alex was becoming a good friend. She sensed that the lieutenant felt a deeper attraction toward her, but consistently he remained preoccupied with something that held him back.

"The only reason I'm here is for my country's freedom, or I'd walk away from it all," he confided to her as they came to the Kamenny Bridge. The motionless water looked as black as India ink; a color exaggerated by the snow-covered banks framing the canal. She leaned over the balustrade, looking down at their silhouettes undulating on a background of lamplight. "I can't leave my friends now," he continued. "I got them here. And I'll see them out."

An empty coal scow slid past. She could hear the slap of waves on the prow as they turned away toward the Treasury staff residences. She had learned that he always held something of himself in reserve. He was disciplined and correct. He made no erotic advances, nor were there overtures of love. Alex presented conversation and a kiss for her hand at the front door. That was all.

"Russia is powerful," she offered. "The High Command has promised fifteen million troops. Fifteen million will smother the enemy." She said this with complete confidence and was embarrassed by the certainty of Alex's dismissal of her point.

"Without food? Guns? Organization?" Alex said, shaking his head as they arrived at the bottom of the stair. "Not the way these wealthy amateurs interfere. Even the career professionals are aristocrats. They don't give a damn about the ordinary soldier."

Katya felt as if she had been slapped in the face. She climbed the stairs quickly and angrily grasped the door handle. "Are you suggesting that Russia is not prepared?"

She expected him to back down from that question, but he stood with a solemn face at the bottom step and quietly nodded. There was pain in those black eyes.

"Let me give you an example," he said. "The rail system is a farce. Trains are lost, for God's sake. Sent to the wrong destination on orders from an aristocrat who's never been near the front, given to a clerk who can't read a map, and passed on to a union worker who hates them all. Germans use captured supplies against the men who wait for them so hopefully. We hear your officers complaining of these things. And the Russian artillery: now there's a story," he added sarcastically. "When they do receive shells, Russian guns sometimes bombard their own front-line troops who have, because of dumb stubborn courage, overrun German lines. Communications go to Grand Duke Nicholas in Petrograd before Artillery Command hears about the advance. It's hopeless."

"I can't believe that!" Katya protested, moving away from the door to glare down at him. She felt her lips draw tightly together. "They will make the necessary corrections. You'll see. It must change."

One of the accountants came up with his wife. They looked concerned as they studied Alex, who removed his cap. "Anything wrong, Katya?" her colleague asked. Katya gave him a quick shake of her head and watched them go inside.

Alex was putting on his cap again, ready to leave. He seemed discouraged. "It probably won't change," he said. "It's the way the ruling class thinks. Ordinary people are used like tools, like animals. And children go hungry. That's really why unionists fight against their own aristocracy and not against Germany."

Katya felt another wave of anger. She refused to believe that her class had less than pure motives. They were defending the country against invasion. "That isn't true!" she said, moving quickly down the three steps to stand in front of him defiantly. "Not our generals. Not the Grand Duke."

"Watch and learn," was all he said.

She turned abruptly and walked back out onto the street. After all, she thought, searching her own actions for the first time, I don't think of ordinary people as tools. Surely not. And yet, she had to admit, the poverty was there in the streets. One could see it, smell it . . . if one only took the time. Do I really look? she asked herself. Do I do anything about it? Does the Czar or any of his ministers?

Alex caught up, his breath steaming. "What kind of leader do you think assigns four infantrymen to one rifle, then?"

"I don't know what you mean," she said.

"A soldier is given a rifle to carry, and he's ordered to charge. So he runs across the snow toward enemy lines chased by three unarmed comrades. When he falls, one of those running behind picks up the gun, and then they continue the charge. They pick up the gun, not the man! He's sacrificed. Casualties mean little. At Tannenberg, 92,000 captured and 78,000 killed or wounded. It made Waterloo look like a skirmish."

Katya stiffened, horrified. "Stop. It will change. It must change." She felt sick and turned away to look across the great square in front of the Winter Palace. The emptiness was frightening. "I had no idea . . . and yet," she said, turning back to her doorway. "You'd die for your country."

"I'm prepared to, but I'll do it surrounded by friends. Not like the common Russian, sacrificed by people who don't give a damn — or remember who he was."

She pointed a finger at his chest. "The Czar cares. I believe this."

"No disrespect, but where did the Czar get his military training? From God at birth? Let's be honest. He has no training, yet every decision he makes affects our separate battle. That makes him a dilettante playing Napoleon, and so far he's not doing a good job of it."

She was determined to challenge his point of view. He could not insult the Czar further! "How do you know all this?"

Alex looked sad. "Because my friends are there, at the front, watching."

Katya stared, her mouth tightly closed as she considered his points. She had not told Alex the true nature of her job with the

Czar's Treasury, because all Treasury staff had been sworn to secrecy in a formal ceremony. Alex knew she lived with fellow accountants in a special residence. What he did not know was that the building was provided by the Czar, and that the Treasury staff had, on many occasions, been granted an audience. Czar Nicholas often told Treasury members of the great responsibility accompanying their position and how much he needed their steadfast allegiance. "I must say," she concluded emphatically, "the Czar has my loyalty. He has little to gain in helping the Western Allies. You just don't know him yet."

"That's true. But I know his game."

Katya turned, marching back to the staff residences. She ran up the stairs to her door. Alex's conviction angered her, but she understood it well enough. And the images of children she understood most clearly of all, because she saw them every day. Their hungry eyes made it very hard to reconcile the wealth stockpiled in the Treasury with the thin soup meant to sustain the poor. Still, it had always been this way. She would watch, and think this through. Then she slipped inside and closed the door.

The next day was Sunday, and as soon as Alex entered the Social Center she knew immediately that he was leaving. All the signs were there. He was serious, yet flushed with the excitement of mission. Katya had become expert at recognizing the symptoms by now. He was going to Poland.

He wished her well, confessing how much he had enjoyed their friendship. "Goodbye, Katya," he said, holding her hand for several breathing spaces as if reluctant to let her go. "Perhaps I could write," she heard him say as the empty space in her chest grew cold. "Perhaps we could meet again . . . ." He suggested this hopefully, it seemed to her, before bowing to kiss her hand.

Since Katya had first met Alex, she realized that he would have to leave one day, and thought she had prepared herself for that inevitability. She had known Alex for only a fortnight but sensed this short attachment was not enough. In a desperate moment, she pulled his hand behind her, stretching her arms around his chest as far as they could reach. "Don't go."

Alex held her for several seconds. Soft lips caressed her cheek. She could feel the strength in his embrace that she wanted to believe hinted at hidden feelings, but she was afraid to ask.

"There's no way out," he whispered. "We win or there's nothing left for us. Au revoir."

Then Katya felt him turn out of her arms, and watched him march quickly away.

CHAPTER 6

THE PINSK MARSHES
SPRING 1915

In front of their tent at the edge of a forest not far from the village of Stepan, Alex peered through sparks from a cooking fire and watched Colonel Trojanov approach on the path from town. He kicked Peter's foot so that they both rose together to welcome this Russian colonel who was known to share the Czar's view that a Czech volunteer was more than just another soldier. The colonel had seen for himself that Alex's volunteers were passionate in their desire to serve, and that they wanted to serve well. Alex was aware that, unlike Trojanov, most of the high-ranking officers within the Russian military system viewed Czechs with disdain.

"Good evening, sir," Alex said, saluting.

The colonel straddled one of the logs dragged in to frame the fire. "You may sit," he directed in an easy way, waving aside wisps of smoke. "They tell me that you have ideas about a raid."

Alex sat down with Peter across from Trojanov. "Yes, sir. I've been talking with our most recent volunteers. The Twenty-Eighth Prague Infantry is only five kilometres across those hills. They want to join us. Lieutenant Kechek and I could bring them out."

The colonel leaned forward absently poking the coals with a stick, but Alex knew he was being studied carefully. There were no secrets from those pale blue eyes.

"The Austrians have four regiments holding the high ground between us and the river and you want to lead one regiment out? You couldn't get through," Trojanov said in a scoffing way, although Alex could tell that the colonel still watched him closely.

"Peter and I can slip around them," he offered. "The marsh is no more than chest deep. There's only one sentry tower because the Austrians know that an attack through marshland would be suicidal. They won't be watching for two quiet men." There was no interruption, so Alex continued. "Getting out will be even easier. From behind the sentry system we can fight our way out, if we have to, with surprise on our side. Or we can wade again."

The colonel merely turned his attention back to the fire. "If you're caught, they'd treat you as spies."

"Well, sir. That's the trick. Not getting caught."

He felt foolish in the silence that followed. The colonel poked some coals into a better position under the fire.

Peter glanced over. He was chewing his lower lip thoughtfully.

After several strained breaths the colonel stood up. "Sounds a gamble to me," he said, shaking his head. He broke the stick in half and tossed it into the fire. "I'm not in favor of it, but you may try, if you are that determined," he said, brushing off his hands.

"Any restrictions, sir?" Alex asked, trying to appear cheerful under Trojanov's continued stare.

"Just don't expect us to come looking for you. We'll listen for the hymn."

At three o'clock the next morning, at the edge of a grove of spindly pine, Alex was crawling toward the swamp over ground covered with sweet-smelling needles. Flat on his stomach, he pulled himself across the tangle toward the edge of the Pinsk Marshes with Peter right behind. He swung his elbow forward onto a fallen branch and when his weight heaved forward, it cracked in the still air louder than a shout.

Alex froze, peering across the muddy swamp and tufts of reeds toward the watchtower one hundred metres away, on the hill overlooking the marsh. Had the sentry heard? Although dressed in dark coveralls for camouflage, they were in the open under the moon, away from the forest's shadowy protection. He felt certain someone in the watchtower could see him. He waited without moving until the sweat on his forehead began to sting his eyes, then turned to look into Peter's intense gaze.

Peter seemed business-like, as he usually was in action. Alex could see that his friend's stare was glued to the tower directly across the marsh from them, and Alex remembered that it was always the time just before physical involvement that was most difficult for Peter. Peter had been that way as an athlete, with an almost trance-like focus upon the space between the goal posts. As center forward for the University team, he was quiet, expressionless, always watching the target for his time to strike — the way he was right now.

The marsh narrowed where the outline of the guard's tower shone in the moonlight. Alex didn't like their chances and gave up on the idea of wading across the narrows undetected. Instead, he inched like a noiseless serpent along the bank at the edge of the marsh. The dirt here was damp and cloying, but he continued to slither toward the wide open swamp farther to the west.

When the sentry's hill was out of sight, Alex eased into the dead water up to his thighs. As his boots sunk in, the mud released a stream of gas-bubbles stinking of decay, and he turned away. A cloud of insects flew into his face. Shuddering, he could feel the cold water soak through his trousers. He watched Peter slip in beside him, his face screwing up at the stench.

Alex waded ahead through the sludge quietly and steadily, trying not to breathe in the mosquitoes. He could feel them crowding around his nose, threatening to choke his every breath. He held his hand up, stopping Peter so that they could cover their heads for relief from the swarm. He pressed each nostril closed with a finger, snorting out forcefully until the other was clear. Reaching under his tunic he ripped away the front of his shirt. He tore it again to give half to Peter, then tied it like a mask over his face.

Breathing through the protective cloth, they waded forward again through the muck, stumbling across small islands of matted grass until at last they heaved themselves out of the fetid marsh onto the far bank.

They followed the edge of the swamp, one behind the other on the narrow mud bank. Aching with cold, and pursued by the relentless mosquitoes, they crept along this slippery path watching nervously for any sign of the Austrian encampment. But the area was so harshly inhospitable that they reached the Styn River at dawn unchallenged.

Alex's legs were numb as he waded into the icy river to wash. As quickly as he could, he got out to change into the uniform of a Twenty-Eighth Prague Infantry sergeant which Peter had been carrying in the pack. Then he rubbed life into his limbs through the rough cloth of the fresh uniform. There was no Austrian uniform for Peter so he merely changed trousers, willing to wait for the mud on his jacket to dry.

While studying an area map, Alex accepted the black bread and cheese Peter handed him. His body was beginning to feel more comfortable with the chance to rest, but he knew he could not take too long. Reveille would sound shortly. He pointed down the path beside the river. "Kolki is another half kilometre down this trail," he said. "I'll meet you right here . . . soon as I can."

Peter appeared unconcerned — busy with the job of hiding Alex's muddy clothes in the brush. "I'll be here," he said casually. "Take your time. I'd like some sleep."

Alex stuffed the last bit of bread into his mouth, shook hands and walked down the path feeling very conspicuous. He determined to act as if he belonged. He had to pull this off.

Hiding in brush outside the camp area near the latrines, Alex waited for bugle call. He was aware now of just how tired he was, and looked uneasily back along the river toward where Peter waited for him, unable to help.

He felt quite alone, and so he tried not to think of the penalty for capture. A firing squad, he thought. My God . . . would I run or quietly submit? I think I'd run.

As traffic to the latrines grew, Alex fell in with the pattern, and entered the tenting area unchallenged. Walking cautiously through the encampment, it did not take him long to find the men of the Twenty-Eighth Prague Regiment sitting at small fires, boiling their morning rations. He felt a rush of joy, until he noticed that they looked up quizzically as he slipped into the largest circle of men to sit on the end of a log.

"Good morning," Alex said in Czech, conscious of their curiosity. He regretted that he had not thought out his approach more carefully. Three men suddenly stood up like sentries in a protective screen around him. Another, who looked like a gypsy, went to one knee in front, hooking the tip of a knife under Alex's crotch. He stared intently up into Alex's face. "You don't belong here. What're you after?" he demanded.

Alex looked down at the soldier. This was no beginner. The gypsy had hard eyes and it was obvious that he was not one to listen to elaborate explanations. "I'm here to lead you out," Alex said simply.

Again he was taken by surprise. Once he had identified this purpose, the man broke into a wide smile and brandished his knife like a sword. The others laughed. "We'll leave right away," the gypsy said.

"Sit down," Alex protested, looking around nervously. "We have to prepare."

"No need. We've been ready for months, . . . just waiting for the right sergeant to lead us." The man with the hard eyes put away his knife with a wink. "Here, lie by the fire. Rest. Eat some bacon. We go to drill in one hour."

Parade was called for inspection with full packs and light weapons. The Czech conscripts were quick into formation. The Austrian officers must have been satisfied by the speedy compliance because they gave only cursory review of the platoons and did not notice Alex in the back ranks trying to blend with the rest. He slowed his breathing and tried to ignore the knot between his shoulder blades. The thought of being captured by the Austrians was too frightening to consider. It simply must not happen. He must be lucky today. He knew none of these men, but believed they would not turn him in. They had no reason to; they wanted out.

Something past the line of tents caught Alex's eye. Following the curve of the river he caught glimpses through the brush of a motorcar driving busily toward the camp. A black sedan turned onto the packed-dirt parade square and stopped in front of the assembled troops. The driver got out and Alex watched anxiously as the rear door opened. My God, he thought. It's Schumann! I'm finished.

Schumann straightened the hem of his jacket, taking his time to look over the two thousand assembled troops of the Twenty-Eighth Prague Infantry. His walk was a casual saunter as he slowly approached the commanding officer who had turned toward the visitor from the center of the parade.

Alex fought back the panic. What could he do? Where could he hide?

He saw the gypsy glance at him with a curious look. Fear must be written all over my face, he thought. Calm down. Don't attract attention. Alex stretched his neck to a normal position and looked straight ahead. As Schumann ambled toward the company, Alex held his breath, his heart pounding.

"Attention. I bring greetings to you men of the Prague Twenty-Eighth Infantry from His Royal Highness Arch Duke Karl the First,"

Schumann called loudly. "His Excellency wishes to commend you for your progress in training, so that you stand ready to serve Austria, as full members of His Majesty's army. This is a great honor that you have earned."

Alex watched as Schumann turned to walk slowly back toward the center company.

"It is especially gratifying to me that you should be so honored, because it was I who recruited you, giving you the opportunity to participate in our great quest." Alex strained to watch as Schumann continued to walk toward the third company. "The Austrian and German armies will forge a new empire . . . stretching from Hamburg to Baghdad. You will be part of this!" he shouted.

Schumann was walking back again. "You will share the prize through your loyalty. For those who do not promise full loyalty . . . let me assure you that justice will be swift. You and your families will be hunted down . . . and will surely . . . by the will of Archduke Karl . . . pay the ultimate price . . . as traitors."

Alex tried to swallow with a dry throat. He felt as if Schumann somehow knew that he was only twenty metres away, but Schumann merely turned toward the commanding officer and gave an off-hand salute before striding quickly to the car.

To his relief, the car drove back down the road by the river, and the drill period was impatiently turned over to non-commissioned rankings so that the Austrian officers could retire to the mess tent for breakfast. Alex slowly let loose his clenched fists.

As soon as the last officer disappeared inside the dining tent, Alex took a position at the front of three companies of the Twenty-Eighth Prague Regiment as their new sergeant, marching them up the road to the north where Peter waited. This was accomplished without complication except for his own extreme discomfort. He should have instructed the gypsy with the knife to lead them away from camp, he realized. Too late now.

To the few remaining stragglers who watched, it must have seemed to be the usual morning drill. From what Alex had gathered, the other regiments were encamped to the south, and by the time he had covered only two hundred metres, the road took a turn conforming to the river. Once around this turn, the column snaked in behind the high ground to their right and with the marshes on their left, and he felt less vulnerable.

Peter stood at the side of the dirt road in a jocular way, saluting and acting the part of an inspecting general as two thousand men in columns of four marched past.

"Let's get the hell out of here," Alex said, clenching and unclenching his fists, trying to make the trembling go away.

He waved over the gypsy with the hard eyes. "I'd like you to pull a few men and take care of any sentries at the head of the marsh. We'll cross over at the narrows."

The gypsy reached up slowly to touch his cap. "No trouble at all," he said with a business-like expression. "It will be my pleasure."

Three hours later, on the verge of exhaustion, Alex waded out of the marshes. Wet to the chest and stinking of mud, he brushed the last few bullrushes out of his way at the edge of the swamp to stand unsteadily on dry land again. Puddles formed on the dirt beneath his boots. He flexed his feet trying to feel his toes.

Peter slipped climbing up the bank and his hand buried in the muck. "Shit!" he complained. He tried to clean his hands on his pants, but two men of the Twenty-Eighth Prague Infantry each grabbed an elbow and hauled him up the slippery bank.

"Come on," Alex called to the men wading the last few metres out of the marsh. "Almost there."

He started walking toward the village of Stolin and the regiment of ragged men followed. Every step was an effort, but Alex allowed himself a smile and swung his arm over Peter's shoulder when they reached the edge of the village.

Then the lusty singing of "Hej Slovani" grew louder as the regiment marched down the muddy main street to where Alex could see Colonel Trojanov waiting at the entrance to the village library, where he had made his headquarters. Trojanov beckoned.

"Well, Branda. There's your song again," the colonel said over the noise of the proud voices marching past. "A little sooner than we expected."

The colonel's aide approached, and Alex heard the order given by Trojanov: "Get the papers ready for Lieutenants Branda and Kechek. Shall we say . . . for meritorious service to Russia? But right now, some tea. I'm going to talk to these fellows. I like idealists when they're high, not after their dreams have been crushed out of them."

• • •

Katya woke early on Saturday morning feeling good about the life she was leading in St. Petersburg. She and Marie would have a full hour of ballet instruction, then breakfast, before spending the rest of the day at the military hospital which now seemed to her to be more important than a full day at the Treasury. Under the strain of war, the Treasury was demanding enough, with the almost frantic sale of war bonds. The community of aristocrats was anxious to pledge money to support the Czar, and this, she agreed, was vital. But at the hospital she served in a direct way, calming some of the men who struggled with unfamiliar feelings of fear and depression; this was important too. The decorated veteran who had lost a foot. The red-haired youth from Smolensk who was convinced that his village had been overrun and family scattered. Katya discovered that she was clever at getting these wounded officers to talk to her as they might talk to a caring sister or an attentive sweetheart, and she hoped it would help them face the doubt that haunted their days.

"Do you think she could ignore this?" one pale young man had asked, the intensity of the question crushing his forehead into sweaty folds.

Katya braced herself before reaching out to where his arms crossed on the table in front of him, putting her fingertips on the end of the bandage where his right hand should have been. When he closed his eyes in embarrassment she was frightened that she might have overstepped herself.

"Of course she will," Katya said confidently, bracing against the emotion rising in her throat. "All she wants is to see your face. That's all she wants."

And how many times had she helped write letters, putting into words those fears which had enfeebled brave men? The answer was: as many times as she had fought for composure in order to smile benignly as if all would be as it once had been.

Ballet class rescued her from these deceptions three times a week, but at times she wondered whether the escape into dance was simply a different deception.

In the ballet salon on the second floor of the Winter Palace, six high windows formed the southeast wall. Katya pulled back one of the drapes to look out over the great square and down rain-swept Nevsky Prospect. There were few foot-travelers on the windy street where long puddles against the curbstones were lashed by sleet and rain. Marie stood at her side looking out onto the slushy boulevard until they heard the ballet mistress call them to order. Quickly Katya ran to her place facing a mirror that stretched the full length of the room from floor to ceiling.

Two sharp raps of a staff began their lesson. "Posture, ladies, posture! Where is your center? You are not peasants in the field. You are graceful statues. Pull up!"

Madame barked her commands in a manner as severe as her hairstyling, which pulled her sparse gray hair tight to the scalp, exaggerating the length of her thin face. "A plie is not stooping for potatoes in the dirt. It is a graceful bending and unbending. Give me the impression of absolutely no effort at all. Ready? Begin."

With one arm curved gracefully to mid-thigh and the other resting lightly on the barre, Katya and the ladies of the court flexed and straightened their knees through first position to the fifth.

She loves this, Katya thought, watching the Grande Dame in the high mirror which was more than twice her height. Four princesses, one grand duchess, three ladies-in-waiting and two staff members make a perfect focus for this tyrant's lust for control.

"Slowly, Katherine Elenskaya. Slowly. You are not in a race. This is your country's beloved soul.

"Tendus, please. Shoulders down." Madame tapped her staff so that the sound echoed sternly up and down the comfortless room, while ten ballerinas-for-a-day faced yet another demand to "stand tall." They were dressed in white tunics tied at the waist, wide sleeves to the elbow, matching cotton pants pegged at the knee and heavy woolen stockings rising to thigh level above satin slippers.

How Russian this room is, Katya mused to herself. Cold and stark, and yet members of the Royal Family come here to be castigated by this old tyrant. One simple wooden chair stands alone on the floor for the exclusive use of Madame, but in all these months I've never seen her use it.

Katya listened to the piano as she worked. No expense has been spared for this beautiful instrument, she noted. The best that money can buy and it is never very far from Madame.

The piano was played unobtrusively by a frail-looking woman who somehow knew exactly when to start and exactly when to stop. Her gaze rarely left Madame. Katya had once wished she could play, but had known almost immediately that her style would not be for pedestrian background rhythm and cues. Rimsky Korsakov perhaps, loud and dramatic, but not like this, she was certain.

Without turning her head, Katya moved her eyes to the reflection of Marie Romanov. Marie was a heavier build than Katya and clung to the barre with a touch more determination than one would expect to find in, say . . . the rehearsal room back stage at the Mariinsky Theatre.

"Katya! Pay attention. The degage combination, begin." The brass tip rapped hard on the polished floor.

Katya could feel the burning in her thigh when she pushed her toe. "Out and close, front . . . side, back and side. Releves. On demi pointe. Up, up, up. Lift."

She moved her mind above the pain until her face took on a look of beatific rapture. She watched the peaceful image in the mirror working calmly on and on. It was an image ignorant of the hot agony building within the human form in front of the glass.

But Madame saw it. Her serpent-like eyes darted from student to student, and for the first time, she gave Katya a thin-lipped smile. "Don't lose it," Madame hissed, her eyes shining in recognition of the internal battle Katya was experiencing. "Grand battement to tendu, s'il vous plâit. Begin."

The ballet mistress stood right behind her, where Katya could see Madame's suppressed energy in the mirror. Katya fought to hold the burning under control. She tried to join the body reflected inside the coolness of the glass. She felt a new relaxed power, and worked on as Madame marched behind the line of dancers, tapping her staff to call the count. "Six, seven and eight. Change sides. And one, two, three . . ."

Katya was aware of dampness now. Her face, her shoulders, even her arms were wet and this cool sensation urged her on. She heard a low rumble from outside on the street and knew it must be another convoy of trucks. But she quickly put this out of her mind. This is my time away from war. There has to be somewhere I can hide.

Madame's intense face was full of a strange pleasure as she stood near Katya. "Shoulders down. Turn out. Seven and close, eight and close. Done."

Most of the ladies at the barre stopped, sagging in fatigue as the final count was called, and the leg, which had been stretched high to the side, was returned to fifth position. Some stopped altogether, even though Madame called the next drill. Then they, like Madame, watched Katya.

"Battement cloche," came the call, more as a challenge than a directive. "Do not clutch at the barre. Rest the fingers gently. Begin!" The piano played again.

With left hand lightly on the barre, Katya, Princess Olga and Princess Tatiana lifted the right leg high in front without a bend in either knee. With a sudden pull, her straight leg swept down, then high behind, to be held motionless for a heartbeat while the right hand floated in an arch toward the horizon.

"And two," Madame ordered.

Never before had Katya felt such relaxed strength, and she exalted in it. Her hip was a fluid, flexible coil turning through its full range of motion over and over until Madame instructed, "Left leg."

By now Katya worked alone. The cooling water flowed down her face and she welcomed it. She was in that other world behind the glass.

She looked at the ballerina in the mirror, while the others watched her. This attention only made Katya stand straighter, whipping the other leg high and behind with new vigor, again and again and again, once more, once more, and again and again, until Madame, looking triumphant, her nostrils flaring, called, "And close. Very good, Katherine Elenskaya. You're a strong young woman." Under the cover of applause from the attending ladies, she whispered in Katya's ear, "Life is a ballet. You will do it well, won't you?"

● ● ●

Katya secretly relived her ballet lesson while she waited for her turn at bridge in the officers' card room at the hospital. As she watered a potted palm, she reveled in the feeling of the muscles in her hips and thighs still tight from exertion. She and Marie played as partners in the games room, which opened out onto a pleasant courtyard garden. Their opponents were clean-shaven and trimmed, crisp in their starched shirts. Tidy uniforms reflected the respect for their company; their eyes showed the gratitude. Other officers stood by, casually watching. One had his right arm slung in an ironed white cloth. Another had no right arm at all. Katya excused herself to fill the watering can.

Down the hall in the janitor's closet, a bent old man rinsed a dirty mop in the sink. "Sorry, Miss. There's another closet like this, just below in the basement. If you wait a minute or two, I'll fetch you some."

"No, don't bother. I'll get it," she said, looking for the stairwell at the end of the hall.

Downstairs, there was a woman working at a deep, square sink. She took a blue enamel jug from a cart full of jugs and emptied the cloudy yellow contents into the sink. Then she rinsed the jug under the tap, emptied it again and returned it to the lower shelf. She was perspiring, just as Katya had perspired at ballet, but this woman looked strained, not exhilarated, Katya could see that. Neither was her hair in order; it stuck to her forehead in wet strands. She kept trying to wipe the sweat and hair from her eyes with the back of her wrist. Katya saw dirt under her broken nails. The air was foul. Oh, my God, Katya thought. Those jugs are full of urine!

The woman looked up as Katya approached, and her face darkened.

Katya knew at once that the woman could see who Katya was and what she represented. It was in the hands. The woman's hands were thickly muscled and rough. The leathery skin indicated the hands of a factory worker. Katya's skin was smooth and clean, the hands of an aristocrat.

As they stood there examining each other, Katya felt awkward about her class for the first time in her life. "I'm, I'm sorry to interrupt," she said self-consciously. "I'm looking for some water."

The woman took another jug of urine and, making a show of it, poured the contents slowly into the sink. She held the jug under the tap and turned to look at Katya again before lowering her gaze to the watering can in Katya's hand. Without a word her eyes shifted back to Katya.

"For the potted palms," Katya said, as if to explain.

The woman's eyes were dead, her expression unchanged. "For the potted palms."

Katya's cheeks grew hot. "We have three. Up . . . upstairs."

The woman put back the rinsed jug. "I wouldn't know."

"What happens down here?" Katya asked.

The woman seemed startled, searching Katya's face before answering. "Casualties are brought in. Men die. Boys die. Some from fever. Some from gangrene. You can catch a whiff of it from down the hall." At this the woman's composure appeared ready to crack, but she recovered almost immediately to focus her anger on Katya once again. "Want to see?"

Katya hesitated. The men down here were uneducated. What were they like, really? She knew the woman despised her . . . but as the Czar said, we are all Russians . . . Alex said they were courageous. "Yes, of course," she replied.

Walking down the dim hallway, Katya nervously offered conversation to the woman pushing the cart full of jugs. "Do you live far from here?" she asked politely.

The woman gave her a sour look. "What the bloody hell do you care?"

Katya, shocked by rudeness she did not understand, was ill-prepared for the sight of the one ward crammed with men, most of whom lay on straw pallets. The naked ones had a blanket. Those on the floor wore uniforms from the field. She looked around the morbid, windowless room. It was crowded and dirty, the air sour with the stench of infection. A priest stood at the far end, his gray beard spilling down the front of a black robe. It occurred to Katya that his gloomy presence must be terribly unnerving to the dying. What a dreadful place, she thought. Surely we can do better.

Katya felt a tapping on her foot and looked down. "Nurse," said an unshaven, unwashed soldier who reached out from his mattress on the floor. "Is there anything to eat?" Katya caught a whiff of the man's stockings and felt her stomach lurch. She tried to conceal her discomfort by turning away, covering her mouth while fighting for control. "I'll find something," she called back over her shoulder as she stepped into the hall for relief.

There she saw the smirk of the woman who had brought her here. Katya straightened up, not wanting to show her qualms. This woman has no respect for aristocracy, she reminded herself, but I'll be damned if I'll add another sneering story to her list. Russians from all stations in society must work together.

"Where's the kitchen?" Katya demanded.

The woman pointed down the hall.

"I will get something for him. Then, you will show me the laundry room."

• • •

Katya re-entered the games room with her watering can. Trying to be inconspicuous, she refreshed the two remaining potted palms before returning to the card table. She stood quietly in the background, realizing that her good mood had vanished. Tired now, she wondered despondently how much of an effect all their work for the war effort would have for those men in the basement. In her mind, a voice answered: They'll always be in the basement, won't they?

One of the officers broke into her thoughts. He was telling a story while he shuffled the cards. "If I don't get back to the front soon, my canary won't get fed. And someone might filch my good leather couch."

Katya thought about the pampered canary. She thought about the hungry conscripts in the basement. It was just as Alex had said; the bourgeoisie — her class — was either ignorant of, or insensitive to, the realities facing a rank-and-file soldier. She was becoming uncomfortably aware of how many of her friends showed more interest in possessions and posturing than in far-reaching ideas.

Suppressing her disenchantment for the moment, she put her hand on Marie's shoulder. "I apologize, gentlemen, for spoiling the game. I'm afraid I'll have to steal the Grand Duchess away. There's much to do downstairs."

CHAPTER 7

VIENNA
SUMMER 1915

Oberleutnant Schumann waited uneasily as Karl the First, heir presumptive to the Austro-Hungarian throne, stood looking out across the Danube from his elaborate royal office. The slender archduke stroked a moustache designed, no doubt, to add an aura of maturity to his scant twenty-eight years. Schumann was therefore surprised when the archduke turned angrily upon a terrified defense minister, the only other person in the cavernous room.

Schumann felt little respect for the inexperienced pretender to the throne, and nothing but disdain for the minister, a little man with a white face who looked as if he might faint. As the officer in charge of the failing program for Czech recruitment, Schumann had to admit to a considerable tension of his own; but he would refuse to show it. And that was the difference.

"This latest desertion is inexcusable," said Karl. Schumann knew that he had claimed the throne just after his uncle, Archduke Ferdinand, and aunt had been gunned down by that lunatic in Sarajevo. Now he watched as Karl pulled his arms down behind his back in a stern gesture which emphasized the twelve gold braids looping across the chest of a sky-blue jacket. His shoes were like two black mirrors as they clicked across the white tile floor. "Oberleutnant," he called.

Schumann began to perspire despite a breeze fluttering the white curtains covering one of the open French doors. He was certain that his career was over or at least severely damaged, but he was determined not to cringe. "Commander?" he replied, trying to assume a detached military manner.

"That regiment is permanently dissolved by royal decree. I want discipline and trust restored to the front line troops. Understood?"

"Sir," Schumann responded quickly.

"Any man caught calling across the line is to be shot where he stands. Understood?"

"Sir." Schumann heard his voice grow stronger in response to what he perceived as orders, rather than the expected personal attack.

"Mix the Czechs up with other racial groups, and offer rewards for information relating to treason. Most importantly, take soldiers from the universities and leading families. Put them at the front in the most exposed sections. They will be our vanguard against Russia."

"Exactly as you wish, sir," Schumann said with growing determination. The tension in his neck and chest was excruciating. He wanted to dab his forehead with the sleeve of his jacket, but of course he would not. He would hold on.

"That is all I ask," said the emperor, turning away.

"Minister!" he then called, in a voice loud enough to jerk the white-faced man to rigid attention.

The voice replying was tentative. "Yes, Majesty?"

"Czech youth has been corrupted by traitors. Loyalty to the Austrian Crown has been compromised. It is obvious by now that there exists an underground organization. Can you report?"

"Yes, Majesty," the minister said so softly that Schumann turned his ear closer, not wanting to miss a word. "My department has been gathering information for some time now. We know exactly who they are." The minister paused and Schumann strained to catch every nuance. "Go on," he heard the emperor say, and the minister hurried to the point.

"The leader, sire, as you expected is Professor Thomas Masaryk, who has just been joined in Paris by an academic colleague. These two are actively organizing a Czech revolution, and at the same time are writing the charter for a democratic republic which they want signed by fifty prominent families. They plan to recruit a Czech army from prisoner-of-war camps to fight for the Triple Entente."

"This will be crushed!" the emperor insisted. "What support do they have?"

"Unfortunately, they are well organized. The administration of the Falcon Athletic Association works with Masaryk. As a result, there is a very effective network throughout the kingdom."

Schumann was disappointed when Emperor Karl merely waved his arms in agitation as if symbolically swatting Masaryk away. *The man is too inexperienced, too liberal,* he thought. He had been convinced by the disturbing rumors among military men that their own emperor was secretly looking for ways to ingratiate himself with the Western Allies — perhaps with a separate peace. *Does the emperor realize how embarrassing it was to feel the constant sneer of Prussian self-assurance?* Schumann still cringed at the thought of the music-hall joke about the conversation between a German soldier and an Austrian soldier:

German: "Our guns are better than yours!"
Austrian: "So they are."
German: "We win more battles."
Austrian: "You do indeed."
German: "Our generals are greater."
Austrian: "Absolutely."
German: "Well, what are you proud of?"
Austrian: "We have a most remarkable ally . . . ."

Schumann clenched his teeth remembering the sharp sting of that insult.

"Outlaw the Falcon organization," the monarch commanded, touching his thumb to a forefinger as if checking off a shopping list. "Arrest the Falcon administration immediately."

Then he continued the royal decree in a lower voice as the thumb moved down the line of fingers. "Eliminate Masaryk. He is far too dangerous."

Schumann was impressed. "Yes, Majesty, it shall be as you command," he heard the man with the white face say, this time in a more relaxed voice.

"How?" the emperor asked, so softly that Schumann almost missed it.

"Majesty?" was the puzzled response.

"How will you deal with Masaryk?" Karl asked with a sharp voice. "He wants to become the first president of Czechoslovakia. I will stop him."

"Oh. Yes, of course, sir. . . . Poisons." Schumann's eyes widened at the minister's response.

"Poisons? Do you invite him in for some wine?" the emperor asked sarcastically. "Won't that be a little obvious?"

"Oh, no, sire. Quite subtle, I assure you. We merely find his laundry and then treat the collar of his shirts or the waist band of his underclothing, . . . wherever it touches the skin firmly. The victim succumbs over a period of five or six days."

"We won't have an executed martyr on our tally sheet, will we?"

"No, Majesty, just another victim of blood poisoning."

"See that it's done then," the emperor said. Schumann half-turned, preparing to leave, when he heard his monarch ask the ashen-faced civil servant a final question. "How do you know so much about all this poison business?"

Schumann held his breath.

"Well . . . experimentation in the prisons, Your Majesty."

The emperor frowned before issuing the cold command, "Go now."

Schumann walked to the door, opening it for the minister who quickly followed him out. He watched in mild surprise as the minister closed the door gently behind them and then whispered into the mahogany panel: "Hypocrite."

● ● ●

The next day, in Prague, only two hundred kilometres through the mountains to the north from Vienna, Anton Branda, as president of the National Falcon Athletic Association, sat with three stern men around a bare dining-room table in his home. Dr. Scheiner carried in a tray of glasses and a pitcher of fresh water from the kitchen. Although the drapes were drawn for privacy, the room was still bright from the July sun pressing down on the white-washed cottage. Light exaggerated the doubt and suspicion on each face. Guarded eyes studied a woman in a lightweight Italian suit. She was speaking with such intensity that the two pheasant feathers on the side of her hat shook with the emotion flashing in her eyes.

"Professor Masaryk is certain that the French will accommodate a Czech army to fight alongside the Allies on the western front," she said. "Once that happens, it is only a matter of time before Britain and France recognize Czechoslovakia as a new nation: The Czech Republic. As our reward, recognition will be fait accompli. The first step is to send an army into France. Why won't you cooperate?"

"May I attempt to answer the young lady's question, Chairman Branda?" the secretary asked in a patient voice.

"Of course. The floor is yours," Anton replied formally. While he watched Dr. Scheiner turn his barrel chest toward the woman, he could see the perspiration on the bald top of his head gleaming above a wreath of white hair. He too felt uncomfortable in a three-piece suit.

"It is an important question, one which I feel we will soon be forced to attend," Scheiner began. "But there are several reasons why we do not cooperate. For one thing, if you will forgive my lack of diplomacy, we've only just met. For all we know, you could be working for the Austrians as agent provocateur, and the topic here is treason."

Anton allowed her to interrupt, and she continued in her confident tone. "Sir, there are not more than twenty people in all of Prague who are unaware of your views on freedom. The only reason the Austrian secret police have not arrested you by now is you haven't been a concern — that is, until the desertions this spring."

At this remark, all heads turned to look at Anton who leaned forward, placing his thick hands and forearms on the table with a smile. He felt again that surge of pride when he picked up a letter from the table in front of him. "I recently received this from my son, Alex. We must be careful about such information, of course, but I wanted my friends to know that our efforts have succeeded in sending close to thirty-five thousand young Czechs to stand with Russia. Strange thing . . . I planned to answer my son's letter this evening and I was surprised to find that it will be the first I've ever written to him."

Scheiner broke in, addressing the woman in the Italian suit. "Let us accept for the moment that you are truly a messenger from Paris. We are admittedly wary of strangers. Perhaps we are slow to change. But it seems far more reasonable, to some of us, and I must admit still a minority at this time, that we should throw all of our support to Russia. Russia will liberate us from the Austrian yoke, as fellow Slavs. This is a far-reaching decision, to be made carefully without rush or hysteria."

"Sir, may I inform you as politely as possible, that you no longer have the luxury of time needed for an academic examination." She was standing now, and Anton could see that this aggressive posture had them all frowning again. "Germany is negotiating with Russia, at this very moment, for Russia to leave the war. They promise Russia the international recognition Czechoslovakia will never see, if you delay any longer. Rumor has it that the pro-German movement is gaining strength among Russian leaders, and that even Rasputin, the mad monk who whispers in the Czarina's ear every night, is in German employ."

"Silence, Madame!" Anton demanded. "There is no need for obscenity and gossip during this discussion."

"You're quite right," the visitor said, picking up her purse slung over the backrest of a high oak chair. "There is no need for exhortation, or argument, because there is no more time. You must decide who will help you the most. Then make certain that they win the war. Goodbye, gentlemen," she said, opening the front door.

It was then that Anton saw the portal blocked by an Austrian officer who waved his arm in a signal. Suddenly, there was the sound of boots as soldiers ran to surround the house. The grim-faced woman was pushed back into the room, and the directors of the Falcon Athletic Association slowly stood up from the table, scraping their chairs on the hardwood floor, their faces the color of chalk.

In those few seconds Anton felt true fright for the first time in his life. His part in the game was now finished, he knew. Only two months ago Germany had torpedoed the *Lusitania*. If they are willing to drown twelve hundred innocent passengers, what possible concern could there be for a stubborn old Czech? He saw the woman try to wrench away from the officer's grasp but her arm was jerked behind her back until the fight drained from her eyes. When she cried out, Anton seized the distraction to make a dash for the fireplace with his membership lists.

From behind, Anton heard the officer curse to see him kneeling in front of the hearth, pouring paraffin oil onto the papers in the grate. The officer hurried over to intercept him, kicking with stout boots again and again to make him stop. But Anton felt nothing. He knew that he must destroy the files and refused to be distracted by the jolts to his rib-cage until he was able to strike a match and watch the papers burst into flame.

• • •

In the first light of morning, Oberleutnant Schumann watched his six prisoners walk warily from the brig onto the armory parade square. From their faces it was readily apparent that none of them had enjoyed a good night's sleep, and this was as it should be, he believed. If he was disappointed at all, it would be because they were so well dressed. He wanted them reduced to a pitiable state. The five men were unshaven, of course, but they had been brought to the armory's brig directly from their meeting, still wearing three-piece suits. The woman, in her gabardine outfit, gave the impression that she might be off to town. But no matter how they wrapped it, they had to face those twelve rifles on the other side of the square. There was no dodging that inevitability.

Schumann waited until the traitors stood in their undisciplined line in front of a concrete wall five metres high, then he gave a quick nod to the lieutenant on duty. He saw that the prisoners looked around this special area. They might as well, he thought. It would be their last view of this world.

The main armory building with its indoor parade square was in front of them across a slightly sloping cement deck. The administration and interrogation section of the armory comprised three floors on their left. The only vistas remaining were the views of the empty parade ground which stretched one hundred metres to their right, and the open sky above. Not much. And they deserved no better.

He listened with approval as the young officer snapped out the order: "Squad. Parade!"

Twelve soldiers marched smartly out of a dark tunnel onto the cement square for their first execution. It was time to blood these young men. They came to a halt in front of four unobtrusive yet strategically placed drains set flush into the smooth decking. The deck could be washed down without much effort.

There certainly would be no effort in the disposal of Anton Branda. There would be an unmarked grave. No grand stone. No ceremony. Nothing. That son of his, or anyone looking for a martyr, would never find a trace — if military justice held sway. Schumann renewed his determination to see that it would.

Schumann studied the last of the Falcon Association's leaders. They were quiet — sullen even — except for Branda. This man was calm. He seemed more interested in staring across the parade square toward the hillside beyond the north wall.

Damn! Schumann quickly motioned the lieutenant to put on the blindfolds. The young officer marched crisply across the deck to

Anton Branda, offering a strip of rough black cloth. Branda declined with a shake of his head, and the inexperienced officer went to the next man. Dr. Scheiner, too, shook his head.

Schumann felt his annoyance spread across the back of his neck when the stupid ass was turned down by every man there, undoubtedly on cue from Branda. He'll hear about this. There, at last the fool has come to his senses. He did not ask the woman; he simply tied the cloth over her eyes.

He watched the young officer turn toward the firing squad — and then stop unexpectedly to walk back to Branda. Perhaps the Czech was not so brave after all and needed a blindfold. No. He merely handed the officer an envelope, and the lieutenant, looking unsure of procedure, turned for a sign from Schumann.

It might be a letter with an address for the prisoner's mutinous son, Schumann reasoned. He met the officer's questioning glance with a nod so that the lieutenant accepted the envelope before turning to march back to the line of marksmen.

This was the moment Schumann relished, when weaknesses in character were revealed. Raw nerves, agonizing throughout the long night, might stretch to the breaking point. Even the strongest will could collapse into a pathetic, blubbering mess when staring at a combat rifle. His squad had been trained with two sharpshooters for each prisoner, aiming at the heart. They were to fire on command without hesitation.

He gave the first order: "Fertig!" and listened to the slap of hands on the rifles and the smack of the lead foot stamping into position. This usually got everyone's attention. Clinically, he checked the faces of the prisoners who, he predicted, would bow their heads to the ground. And this they did, he saw as he worked his eyes down the line — until they came to Branda!

The fool had placed his hand on Scheiner's shoulder and Scheiner had turned to give a smile in return. In a voice rising angrily in an attempt to regain Branda's attention, Schumann drew out the next order: "Zielen!" and was momentarily satisfied when he saw Branda turn his head to look him straight in the eye.

But just as quickly the stare was gone. He felt cheated, and was distracted again when Branda looked away up the hill — and waved. The man raised his hand high over his head and gave a slow wave. What was this fool waving at? The city? His cottage? That was it, his goddamned cottage. And that was his last thought?! Then so be it, Schumann decided, and called out sharply: "Feuern!"

There was an explosion of sound as rifle-fire reverberated around the enclosed square. Schumann checked his squad for reaction. A vein in the neck of the soldier nearest him beat with an observable pulse, but he was satisfied that they had maintained their poise as they looked down smoking barrels. It was only then that he walked slowly up the tilted deck to examine the prisoners, being sure not to step in any of the rivulets of blood that swerved their separate paths toward the drains. Their cheeks rested on the wet concrete, mouths agape, with sightless eyes staring back toward the feet of the firing squad.

Schumann took his time, in a clinical way, with pistol in hand, looking to see if a bullet to the back of the head was required. He aimed his pistol at Branda's peaceful face, but he did not shoot. There was a twinge of disappointment that the job had been finished so quickly. He could feel his men watching, and he hoped they were learning something about professional objectivity and an officer's care for detail. It was difficult to know for certain just what encouraged respect from the rank and file, but certainly it must be times like this, he supposed.

When satisfied that the sentence had been served, and his credibility with superiors rejuvenated, no doubt, Schumann return-ed the pistol to its side holster. He nodded silent approval when the squad snapped to attention, their polished boots stamping as one. Under the lieutenant's command, the soldiers turned left and marched crisply away. Schumann gave the traitorous remains one last casual scan. Then, with a smile of detached satisfaction, he followed the firing squad into the tunnel.

● ● ●

Katya lay fully clothed on her bed in the Treasury residences. Her head rested on the pillow staring at the ceiling. Her feet were together, her dress folded perfectly. I must look like a corpse, she thought angrily, resenting the biological fact that she, like most women, had to surren-der several days out of each month to Eve's curse.

It was so intrusive, so unnecessary and so damned inconvenient. I'm not ready for children, she thought, and there's work to be done.

She was not absent from work often, because she found no joy staying alone in her room. She liked her job, preferring to remain active. But sometimes it was necessary to miss a day here and there. It was just so potentially embarrassing. A stain. An odor. Unthinkable. The headache and the waterlogged feeling she could handle, but the damned inconvenience was too much.

At times Katya felt guilty about the bitterness she laid on her mother's memory. Perhaps it was anger. Anger or disappointment, she didn't really know. Mother told me nothing, she mused, but should have. Of course, it could have been the case that nobody told her. She showed me how to put cotton rags under several suits of old undergarments, with a second and even a third set ready.

But there had been no preparation for the fright of the first time. Nor was there any explanation, or sympathy, or discussion of this function as being normal. It was just assumed that one suffered, and that one was to accept that fate. Well, I won't, Katya promised herself. Marie was a registered nurse and had taught Katya the physiology behind the monthly cycle that arrived with such irritating monotony. But it should have been Mother who prepared me for this, she thought.

A soft knock on the door forced Katya out of her self-absorption.

"Come in," she called.

Marie stepped inside, looking concerned. "How are you?" she asked. Marie was dressed in her nursing uniform: an Oxford-gray skirt with sensibly wide straps over each shoulder, a white, long-sleeved blouse and a matching winged cap with a red cross on the front. Over this she wore a white apron.

"Terrible. You?"

"Fine. I've got some news about your Czech friends, if you like?"

"Thank you, Marie. Please sit. I'm sorry to be so cranky. What is it?"

"Those Czechs might just make it. A friend got back from Finland yesterday full of the latest news. Thomas Masaryk met with a tight circle of friends in Paris where they've written a constitution with a new democracy like the United States. And they have the written blessing of fifty leading Czecho-Slovak families. The French government is urging Britain and the United States to agree."

"Alex will like that," Katya said, feeling a little more enthusiastic at least.

"One thing though," Marie cautioned. "There was an attempt on Masaryk's life while they were meeting."

"He was shot?"

"No. Something worse, I thought — a treacherous thing. His laundry at the hotel was treated with venom, ... from a viper soaked into the collar of his shirts and then dried. When his body warmed and had absorbed the venom, he became weaker and weaker. Everyone thought it was simply a sixty-year-old man reacting to the rigors of debate. Then he collapsed and someone spotted the rash on his neck."

Katya was shocked. "What did they do?"

"Baths. Leeches. Some blood-letting. He's all right now."

"But they'll try again," Katya said.

She watched Marie consider this remark with a shrug. "He's in the United States right now gathering funds from the émigrés."

Marie walked toward the door at the sound of someone approaching in the hall. "I've ordered tea for us. You know, they might just do it, if America helps."

* * *

On the beach below the Monterey Presidio, long ocean waves rolled in from the Pacific. Victor watched the sun shine emerald-green through their curl just before they tumbled across the sand. High dunes stretched north as far as he could see while his platoon, all dressed in olive-green shorts and singlet, ran barefoot through the froth of broken surf. He felt so alive, running like this and savoring his youth.

"Almost home, men. Pick it up," Victor shouted over the steady resonance of the breakers, squinting into the sun as he watched a staff car the color of sand drive up the beach toward them. The car stopped to wait for the runners, and as they approached, a uniformed officer waved him over.

"A two-star general from Washington wants to see you, for cripes sake. You better get dressed fast, Lieutenant. Damn fast."

Soon Victor was ushered into his commander's office where he saluted the colonel and an officer he had never seen before.

"At ease, Lieutenant," the colonel said. "Let me introduce General William Graves, from the War Department. He'd like to talk to you. Have a seat."

"Thank you, sir," he replied, sitting down while he studied the general's serious face. He was impressed by the youthful appearance and lean physique. The look of a scholar, Victor thought.

The general took a little time to examine him before speaking. "Lindal, I won't beat around the bush here. We've been looking you over. We're hopeful that you're ambitious enough to get in on an important project."

Victor breathed a little easier. He had enjoyed several fleeting associations with young women from Pacific Grove and had worried about complications that might arise from recent strolls on the beaches for midnight picnics on the salt-white dunes. "I'm interested, General, especially if it gets me to Europe."

"Now hold on a minute," Graves said quickly. "No one said anything about Europe. We're not involved, and we don't see that happening. That's official."

"And we sure as hell don't want any damn rumors getting around," added the colonel. "Are you with us on this?"

"Yes, sir," Victor said agreeably. "Of course, sir. I was just theorizing. What I assumed, was that Intelligence Division would want planning done for every possibility, no matter how remote."

The general nodded, but Alex knew he was being studied carefully. "Tell me again the languages you speak fluently besides English."

"French, Russian and Czech, sir."

"He's been teaching English and Russian here for the past ten months, General."

Graves' brow was furrowed with something important. "You sure of your Czech?"

Victor nodded. "Came to America when I was eight, sir. Mother kept me at it."

"He's got an eye for the ladies, but he's diligent, General," the colonel added.

"Could that be a hair in the butter?" Graves asked with a stern look.

"No, sir," Victor answered quickly.

Graves reached for his cap. "Very well, I want you to come back to Washington with me. You're going to help steer a Professor Masaryk around. Ever heard of him?"

"Oh yes, sir," Victor replied confidently. "He's the president of Czechoslovakia, in exile. Speaks English. Met an American woman at the University of Leipzig where she studied music. And you know . . .

I just realized, that was back in 1879. They were married in New York thirty-six years ago. Amazing."

The general nodded while studying Victor's surprise. "Well, you've done your homework. If you have a yen to see the world, you'll be helpful to him."

Victor felt his excitement grow, but he kept quiet. Of course, he realized, it would be natural for the Czechs to use the United States as a model for their new republic, and he would be the perfect bridge between old and new. "Sounds promising, sir."

"Promising, it is," the general replied. "Provided you can keep Masaryk alive. Had one attempt already. But he made it, with a scare. Keep your eyes open."

Victor watched carefully as General Graves turned to the colonel. "You'd better promote Lindal here. He'll be more impressive in Washington as a captain." Then, turning back to Victor, he said: "The Czechs are raising funds for an army. You be of service to them and keep your well-trained, expensive ears open for us. Find out all you can about these folks." He prepared to leave, but stopped again to add: "One more thing, Lindal . . . give us all you can on the Russian situation."

"Russia, General?"

"Yes, Russia," he said, looking deadpan at Victor. "We're planning for every possibility. No matter how remote."

● ● ●

In the cavernous main room of the Treasury vault, Katya stood beside Ordinov and the rest of the accountants watching uniformed soldiers swing open the castle-like door at the far end. Except for Ordinov who was, as usual, formally attired, they were dressed in forest-green coveralls. A freight train with cargo doors wide open waited in the tunnel outside.

"All right," Ordinov said. "Shall we begin?"

The others walked to their stations, but Katya hung back. "Why go to all the trouble of moving to Moscow?" she asked. "The Treasury should not leave our care."

Ordinov was uneasy about his answer, she thought. "With this spring's thaw, the German navy can steam within a kilometre of our building. That is the main reason."

Katya made a wry face.

Ordinov sighed. "There are other problems," he said in a very troubled voice.

A cart with metal wheels and loaded with crates was pulled across the shining cement floor by two soldiers with their shirtsleeves rolled up. The crates were tagged 'January 1916' and each had its own identification number. Treasury accountants recorded each tag before escorting the cart onto the freight train.

Katya stood her ground, waiting.

"And political problems," Ordinov finally admitted.

"All the more reason," Katya argued. "Politics change minute by minute. We are responsible for the wealth of a thousand years."

CHAPTER 8
PETROGRAD
WINTER 1916

Alex grasped a handhold as his truck rumbled across a rough stretch of cobbled street on its way to the Fortress of St. Peter and St. Paul. Even though it was close to Christmas, Alex and Peter had been summoned by the Czar to Petrograd all the way from the front near the Pinsk Marshes. The emperor planned to present twenty crosses of the kingdom, as well as five medals of St. George, to Czecho-Slovak soldiers in recognition of their bravery.

He heard the driver's door slam shut and a friendly voice call out: "All right, lads. It's time for a wash and new uniforms before dinner. Follow the corporal." The order came from Colonel Jan Syrovy. Alex knew him as a big confident man in charge of the Hussite Regiment who now jumped down from the back of their trucks, shouldering duffle bags and making their way into the fortress.

Alex followed along with the crowd to a large barracks room where men stripped down for their turn at the shaving bowls and bathtubs. A crew of tailors prepared to outfit them with the new Czech dress-uniform: dark blue trousers with a two-inch white stripe down the full length of leg and a blood-red coat. Two lines of bright brass buttons arched over the chest from throat to waist.

While alterations were made to the uniforms, Alex read the citations commending each award. "Hey, Petya," he called, "it says here you're a hero who needs a haircut."

He laughed at Peter's rude gesture, but could see that Syrovy, who was almost completely bald, glared fiercely at the hair growing over Peter's collar. Alex had seen that look on his father's face.

The gold embossed card he was reading told how Syrovy had distinguished himself by capturing one hundred men and officers of the Thirty-Third Austrian Regiment in a daring raid. With him on this sortie was a Czech whom Alex recognized from his first night at the Petersburg Social Center. It was Lieutenant Rad Gaida, the twenty-six-year-old former pharmacist with the medical corps, and a man of great confidence. Gaida, it appeared, did not remember Alex.

"Damn it, tailor, I want a captain's uniform tonight!" Gaida bellowed. "I was acting-captain herding the Austrians, and I'll be one at the presentation." This bawl was greeted by rude jeers from his fellows, but Alex noticed that Gaida kept on until the tailor gave in.

Gaida was not a large man. He had the build of a trim gymnast with a bearing which spoke of strength and action. The would-be captain had high cheekbones and a soft brown moustache. However, it was not his slim features that attracted attention, but more his manner and confidence. He gave the impression that he was naturally in command. Gaida made decisions rapidly and firmly, possibly as a result of his medical training. It appeared to anyone who was watching him that he believed himself to be a born leader.

"Brother!" Gaida called across the room to Alex as the tailor sewed on the insignia of a captain. "If Colonel Syrovy and I get one medal for one hundred of the enemy, how many medals do you get for persuading two thousand Czechs to cross over?"

"Probably the same medal, brother Gaida," Alex answered, surprised at his extroverted manner in front of the grinning spectators to this performance. He was not usually given to exhibitionism, but in this instance Alex decided to give Gaida a chance; after all, they still had not really met. Ambitious he may be, Alex thought, but he does have his charm, so Alex continued in the spirit of the moment. "We all know how easy it is to get anyone to quit the Austrians."

The entire company broke into a cacophony of laughter at this exchange, so that Gaida extended his hand to Alex with a broad grin. "Brother Branda, I shall have dinner with you tonight. I want you to keep me laughing."

"As you wish, Acting-Captain Gaida," Alex said with a smile. "I'll soon have you choking on your borscht."

Thus began a happy and informal evening for the twenty-five comrades who relaxed, enjoying their growing bond of friendship while they prepared for the Czar's ceremony.

Alex had hoped to break away and travel down Sadovaya Street to the canteen, to see if Katya was there. Through the months on the Polish front he found he could not forget her haunting image. Nights had been filled with the memory of her fragrance, her happy smile. Now he was almost fearful of facing reality. What if she's found someone who does not have my burden? Is she well?

Alex approached Colonel Syrovy who, naked from the waist up, was shaving the top of his head with a straight razor. "Excuse me, Colonel. Could you tell me if I have time to go into town tonight?"

Syrovy turned from the mirror with a wicked grin. "Nocturnal meandering, even though you look ready to drop. Not tonight, lad. You're stuck with us."

He was right of course. There was nothing to wear. Their combat gear was being washed and repaired, so Alex gave himself up to the anticipation of a noisy mess-hall dinner.

At first there was much joking with exaggerated laughter, but as time wore on, the joking had run its course. There was almost complete silence as servants cleared the long table to place overly generous rations of tea and vodka on the sideboard. The men were thoughtful for a number of reasons: they were tired and far from home; they were fearful for their future; they were full of hot food for the first time in weeks and they were clean. Alex watched as they unfastened the side-neck buttons of their borrowed cavalry blouses and leaned back, appraising the fresh fruit and cheeses loaded on giant silver trays. Clumps of purple grapes were intermingled with squares of white cheese and slices of pear and apple. The heavy aroma of fresh coffee was overwhelming. All of these sensations demanded time for contemplation.

With elbows on the table Alex leaned his chin on two fists. He was tired, but there was business to be done. "Colonel Syrovy, can you give us any news from Paris? It's difficult to keep track of the situation without mail or papers."

The colonel lounged back on his chair with legs stretched out across the seat of another. He fondled a full moustache before delivering his answer.

"Yes, I can," he said in a slow voice. "There are two pieces of news . . . thought-provoking news. We are caught in a complex game of chess that you must understand."

The dinner companions uttered no sound.

"Germany's on the move again in France. Things are going badly and the Western Allies are vigorously trying to persuade the United States of America into the war. As a result, President Woodrow Wilson asked for a new definition of Allied war aims. Their restatement has just been released . . . The West agrees that we should be an independent democratic nation — Czechoslovakia."

Alex smiled. There was a murmur of approval around the table that quickly faded waiting for Syrovy to continue. "This means they want us on the western front. We will leave Russia."

"Leave Russia?" Alex was surprised. "Why? What will our comrades think of us? We've gone to a lot of trouble to earn a little trust."

"What about Trojanov? The best damned Russian officer we have," Peter added.

"Russia? The Allies believe she's failing," Syrovy answered unemotionally.

"All the more reason to stay and help," Alex said.

"If she's failing where did all this come from?" Gaida asked, gesturing around the table. "It's very impressive."

"It's supposed to be," Syrovy growled. "Don't you recognize horseshit when you see it? I brought you all here to learn something. It's all sham and horseshit. Everything's horseshit," he concluded, pouring a glass so full that the vodka hung quivering on its rim.

"Come on now, Colonel," Alex chided gently, trying to regain a lighter tone. "You don't think everything's a sham, surely. We dedicate ourselves to some powerful principles, don't you think?"

The colonel drained the glass with one swift tilt of his head before restating his position. "No, I don't. People maneuver for power or money. It's that simple. All the words, all the promises, all are horseshit."

"But if you consider–" Alex began.

"I will," interrupted the colonel, standing unsteadily to place two muscled fists on the table. He then leaned over to growl at the attentive group, "I will consider, when any one of you, the intelligentsia of Czechoslovakia, can tell me one thing that isn't horseshit."

Syrovy glared into each face while Alex ran through a list of possibilities, silently trying to select an absolute that would end the debate. Religion, he thought, but corrected himself quickly. No, no, Syrovy would have a field day with the church. Politics then? No, nothing there either.

Alex watched Syrovy smile and straighten up. "Think on it, m'lads. Take your time. Let me know when you've found something." The colonel then turned and walked carefully off to bed.

As the others drifted away, Gaida asked no one in particular, "I wonder how they expect to get us to France?"

"North through Archangel," Peter offered.

They all considered this possibility. Alex decided that Peter must have been privy to new information because of his recent promotion to captain.

"As for me," Alex said, "I'd prefer to fight Austrians. Good night."

● ● ●

The early part of the next morning was taken up polishing buttons and shining leather for their eleven o'clock presentation. A rehearsal was called for nine-thirty, and one hour later Alex stood with the rest of the medal winners in the small anteroom waiting for the Czar to arrive. The noise from the guests arriving in the adjoining ceremony room kept the Czechs nervously visiting the porcelain chamber pots stored in a mahogany cupboard. "Come on now," Syrovy teased. "Mustn't be nervous. He's only a bloody Czar."

● ● ●

Katya entered the ceremony room walking past Cossack guards who stood seven feet tall in their Astrakhan hats. Twelve chandeliers hung from a painted ceiling, and light green drapes, the color of willow leaves, hung from French windows towering above the crowd. Nicholas Romanov and his son, Alexievitch, sat at the end of the room on a burgundy throne. Both were dressed in Cossack uniforms.

Katya's pulse was racing as the Czechs slow-marched down the center of the hall, their scarlet tunics and buttons creating a slightly blurred reflection in the shiny waxed floor. They halted as one man and then turned left to face the crowd standing against the windows. She could barely hear the soft-spoken emperor's words of praise and welcome. "These brave Slavs have distinguished themselves for Mother Russia in a most unique way . . . a record unsurpassed. In all their special assignments . . . only forty-one lost, and only ninety-five wounded . . . truly remarkable . . . ."

As she watched Czar Nicholas come down the line to make the presentations, she wondered how Alex would respond to a monarch who claimed to have been placed on the throne by the will of God, and certainly not by the democratic process. She watched Colonel Syrovy while the Czar pinned on the first medal. The colonel simply stood in place; probably Alex would do the same. However, when the Czar moved to Alex, he unexpectedly turned to the audience and said: "This brave young man crept through no-man's-land to lead two thousand men of the elite Twenty-Eighth Prague Infantry out from behind enemy lines. It was a most courageous act. I am certain his family is very proud."

Alex looked dumbfounded. His cheeks grew crimson, but he looked straight at the sad-eyed patrician and then saluted with all his heart. It was only after the Czar had passed on down the line that Katya saw Alex relax enough to allow his eyes to wander over the audience. Unexpectedly he looked right at her, and froze.

Katya watched as Alex stood like a wooden carving during the closing speeches and the withdrawal of the Czar. The guests and the medal recipients followed the royal pair to the luncheon buffet set across the hall. Then Alex strode wordlessly across the floor, while she waited. Her fingers rested lightly on the ruffles near her throat until he stood in front of her, then with a smile she reached out to touch the medal on his chest. "Hello, Alexander. Congratulations."

He held her hand for a long time, caressing her fingers, as if unable to find the words he wanted. "You're all I've been thinking about for nine months . . . the dream stops for a moment . . . and you appear." He looked bewildered. "Where did you come from? How did you get here?"

"But Alexander . . . my dear Alex," she said. "This is where I live." She smiled, as he held her gently to him, breathing in the same deep rhythm. They stood like two dancers caught in a photograph, until the sound of staff clearing away chairs interrupted the moment and he stepped back, smiling.

She accepted the offer of his arm, walking slowly beside him down the carpet of a long hallway to join the buffet. But Gaida stood at the entrance blocking the way.

"Katherine," Gaida said with a grin. "It's wonderful to see you. Please, join me for lunch." He took her hand and was about to fold it over his arm when Katya saw Marie approaching.

Katya curtsied, saying, "Grand Duchess Marie, may I present Lieutenant Branda and Captain Gaida?"

"Yes, Katherine Kazakova, I've been watching, and thought that as a good friend, I should meet these men who are such a topic of conversation."

Alex took the duchess's gloved hand and bowed over it. Katya noticed that he did not touch his lips to her glove. "Your Highness," he muttered.

Marie offered her hand to Gaida. "I hope you will forgive me, Katherine Elenskaya, but I must steal away this handsome soldier. I have so many questions."

Gaida looked pleased, kissed her hand and said, "Of course, Ma'am. It will be an honor."

"She is the granddaughter of Nicholas the First. A remarkable woman," Katya whispered as Gaida escorted the Grand Duchess to the table.

"Remarkable because of her royal title?" Alex asked carefully.

"No. Because she's a modern woman. Marie . . . I mean, Grand Duchess Marie, is also a nurse at the military hospital. She serves rank-and-file soldiers as well as the officers."

"Impressive," Alex said. "I take you to mean she's modern because as royalty she's not expected to tend patients from the working class."

"Well, more than that. She also skis, wearing men's pants. When I first came to Petersburg she was fined twenty-five rubles for smoking in public. She was furious, demanding to know why men were not so restrained. But I suppose I was thinking more of her annulment. She was married to Prince William of Sweden but cancelled it," Katya said, almost triumphantly.

"Cancelled her marriage to a prince? That is something," Alex said with an approving nod. "Why would she do that?"

"She said he was cold and formal, but more importantly, she hated to be away from Russia, living what she called a life of idleness and isolation. What do you think?"

"I think I like her. As you say, . . . she's modern."

Over a luncheon of seafood, Katya tried to explain her position as actuary, without alluding to any sensitive topics.

"There's really not much to it," Katya said. "I suppose it's only a matter of reliability and loyalty to the Czar. I certainly don't get shot at, as you do . . . for your loyalty."

"My loyalty is really to friends and home," Alex pointed out. "I see the Duma has changed the name from St. Petersburg. A shame for the grand old city," he said.

Katya felt a frown. "Another stupid inconvenience, all because it sounded too German. Petrograd is a war name, that's all. Foolishness."

The Grand Duchess beckoned to Katya from across the wide room. "Alexander, I must go now, but I'll be back for dinner. It will be grand, and we can talk, and dance. How long do you stay?"

"Damn. I hadn't even thought about it," he said in exasperation. "We leave by train in the morning."

"Oh, dear," she said, frowning again. "Well, we mustn't dwell on that. I'll see you at dinner," and reached up to kiss him on the cheek. "Save me a chair beside yours."

"Of course," he smiled. "Even if I have to fight the Cossacks for it."

She laughed and said, "Well, after all, I am 'Kazakova', which means daughter of a Cossack." She reached up and wiped his cheek with a handkerchief.

Alex smiled, but it quickly faded when Gaida spoke from behind him: "Fight the Cossacks, or fight me." His mouth was set in a thin smile that did not reach his eyes. Gaida then turned to Katya and the eyes grew warm. "Katherine, I hope to see you this evening."

"Rad. How nice to have you back. I saw you at the ceremony. It's wonderful to see you all again . . . I'm sorry, I must run. Goodbye. Goodbye, Alexander."

Gaida turned again to Alex and said in a low voice, "I want you to leave us alone tonight," then turned to follow Katya as she hurried across the room to Marie. Alex stopped him by reaching out to grasp his elbow, holding him back with one firm hand. "Sorry. She's dining with me."

Gaida tried to pull his arm back from Alex's grasp and seemed surprised to find that he could not. "Let go of me, Lieutenant. You can't handle a senior officer."

"I'm just getting your attention. And how senior is the rank of Acting Captain?"

"Ha. What have we here?" he heard the deep voice of Colonel Syrovy say. "Fighting coq, at first glance. Or is it really two guests under the Czar's roof, acting foolishly the day before they go back to the Polish front with their beloved colonel?"

"Probably the latter," Alex said, releasing the grip on Gaida's arm.

"Yes, I thought so," Syrovy said, still watching Gaida's reaction. "In nature the females of most species do the choosing, and so shall it be tonight. Agreed?"

"Sounds logical to me," Alex said, now feeling a little foolish.

"And it sounds even more logical when the colonel in command says it, I would expect?" Syrovy asked good-naturedly.

"Yes, sir," Alex agreed, offering his hand to Gaida. "There are more important problems."

Gaida took his hand, but walked away with a scowl.

●　●　●

That evening Katya sat beside Alex in the lavish dining room hoping the meal would last for hours; and it did. The heavy oak table was set entirely with silver, the way she liked it: the cutlery, the candlesticks, the condiment shakers, the etched containers of black Beluga caviar, and even the frosted champagne buckets packed with shaved ice.

Katya smiled, happy to share the court atmosphere with Alex, although she believed that as a non-Russian he would probably never fully accept the monarchy. But perhaps, she hoped, he might understand them a little better.

"I hated to leave you and Rad, but we had a shift at the hospital that I couldn't miss. Some of the women put in a full day at a factory before working the wards — so it wouldn't do for us to be late." She sipped a spoonful of a delicate cucumber soup. "I hope this is robust enough for you."

"It's not what we're used to, but it's very good," he admitted, and she noted that he was more relaxed now. "I'd be happy with the fish-paste sandwiches we made."

Katya refused to acknowledge Gaida's dark glances from the other end of the table where he sat beside Marie. She knew that Alex had seen Grand Duchess Marie intercept Gaida as he entered the dining room, and she wondered whether Alex understood why. Katya had applauded Marie's plan to commandeer Gaida for the entire evening.

Waiters carried in plates of white fish in thin strips lathered with an intoxicating sauce. Onto a side table, they hefted a sterling silver barrel from which they poured a white Bordeaux wine into decanters.

"Oh, Alex, you must try the wine," said Katya proudly, as if she were showing a friend through her own cellar. "It's very special."

After the servant had poured from a crystal decanter, she watched Alex take a sip. He paused, and took another. "Spectacular," he said. "I wonder what it is."

"I can tell you," Katya said enthusiastically. "This is the famous Chateau D'Yquem of 1847. It's a great compliment. The Czar's brother bought the last four silver barrels for 20,000 francs; the highest price paid for wine in the last century. He's trying to thank you."

Alex sat quietly savoring the apple-sweet Bordeaux. "For some strange reason it makes me think of hiking with my father in the mountains, and drinking cold creek water. And I remember spring nights and beer with friends after football." She watched him sip the wine again. "I am very grateful for this experience," he admitted.

After the game birds stuffed with rice, Alex asked, "Do you always dine this well?" His question immediately brought back her worries about the war.

"No, no, of course not," Katya said. "This is a special night, but we do eat far better than most. I don't believe his Majesty is aware of that reality, however. It is imperative that he learn how badly off some of his citizens are."

"Imperative?"

"Yes," Katya said, "that's the word." Marie had admitted to her that the war was not going well. "Oh, the Czech Regiments dazzle us, but you're only thirty-five thousand volunteers. The Russian army loses that many men in one week just from desertions." She found her temper rising and thought that it was just as well that each course of the meal was punctuated by entertainment because it interrupted talk of the damned war.

The performers stood in front of a roaring log fire, facing the responsive audience. The arrogance of a young pianist was melted by noisy applause for his Chopin. So delighted was he that he stood, bowed, and then strung together a dazzling medley of Russian folk music that had the soldiers standing and shouting at the end. Some men got up to dance, leaping athletically in response to the familiar melodies. Katya watched Alex who seemed fascinated by the Czar and Czarina as they laughed and clapped with their children.

Then a haughty young artist played a mesmerizing violin and Prokofiev's romantic airs held the table in a hush. He was joined by the triumphant pianist and together they accompanied a soprano who threatened to set the crystal of the overhead chandeliers tinkling with her vibrato. During dessert of custards and pastries with whipped cream and strawberry halves, a tenor from the Don Cossacks sang songs of love and courage and the homeland. Like a skilled lover, he drew exquisite torment slowly from each heart. It was a dinner Katya would remember for the rest of her life. No matter how her future turned out, this night she would cling to.

Not long after midnight, the mild-mannered man who controlled that future, and the lives of everyone in that great dining hall, stood to pay his respects.

"My dear guests, I cannot express how much joy your pleasant fellowship brings to the Empress and me, especially during these trying times. God will see us through, I am sure. We have been blessed, you see . . . with brave young men such as these gallant heroes who share our table tonight."

The Czar waited for the polite applause. It was especially polite from Generals Brusilov and Lvov who Katya had heard were becoming more and more apprehensive concerning the Czar's interference with the military. And so it was somewhat to her relief that his final announcement was only to add, "These men have earned their spurs. I am re-assigning the Czech Volunteers. They are now to be known as the Czecho-Slovak Rifle Corps, and will serve with the Russian Eleventh Army in Ukraine. Good fortune to you all."

At this moment the twenty-five medal winners stood up from their seats to move in front of the great fireplace. Each had a slender glass of vodka in hand, and Katya was delighted to hear Syrovy say: "You, brother Branda, are idealistic enough for this pleasant task. Give the toast." Katya stood expectantly, wondering what he might say as he waited for the rising noise of the hand-clapping to fall silent before he spoke.

Alex began: "To the Emperor of all the Russias, we solemnly declare our gratitude for your recognition of Czecho-Slovak loyalty and your generous attention to Slavic unity. We swear allegiance to your Royal Highness against the enemies of Russia." Then he raised his glass, paused and chanted: "Long live the Czar."

The guests raised their glasses, and in chorus with the Czechs, shouted as one, "The Czar!" then drank from their glasses.

However, the men of the new Czecho-Slovak Rifle Corps waited to seal the moment. They thrust their raised glasses toward Nicholas Romanov, drained the vodka with one swift tilt of the head, and threw their tumblers into the back of the great stone fireplace. Puffs of blue flame burst against the black background as the dregs of vodka exploded.

The Czar was pleased, Katya could see. He smiled contentedly while searching the eager young faces of his new regiment. He slowly raised his glass to them, then drank the contents — and then in one sudden and unexpectedly vigorous action, smashed his own glass on top of those thrown just before. A symbolic bond, Katya thought, and she felt an electric thrill as the Czechs roared approval.

Much later, Alex pulled chairs up to the hearth where he and Katya sipped wine as they talked through the night. The other guests had long gone, and the two of them were alone in the dark except for three candles and the fire, which Alex replenished from time to time with pine logs oozing bubbles of crackling pitch.

"That was wonderful," Katya said smiling, and feeling more contentment than she could remember. "What a paradox," she said. "Your father is anti-monarchist, yet you toast a monarch's health. As a school teacher you'd preach the new liberalism, yet you fight for the old aristocratic ways."

Alex shook his head. "I'm not fighting for the aristocracy. I'm fighting beside them. My father works for a democratic Czech nation. I do the same. We're moving away from the monarchist structure you enjoy here. The Czar is ingrained in every facet of the culture, but as the world evolves . . . I don't know. I haven't settled on it yet. Every society needs that permanence, that mortar. He represents Russia's soul. But that won't stand up if there's hunger . . . or neglect."

"Of course I enjoy aristocracy," Katya said sharply. "I was trained for it. I worked for it. I've earned it!" Her face tightened. "And it's slipping away."

She saw him frown. "Let's not talk politics. Our backgrounds are so different. We can't change that. I like to see you laugh, because then I know the world is all right."

"I'm not sure that it is all right. I'm afraid we're changing, forever. All of us," Katya said, watching the cherry-red coals. "He believes he's God-like. What a mistake. The Czarina too. They're both oblivious to reality. Maybe he's never seen ordinary people. It's alarming! He must look!"

"How bad is it?" Alex asked. He looks uneasy, Katya thought. Am I too intense?

"Perhaps . . . hopeless," she finally answered, trying to appear calmer. "It's so hard to know which turn to take. Marie says our only real chance is a constitutional monarchy, like England. We have to end this ghastly war before the people are bled white. The Duma works toward a constitution, but the Bolsheviki are pulling in another direction. They may be too powerful . . . or we may be too stubborn!"

"Do the people want a monarchy? Even like England's?"

Katya shrugged. "I can't tell. Sometimes I think not. I can see it in their faces. Even when I'm trying to help them, they don't trust me. The Social Democrats and their Bolshevik wing want to destroy the monarchy. The Czarina is completely opposed to her husband ever listening to the Duma or the people. She believes that he represents God in Russia, and demands that this idea not be degraded. Alex, it really is too frustrating. She acts like a religious mystic with Rasputin, that uneducated beast whom she keeps about, hoping this 'other man of God' can cleanse her son of his dreadful haemophilia. A fall, and Alexievitch could die. Something is very wrong! We're sliding toward the abyss. I'm not sure how this will end . . . or what I should do." Her eyes ached. She put her hands over her face, hunching forward.

There was a long pause before Alex spoke. She heard him struggling with his emotions. "Katya, I feel so, . . . so strongly for you . . . but I can't pull my energies away from my purpose, to rescue you . . . us . . . even if I knew how."

Katya looked up, serious and composed. "What is it you want?"

"But I've told you," Alex said. "I want nationhood, and an end to this nightmare."

"But what about your personal wants?" she persisted.

"I don't have any just now," he said, looking away. "We have this task — this impossible task. Put together an army, fight a war, win it and then produce a free nation. Ridiculous, but we must try." He continued as if apologizing. "Look, right now I can't think about me. After the war I can, and we could talk then. Let's make a pact. We meet in Prague when the war is over, any Saturday at noon . . . on the Charles Bridge under the statues. What do you say?"

After a long pause Katya looked at him. She tried to keep her feelings in check. "Maybe we should think about it. I could agree to Prague, because I don't know if the Winter Palace will still be here."

She got up to open the drapes and stood looking out, still considering the idea. Katya wondered why she hadn't agreed to meet him. She wanted to, but something held her back — there was a cold spot in their relationship, perhaps a hole — she hadn't fully analyzed it. It was just that Alex had not yet made commitments. There had not been any real intimacy yet, and she understood about that. *He has his duty; . . . I have a career, . . . and not many young women can say that. Most women might be chained to the usual course: love, marriage, children and servitude, but I'm not. I have a career, and even though my instincts tell me I should be with him, I'm not sure.*

• • •

A weak, gray light streaked the winter sky as Alex followed Katya across the snow-covered square in front of the Winter Palace. She had both surprised and pleased him by taking four large wicker fruit baskets and stuffing them with leftover food scraps. *Stealing from the Czar's table? Not the action of an unfeeling grandee,* he thought as he followed her down Zinoviev Avenue toward the harbor. After a short walk they approached the rear of one of the storage buildings where Alex could barely make out piles of rags on the loading dock. There were wooden posts every five metres holding a low roof, which added to the darkness, but as his eyes adjusted he realized that the mounds represented perhaps fifty people asleep there. He stepped back, appalled. He had just spent an evening in the luxury of the Winter Palace enjoying the most expensive wine purchased in the nineteenth century, while just a few hundred metres away families were trying to survive another cold night. He shook his head, disbelieving. "Is this common?" he asked.

Katya looked down. Was she embarrassed that a visitor should see such neglect, he wondered, or embarrassed by the conditions in her capital?

She looked troubled and began cautiously, "I saw some children the other day . . . outside the foundry, . . . covered in soot. There was a little girl, only two or three, coughing. I said to Marie, 'One would think that the mother would see to that,' and Marie looked at me suspiciously from under those wide dark eyebrows of hers."

Alex waited as Katya appeared to struggle with the scene in her mind.

"When she didn't answer I thought I was being vague, and asked, 'Why don't they leave the children at home?'"

"Marie took time with her answer and I couldn't help feeling a bit naive with the patience in her voice. 'That is their home,' she told me. 'And at least the foundry's warm.'"

Alex watched her lips pull tight as if the memory drew pain.

"Marie tried to explain, and that only made it worse," Katya continued. "Marie said that the workers choose to leave their place on the farms for all kinds of romantic notions. Most run away from reasonable debt owed their landlords, she claimed. They come to the city for work, and once they get it, they want even more benefits from us. It's always the same. They always want more. The unions just goad them on, which means, Marie believed, that they must take a share of the blame in risking the ruination of our country."

Alex could tell she had not finished. He would let her get it out.

"I assured Marie of my reverence for the Czar," she continued. "But I had to say: If His Majesty asks his subjects to fight for Russia, shouldn't we care for their children?"

"Marie wouldn't look at me. 'Be careful, Katya,' she said, 'you're beginning to sound like a socialist.' Well, I felt like a fool." Katya bit her lip, as if to say no more.

Alex saw the questions in her eyes but knew he had no answers, so he turned toward the platform.

"Don't disturb them," Katya cautioned. "There are too many. Just leave the food."

Alex placed the baskets on the loading platform at intervals. As he put down the last one, he became aware of the pale face of a young girl, perhaps six years old. She looked up at him with unblinking eyes. She was shivering, and he stood staring helplessly until he felt Katya pulling him away by the arm.

They stopped at the passage entrance where he looked back. Katya turned to face him in the half-light and he could see that she studied him with a look of wonder on her face. "Why, Alexander . . . dearest Alex," she said incredulously. "You're crying." She took his hands, kissing his fingers. "I'll meet you in Prague," she whispered.

CHAPTER 9

KIEV
SPRING 1917

Alex peered from the window of a first-class train carriage rolling slowly out of Petrograd, bound for the Polish front near Brest-Litovsk. This last lofty gesture by Czar Nicholas, of giving them a private car, only saddened him, because from his luxurious seat he could see refugees trying to survive on the edge of an indifferent city. He could see men lying in crates

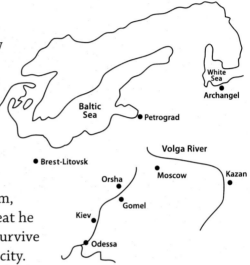

hoping, he supposed, that it wouldn't rain that night so they could at least sleep, if not be warm. Other figures hunched around small fires trying to fan life into the spluttering wet coal they had stolen from black slag heaps. It seemed to him that they clung to life through sheer stubbornness, even to the exclusion of dignity.

He was distracted from his meditation when Colonel Syrovy strolled up the aisle to where Alex sat alone. Gaida and Peter followed. The colonel sat down opposite, looking concerned. Gaida stood watching. "So, my young visionary," came the low rumble of Syrovy's voice. "Having trouble with the purity of your absolutes?"

"No, brother Syrovy, truth, love and beauty exist . . . but in some places one must look harder for them."

"A thing of beauty is a joy forever. Is that it?"

"Exactly."

"I for one do not believe that," interrupted Gaida, folding his arms — trying, Alex guessed, to look like a referee at a chess match. "If you're searching for beauty, then I'm afraid you are heading in the wrong direction. She's back at the Treasury Building in Petrograd, my son."

Alex frowned. Gaida is twenty-six, he thought. I'm twenty-four. So why is he saying 'my son' to me?

There was, Alex had to admit, a twinge of anxiety when he first recognized the potential competition for Katya from this handsome extrovert. But he was also irked because Gaida still wore the insignia of a captain.

"There'll be no time for romance," Alex reminded him, "but I'd like to know why you're still acting like a captain . . . Lieutenant."

"When the Czar renamed our regiment, I stood before him as a captain. I was automatically a captain as a medical officer, and so I shall remain. We'll be lucky to get promoted from now on; besides, I've decided to leave medicine — a frustrating and depressing task — and turn my talents to command. Correct, Colonel Syrovy?"

"It's not my army," Syrovy grunted. "I suppose we could use more officers while three Czech regiments try to form a spine on the Polish Front. I'm taking Alex and his Falcons with me to Lvov. Captain Kechek will command the Third Regiment at Brest-Litovsk. Gaida will take the Second Hussite Regiment to Minsk. Winter won't be easy, but by the New Year we might know where we're headed. That's all for now," he concluded, slipping away to the far end of the coach to doze.

Peter said nothing, but Gaida could not stay quiet, calling out in a happy voice, "Ahh, Minsk, and the Pinsk marshes again! And the women . . . all gorgeous. Virgins, every one." The men's laughter only encouraged Gaida, who started singing to a slow clap that even Alex couldn't resist. "Oh, that Minsk from Pinsk, I never shall forget . . ." and Gaida signaled for everyone to join his song.

"That Minsk from Pinsk, I'm dreaming of her yet."

Later, as the singing died away and lights from the city gave way to dark forest, everyone settled down to read or to sleep. Alex went over to Syrovy, even though he felt self-conscious, never having advertised himself before. "Captain Gaida, Captain Kechek . . . why not Captain Branda? Is it my stammer?"

Syrovy looked straight into Alex's eyes. "Rank is not that important to leadership. I'm just not sure whether you're cold enough to command. Idealists don't make great officers. Too trusting. There was one, Marc Antony; look what happened to him."

Alex returned to his seat to think about that remark. He peered out through his own reflection in the window, charting their progress toward the southwestern front near Cracow. The train whistle shrieked into the night.

* * *

Alex and his men trotted after Syrovy through a small wood. Off to the left he could see wheat fields covered with snow and dotted with the black figures of deserting Russian troops. "If those bastards would stop and fight, we could give the Germans something to think about," Syrovy growled while he caught his breath.

"One million new recruits in full retreat. They'll all wind up in Kiev, if this keeps up," Alex said, wiping sweat from his eyes.

"Ready, lads?" Syrovy barked. "Here we go."

Syrovy charged out of the trees toward an advancing German patrol. Alex and his men chased after him, slowing only to shoot at surprised German troops who had difficulty finding cover.

"We've got them!" Syrovy called just as a grenade landed close by. He put his hand to his right eye and fell into the ankle-deep snow. Alex and his Falcons increased their fire until the Germans ran into the trees and disappeared.

By the time Alex got back, a medical team was packing Syrovy's eye socket with cotton wool. "Branda!" Syrovy called. "Get over here." Syrovy was pale and sweating. "Take command — Captain. I'm due for a bit of medical work."

Alex searched Syrovy's face carefully as they put a blanket around him. "I don't think I'm the right one."

"What in hell does that mean?" Syrovy growled, pushing up on one elbow.

"I mean, I wouldn't fight this way. The frontal charge is medieval."

"And just how the hell would you do it?"

"The American colonials fought the British red coats like Indians — and won."

Syrovy rolled onto the stretcher. "Get me out of here," he said to the litter bearers. "He's mad. Trying to fight a war where no one gets hurt . . . I need a drink."

Alex had, so far, remained untouched in battle. The Falcons stood in awe of his luck and envied the visual overview of the battle scene he possessed. They speculated that he somehow sensed danger before it actually appeared. Alex dismissed any talk like this as mystical nonsense, pointing out that Falcon Company had the lowest casualty rate of any regiment on either front. He attributed this to the fact that they were sportsmen with proven agility and remarkable reflexes.

Above all, Alex was convinced that the special eyesight possessed by goal scorers would also benefit them as warriors. "That's why I chose them," he recalled. "Athletes — all trained by my father. I'm not going to send them charging into entrenched gunfire just because a textbook says so."

He knew that his men were grateful for his particular view of warfare, and that they were determined to make it work. Surely, Alex reasoned, they all sensed that the end of Russia was near, and must dread the thought of being ordered to make the sacrifices which were constantly demanded of the peasant soldiers on their flanks. So he designed sneak attacks in the dark, and hid his men under camouflage by day to make any German advance as awkward as possible. Alex supposed that Syrovy would hear these reports at the hospital, and he wondered whether the colonel would argue with the results.

He didn't. In five days Syrovy was back in the trenches wearing a black leather eye patch as if it were a medallion. The patch had become the focal point of his face because his head was shaved completely bald, and he determined to keep it that way. "It's clean and it's neat," he explained.

"You look like a pirate," Alex said, amazed at the man's nonchalant attitude to such a devastating injury. "Am I a lieutenant again?"

"No, not yet," the colonel said. "I'm not completely sure of my vision. You might still be useful. . . . By the way, this telegram came for you. Miss Kazakova, I believe."

The occasional letter, and nights filled with dreams of her face and her fragrance, had been Alex's only contact with Katya for months now, so he opened the envelope carefully, knowing he would save and re-read it many times. He was grateful for the Red Cross mail services that struggled out to the front, but wished at the same time that he could somehow get a letter to his father, from whom he had heard nothing since crossing over no-man's-land into Russia.

Dearest Alex (stop) Have bad news (stop) Father suffered heart attack and passed away (stop) I go to Kiev March 10 to arrange things (stop) Can you meet me there? Katya.

As Alex looked up, Syrovy turned away to stare out the window. "You can have six days. No more."

Alex was incredulous. "You read my telegram?"

Syrovy gave a nonchalant shrug. "I'm your colonel."

•   •   •

In Kiev, Alex found Katya in the cemetery behind St. Basil's Church. She wore a black coat and veil. He searched her sad face and reddened eyes, then pulled her tightly to his chest. They stood beside her father's headstone under the Turks-hat dome of the church, its gold and blue stripes twirling toward heaven and everlasting life. There was nothing he could do but pat her shoulder reassuringly while she leaned against him. He looked out over the river from high on the west bank, watching sea birds bouncing on the wind. A light spring rain fell on the chestnut blossoms sweeping down the hill.

"He's gone," she said, weeping softly.

As they clung to each other, Alex supposed that the tears were not completely for her dead father, but perhaps for the fear of loneliness as well, or even the relief at being together again for a while at least.

When she was ready, he walked her down the long hill to the river, turning at the Dnieper esplanade to follow the railing along the water's edge. Here he felt an unexpected sense of comfort just being with her. He stopped to hug Katya again, ignoring glances from pedestrians out for their evening stroll. This openness was unusual for him, he realized, but he was relieved to find that Katya did not seem bothered by it. She merely put her head on his chest and squeezed her arms tighter around him.

Further along the esplanade they traversed their way up the zigzag path to the top of the embankment and then turned onto Garden Street toward the Balalaika Cafe. Alex felt himself smile as soon as they entered. The cafe was crowded and the buzz of happy talk was not at all like Petrograd, which now seemed to be devoid of all opportunity for laughter. In Kiev the gardens and trees reminded him of home. Inside the cafe there were bright checkered tablecloths, busy waiters and a trio of violinists. He hung up their coats and felt his shoulders relax comfortably.

"I feel sinful, I'm enjoying this so much," Katya said over her second goblet of red wine. "Why am I not sad . . . am I wicked?"

"You've cried it all away," Alex said, raising his glass in a silent toast. "The only sin is this Chicken Kiev," he grinned, taking another buttery mouthful. "I didn't know anything from Ukraine could taste so good."

"This is our national dish," she protested, "and you are on dangerous ground."

But Alex went on. "I once came across a Ukrainian cookbook and read it from cover to cover."

"So? What did you learn?"

"Well, it was so unusual," Alex said, putting down his fork and pausing for effect. "All the recipes started off the same way: First, you steal a chicken."

She stared at him in surprise, and then laughed so loudly that most of the diners turned to share the moment.

He laughed and stood up. "Shall we dance?"

A gypsy trio struck up a sweet melody. The diners hummed along with the violins. He swirled her around and they sang "Dark Eyes" and "Two Guitars" all the way through. The war was forgotten for a time.

Alex enjoyed a new sensation washing over him as he looked across the table at Katya. Is this love? he wondered. Is it time to accept this new fact? He had known her for more than one year, but in that year there had been only ten days to spend any time together — mostly in the kitchen of the Social Center and that one night beside the Czar's fireplace. But he felt so close to her now. There was no longer room for doubt or self-consciousness — caution, of course, but now they were free to choose unhurriedly and at a distance from the war. It was not a breathless decision from the heart made by the very young. It was a mature response to a new condition.

The trio played "Kalinka" as they left the restaurant, and the fading beat of clapping hands followed while they walked away down the rain-swept street. The night air smelled fresh. Wet pavement reproduced each glittering light that beckoned from the entrance to the Grand Hotel at the end of Vasil'kov Avenue. There, Katya had rented a large room boasting a gargantuan feather bed where a couple could sink away from the world into a cloud of eiderdown.

Alex was suddenly stunned to realize that he did not know how to act. He had been with girls before but only in hurried encounters on a path in the park, or outside darkened front doors, looking for a stolen kiss. Anything more than this would evolve only after months of engagement before marriage. So for now, he was not sure what to do.

Katya had turned out the lamp. He watched, motionless in the dim light reflected from the street, as she hung her clothes over a chair. With arms folded across her bare upper body she moved quickly into bed wearing only a linen undergarment pegged below the knee.

Just as quickly he stripped down to the bottom half of his underwear and slipped carefully under the covers beside her.

When she turned to face him, he held her lightly, not sure where this should lead but satisfied for now that at least they were together. In her bed there was no fear, only a warm weakness, because the close contact assured him that here was a new bond between them.

Rain rattled against the window and the faint light from outside slanted across her face. When she moved, he could feel her bare arm touch his, and long hair spilled softly onto his chest. His senses were acutely alive. Even though in his bedroll at the front he had often imagined what it would be like to be with Katya like this, he did not anticipate the intensity of the first time. He was aware of every movement, every breath, every touch.

He kissed her neck as softly as he could, listening to a pulse pounding in his ear, remaining alert to any signal of refusal or embarrassment. Helpless with fascination, he kissed her shoulders, her face, the notch at the base of her throat.

When she pressed her soft chest to his, he felt a sudden panic and rolled onto his back, breathing rapidly. My father is watching us, he thought. No distractions, he'd say. And there would be her father, watching from the grave for those who would take advantage of her vulnerability. He lay staring at raindrop shadows rolling across the ceiling, until he felt her hand slip into his.

Alex rolled toward her and they embraced to the point of torment. His hands explored, trying to imagine what could not be seen in the dark. Somehow her undergarment had vanished, and he quickly slipped out of his own. Fingertips touched everywhere, memorizing for later when he would be alone again, separated by the terrible war. Sometimes she guided his touch, and when her hand rested lightly on his thigh, he thought that his blood had turned to fire. His mind could think of only what she touched. He was reduced to one singularly intense focal point until the tension burst convulsively.

Katya sounded as if she were drugged, and very near sleep. "Alex, my love . . . we have each other now. But you . . . we didn't actually . . ."

"It's not the right time, Katya," he whispered.

"Oh?" answered the drowsy faraway voice.

"War is not a time for babies."

There was a pause of many seconds. "Is it religion?"

"No," he smiled. "It's just . . . the time is out of joint."

"What's that?"

"Hamlet," he answered, but she was gone, off to a deep and heavy sleep. He waited before continuing, "Oh cursed spite that ever I was born to set it right."

He stayed awake long enough to ask himself: am I like Hamlet then? Carrying the burden of a father's promise and idealistic to the point of inaction? How long can I keep control near her? Not long, I know . . . this war must end. I have to get away. He allowed his thoughts to drift away into a deep warm pool — purple at first, then dark blue, and finally ink black.

It was after nine when he awoke, looking into her smile. "Good morning," she said. "My first night in a hotel with a good-looking man, and I'm still chaste."

"Yes, my beauty," he said, trying to sound light, "but without worrying if anything went wrong." He could see how thoughtful she became with this remark, so Alex continued carefully, trying to explain himself. "I couldn't risk bringing a child into the nightmare of war or leave a woman helpless, alone with that kind of responsibility. I couldn't do it."

"Not helpless," Katya said, without arguing. He was not sure if she felt offended or not — just as long as she understood his logic.

"All right, not helpless, but in a hellish spot," he said, leaving their warm bed for the washroom.

A few minutes later, Alex rang for the porter, ordering eggs, mixed grill, crisp white-flour rolls, marmalade and sweet tea. He knew the cost of the meal would be outrageous because of shortages, but he didn't care. He insisted that she climb back into the bed without worrying about clothing or hair or makeup — or shyness. "Picnic with me for five days," he persisted, "au naturel. We rest. And we stay right here."

He paused to watch her laugh before joining her in devouring the food like two happy savages on a deserted beach. As the last mouthful was finished Alex took Katya in his arms, brushed imagined crumbs from his mouth, and covered her laughing face with kisses. They made love again, but only in their careful way, with Alex now painfully aware of how difficult it was becoming to remain true to his resolve. In the end they fell once more into a languorous sleep as if to prepare for their unsettled future.

In the early afternoon of their second day together, he strolled with Katya down the switchback hill through flowering chestnut groves to the west embankment of the Dnieper. They were detached from all other traffic, lost in that isolated world familiar to children with dolls, or to lovers. But he smiled at passersby with nodded greetings, amazed at the pleasure to be found in an act as simple as walking a dog or lifting a child up onto the wall for a better view of a boat on the river. In the park there were carts with melons for sale.

"Shall we have dinner at the Balalaika again tonight?" Alex asked with a smile.

"Oh yes, it was wonderful. . . . I so enjoyed myself." Suddenly she stopped. "How can you pay for all this?"

Alex laughed. "It's hard to believe, but I've been an officer in the Czar's service for over two years now, and we do get paid. Not very much, but there's an extra benefit."

Katya frowned. "Benefit? And what could that possibly be?"

"On the Polish front there's nowhere to spend it," he said, smiling at his own joke. "We formed a bank for ourselves because there's nothing back home. The Austrian military won't pay us for deserting. I suppose the French government will become our paymaster when we take the ship out from Archangel for France." He stopped talking because Katya had suddenly stiffened.

"When do you leave?" she asked quietly, while looking down at the pavement.

"I don't know," Alex said, angry at himself for breaking the mood. He saw her disappointment and in a flash was convinced he had been right in not consummating their new love. He renewed his determination to control himself for the rest of their time together; otherwise, he knew that he would never be able to leave her.

"We've been waiting so long for orders to head north for Archangel, but of course that can be done only in the summer when the port is free from ice. We've tried fighting our way through the mountains. That didn't work. To tell the truth, the government has been so painfully slow that I don't know if we'll ever leave. Besides, the most important rumor is that America will soon join the western front. It shouldn't last long after they come in."

She looked slightly less strained at this comment, even hopeful he thought, but just then Katya stopped, staring in disbelief at a newspaper kiosk. The headlines of March 12, 1917 shouted out: PETROGRAD ARMY MUTINIES.

Alex put down a coin before snatching up a copy of *Kiev Lianin* to read aloud. "General Trojanov, commander of the Northern Front reports: 'I am hanging on by a mere thread. The control of events is slipping from my hands. I am afraid the worst is waiting for us. Soldiers stationed in Petrograd have mutinied. The rebellious troops have seized public buildings and members of the Imperial Cabinet are held under house arrest.'"

Alex began skipping over the front page, reading subtitles: "Duma Ignores Czar's Decree." "Lvov Refuses to Dissolve Parliament." When he had read enough, he folded the paper and looked out across the gray river where brisk spring winds had picked up a white chop. "Well, the Czar can't help us now. He's got his own troubles."

"I must get back to Moscow," said Katya, suddenly breaking into his thoughts.

"Why Moscow?" Alex asked in a puzzled voice. "I thought you were in Petrograd, with the Treasury."

Katya looked vexed, he thought, but only for the flash of a second. "What I was referring to," she added, "was my changeover train to Petrograd. There is no direct train during the afternoon."

"You're leaving today?" he asked, feeling a little lost.

"Both of us must leave. Things are going to change very rapidly now. Maybe for the better. Parliament will take control, and Prime Minister Kerensky will reunite the war effort. Russia can be saved."

Alex shook his head slowly. "I'm not so sure. Is the ordinary Russian willing to fight for somebody else's land? But you're right, I have to go back. It's my birthday tomorrow. I'll be twenty-five."

He felt an empty, lonely feeling as he said this, and suddenly realized it was the same chill he felt as a boy when his mother had kissed him goodbye. She could be in the city at this moment. I wonder if she remembers it's my birthday. He held Katya close. "Katya, please write me. I'm not sure I can make it without knowing you're all right. The post will find us somehow."

"Yes, of course, my dear Alex. And you write as much as you can to the Treasury office. It can't be much longer now. Can it?"

"I hope not. But if . . . you . . . or if-if something goes wrong for us . . . you'd tell me wouldn't you?"

Katya looked deep into his eyes as if she could see his torment. She must have noticed his struggle with the stammer that came every now and then. She hugged him tightly. "Don't worry about that," she said.

He reached inside his coat, struggling with the pin to the only decoration on his tunic. "When everything's settled, we'll meet and plan. I don't have a ring. Will you keep this?" Alex asked. He took the Cross of St. George, presented to him by the Czar in Katya's presence, and placed it on her upturned palm.

On the train to Moscow that evening, Katya sat staring at his medal, a symbol of . . . of what? Their short time together. That was hardly a satisfying substitute. Or was it a symbol of their future, insecure at best? She decided it represented the importance of his feelings for her, and that this would have to do for now. He still put the safety of his friends before her, but she would not interfere. He'd made a promise to his father, and she understood the importance of that. Besides, she had her duty too. The time certainly was out of joint.

Katya looked down at the white enamel bars and the two gold points at the end of each arm of the cross. Ruby chips decorated the glittering field of white with an eye of silver staring out from its center.

She felt a twinge of shame. She hadn't told him that the wealth of Russia had been moved under excruciating security to Moscow, that she had been sworn to secrecy and that this was a vow she was determined to honor. Petrograd was too close to Germany. Invasion across the Baltic on the shaky northern front was always a possibility, and so, little by little, the coins, the bullion and the gems were verified, moved and listed: 230 tonnes of gold bullion; 115 tonnes of silver ingots; 90 percent of the nation's coinage and paper currency; 70,000 wafers of pure platinum; the crown jewels; and cut gems without settings in 1,678 leather bags.

Good God what a load, she remembered. I suppose I could have told him. He'd be impressed, I'm sure. She thought of the future. Can our system survive? If we work hard and it does survive, will Alex be a part of it? He's now a decorated officer, accepted by the aristocracy . . . but would he want that life?

Katya straightened up, looking past her reflection in the unsteady train window, out into the darkness. I don't have to show off to Alexander. Duty, that's what I must tend to now . . . even though — and here she recoiled at her own rebellious thoughts — the Czar may be wrong. She held her emotions tightly, not daring to give shape to her hopes for the future, nor substance to her fears for the safety of Captain Alexander Branda, who was once again a soldier, and not just the man she loved.

A plum red sedan drove Katya from Moscow's South Gate Station to the new living quarters for Treasury staff. It was seven o'clock in the evening, March 15, and she was puzzled to see that the transportation had been sent over by the Provisional Government, not by the Czar. She was met at the apartments by Marie Romanov, her long black hair tied at the back and spilling over an Oxford-gray nurse's cape.

A sombre look on Marie's face disturbed her. "Grand Duchess Marie," she said with a curtsy.

"Katya Kazakova, when will you stop calling me Duchess? I'm a nurse now. Besides," she continued, searching Katya's face, "have you heard the news? No. I can see you haven't. The Czar has abdicated."

"Dear God, it's come to this." Katya slumped in a chair. "Will we ever return to sanity?"

"If you mean to the old ways, you'd best forget them. Right now our worry is how to keep control. The Duma and Prince Lvov are our only hope. They must somehow, miraculously, liberalize Russia. I'm not even sure if England will help us. It's a disgrace! My own relatives and friends in London abandoning us to Lenin — that wolf! Kerensky and the Provisional Government have their hands full all right. He's issued orders to Mr. Ordinov about relocating the Treasury yet again. You have a meeting at ten o'clock. I'll help you pack."

Marie stayed behind to complete the packing while Katya took her silent place in the auditorium with the rest of the Treasury staff. The shadowy ceiling had been painted to depict Hades, and from the top of walls of red velvet paneling, plaster faces of imps and goblins stared down at her. The loges above the main floor were empty, as was the balcony. It took only the first three or four rows of seats to accommodate everyone. Such a small crowd exaggerated the emptiness of the hall, and a lack of stage lighting only increased the gloom. The strain showed on each face. The children were quiet; unnaturally quiet, she knew, as they leaned against their parents for comfort.

At ten, President Ordinov walked to the lectern and announced: "Ladies and Gentlemen, I present Alexander Kerensky, Minister of Justice for the Provisional Government and Commander-in-Chief of the armies of Russia."

Kerensky was dressed in the rough, olive-colored cloth of army field uniforms. He wore leggings wrapped to his knees from the top of his clumsy army boots. He looked harried but in control.

"Good evening, ladies and gentlemen, I apologize for calling you on such short notice but I must inform you of the issue at hand. We are talking about the future of Russia," he said dramatically. "You and I have a large share in her destiny. You are well aware that there are forces plotting to bring about the total collapse of our system, only to remake it in a corrupted form of socialism."

In his army uniform he was sweating now, and paused to wipe his forehead below a thatch of wavy brown hair. With a new clarity, Katya could see his desperate position.

Again Kerensky spoke. "I refer of course to the Bolshevik menace, and the leader of those vicious sewer rats, Vladimir Ulyanov — more commonly known by his revolutionary name, Lenin. Well I can tell you, my friends, that my father, as headmaster in Simbirsk, handled this wily schoolboy, and I will handle him now." A burst of clapping echoed throughout the hall.

Katya could see flecks of saliva at the corners of his mouth as Kerensky paused to drink water from a nearby glass. Calmed somewhat, he spoke again.

"I'm going to ask you and your wives and children to stay with the great Treasury of Russia and keep it safe. I want you to leave tomorrow morning as soon as you have finished checking the manifest. You will live in special cars on a special train and I have assigned one hundred veteran guardsmen for your protection. The train will be loaded after this meeting from which time you will be responsible for the future of our country's assets."

He clutched the sides of the lectern, staring down at them, shaking his head as if bewildered by the enormity of the situation. "It's everything we have."

Katya watched without breathing, as the intense Kerensky began again. The stage curtain behind him seemed to crowd him in closer. She could feel his fear.

"If the Treasury falls into enemy hands," he said in a low voice, "a way of life is lost forever. It is not an exaggeration to say that Russia's future rides with you on that train."

The silence consumed her as Kerensky searched each nervous face in the audience. Then suddenly he straightened up. It was as if he had just thrown dice down a long table in a gaming house and he was stoically business-like again.

"Upon completion of the loading, you will check all seals. Discuss any questions with Mr. Ordinov. Your destination of course must remain a profound secret. There will be no communication with family or friends. I apologize for this security, but so much depends upon you. For now, goodbye and God-speed. . . . I have a thousand emergencies."

Numb and in shock, Katya stared in disbelief as Kerensky marched off stage to disappear behind the curtain. When her eyes drifted up to the ceiling she sucked in her breath as she caught sight of a grinning carved Satan. She stood up quickly, angry that she could be frightened so easily, and hurried through the lobby to the street.

Back at Marie's apartment, Katya slumped on the edge of the bed. "Where are you going this time?" Marie asked.

"We don't know . . . and couldn't say, even if we did."

"What about that brave young Czech of yours?"

"Still very brave, but none of us is so young anymore. Please, Marie . . . please write to him, try to explain, . . . explain why I can't write. Good Lord, he might not understand. You must explain. Tell him I'm incommunicado. And please, you must be careful. You are in dreadful danger."

Katya put on a fur coat so black it reflected the shimmering candlelight. She picked up her suitcase, turning toward Marie's sad face. Neither woman could speak, so their parting embrace was held, waiting for the words to come. It was Katya who broke the silence with a question. "It can't last too much longer. Can it?"

As Katya rode east through the city to Ural Station, her eyes filled with tears. The Treasury's driver tried to drop her right at the train, but was stopped by soldiers at a high, wrought-iron gate; so she took her own bag and walked to the farthest platform quite isolated from the rest. There she found a frenzied scene. One last train waited on the last track where sweating soldiers in shirtsleeves unloaded trucks backed up to the loading platform.

In a half-light coming from the train's freight cars, the men chosen from the Palace Guard to accompany the Treasury rolled carts laden with mahogany cases full of bullion onto the train. Nervous accountants checked the seals on each case, supervising their storage space on the train. Leather sacks, which were full of gems and jewelry, Katya knew, were sitting unattended in a heap on the platform, and still the trucks kept arriving to discharge their opulent cargo. There was a strange absence of talk, it seemed to Katya. The trucks, she noticed, were ordered quickly away. Although the train was supposed to be a secret, it was natural to assume that the guards knew what they were loading. Obviously, someone had told them how important it was that secrecy be maintained — for their good, as well as for the government's. At last all the cargo had been stored, and each freight car door rolled shut.

At the sleeping car, Katya found her name on a posted list: 'Kazakova, third compartment.' The room was small but elegant: a narrow bed; inlaid wood on the walls; a tiny lavatory behind a narrow door; a commode for washing, with a head and shoulder mirror above it. She pulled open the storage cupboard above her bed and put away her suitcase. Then she sat on the bed next to the window. There was a wheel to manipulate metal shutters on the outside of the glass like Venetian blinds. She peered outside at an angle. The platform was dark and deserted. A hand-held whistle sounded. There was a pause, and then the Treasury train slowly began rolling eastward toward the Volga River.

* * *

Alex found his regiment two hundred kilometres northwest from Kiev in the corner of a Ukrainian field near Orsha. Colonel Syrovy looked up when Alex entered the damp barn they were using as a temporary headquarters. "So, the Falcon has returned — perhaps from a love nest." Alex knew that the colonel expected a reaction, but he merely smiled.

Alex enjoyed Syrovy's company. He had a lot of his father's qualities, along with a renegade's philosophy which Alex found challenging and surprisingly attractive. He would enjoy telling him about Katya one day, but not now. He didn't want to think about her in their warm bed at the Grand Hotel. He preferred to store that memory for private reflection. "Your eye looks like a glass of cheap red wine," he said to the colonel. "Have you been peeking though keyholes again?"

Syrovy leaned his elbows on an empty window frame. Icicles dripping in the spring sunshine hung from the roof's edge. "You're a sly one," he laughed, rubbing the pink crease where the strap to his eye-patch cut into his forehead. "I've been squinting through this damned telescope. Here . . . you can see the Carpathians. I could spit to them. If we flogged our Russian comrades to some kind of sustained effort, we could fight our way home."

Alex took a long look across the sunny sky toward distant white peaks. "What a nice thought. We could be skiing this spring." He made another sweep and then abruptly folded the long brass scope with a series of clicks. "What would we find if we got there? Austrians, waiting for us. Nothing's changed. So we sit and watch Russia writhing on her own sword. I tell you, we'd better get to Archangel in a hurry. It'll be summer before we know it. Maybe Masaryk can get us on a boat by then. God willing."

"A good bet," agreed Syrovy with a grin, and Alex could feel him watching closely. "I've got some news for you," the colonel said. "America is waiting for an excuse to enter the war as our ally. It can't be long now."

CHAPTER 10

PETROGRAD
SPRING 1917

Colonel Syrovy sent Alex and Peter on leave to the capital city for a report on Russia's deteriorating situation. As soon as they arrived at the barracks for the Fortress of St. Peter and St. Paul, Alex dropped his carry-sack on the floor beside Peter's bag. "Petya, look after this for me, won't you? Be back soon."

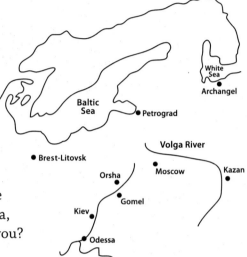

Out in the auto compound, he found the non-commissioned officer on duty. "Any transportation for the Social Center?"

The corporal had doubting eyes and searched Alex's face coldly. Eventually he shrugged. "I can let you have a bicycle," he said. "Better watch yourself though."

Alex swung his leg over the seat of a sturdy Royal Enfield and pedaled his way down Nevsky Prospect with the bike emitting a measured squeak for each circle of his pumping legs.

The great buildings of power sat dark and unattended: the Admiralty, the War Ministry, the Kazan Cathedral — silent, ominous monuments to monarchical stability, he supposed. But even though this section of the city seemed deserted, he sensed there were those who watched.

Leaning the handlebars against the front of the Social Center where he had first met Katya, Alex hurried up the stairs. There were only a few soldiers inside. He did not recognize them, and they showed little interest in him as he entered the main room. Katya was not to be seen. Why no letters, he wondered? Grand Duchess Marie had been vague: 'Incommunicado.' Why?

He walked through to the kitchen, half expecting Katya to be there smiling her happy welcome, but there was only an elderly woman who turned from the stove with a glance that asked his purpose. Alex bowed apologetically and backed out. Turning toward the buffet-table he recognized a familiar face.

"Hello, I hope you remember me," he said to the serving lady.

"Yes, of course, sir." Her face flushed. "You're Miss Kazakova's friend."

"Have you seen her? Does she still come here?"

"Oh, dear," she said, a little anxiously. "No. No, I'm sorry. It's been nearly a year. She hasn't been back."

Alex nodded, trying to think of other questions that might solve the mystery; anything to answer his need to find her, or at least to determine if she was safe.

"Does anyone know where to contact her?"

The woman left the room to ask her partner, then returned shaking her head.

"Can you tell me who might know?"

The woman shook her head again.

"Any suggestions?" he asked in exasperation. "Somebody's got to know where sh-she is."

The woman became flustered. "I don't know anything anymore," she admitted in a frantic voice. "Everything's upside down. Nothing's the way it should be."

Alex stepped back. "I'm sorry. I'm very sorry. Thank you just the same," he said quickly, trying to hurry away.

Out on the street, he paused, trying to think his way through the problem. How do I find Katya? He looked around, gave up with a shrug and then began to pedal the squeaking bicycle back to barracks. The buildings were dark. Gas lamps were flickering, unattended. The deserted streets were littered. Where can I look now? Maybe I can find someone tomorrow at the Treasury, he thought, pumping his legs faster.

Without warning, something hit him on the side of the head sending him sprawling hard onto the road. There was a flash of pain. His vision blurred, but he struggled to remain conscious because he could hear people coming close. Someone pulled the bicycle out from under his legs. He could hear it squeaking away down the street. Someone else rifled his pockets; he could move his arms only weakly in protest so that his reactions were well behind the act. He heard voices, but could not focus on the faces.

When he regained full consciousness they were gone, and the bicycle with them. He pushed himself up holding his throbbing head, trying to find his balance. Following several lurching steps he gradually recovered enough to begin the walk back to barracks.

After he had cleaned the cut on his forehead, Alex joined Peter in the near-empty mess hall for a late supper. A moon-faced Russian officer came over to hear Alex's account of the attack. "The city's gone to hell," he said pulling up a chair to their table. "Mobs steal everything. You're lucky they didn't kill you."

"I was stupid for not being careful. Petya, this thing isn't over yet. Almost three years of combat and I get taken by some street thugs."

He admitted reluctantly to himself that his thoughts of Katya may have distracted him. He had to stay alert. The game was still on.

The Russian officer continued. "The goddamned Bolsheviks disrupt everything." He stared into his mug of black tea as if reading their fortune. "One night I was going to the Bolshoi across town. No bloody trams. A few days later at intermission for the Prokofiev recital, a student jumps up on stage to make a speech denouncing the Provisional Government. He demanded that all legal and administrative authority — across the whole of Russia, mind you — be given over to the Soviets and their local councils. It wasn't even mentioned in the newspapers. They were on strike. Every day one factory or another closes down. Workers march to the square in front of Marion Palace to make more speeches. Sometimes they march right into the Duma and parliament stops. I tell you," he said, jabbing a thick finger at them both. "Prince Lvov and Kerensky, his new bed-fellow of convenience, haven't got a bloody chance. Every damned one of the street thugs waits for Lenin. And God only knows what he's capable of leading them into. I tell you he's trouble. Germany didn't arrange his passage from Switzerland to Finland for nothing."

Alex and Peter watched the disenchanted Russian walk away, just as a stern-looking duty officer approached their table. "All right then," he said. "I need you for a small job tonight. And it needs to be done properly."

Alex nodded. He had nothing more to do, and looked over to Peter who merely shrugged. "What's up?" he asked, turning back to the duty officer. "I'm free."

"Kerensky wants an honor guard for a visitor. Not a big event. In fact the quieter it is, the better. Take four men to Finland Station for the eight o'clock train from Helsinki. They must be internationals. No Russian troops to be used. Understood?"

"I understand," Alex answered tolerantly. "Who's the visitor?"

The duty officer looked around before answering in a conspiratorial tone, "Lenin. He's coming tonight."

"But the Czar banished him," Alex said.

"Well, now the Czar's abdicated, so it's back from exile for Lenin. That's why Kerensky wants no fuss, and no Russian guards. Just five of you."

Peter broke in. "I'm going too."

The duty officer made a gesture of futility. "Six then, but no fuss. Be early. Take him straight to Bolshevik Headquarters at Kshesinskaya Palace. The fewer who know he's here, the better. Field uniforms only. Nothing fancy."

Peter went to conscript four men while Alex finished the meal. Meeting later in the compound, Alex gave the soldiers their instructions before loading them up in an armored car. Off they drove to Finland Station. Peter drove east toward the town side of the Neva River while Alex looked across the black water to the Winter Palace on his right.

"The Czar's over there, a virtual prisoner, while the man he exiled has the nerve to swagger back in . . . things have changed all right."

Peter grunted. "A nice prison though. . . . We had quite a night there, that once."

"Great night," Alex agreed, remembering the dinner with Katya and talking by the fire afterwards. "How does all this end, I wonder?"

"The Czar will surely hang that little bastard Lenin for a start," Peter offered.

"You think so?" Alex asked. "I'm not sure. Would the Council of Workers let that happen?"

They both pondered that question until their car pulled up at Finland Station. The clock on the outside of the station wall chimed seven as Peter parked the armored car near the main entrance. Alex looked around uneasily. The square in front of the station had several hundred people watching a crew of determined men roll into position the biggest searchlight he had ever seen — one that promised to attract large numbers of people to an event supposed to be informal.

Voices from onlookers called out words of encouragement to the men who wrestled with the searchlight, and they laughed when sworn at by the struggling technicians.

Some energetic men and women were busy hanging Lenin's picture on the station's wall. Tight ropes stretched wide banners between lampposts at the edge of the square. These pennants shouted their greeting in loud letters: **WELCOME COMRADE LENIN.** There was also a demand printed in dripping red paint: **ALL POWER TO THE PEOPLE.** Alex looked around the edges of the square. There were no police uniforms to be seen.

Frowning, he spoke in a low voice to Peter, "They're looking to make this quite a night." He walked over to the honor guards. "I want two of you to stay with the car and two at the main door. Brother Kechek and I will be inside."

He stepped into the station waiting-room already crowded with Bolshevik officials who were arguing angrily about where the speeches should be made. Thirty or more sailors in blue casual-dress excitedly laughed and poked at each other as if waiting for a prize fight to begin. A band, partially hidden by the sailors, sat on low chairs. Fueled by nervous energy, they kept tuning their instruments, practising in short bursts at a volume demanded to be heard over the rising noise of the crowd.

Alex pressed fingertips to his forehead trying to touch the ache inside. A middle-aged man in a dark suit pushed his way through the din until his face was inches away from Alex's nose. He spoke emphatically, introducing himself as a minister from the Duma. "When Mr. Lenin arrives, get him out of here to the Kshesinskaya Palace as quickly as possible."

Alex could smell the heavy pall of brandy on the man's breath and was mildly interested by the minister's agitation. Who's in control here? he wondered. Perhaps no one, unless it's me. This is not good. There could be a riot.

As Alex went out to get Peter, the searchlight went on with a loud thunk, and the crowd cheered as the bright shaft of hot white light stretched stiffly up into the twilight sky. He heard them applaud as if they already welcomed the thousands who could see this invitation written in the dark, and there were shouts that seemed to come from far down the road. By the cheering, Alex knew that in some way they saw the light as more than just a beacon.

Alex gave firm instructions to the two soldiers in front of the station door. "Nobody else gets in." It was past eight o'clock by now, with the crowd growing rapidly. He looked back down along the road at the steady stream of pedestrians hurrying to the station for a glimpse of, or perhaps a word from, their new messiah. He ushered Peter back inside the stifling room to wait.

By ten, the square outside the station was packed with excited men and women of the working class. Alex was surprised to find the mood of the crowd remained enthusiastic, even jovial, past eleven o'clock and on to midnight, although the train had still not arrived. Peter's uniform had damp stains under the arms, and so had his.

When the approaching whistle finally sounded, a loud cheer called back in response. The talk and laughter subsided into an expectant hush as the train shuddered to a stop. Stationed between the crowd in the waiting area and the double doors to the platform, Alex waited quietly, looking through the window, straining to see past the steam clouds. Within seconds a short man in a black suit scurried down the steps from the train to the loading ramp. As he came closer, striding through the mist, Alex saw the familiar face and bald head the color of chalk. In one hand the controversial passenger carried a crumpled cap; in the other a small case. When Alex held the door open, those in the waiting-room could make out the familiar goatee and they began to shout and clap their hands. "Lenin! Bravo! Bravo, Lenin!"

Alex watched the visitor approach. The face remained passive even when the crowd outside began to cheer on its own while excited faces pressed against the windows of the station, straining to see. The band struck up "La Marseillaise" — which so roused the cheering, frantic crowd that Alex supposed the music would have been drowned out had it not been for the hundreds who sang or wept. They don't even have their own song, he noted. Nevertheless, with the borrowed anthem, their meaning was clear enough.

Lenin showed little reaction to the clamor as he strode the length of the platform to enter the imperial waiting-room. He stopped in front of Alex and studied the unfamiliar uniform. Lenin said something which Alex could not hear even though he cocked his ear closer. "Captain Branda. Czech Rifle Corps," Alex shouted back.

Lenin only nodded, and Alex watched closely, trying to pinpoint the exact moment when the man who had returned from exile understood why unofficial internationals were tending to his arrival.

It did not take long. Lenin looked directly into Alex's face, an action which Alex took as encouragement to get on with it, so he led him to the centrally positioned podium. Peter and Alex stood behind Lenin, one on either side.

Alex tried to look composed while the Menshevik Minister of Labor made a speech of welcome in a slow soothing voice. The man turned in Lenin's direction after each sentence, grinning slyly as if he shared some private joke. But Alex saw that the little man did not even look at the minister, apparently preferring to study the faces in the crowd. "Comrade Lenin," the man intoned. "In the name of the Petersburg Soviet, and for the whole revolution, we welcome you to Russia."

At this public mention of the word "revolution," Alex shot a look at Peter. Lenin continued to stare into the crowd, treating the speaker as some annoyance which had to be tolerated.

"We believe that the first task of the revolutionary democratic movement is to defend the revolution from within and from without. This goal requires union, and a closing of democratic ranks." The minister looked over to Lenin but there was still no acknowledgement. "We hope you will pursue these goals with us," he concluded meekly.

There was polite applause when the minister picked up his notes and moved away from the podium, his appeal for cooperation done. The applause died away into a sudden hush when Lenin stepped forward. Alex scanned the intense faces in the crowd. There did not seem to be any trouble-makers here, he thought. Rather, this gathering seemed to share an atmosphere more electric than the anticipation before a great overture. Alex wondered how Lenin would respond to the minister's appeals for cooperation, and watched Lenin carefully while he and Peter stood frozen in their places.

Lenin stood quietly in front of the minister, appearing to study those in the waiting-room, perhaps noting who was there and who wasn't. Alex followed his stare into the far corner by the toilets where ten sailors stood behind the seated band, all eyes riveted on the man at the podium. Alex sensed that the fascination with this zealot, as some called him, seemed to be growing in power with each passing minute.

Lenin stood without comment, until all that could be heard was the hum of the searchlight outside. Alex's tension grew while the station clock ticked on. There was a steady throb behind his eyes. The air crackled. Ha! Alex suddenly realized, he'll ignore the minister completely. Then came the moment when Lenin finally spoke. He stretched ram-rod straight, leaned forward like a chanting priest, and fairly shouted: "Dearest comrades, soldiers, sailors, workers. I am happy to welcome you to the victorious Russian revolution, and greet you," he shouted, sweeping his pointed finger across the wall of faces, "as the vanguard of the worldwide proletarian army. This war against imperialism is the beginning of civil war throughout Europe!"

Alex braced himself as the room erupted into boisterous cheering. He was certain that this was the moment when mayhem might occur. Then he heard Lenin shouting for attention once again, and some control was restored. But not for long, he feared.

"The worldwide Socialist Revolution has already dawned. Germany is seething," Lenin called out with passion. "Any day now, European capitalism will crash. The Russian Revolution, to be accomplished by you, will prepare the way for a new epoch."

Peter was frowning. Alex looked around the room for the first signs of mayhem.

"Long live the worldwide socialist revolution!"

At this, the crowd went mad. People outside screamed and cheered, pressing against the windows and threatening to burst through. Alex grasped Lenin by the arm, pushing him toward the main door to follow Peter who cleared the way.

With the help of the two honor guards, they forced their way to the armored car. The crowd churned in frenzy, happily pressing toward Lenin who now clung to Alex in fear of being carried away.

At the car, Lenin jumped up onto the hood and the crowd cheered until he held his arms up for quiet. Then the revolutionary made another short, passionate, shouting speech. "We shall take no part in shameful imperialist slaughter . . . lies and frauds . . . capitalist pirates! Peace. Bread. Land!" The mob howled.

Alex pulled Lenin into the car by the elbow. Peter sat behind the wheel beckoning in futility to his honor guard; finally waving them goodbye. Alex looked into Lenin's impassive face and said, "We've been told to take you to Kshesinskaya Palace, which is now Bolshevik Headquarters. What are your wishes?"

There was a change in Lenin's face. He appeared to look at Alex with new interest. "The first person in six days to ask what I want.

Yes, to headquarters. But slowly." Alex peered out through the windscreen at the blur of faces leaning forward to look in, with a smile for their hero. People thumped good-naturedly on the steel-plated car as Peter pushed cautiously forward through the mob which somehow moved out of the way just in time.

Crossing Sampson Bridge to the Petersburg side was a nerve-wracking crawl because Peter said he was afraid that they might squeeze someone over the rail into the black water. They stopped at every intersection to let Lenin climb onto the roof for another wave and short speech to ecstatic crowds. It took hours to travel four kilometres to the residence of Matilde Kshesinskaya, Petrograd's favorite ballerina and the Czar's favorite mistress. They finally arrived at three in the morning. Alex could feel the strain; he wondered how this night would end.

As Alex got out of the car, he scanned the building. Now a political headquarters, the once gaudy palace looked appropriately stark. He and Peter followed behind Lenin as he was ushered into the main floor dining room where some tea, bread and pickled herring was waiting for the visitor. While Lenin ate, Alex watched important union leaders and professional revolutionaries whisper to one another. Waiting so anxiously for what, Alex wondered. Words of revolution? Or a plan? Others appeared to be nervous. Perhaps the brave words were pushing them too quickly toward confrontation, and they waited for the moment when high emotions might falter, so that reason could bring forward the moderate path upon which some might feel more comfortable.

Peter and Alex sat by the door out of the way. "This is strange," Alex whispered. "Look at their faces. Peaceful. Contented. Their messiah has arrived, and victory will soon be theirs. He tells them so. Down with war. Immediate peace at all costs. They're certain it's about to happen."

When the decision-makers moved Lenin up the wide staircase to a conference room, he paused in front of Alex and Peter as if expecting their continued escort, and so they fell in behind, to stand just inside the door which closed after them. It was nearly dawn, but Lenin was still enthusiastic, showing no signs of fatigue that Alex could see. Two alert eyes studied every speaker.

In this smallish third-floor room, Alex tried to examine the political games he was privy to. It appeared to him that those conservatives close to the inner circle of socialism now tried to influence, or at least test, this little man whose strength and confidence flourished by the minute. Someone Alex did not know mentioned "unity" and Lenin politely deflected the topic toward "revolution." Another voice spoke pointedly about "the will of the majority." But Lenin merely countered with a comment about the "power of the people." Alex tried to contain his awe, while marveling at Lenin's skill. They couldn't shake this fellow.

In a room where so many were dressed in working clothes, an older man in a business suit became pointedly aggressive, arguing that "it will take a long time to educate the people to socialist theory."

Lenin, in response, matched the gentleman's truculence with a sneer, saying, "There will be time for the luxury of theorizing after we seize power!" And Alex was surprised to see that this terse comment, without the benefit of diplomatic language, set the room into noisy argument.

"The raving of a madman!" "Indecent." "This is claptrap!"

As the din rose, Alex saw that Lenin merely took another bite of herring, then looked over to the far corner by the shuttered windows — where a woman with short brown hair and an expressionless face was watching the commotion.

"Alexandra Kolontai," Peter whispered.

Lenin stared boldly at Kolontai. Their eyes met and held for a few seconds while the noise grew. But then the opposition was formalized and the discord brought to silence by Ivan Goldenburg, the veteran Social Democrat and leader of the would-be unifiers whom Alex recognized from the newspapers back at the barracks.

Goldenburg seemed determined to curb Lenin, clearing his throat like a stern schoolmaster before saying, "Lenin has raised the banner of civil war within the democracy. It is ludicrous to talk of unity with those whose watchword is schism, or those who place themselves outside social-democracy. This is madness! You must remember, sir," he said, waggling his finger in Lenin's direction, "there is no political party in Russia willing to take on the entire burden of power by itself!"

As Alex watched this fascinating play, Lenin unexpectedly banged his hand down upon the table before any applause for Goldenburg had a chance to begin. Every head turned as Lenin leapt to his feet in a room now stiff with silence. In a voice designed to shake them by the scruff of the neck, he spat out, "Yes there is, you bloody fool! Yes there is a willing party. A party thirsting for power. They're downstairs right now — and they're waiting for me!"

Alex quickly scanned the room. Every man there was frozen with the challenge of this fanatical, this obsessive, belief. Things were moving too quickly for them, he guessed. He kept his eye on Lenin who was peering again into the far corner where Kolontai stood with a closed-mouth smile of victory.

Lenin moved determinedly toward the door, where he stopped in front of Alex. "Comrade, your job is done," he said. "Get some sleep. Then tell your Czech friends the war will soon come to an end."

Alex felt his pulse race at this thought: an end to the war!

Alex hurriedly opened the door and then put a hand on the balustrade overlooking the foyer while Lenin and Kolontai scurried down the broad staircase. Alex was tired, but he felt Peter's slap on the shoulder and saw the smile. They both watched as the two revolutionaries arrived at the landing halfway down where the staircase made a turn before descending to the main floor. Here Lenin looked out over the foyer below, crowded with a mass of upturned faces. The expectant crowd stood quietly waiting. Lenin glanced back up the staircase where the politicians gathered along the railing to stare down with what seemed to be considerable apprehension — worrying perhaps about how much power remained for them.

Then, like an official at the start of a race, Lenin turned to the crowd, "Are you ready?" he asked.

One hysterical cheer was answer enough.

CHAPTER 11

CAMP FREMONT
SPRING 1917

Victor waited for General Bill Graves outside the War Department office in Washington. It was the first week of April and two days after Lenin's triumphant return to Petrograd. Victor could sense the worry up and down the halls of the War Department as he watched a shadow pace behind the frosted glass door. An emphatic voice from within complained, "We've got to get ready."

Victor could not hear the response, as it was no more than a mumble, but he could see that the figure kept pacing. The first voice continued. "Those crazy bastards could make the move anytime. I want some people in position to help us."

Again there was a softer, muffled response just before the door opened, and an aide beckoned Victor inside.

"General Graves," the aide said, closing the door behind Victor. "I believe we've got just the right man. Maybe you remember Captain Lindal, out of Stanford? A rugby player the ladies seem to admire."

Victor marched across the soft carpet, cap under his left arm. He stopped in front of General Graves' desk and saluted smartly as the general stood up in front of a portrait of President Woodrow Wilson. The general's face had a healthy look to it. The tinge of color might have had something to do with the high khaki collar or the Bolshevik problem — it was hard to tell which — but his primary impression was that the general was physically fit.

"Of course I remember him," General Graves said. "He's been working with Masaryk."

"Yes, sir," replied the attentive aide. "Fundraising. Speaks Russian and Czech."

"Hmmm," Graves nodded. "Sit down, Lindal," he said in a friendly voice, smiling as he looked Victor up and down. "You've been doing a good job for the Czech patriots. Maybe you can do some more." He paused as if for further consideration. "The president is determined to help these folks forge a democratic republic right in the middle of Europe."

"Well, sir, I'd be happy to help."

"Good. Good. I'd want you to spend some time working with me at Camp Fremont in California. I'd like to begin next month. When the camp is ready — and we'll be starting in tents — we're going to mix some new recruits in with our regular army boys from Manila. I don't suppose I have to tell someone from General Staff that Congress will likely declare war against Germany in a few days. We've been inching toward it long enough, and if Russia drops out, the Western Allies will need us badly."

To himself, Victor reflected on how rapidly America was reacting to Lenin's audacious move: a new training base; military conscription for men twenty-one to thirty years of age; and tomorrow a declaration of war. Was the fear of Socialism really that powerful? Of course Americans were well aware of their cultural attachments to Great Britain — obligations, some would even argue. The sinking of the *Lusitania* made it plain that the United States would go to Britain's aid sooner or later. And now, with Russia failing, help on the western front was vital to the Allied cause against Germany.

"Congress is scheduled to make the announcement tomorrow, sir," Victor offered. "April 6, 1917 will become a date to remember, I would think."

The general looked at his aide with what Victor took to be a little surprise. "Tomorrow? Well, all right then. If I can get control of a training camp I'll put together a bunch that'll knock Kaiser Bill off Vimy Ridge like scum off a Florida swamp." Graves smiled as he smacked his fist into the palm of his hand. "Vic, you keep working with the Czech dignitaries. Later, you can come with me and we'll build Camp Fremont. I'll stay in touch."

"Sounds fine to me, sir. Thank you very much."

The general stood, offering his hand. "You're going to see some of the world when we join this war. There's a lot of adventure out there, and women, but I've heard you know all about the ladies. You've got to be prudent with the painted cats, you know."

"Yes, sir. It would be foolish to quench your thirst from a muddy creek." He felt the general watching closely. There were no secrets to be hidden from those eyes. When Graves nodded, Victor saluted and left the office.

Walking down the hall he reflected on his reputation. Sure he liked girls — always had. Nothing wrong with that. But a small worry had him thinking lately. They all seemed the same somehow, and sometimes he wondered: could I ever love just one woman for a significant period of time? That question gave him pause, but he refused to dwell on it for long. He gave a shrug. We'll see, he thought to himself. Camp Fremont will be right on Stanford's doorstep. Maybe Miriam is still on campus. She used to like his chestnut-colored hair.

Five months later, Victor looked out from the front passenger seat of General Graves' staff car as it drove along Santa Clara Avenue away from Menlo Park and up the newly macadamized road toward a sign announcing: CAMP FREMONT. HOME OF THE EIGHTH INFANTRY.

Here, a guard stepped out of the gate-house to snap a salute for Major General Bill Graves who sat by himself in the back.

Their driver stopped in front of some new field-houses where waves of heat shimmered above the glare of fresh paint. Victor stepped from the front seat into the breeze off San Francisco Bay just three miles to the east. He removed his cap to let the wind dry his hair while he studied the rows of canvas tents crowded under green oak; he heard a master-sergeant shouting encouragement to recruits on the field behind the huts.

As they walked toward the training field, he wondered why the general had brought him along to a combat preparation camp, but decided that he would find out soon enough — all in the army's considered time.

Young men charged across the field one after another with their Springfield bolt-action rifles held stiffly in front of them. They looked uncomfortable in their prickly wool pants with combat boots to the knee; their khaki shirts soaked with sweat. The trainees wore the flat-brimmed scouting hat as they ran; a leather chin-strap was cinched tightly under each resolute jaw, and Victor recalled the times when he had dreamed of joining the Boy Scouts to wear a hat like that, back in the days when the requirement of "earning and banking two dollars" had proven too big an obstacle for him. Now, he wouldn't mind some hard training.

They could keep the bayonet work, though. Victor watched a wiry soldier try to thrust a sixteen-inch steel blade through a loop at the end of a stick held by the sergeant. Four small boys sitting in the shade watched happily, waiting to applaud each hit. The general chuckled, clapping his hands to add support for their cheers. From somewhere over the rolling hills Vic could hear the grumble of light artillery.

Graves took his time climbing the stairs to the administration hut. He kept stopping to watch hard-working teams in their stained undershirts struggling through the obstacle course, but when a well-tanned man came out onto the porch he quickly moved forward to shake his hand. "Vic, meet a good friend, General John Morrison."

Victor saluted while Graves continued talking animatedly. "John, this is my assistant, Vic Lindal. We're here for a look around."

Victor followed them across a wooden floor into the sparse office where a rotary fan oscillated on a high stand. "How are the citizens of Menlo Park taking to their new neighbors?" Graves asked.

The general made a gesture for Vic to sit. "Good, Bill. Good. It's great to see you. Well, I have to confess . . . at first they didn't much like the idea of living next door to a camp that'll be ten times the size of their village and the end to their quiet country life. But no one complains about the economy — she's perked up a touch. We spent almost two million setting up. We buy four hundred gallons of milk every day, newspapers, ice cream, candy, haircuts — you name it. And they sure as hell like the paved roads and gas-main. The Knights of Columbus are real pleased with the playing fields and rec centers. You know, they do a damn fine job . . . got all kinds of leagues going for the men. The only person whose nose is out of joint is some guy named Crane. Local postmaster. Said he was swamped. But he can go to hell now. We built our own P.O. Oh yeah, . . . they also get a spur off the Southern Pacific, a new library and a new movie theatre. Things are looking swell . . . 'cept the nearest place to get a drink is San Jose."

Graves smiled. "Well done, John. What's our strength?"

General Morrison reached over to the wall where a clipboard hung on a hook. "Here we are: 573 officers, 6,744 enlisted men, 7 coloreds. The total would've been 10,000, but there was a screw-up. Some of the Manila bunch went to Camp Lewis by mistake. We'll get that straightened out."

"Well, when you do, start picking out five thousand of the best for me. . . . And make certain that all forty-eight states are represented, won't you? What's the program?"

"Everyone takes boxing. Compulsory. Six days a week." The general turned to Vic as if to include him in the conversation. "Helps the backbone, I think . . . and there's a lot in boxing that carries over to bayonet work."

Victor nodded.

"How do the troops like it here?" Graves continued.

"Camp Fremont? They think they've died and gone to heaven. Hell, the regulars from Manila can't believe it. Stanford campus filled with girls. All the candy stores packed in the evening with girls everywhere. Six marriages already. They've never seen a camp like this one — just like home."

Vic saw a quick glance from Graves. He took it as a warning that the general would not abide any tomcatting when on assignment at Camp Fremont, no matter how many girls there were. Graves wants me toughened up, Victor had decided earlier. Whatever the reason, I wouldn't mind getting back in shape after all those fundraising tours. Maybe I could get away for a run with Lefty and the rugby boys — it's been more than two years. He thought about Miriam again. Maybe later . . . but only maybe. "Well, John, let them enjoy it while they can," he heard Graves say. "We'll all be very busy soon enough."

"Yeah, France will be a shock," General Morrison said with a serious face.

"How are you preparing them for that?" Graves asked.

The commander looked pleased with himself. "We've got evening French classes, and the camp newspaper carries a French conversation lesson every day."

"Excellent, John." Graves nodded. "Keep up the good work. Captain Lindal and I will stay around a while. He's going to get in on some of the training, and I'm going to put together one hell of a division. The War Department should be calling anytime soon." Graves then became silent, chewing his lip for a long while.

Victor watched closely as both generals turned in their chairs toward him. What's up now, he wondered, forcing himself to remain calm. He knew that in the army you shouldn't let change push you off balance. The unexpected was an old, old game, and he would simply let it unfold.

General Graves cleared his throat. "Vic, I'd like you to spend a little time with our allies in Japan."

Victor tried not to act surprised. He was willing for anything, especially with General Graves. He liked the man. Graves was educated, a straight-shooter, and Victor was willing to give the general his complete loyalty. "Of course, sir. However, the general will remember that I don't speak Japanese."

"But you do speak the language of engineers — John Stevens, to be specific. A highly qualified railroad expert with a core of hot-shots from the Great Northern in Yokohama. I want you in position. And if the situation ever develops, you'll go with him into Russia, just to keep an eye on things. The Trans-Siberian is worn out. If we're helping our Russian allies, the engineers have to fix the damn railroad first."

Graves took off his glasses and put each lens in his open mouth to exhale on the glass which he wiped clear with a white handkerchief. "If we send you in through the back door at Vladivostok, maybe you can get a sense of what's going on. President Wilson applauds the new situation in Russia. The Czar's abdication and the new, liberal Provisional Government means the Allies are all democratic now, and we'd like to keep Russia supplied and able to stay with us in the war."

"Vladivostok? Certainly, General. I'll be ready."

"Good. That's fine, Lindal, fine." The general paused. "I also want your best appraisal of the Japanese presence in the region. And what about Russia? If we get you to Harbin, Manchuria, that'll probably be a rich source of information for you. Lots of frightened Russian diplomats there already." Graves turned to General Morrison. "Let's get him going right away."

Victor was impressed. Things were moving rapidly, very rapidly, and he listened carefully as Morrison responded. "Certainly, Bill. Right away. But don't you think we'd better promote Lindal? The Japanese will wonder what the hell a captain is doing there on an unattached assignment with a bunch of railroad engineers."

"Jumping Jehosophat. Are you his shill or something? Vic's been with us for only a year and a half." Graves drummed his fingers while he thought. "All right. Give him the rank of major, but you balance the budget."

"Anything you say," Morrison continued smoothly. "And if we send him into Manchuria to set up? He'll be dealing with some high-powered people in Harbin."

Graves looked up with a scowl. "Jehosophat. All right. A flipping lieutenant colonel then. But only if we go into Harbin to set up shop — understood? The president's sweating blood over this Russian situation . . . thinks somebody had better stop those damned bomb-throwers, but politically our hands are tied. The option of using force against Lenin's Bolsheviks is virtually impossible and morally ambiguous at best. We can't attack Russia. They're our allies — like Japan. Except Japan would pull the rug out from under us if given half a chance. They want to expand. No doubt about it. But no matter, that's all conjecture. The War Department promised me a division in France! That's where this war will be decided. On the Western Front."

Victor's head was light from the excitement. It wasn't like the feeling of a headache, it was more like the readiness before a rugby match and it felt good. Never take the army for granted, he decided. He would follow General Bill Graves down any road coming their way. The Japan trip sounded like a boondoggle. To Russia? Impossible. But if General Graves got to Europe on the Western Front, so much the better. "I'm all for that."

CHAPTER 12
KIEV TO BORISPOL
SUMMER 1917

Katya stared listlessly through a window of the Treasury train. For almost a fortnight they had been sitting on this unused spur hidden deep in the Ural Mountains northeast from Kazan, far from the war. Outside, guards on duty near the forest's edge threw lunch scraps to a timid black bear in an attempt to stay amused for the remainder of their four-hour watch. Katya glanced at them occasionally from the railroad car that had been designed as a model schoolroom. Here she paced the aisle between eleven children working at their desks. A global model of earth swung from a string in the corner; the map of South America covered one wall; ink etchings of jungle animals peered down from above the windows just as they had for six months now.

She was ready to admit that the novelty of hiding on a railroad train had worn off for the children. It certainly had for her, because there wasn't much to do, and time dragged by, giving everyone far too much time to worry. Quite unexpectedly, Katya discovered that in spite of the one hundred and thirty people on board, there was really no one for her to talk to.

Essentially there were eight accountants on the Treasury staff directed by President Ordinov, who acted for the most part, Katya felt, as a strict father. Four of the men traveled with their wives and children; three others were unmarried. Katya found, to her discomfort, that she was the only single woman, and there were times when she sensed that her free state was a source of hostility for the wives,

who, although not much older than Katya, were not as friendly as
they might have been. They seemed determined to count, record and
resent any glance or conversational crumb the men, especially the
married men, might send her way.

Katya was on good terms with the service personnel and the
sentries, but she soon found that Mrs. Ordinov was her only real
source of human contact. She found as well just how difficult it was
not having anyone her own age with whom she could exchange ideas.
The men had accepted her when it came to work — although Rovskoy
was not to be trusted — but there was no work, and Katya had made
up her mind that any informal relationship with unmarried colleagues
would just create problems, not to mention gossip. Therefore, she had
joined in willingly to organize a school curriculum for the children,
and she spent long hours monitoring their assignments.

The youngest boy raised his hand.

"Yes, Sasha."

His tie was crooked, pushing one point of his collar up while the
other was down. Clearing his throat, he asked, "Miss Kazakova, how
long has the war been going?"

The older children only glanced his way, showing little concern.
Their eyes darted toward him, then to their teacher while they
continued to write.

"It began in the summer of 1914," Katya said quietly. "And it's
now 1917."

Sasha looked down at the desktop. "Was I five?" he asked.

"Quite correct, Sasha. Good."

The boy smiled and went back to his sums. Katya sat down at her
desk, her eyes lowered. And I was twenty-one, she remembered.

She re-read a letter from Marie Romanov who had remembered
Katya's July birthday. It was a brave note, Katya felt, even though
she could sense the fear hiding among its happy words. Marie had
been determined to overcome the rising animosity toward her and all
landed gentry, by working at common tasks alongside working-class
colleagues. The taunts and sneers were constant, soon to become
vicious. Where once there had been reverence, threats were now
commonplace. The shock from this change had encouraged Marie
to volunteer for service near the front, where she threw herself
tirelessly into nursing. Even there, in the sickening field hospitals
with their ghastly stock-in-trade, she could not escape the ridicule

and the hatred, and for her own protection, the head surgeon who was a family friend, transferred Marie to Moscow. "And here I met Sergei," Marie had written.

Katya understood these words all right. Short, simple and unadorned as they were, the message was expansive. It was an ancient announcement to be shared by friends. It spoke of a search completed; a private celebration between two women who, although having little stability in the present, had found the promise of a future for one, and this gave strength to the other to believe that those things that really mattered were still within reach.

She looked around her classroom. The children were still at work.

Katya was torn. She was happy for Marie, but without communication from Alex, and feeling trapped, her confidence faded daily. Marie had heard nothing from Alex. Not one letter. Of course Marie, whose job it was to receive Alex's letters, was near the front and on the move constantly, so mail was difficult to deliver. The real problem might be that Marie no longer received any mail at all. Marie pretended to joke: "The impassioned and newly empowered postal zealots who censor my letters to shreds have now stopped sending even the shreds."

There was a silent undertone to this which made Katya cringe in the middle of the night: Alex might have been killed. Trying not to call out or cry, she would hug her pillow and change her dream to Alex and their room at the Grand Hotel in Kiev.

Alex, who had convinced her that she was attractive, at least to him. He had even called her "beauty." This memory gave her a certain contentment, but she wondered how long it would be before she fulfilled her promise as a woman. Could Alex ever find her? Was he even alive?

During these dead dull days her mind wandered, and the scenes she dreamed of, and the sensations she felt alone in her bed, caused her worry. She wondered whether Marie ever felt guilty about the body's response to dark thoughts. Of course, the Grand Duchess had been married once. Katya wanted to ask her about the torture of her insistent fantasies.

She glanced around the class again, nervous that her thoughts might somehow be in view.

Katya had noticed the way the young guardsman, Constantine, watched her. He had grown a soft brown beard — trying, she supposed, to make himself look older. She had to admit she enjoyed the courting dance, a sort of reassurance. And what about Pasha, the pathetically shy accountant who had timidly tried to enter her compartment one night? She had actually considered letting him in! Alex, are you alive? Soldiers get shot. Young soldiers die before they can complete things that really matter. Where are you?

Katya shook her head trying to talk some sense to herself. Abruptly, she clapped her hands. "Come to order please. I want to check your answers."

●   ●   ●

Alex looked back into the dark trees where they lay hidden just seventy kilometres north of Kiev. Chased steadily southward from Poland, the Czech Rifle Corps prepared to defend Germany's next target — Kiev, the ancient trading city located on the west bank of the Dnieper River. The Russians, he had heard, were committed to an all-out effort to stop any further German advance.

Trying to keep his breathing quiet, Alex listened for sounds of the following German troops while he wiped the sweat from his eyes to peer into the dark. Nothing moved. He didn't mind the dark because, with his experience in sport, he felt he had a better chance than if he were lined up in the light of day marching into the cross-hairs of a waiting gun. That horror was not a contest of skill and physical strength; it was contrived slaughter — the outcome depending upon which side had the most men to sacrifice. He abhorred the thought of being killed by some mindless fool from a distance. He wanted at least a chance. And so, until the next morning, at which time the Russian High Command had ordered them out of the action near Kiev, he would be very careful. The Czechs were to be sent across the Dnieper River to Borispol, as if they could not be trusted. Russian commanders were having more than enough trouble with their own troops and did not want to worry about internationals. Alex determined with his friends not to get hurt in someone else's war.

He heard a little noise through the trees and made ready to fight, hoping they were German troops and not Austrian. The thought of ever being captured by the Austrians gave him a chill. His friends had often talked about the fate awaiting any captured Czech, especially those who had deserted the Habsburg Empire.

"Alex, train tracks over here," he heard Peter whisper, and he started toward his friend's voice. As he stepped between two trees, silhouetted for an instant against the sky, he heard the explosion of a rifle and felt a burning near his waist.

"Damn!" he grunted in pain, falling to the ground while three rifles near him answered. He squeezed his side hard, waiting until the noise stopped. When it was quiet again a lit match was held close by.

"How bad is it?" Alex asked angrily.

Peter cut away his blouse and Syrovy peered at the oozing mess. "Not bad. They tore a chunk out of you, but it's hardly bleeding. Just your roll of fat. Lucky. If you weren't so plump it would've hit your kidney."

"Plump." Alex winced. "If I were any thinner it would've missed me." His attempt at a grin was more like the expression of a man who had just cut himself shaving, but Syrovy and Peter laughed anyway.

Peter wrapped the wound tightly at the waist with a roll of first aid linen from his kit bag, then helped Alex onto the train while his troops loaded most of the abandoned fighting equipment into storage cars. Captain Gaida and his regiment stayed near the edge of the forest slowing down the German advance. Soon they were all loaded and rolling toward their new quarters at Borispol.

Alex lay on the rough floorboards of the freight car for three sleepless hours until morning, when he was able to climb stiffly out into the huge railroad storage yard for the city of Kiev at Borispol. They disembarked onto a dusty maze of empty train tracks, to lounge in the sun.

A crumpled brown car drove over to the boxcar where Syrovy waited. Colonel Trojanov, the Russian officer assigned to the Czech Rifle Corps, got out looking as if he had not had proper rest in weeks. He shook hands and then strolled away from the troops with Syrovy and Alex. They stopped about fifty metres away from the few trains that remained in the railroad yard.

He pointed west toward the river where the small village of Borispol sat near the bridge about three kilometres away. It looked green and peaceful but Trojanov said, as if reading their thoughts, "The villagers don't want you there. There are too many of you now with a lot more arriving soon."

He pointed across the compound. "There are your new military barracks, General. We call these Zemlanky. They should keep you snug for as long as you stay." Trojanov's gesture indicated twenty-five thatched roofs lined up in five neat rows, each being fifty metres long and twenty wide. The main feature was, however, that each roof stood no more than waist high.

"A bit cramped, don't you think, Colonel?" Syrovy remarked dryly.

"No, no, my friend. Maybe you haven't seen Zemlanky before. Each one is dug three metres deep under that roof. Cool in summer, warm in winter. They'll suit your purposes. The Russian army won't need them again," he added.

"How long will we be here?" Syrovy asked.

Alex watched Trojanov's face for the answer. There was an uncharacteristic lack of spirit, he thought, and this notion was confirmed by the Russian's pensive answer: "No one knows. You will assemble every Czech unit here, and wait for instructions. The situation is completely liquid at the moment . . . but it remains, after all, a Russian war and we still have six million fighting men. Your dismissal was a political decision. However, you will be left with the thanks and recognition that only a military colleague can offer. Career soldiers know what you fellows accomplished. Politicians never really understand."

Alex followed Syrovy and Trojanov back toward the trainload of Czechs now assembled as rank and file on a clear space to the side of the maze of tracks. More dusty trucks arrived to disgorge a varied collection of men who fell in beside the squadrons of battle-hardened troops. There were so many Czechs in so many different uniforms, that it looked as if every brigade in the Russian army was represented. Section officers called them to attention. May sunshine warmed their necks as Trojanov took a long last look at his command.

"Brave Czechs," he called loudly. "I thank you for your devoted service. And now, under the authority of Russia's Sixth Army, I turn this command over to your newly appointed leaders: General Syrovy and Major Kechek." There were cheers for this announcement, and Alex gave Peter a slap on the back. "Well done, Major. Congratulations, General. Well deserved."

Trojanov continued. "Thomas Masaryk, your president in exile, will come to Kiev in just a few days to instruct you further. God save the Slavic race!"

Shaking hands, Alex heard him say to Syrovy, "Well, Commander, here is the beginning of your new Czech army with more than forty thousand men who were courageous enough to desert Austria. Take your officers to the Shevchenko Opera House in two weeks to learn their future. I did not say to them 'Long live Russia' because I no longer know what Russia is.'"

Trojanov saluted and then got into his car.

Alex called out: "Three cheers for Colonel Trojanov!" The troops responded with three enthusiastic hurrahs, kept in time by his prompting "hip, hip." Then he stood beside Syrovy, saluting the sad face looking back at them from the rear window.

"Dismissed!" Syrovy bellowed, and the tattered lines of men found their way to their new quarters. Alex, Peter and Gaida waited for instructions.

A hand slapped him on the back. It was Syrovy. "All right now. Don't look so glum," he said confidently. "We've got time to whip this bunch into shape before we trek off to France. And just look what we've got." He read from Trojanov's list: "112 carpenters. 81 tailors. 76 machinists. 89 bakers. 67 blacksmiths. 52 butchers. 138 cooks. 18 physicians. 6 dentists in a force of 42,000 men. That's a hell of a start for a good-sized town — all we need are some barmaids."

"Rad," he called to Gaida. "I want you to get this place organized. Set up the bank. Go buy enough sheep to make everyone a coat. Archangel's far, far to the north. Sooner or later, we're going to run into winter."

Turning to Alex and Peter he said, "Have you two figured out how we get to Archangel yet? No? Well until you have something better to do, I want you to find trains. Set them up in the yard and get them in good running order. We have to keep this troop together. Away you go."

• • •

By the time Thomas Masaryk, the aging and unofficial president of Czechoslovakia, arrived in Kiev three days later, the New Czech Army dominated the east bank of the Dnieper River looking across to the ancient city of Kiev. On a warm night in August, Alex crowded into the Shevchenko Opera House with two thousand others to hear Masaryk speak.

Alex had a clean uniform with a fresh dressing and ointment for his wound. He sat examining the carved gargoyles peering into the audience from above the burgundy curtain. Sitting beside Syrovy and Peter, his hopes were high as the sixty-eight-year-old leader strode nimbly across the stage amid thunderous applause. Masaryk, in the glare of the footlights, waved and brushed back his white hair self-consciously before stepping forward to describe the turmoil that was Russia. And then he spoke of that which they longed to hear.

"My boys, you have waited such a long time, . . . some of you almost three years, but we've made progress. Edward Benes is in the United States of America at this moment, enjoying the support of Theodore Roosevelt and Woodrow Wilson. They will help us." There was applause and excited talk at this announcement. "From Italy, a guerrilla force of twenty-two thousand Czechs waits for you on the western front." More applause, as Masaryk mopped his forehead with a handkerchief.

This is what we need, Alex thought. He could see the excitement on Peter's face. Only Syrovy appeared business-like as Masaryk continued. "On his tour of the United States, Benes has collected support funds in excess of one million dollars from Czech émigrés." Still more hand-clapping and smiles, but Syrovy allowed only a slight nod.

"But my boys, I've been saving some special news for you. I know the situation is confused, and there is still a long way to go, but I want you to realize that we now have tangible hope — not just the promise of a dream, but ink on an agreement. After months of negotiation I have just been informed that the French government has, only days ago, officially recognized our Czecho-Slovak force as an ally, and part of the French army!"

Men stood now and the applause rang out, mixed with happy shouts, arms raised in salute until Masaryk brought them back once more with a caution. "There is still much to do. Be prepared! I am going to Moscow tomorrow to see Prime Minister Kerensky about passage north through Archangel. A ship to the west — then we'll be on our way, my boys!" This statement brought wild shouts as suppressed hopes and fears were at last given vent. The theatre became one great cave filled with cheering and singing men.

Syrovy interrupted the moment by pulling on Alex's sleeve. Along with Gaida and Kechek they left the theatre to find a cafe before the happy mob came out.

"Don't believe everything politicians tell you," Syrovy said.

"Lenin will never let us through the Petrograd district," Peter added with a worried look.

"Come on, don't be so pessimistic," Alex chided. "The head of our country isn't going to lie to us."

"Not lie," Syrovy admitted, adjusting the strap on his forehead, his one good eye staring intensely out at his mates. "He's just too damned cavalier to be practical. How in hell do we move forty thousand men through the middle of both a war and a revolution?"

"We're stronger than ever," Alex argued. "The Allies will back us."

"Then why do I have this sinking feeling that we're becoming more and more isolated? More and more vulnerable," Syrovy worried out loud. The lines on his forehead seemed deeper than usual. "How do we get out of here?"

"Lenin won't let us through," Peter repeated, with his jaw set firmly in place.

Gaida, unusually quiet and thoughtful, stroked his light moustache. "Gentlemen," he said with a wry smile, "I can only suggest that it's going to be a very interesting journey."

Alex fretted as the Czechs languished in Borispol while summer became autumn. Their numbers grew each week, so that drilling newcomers became the main activity. Alex and his Falcons busied themselves with the collection of abandoned trains — obsessed with the urgency to be able to leave when the moment came.

At night he prowled near German lines raiding train yards with Peter and Jan, looking for unguarded engines. They would watch from the shadows until sure that a crew had gone until morning. Sometimes they worked through the night making temporary repairs, or stealing fuel to make it back to the great rail storage yard at Borispol.

Once there, machinists and carpenters refurbished the cars with bunks and stoves. The outside walls were double-planked for protection. The inside walls were painted by homesick men with murals of Bohemian scenes; the mountains, trees and flowers they dreamed of. A few cars were transformed in such detail that Alex could imagine he stood in the center of a farming village. There were the houses and the sweeping fields at harvest, and on the other wall, the church. No one told him how many trains would be needed, but Alex was determined to have the means of transportation when word came for them to move north to Archangel.

Masaryk returned in October, but Alex thought he was far less enthusiastic as he took center stage at the theatre once again. No longer was there noisy applause, although there was still affection in the hopeful eyes of tired men too long, too far from home. This kindly, indefatigable man who addressed the hardened collection of veteran soldiers as "my boys" had their respect, but they knew something was wrong.

"Things in Russia are not entirely as they seem," Masaryk began, tugging at the vest of his rumpled suit. "I don't think the Kerensky government can last much longer. We must stand back-to-back to protect one another." He shook his fist for emphasis. "Truth always wins. And because our ideals are good, and because we are justified in what we seek, we must — and shall — win."

Alex looked at Peter. Syrovy rolled his good eye heavenward.

"He's saying nothing," Alex growled.

Gaida looked at the floor in disgust, shaking his head.

"Have no fear," Masaryk called into the silent theatre. Grim faces stared back. "But I repeat to you, be on guard, beware! Above all else, do not interfere in Russian politics. I will report back."

The Czechs continued their military exercises, training the new arrivals, blending them in with the battle-hardened troops in anticipation of their journey to the western front. Through Syrovy's binoculars, Alex watched the progress of the Bolshevik revolution in the Kiev area with increased agitation. From the east bank of the Dnieper he could follow the defense build-up of the Bolshevik outposts close to the railroad bridge, in anticipation of the enemy. But what enemy might that be, he wondered — the German army, or Prime Minister Kerensky's faithful troops? There were fewer and fewer workers in the village. Everyone would be forced to choose: left or right? Red or white?

At night, when not on patrol, Alex worried about his father, and dreamed of Katya. Tension in camp cut as sharply as the frigid wind until one day a letter came, which for Alex was like a rush of warm spring air in November. "My Dearest Alex," Katya began. A simple opening really, but it produced in Alex a peculiar mixture of protective instincts and emotions, not the least of which was yearning. "I want you to know that I'm safe, although I can't predict for how long."

While he read, he felt an emptiness that became an ache as the letter told her story. He believed that he should have been with her.

He had realized some months ago that his instincts nagged him daily — not about war, but about building a home. Syrovy made the point in the strongest way one evening when Gaida was blustering about "how manly a good battle made him feel." Syrovy had spiked that nonsense with a simple observation: "When you grow up, you will find that a man feels most like a man when he's in his own home with a wife and child." That barb had ended the conversation, but the message had remained with Alex. He knew Syrovy was right, as he continued with Katya's letter.

CHAPTER 13

KAZAN TO PETROGRAD
WINTER 1917

Katya went to a
meeting called
by Mr. Ordinov.
The Treasury staff
gathered in the
train's conference-
car immediately after
breakfast, sitting with
considerable strain
waiting for their leader.
They were nervous, she
deduced, because no one
had yet seen him this day.

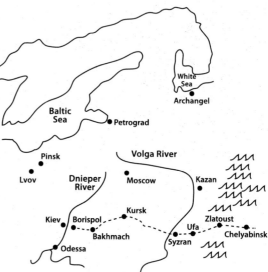

As he entered the car Katya searched his face anxiously for signs.

"Good morning," Ordinov said, hanging up his town-coat and homburg — city garments, looking so out-of-place in the mountains, Katya thought.

He rubbed his hands together, and Katya wondered whether it was because of cold, or fear, while she prayed that there would be some good news from Moscow at last.

"I am sorry to report, that after three days of trying, I can raise neither comment nor direction from Prime Minister Kerensky. A crisis is approaching, and we must have definitive information. What happens to the gold store of Russia in the advent of, God forbid, a successful revolution?" President Ordinov stopped, and with a trembling hand dabbed his face with a white handkerchief.

Katya was numb. What is happening to my life? She focused on the royal seal on Ordinov's handkerchief. A gift from the Czar, most likely, but where is the Czar now? Is he safe? Has he been murdered? His legs blown off by a maniac's bomb, like his father? Dear God!

Ordinov recovered enough to continue. "Any hope of a confiden-tial message through the post is impossible . . . and yet we must know what to do with the Treasury. Do we in fact have to turn it over to Lenin, in the possibility that . . . ."

Here he was drowned out by gasps and protestations from his staff, who refused to believe the possibility of a Bolshevik triumph. They all knew that the key to power for those in control was possession of the Treasury, this vast horde of bullion — the largest in Europe, the envy of the world. Katya wanted it kept for the Czar, or at the very least for Kerensky and the Duma. After all, it was her career. Lenin of course needed wealth for international credibility, to spread his socialism, pitting workers against the ruling class — certainly he must never get his vile hands on one ruble of it!

"You see my dilemma then," she heard Ordinov say. "We must send a man through Moscow to Petrograd for official word from Kerensky. There is no alternative."

The staff again began talking, and Katya watched their worried faces as they calculated the risks. She could see frightened wives sending signals by means of guarded expressions with lips and eyebrows. No doubt they were trying to dissuade their husbands from volunteering for this dangerous errand.

Katya remained deep in her own thoughts as she stared out at the high Ural peaks which now seemed like prison walls. The Czar could have prevented this months ago. My dead father would have known what to do with Lenin. Why doesn't Kerensky throw that ruffian into Lubyanka's darkest cell? What's the matter with them, she asked herself before finding her voice. "I'll go," she heard herself say.

The talking stopped abruptly. Everyone in the conference car turned her way. "Katherine Elenskaya," said the president. "You have our deepest admiration for your gesture, but really, you have no idea — the whole Duchy of Muscovy is a tinder box. It may be ablaze as we speak . . . I . . . I couldn't," he said, his voice trailing off.

The room was in complete silence as Katya stood. She was embarrassed, but determined in her decision. "You have no choice, Mr. Ordinov. I'm the only one here without family." She knew it was desperation that had given her the courage to speak. No matter, she thought, I refuse to let my career slip away without trying. Strangely, it was Rovskoy who spoke up, "It's not a bad idea," he offered.

That evening the engineer took her to Kazan in a four-man maintenance car. As they sped out of the maze of mountains into a northern twilight, it occurred to her that the Urals were much like the labyrinthine complexity of Russia itself. She watched the streaked purple sky, praying that the pink glow to the west did not come from Moscow in flames. She stood on the platform for two hours watching down the dark track, waiting for a train already five hours late, finally giving up to lie on a bench in the station house.

"Like a common gypsy," she murmured, smiling before sleep came, sensing that she was on her own for what was really the first time in her life.

The next morning, in response to her aggressive questioning, the station master admitted that he did not know when the next train to Moscow would leave, and finally confessed that he had not seen a west-bound train for seventeen hours.

Katya overlooked the way he treated her. Once, people in service had used a special tone for the upper class; now there was contemptuous indifference. It made her uneasy, but just before lunch, a train did arrive, so Katya counted herself fortunate when she arrived in Moscow that evening, even though she had very little knowledge of the city, or the location of Grand Duchess Marie's apartment.

There was only one cab waiting at the main entrance to the Ural Station on the east side of Moscow. An old man, wearing worn but meticulously brushed black livery, stood beside a sagging horse. The cloth on his coat was shiny with age, but spotless.

"Can you take me to Zendal Crescent?" she asked.

The old man became animated immediately, touching the peak of his cap before opening the door. "I haven't been up there in a while. Hope there's no guns." He jerked his thumb toward the horse. "Vladu doesn't like 'em." He closed the door and then carefully hauled himself up onto the high seat.

From its holding-tube he pulled a well-worn whip with a wound leather handle; Katya was relieved to see that he only touched Vladu's rump with it. At this nudge, the alerted horse began to plod toward Marie's apartment.

They wheeled beneath barren trees down the wide boulevard toward a residential section of the city which appeared to be empty of people. There was rubble everywhere. Stones and shards of glass from smashed buildings littered the way. Some business sections had no glass in the windows at all; Katya supposed looting had gotten out of control there. Guns rumbled, out of sight in the distance.

When they stopped in front of a brown stone building she gave the old man three times the usual tip, wondering if he too wanted the Czar's world to come crashing down. The horse looked as if there was no hope left for anything at all, but she felt better when the old man touched his cap to say, "A pleasure to be of service, Ma'am." Then she ran to the door of Marie's apartment.

Katya was surprised when Marie opened the door wearing a mariner's woolen toque. "Thank God I found you," Katya said, very near tears as they embraced in relief at seeing each other again. "I've been so worried."

"Well, I'm glad you caught me," Marie said, leading her into a small parlor. "I've finished my dinner break. I was just going back. But I can wait a while." She tugged off her toque and short black hair fell out in a tangle.

"Good Lord, Marie. Your beautiful hair! You look like a man!"

Marie smiled shyly, "Well I'm not . . . but I'm married to one. Look. This is Sergei." Marie picked up a brown leather frame with a picture of a young man in his late twenties. "Prince Sergei Putiatin."

He wore a white dress shirt without a tie, open to the summer sun. His tanned face and wide smile wounded Katya. "So like Alex," she said softly.

"You'll have to change your clothes. You look as if you're going to a ball."

Katya followed Marie into a tiny bedroom with room enough for only a bed and bureau. "I'll get you a bite to eat while you put these on," Marie said, reaching into one of the drawers for clothes she placed on the bed.

Katya unfolded the pants. They were sailors' issue, thick and woolen. She removed her own heavy skirts and tight jacket to put on the ink-blue sweater with a new excitement. The turtleneck was tight around her throat and the close-knit wool scratched her skin, but she felt the warmth those long sleeves offered as she hurried to put on the bell-bottomed trousers. The waist was small and after she had done up the two rows of buttons which cinched up the front flap, the pants held her firmly around the hips. The feeling of freedom surprised her. "Marie, I'm so light. I may never wear skirts again," she laughed.

"Wait 'til you try the shoes," Marie called from the kitchen. "Rubber soles. You can run in those. Sometimes you have to run."

Just before midnight, Katya followed Marie down the back streets toward the Kremlin. They scurried down alleys which, under normal conditions, Katya would never dream of entering. She could see that Marie constantly watched out for the gangs of thugs who, she warned, had been rampaging and looting for days.

"I mustn't let them find who I am . . . or was," she said. "It's like the French Revolution all over again. Only this time it's the Kremlin, not the Bastille, and they're hunting for me."

"Marie, is it that bad? Would they harm you? Or any of us?"

The wide eyebrows lowered, and for a moment Marie looked darkly unhappy, but replied only, "Kerensky moved my family into the Urals with the Czar . . . to Ekaterinburg, they say. I stayed here. Citizenness Romanova . . . and I cut my hair off. Can you guess how that feels?" she asked sadly.

Katya was suddenly frightened for her friend's life and fearful for her own as well. It was only just then that she understood the feeling of the word "revolution."

It was like finding a dead robin as a child: that was the moment when the meaning of death suddenly became real. Here and now, the revolution was real. It threatened all those who looked and dressed and thought like the ruling class. "I have to find Kerensky. Marie, you must get away."

Guns roared near the south wall, and between the thump of each explosion they could hear the rattle of small arms. "Now's our chance," Marie called, grabbing Katya's hand and running toward the monolithic court building across the square from the west wall, thick and unyielding.

Through a side entrance down steep dark stairs they entered the comparative quiet of a cavernous basement. It was set up as another crowded hospital — like the basement in Petersburg, Katya remembered. She must have looked confused or disgusted, because Marie said in an explanatory way, "A regiment of military cadets, young boys really, defend this fortress. The wounded come to us through that tunnel."

While tending to the casualties, Katya tried to appear cheerful even though her depression increased with each frightened young face. One boy of fourteen years made her particularly sombre as she examined his wound. His arm was wrapped in a filthy bandage, stiff from pus and dried blood. He appeared calm — too calm, Katya thought, herself numbed by the enormity of the situation. She had caught an ominous whiff of infection and finished quickly. Fighting panic, she went over to the sink where Marie was washing bandages. "Marie," she said insistently. "I must get to Kerensky!"

Marie nodded her understanding, and arranged with the head nurse to leave first thing in the morning.

During business hours they found their way to the American Embassy, not far from Marie's apartment. A young marine let them in past the gate. She waited while Marie knocked on the door in agitated bursts until finally an anxious face of the housekeeper peeked out over the chain and the door was opened, much to Katya's relief.

Her optimism returned in a rush when Ambassador John Davis came out to meet them in the entrance hall. He wore a tailored blue suit, and in his steady eyes Katya recognized a deep concern for Marie's safety. "Your Royal Highness, please let me help," he implored. "You're in grave danger. Nothing can stop this now."

Marie turned to Katya defiantly. "Mr. Davis tells me I must leave Russia."

"Where could she go?" Katya asked, tacitly acknowledging the truth in his words.

Davis spoke directly, perhaps relieved to hear that he had some support. "Through Romania, and from there to Sweden," he said, glancing at Marie with a worried look.

But now Marie put a hand on Katya's arm. "I can't go begging to my former husband's family in Stockholm after I divorced their son. And what about Sergei?" Katya felt the grip of Marie's hand, and was devastated to see tears welling up in the eyes of the former Grand Duchess. "And leave Russia?" Marie continued, her lower lip wavering. "Never," she said in a breaking voice.

"Well," Davis said to Katya, apparently deciding to wait before arguing with Marie again. "How may I help you?"

* * *

It was the afternoon of October 24, 1917 as Katya rode north from Moscow up the six hundred kilometres to Petrograd in the embassy car with an American flag on each forward fender. Above chromium headlamps, the two flags snapped in the wind while the car raced down deserted country roads. She kept low in the back seat, occasionally looking out through the windscreen between Ambassador Davis and the chauffeur, as they swept through towns and villages. There was no trouble — only some unfriendly looks and hateful shouts which, because of the speed of the car, died as soon as they began, and Katya was certain that the bright little flags helped this swift passage.

She passed the time by thinking of Marie. Katya knew she would be too frightened to think of herself, so she curled up in the corner of the wide leather seat to dream of their ballet classes with Madame at the Winter Palace so long ago.

Weaving through the sandy hills south of Petrograd, they reached the outskirts of the capital in the gloom of late afternoon where, despite increasing darkness, there were still clusters of people prowling the streets. As their limousine drove cautiously past hostile stares, Katya was again relieved to find that the watchers seemed to hold a peculiar respect for the embassy car. The chauffeur was permitted to drive without incident to Kerensky's apartment overlooking the Ekaterininsky Canal. Here a guard swung open the iron gate which admitted them to the protection of a courtyard.

A servant with a sharp hawk-nose seemed to recognize Ambassador Davis, and opened the door to let Davis and his chauffeur inside. But when Katya stepped through the door into a foyer ablaze with gold leaf pillars climbing high toward a domed ceiling, the servant's glare was devastating — and Katya suddenly realized that she was still wearing her sailor pants and toque.

As the door thumped shut and the lock pulled firmly into place, she remembered in a flash of temper that she had left her overnight bag at Marie's. "Chort!" she cursed, and ignoring the servant she walked quickly over to a long elliptical mirror near the staircase. She took off the woolen cap, trying to arrange as tidily as possible the hair splashing down the back of her pullover. I have money in the pouch of these pants, she reassured herself. I will see this through.

She followed Davis upstairs into an echoing room which had been stripped of its furniture and rugs. A table in the center of the hardwood floor was covered with boxes filled with file folders. And there stood Kerensky.

He wore the pants and vest of a black suit and a stiff-collared shirt with the sleeves rolled up to the elbows. He rummaged like a wild man through files of official documents. At first, he took little notice of his visitors, but then he recognized Ambassador Davis. "John! What are you doing here? It's all coming apart, you know."

Davis looked startled for the first time since Katya had met the suave diplomat. His face pulled tight. "How much time do we have?"

"I don't know," Kerensky said. "It's a madhouse out there." He pointed out through the French doors overlooking the canal. "I've only just managed to creep back here from the Winter Palace. We've been there all day trying to determine where we can find reinforcements. I don't even have a car. I have only a military telephone left, and it's growing less reliable by the hour!"

Katya still had not been introduced, so she waited impatiently while Davis went to the window. She was determined to have her purpose acknowledged. "Were you in Malachite Hall?" she asked Kerensky in a conversational way.

"What?" he asked in surprise, looking her up and down with a puzzled look.

"The Winter Palace," she replied. "Did you have your meeting in Malachite Hall?"

"Why. Why, yes," Kerensky stumbled. "But . . ." He stared at her again until Davis came back from the window.

"Forgive me, please," Davis said. "Your Excellency, this is Mademoiselle Kazakova who is here to ask you some questions concerning . . ."

Just then there was a noise from outside on Nevsky Prospect and Kerensky rushed to the window to peer out from the side of the high drapes.

"Damn," Katya said in a sharp whisper.

When Davis gave her a look of surprise, she realized that she must not succumb to the tension. Her job was to obtain instructions for the Treasury train.

Kerensky looked back over his shoulder. "They all seem to be headed for the Palace," he said to no one in particular. "A thousand metres, but they run as if it were only fifty."

Katya looked around the room littered with packing boxes from which the servant took file folders to stack on the table. Kerensky seized one and searched through it before throwing most of the papers into the hearth-fire. Then he handed one or two pages to his frowning servant who re-filed them in an attaché case.

"Mr. Kerensky," Katya said. "This is most important."

"How do you know about Malachite Hall?" he asked. "Who are you, mademoiselle?"

"I am an actuary with the Treasury."

Noticing his skeptical stare, Katya tried to think of something to persuade him into dealing with her problem. "You sent us on a train into the Urals." She saw a glimmer of interest in his darting eyes. "We've been in hiding for seven months now."

"With Ordinov? Good Lord, I hadn't even considered . . . ." His voice wandered off.

"Where is he now?" he suddenly demanded.

"He sent me to find you. We need further instructions," she said hopefully.

Kerensky looked away. "I'm very sorry," he said. "I can't help you. I can barely help myself."

"But you must," she insisted.

She could feel the men looking at her. "If you can't, then who will? You vowed to protect the Czar's Treasury. Then you made us promise to look after it. What are we supposed to do? Must we turn it over to the Bolsheviks?"

She watched his every move as he glanced away, perhaps trying to think of an answer — but instead, he went back to the window. He needs more time, she thought, following him as Kerensky stepped out onto the balcony into the clear night air. Davis came behind them.

Katya looked down onto the lane along the edge of the canal where a group of dark figures called out to one another as they hurried by. The Admiralty was in plain view at the end of broad Voznesensky Prospect and she could see the crowds of people jamming the wide junction where Voznesensky and Gorokhovaya Street met at the end of Nevsky Prospect.

From a ship on the river to the left of the Admiralty's central dome, a probing searchlight highlighted the Winter Palace. The Palace was partially obscured by the War Ministry to the right, but she could see the top of the Alexander column in Palace Square, and more people in the street.

"Look," Kerensky said pointing, "that cruiser near Nikolaevsky Bridge."

"Where are the police?" Katya asked.

Kerensky shook his head. "This government has no control. We're in grave danger. I'm sorry, my dear, this could be the end."

"No! We mustn't think that," Katya insisted. "Look down below on the Nevsky. Prostitutes and cabbies, just hanging about. This is not a revolution yet. It's more like an audience of curiosity seekers."

Kerensky was listening at last, she felt, but when the telephone rang with a particularly irritating insistency, he rushed over to pick it up. "Yes?" he said cautiously, "Captain Kozmin?"

Aghast, Katya followed him inside. She turned to Davis. "There must be some way of saving the Treasury."

She stopped when she saw the look on Kerensky's face. "St. Peter and Paul Fortress just surrendered," he said quietly, putting down the telephone.

"Surrendered?" Davis repeated. "How, for God's sake?"

"The Red Guard took control, that's how." Kerensky said this with a shrug, but Katya could see a terrible pain on his face.

"When the *Aurora* anchored in the river to aim her guns, the Fortress surrendered." He shook his head. "Now the cannons of the Fortress are pointed across the river at the Winter Palace."

Katya was stunned. "All this way and nothing is to be done." Her shoulders ached she was so tired, although she still burned inside from frustration.

The strain on Kerensky was obvious. His skin did not have a healthy look, and there were dark moons under his eyes. "I must finish. Please let me think. Have a rest until Captain Kozmin reports back."

Numbly she followed the servant to a small bedroom, certain that sleep would be impossible. She lay down on the bed feeling the long sleeves of the tight pullover covering her arms firmly to each wrist. The turtleneck collar held her gently at the throat. At least I'm warm, she sighed.

Before first light, Katya could hear a telephone ringing in the distance. Although momentarily confused, she bolted upright.

Remembering where she was, she bounced off the bed to the door and ran down the hall to Kerensky's den as quickly as she could. There he stood with the telephone to his ear and Davis at his side, looking grimly on.

Her heart sank as Kerensky slowly replaced the telephone on its cradle. The look on his face was one of complete dejection. "There's nothing left," he announced. "The Telephone Exchange, State Bank, Post Office, power stations — all gone. My aide tells me there is not one military unit in the capital upon which I can rely. He's on his way here now." Kerensky pulled a watch from his vest pocket. "Six thirty. We must leave. I'm sorry, my dear, it's over."

Kerensky walked across the room to stare for a moment at an Ilya Repin portrait of himself. He seemed to study the painted face which was serious and resolute — not like his own face this morning which showed the scars of too many sleepless nights; his eyes were windows of worry and doubt.

She was surprised when he lifted the painting carefully from the wall. But there was the reason — a hidden safe. Kerensky began spinning the dial. He took his time pulling the door open to remove more documents for sorting. With a serious look, he committed some pages to the flames. The remainder he squeezed into his attaché case before handing it to the hawk-nosed servant. "Wait downstairs for Captain Kozmin," he said.

Katya's mind was racing. The empire of a thousand years was being dismantled before her eyes. Everyone giving in! But then her head jerked toward the sound of running footsteps on the staircase. Her stare fixed on the door long before the knock.

"Come," Kerensky said, and a vigorous man in uniform came inside in a busy way.

"Captain Kozmin," Kerensky said expectantly. "What news?"

The soldier saluted his commander-in-chief before removing his cap. Katya was startled to see that Captain Kozmin, although certainly not more than thirty, had a full head of silver hair — he was remarkable.

"Sir," the captain said in a very hoarse voice. "You must leave now. Lenin is back from Finland. He's going to order the arrest of your government sometime today."

"He's back?" Kerensky looked incredulous. "He knows I've restored the death penalty. He'll be recognized."

The captain remained detached from this theoretical point, it seemed to Katya, although she could hear the agitation in his rough voice. "Lenin has been living in the Vyborg district for a fortnight now, wearing nothing more than a token disguise. He took a tram last night to the Smolny Institute to meet with Joseph Stalin, his new editor for *Pravda*. Leon Trotsky is now head of the Cheka, his secret police, and he is to announce in today's newspaper that you have been consigned to the dustbin of history." He cleared his throat. "They're all down the street right now in Smolny auditorium.

The place is packed with mobs carrying machine guns and a field piece. No one will turn him in, and there is no one left to shoot him."

Kerensky flushed. "Then I shall!"

Captain Kozmin shook his head of silver hair. His raspy voice sounded again. "Sir, I've managed to borrow a car. My lieutenant is outside with the engine running. We believe there is a Cossack Division of House Guards not far from the Summer Palace." He looked anxiously at his prime minister. "Let me take you there."

Kerensky looked up. "Excellent, Kozmin! First rate. Hang on while I change." He was gray with exhaustion and near collapse, but he turned and ran to a bedroom.

Katya felt a wave of exultation wash over her. A Cossack Division! But just as suddenly, there was panic. Kerensky was rushing away again before solving the Treasury problem. Perhaps he couldn't solve it. She looked appealingly to Ambassador Davis.

"I'll talk to him," Davis assured her. "We'd best get some breakfast." Turning to the butler, he asked: "Is there anything in the kitchen?"

The man nodded and led them downstairs.

While the servant cut slices from a deep Mowbrey pie, Davis took plates out of a cupboard. Captain Kozmin poured red wine into tea cups and began to eat with considerable eagerness.

Katya could only think of what might happen to the Treasury should Lenin succeed. She merely nibbled at the meat pie. Would they have to turn all that wealth over to the revolutionaries? God forbid! She looked up when Kerensky strode into the kitchen in combat uniform: military jacket, breeches, boots, gaiters and a fresh shave. The Sam Browne belt slanted across his chest to the broad belt at his waist, all designed, she suspected, to give him a dashing look — an inspiration to the troops. But there was no disguising the fact that the ears were too large for a big head on a long neck. And now, the jammed-down officer's cap pushed the ears out, presenting a picture, she felt, of a clown dressed up to play soldier. She hoped the Cossacks wouldn't notice, or wouldn't mind.

She was startled by a sharp rap on the front door. The brass knocker echoed harshly down the hall to the kitchen.

Kozmin went to the door and returned almost immediately. "Everything is ready," he croaked. "There are roadblocks. But we could make a convoy of our two cars. Perhaps I should lead our way in the Renault," he suggested.

"Well done," Kerensky replied. "If that's all right with you, John."

"Of course. Good idea," the ambassador said, and Kozmin went outside again.

Katya was pleased to hear the confident tone of a forthright plan at last. Kerensky was energized, she noted, even though there was no hiding his ghostly pallor and a twitch at the corner of his mouth. She was reluctant to cause him more bother but knew she had to. As Kozmin moved out the door, she put a hand on his elbow. "I must have a word with you and Ambassador Davis in private," she said.

Kerensky looked a haunted man, but he nodded, and she followed him into the dining room with Davis. "I was sent here by Mr. Ordinov," she emphasized. "Please tell me what we are to do with the Treasury, should the worst happen."

Kerensky squared his chin. "If I can raise an army, I shall send this guttersnipe into the agonies of hell," he announced bravely.

"Then there will be no problem," Davis said, taking his watch from a vest pocket. "It's almost seven. The prime minister should leave!"

"Wait," Katya said urgently, realizing that they were still avoiding the unpalatable possibility of Lenin's success. "What if . . . ?"

Davis looked uncomfortable, but turned to Kerensky. "She has a point. Sir, may I offer you the help of the United States government concerning the bullion?" He opened the door a crack to peek out into the foyer and then closed it again. Dropping his voice, he said, "We are putting some people in place who will be able to help. But only in the worst of all possible circumstances," he added gently. "Would that be satisfactory, sir?"

"Yes, of course," Kerensky said sadly. "I would be most grateful."

He turned to Katya. "Tell Mr. Ordinov and his staff to hold on."

They ran outside into the gray chill and climbed into the idling limousine. The driver was loading extra petrol cans in the trunk. "Good man, Robert," Davis called.

Kozmin had the gate open, and the Renault drove out ahead of them.

Kerensky lay on the floor and Katya threw a car-rug over him before she and Davis sat down. "Robert, let's go!" shouted Davis, and the chauffeur drove through the gate ready to pursue the black Renault.

The guard had disappeared, so the chauffeur stopped and started to get out of the car to close the gate. Davis said, "Keep driving. I'll get it." He sprang from his back seat running for the gate, swung it shut, then jumped back into the car.

And so it was, Alex, that in the quiet of dawn I, dressed as a sailor, threw a car-rug over the last elected prime minister of Russia who was lying on the floor of the embassy car under my feet! We raced south along Zabalkansky Prospect with the borrowed Renault leading the way and when we cleared Petrograd, Kerensky got into the Renault with his two aides, and they sped off to Czarskoe Selo in the west, in search of a Cossack army. I wished them Godspeed. By eleven o'clock that night, Lenin had given the command for the revolution to begin, and the *Aurora* fired blanks over the Winter Palace as a challenge to surrender or fight.

By 2:00 a.m. on October 26, the Winter Palace, defended only by a regiment of women and some Cossack Guards, surrendered to the street gangs of workers and sailors. Lenin's new thinking was so persuasive that not a single shot had to be fired.

I can't tell you where I am right now. Please meet me where you said: on the Charles Bridge in Prague. Any day at noon, when the war is over. Until that day, I'll miss you. Katya.

● ● ●

Alex sat on his bunk thumping his knee with a clenched fist and staring at the letter in his other hand. Slowly he came to face the fact there was nothing he could do for her — nothing at all — so he sadly folded the letter and returned to the task of being a soldier and finding some way out of Russia.

Five days before Christmas, he sat in the crowded Zemlanky with fifty others, like a sardine in a crowded tin — a very smelly tin. He leaned back against the frozen wall hugging his knees, grateful nevertheless for the pit that hid them from the sting of the wind whining over an empty parade square above, sucked dry by the merciless howling draft. Looking up the three metres of high dirt walls, Alex said to no one in particular, "Perhaps the Russians know, after all, how to hide from winter."

When Masaryk came a third time to Kiev, Alex noticed how tired the statesman appeared in the harsh footlights, as tired perhaps as the fading red curtain behind him. The knees of his pants were two bulbous bags, with no sign of a crease. Alex shook his head slowly, his lips pursed. Masaryk did not look like the president of a nation. "You are alone in a disintegrating society. But now you stand recognized as an ally of the western powers."

There was only scattered polite applause, Alex noted, probably because the audience, who had heard the theme before, had not yet grasped the significance of Masaryk's statement. They came alive a moment later when they heard the rest: "I am happy to tell you that after two years of negotiations . . . England, France and the United States have signed a decree recognizing Czechoslovakia as an independent nation. We now have a country to call home. And we now have a country to which we can return!"

The men came to their feet with a roar of approval.

"That set them off," shouted Syrovy over the din. "I wonder how we get there?"

When at last the excited audience had retaken their seats, Masaryk continued. But Alex, watching closely, concluded that he did not relish his job. *We've been at war for three years now. Would he ask us for more? How long will it take,* he wondered as the old man began again.

"I am sorry to tell you that getting to the west will be difficult. The Dardanelles is cut off by Germany's ally Turkey, and even if we could get around the shambles of Moscow and Petrograd, Archangel will be frozen for another five months. The Germans will march on Ukraine as soon as the Bolsheviks sign a peace treaty. This leaves only one direction to go . . . and that is, to the east."

Alex shook his head as the enormity of this proposal sunk in. A rumble of incredulous shouted questions interrupted Masaryk. "In this weather?" "How, for God's sake?"

Masaryk silenced them with raised arms, cutting his conclusion short. "Simply put, there is no other way! I will arrange your passage to Vladivostok by way of the Great Siberian Railway. The French, British and American navies will take you to France from there. I will tell you your date of departure as soon as I secure the necessary permission from Lenin. It's the best we can do. Goodbye, my boys! Bonne chance!"

As the crowd surged toward the exit doors, Alex pushed his way against the flow until he was able to clamber up on to the stage. Running through the wings to the backstage dressing room, Alex found a door and hurled it open. Masaryk, with coat already on, looked up in surprise as Alex burst in. An aide moved to block him, catching him by the lapels. The other aide drew a gun from the inside of his jacket and watched intently, holding it above his shoulder with a bent arm, the snubbed barrel pointed toward the ceiling as a concession to safety, but the steady frown showing that he meant business.

Alex realized his blunder. "Professor," he said quickly. "It's Alex Branda. Former student. You'll need an escort to Moscow. When you speak to Lenin. I can help."

CHAPTER 14

TO MOSCOW AND KAZAN
WINTER 1917

On the train to
Moscow, Alex had
his first chance since
studying history
under the famous
Professor Masaryk to
talk in a spontaneous
manner with his former
teacher. But now that he
sat across from a president,
words did not come easily.
Maybe it was because the
man did not, just now at

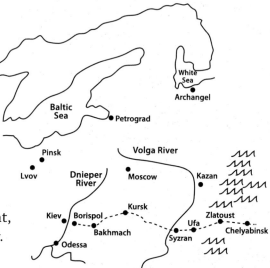

least, look like a national leader to Alex. At sixty-eight, in his crumpled
black suit shining at the elbows and at every point on the back that
had compressed against a chair during his innumerable meetings, he
looked more like a tired grandfather. Perhaps, Alex thought, that's
what he would prefer to be.

He could tell that the old man was tired, and yet Masaryk seemed
to go out of his way to ensure that Alex was included in the tight
little group consisting of the president of free Czechoslovakia and
two sullen bodyguards.

Were they sullen, he asked himself, or simply bored with the
years of searching for recognition in a world changing with every
disastrous infantry charge? Bored they may be, he realized, but their
attentiveness toward Masaryk's safety was at times tender, even
loving. It must be only that they have no time for me.

He sat down beside Masaryk, who rested his arm on the ledge
next to the dusty window. Judging from the litter on the floor, this
car had not seen a cleaning crew for several trips. They both sat knee
to knee with the bodyguards as the train pulled away from Kiev on
its northerly trek to Moscow.

"Well then, young Alexander," Masaryk said cheerfully; above a white moustache, his cheeks were pink from the rush for the train. "Not the glamorous life you expected as a normal day for a politician, I'd wager." His quick eyes flicked in Alex's direction for a reaction. "You won't find much of the aristocratic high-life on this trip." And then, perhaps as an afterthought: "If you do find any, make sure you let us know." This remark brought grins from the two guards.

"Professor, do you have any news about my father?" Alex asked hopefully. "I haven't had a letter in a long time."

Masaryk frowned. "That's understandable. The Austrians have clamped down on Czechs who are out of the country, in order to maintain the illusion that we are still under their direct control. They go out of their way to keep us from communicating."

Masaryk became silent for a moment. "I'll give you a Swiss address. They get our letters into Prague." He wrote on the back of his card, swaying with the motion of the train. "I've been away from Czechoslovakia for almost three years now — traveling around like a salesman to every country but my own. I hear little else than rumors. I would very much like a letter from my wife." He made a gesture of resignation with his face and hands. "Your father is a patriot. I hope he is well."

As the train cleared the outskirts of Kiev, the lavatories were opened. Snapping the brass hook into place to lock the toilet door, Alex realized he had left Borispol so quickly that he had no shaving gear — nothing. He washed his face in the deep metal sink and stared into the mirror. It was the reflection of a tired soldier. The eyes were dull, without anticipation. What was his purpose now? Was it to stay in Russia to find Katya, or to fight his way out of Russia and sail to France? It had been so obvious once; now his mind could not hold the facts together long enough for a clear picture. Maybe he shouldn't be so critical of Masaryk who had been traveling for months on end and never slackening in his commitment to free Czechoslovakia.

He looked again into the mirror at the black hair curling over his collar. It was getting as long as Peter's. Father would send us both to the barber, he mused. A sharp rap on the door brought him back to the present and he returned to his seat.

Once in Moscow, it was Masaryk's plan to see Lenin right away, but there were no appointments available; the Duma was in session so they would have to wait. Somehow Masaryk wheedled his question onto the agenda under "new business" so he and Alex went to the Peoples Hall to find a seat in the gallery overlooking the main floor.

Each row in the balcony was on its own step with its own stiff, church-like pew. The gallery was sparsely populated even though the new regime had decreed that all meetings were open to the public. Masaryk determined to remain in the gallery until their item came up; stretching out when tired, or when the Duma took a break. A bodyguard brought them food periodically — just bread and sausage with a pungent cheese, things they could eat right there as they waited.

Masaryk watched most of the debates, nudging Alex, explaining the procedure, pointing out the strategies which Alex had been willing to ignore until Masaryk chided him. "You say you're a student of history, but you're reading somebody else's textbook. History is here, now, unfolding in front of you. These men are reshaping Europe. Watch them and learn, so that you can make a contribution one day."

Alex felt foolish. Masaryk was right. When did he start allowing himself to waste time? If Masaryk remained so committed at his age, even during all these years away from wife and home, how could he give less? He spelled off with Masaryk, just like two sentries on watch, so that they would miss nothing. When one slept on the benches, the other would listen attentively, making notes to describe the proceedings later.

It was well past midnight the morning of the second day. Alex watched Lenin from the public gallery, empty now except for himself and Masaryk. He leaned his arms on the balcony railing looking down onto the conference table. His view was from slightly above the metal lamp shades which directed harsh lights onto the table where Lenin led his ministers through the long agenda. A stove on the main floor had been heaped with coal, and the center of its hourglass belly had an orange glow. Alex could smell the acid soot, and his eyes grew scratchy in the stuffy atmosphere.

Masaryk's head hung at an awkward angle, his chin resting on the vest of a crumpled suit. Alex folded up his overcoat and gently lifted the old man's head onto it like a pillow, then watched dully as Lenin conducted the long meeting.

Alex could see that Lenin was tired too. Sitting in the head chair, his red-rimmed eyes stared unblinking down the table while speaking to the ashen face of Leon Trotsky. Green blotters and inkwells lay in front of each member of the Bolshevik Party's Executive Committee. One by one, droplets of sweat fell from Trotsky's pointed nose, leaving dark stains on the leather-framed blotter in front of him. Alex noticed that those around the table watched intently and without question. His head began to droop, until a jarring shove from Masaryk woke him up. "Listen to this."

Lenin was speaking: "Perhaps it's time to review what our party has accomplished since the November Putsch . . . and underline what is left undone," Lenin intoned. "Comrade Trotsky, our Foreign Commissar, will now give the simplified list, so that you will all remember why we occupy these seats of power."

Alex knew that Trotsky was recognized for his forceful eloquence, and so he was puzzled when Trotsky stood and began an uncharacteristically timid recital. "Comrades, as you well know . . . since the success of the socialist revolution by the people . . . our Bolshevik party has been given control."

"How?" Chairman Lenin interrupted.

Trotsky looked startled, even confused, Alex thought. "Why, we held the election of November 12th and won."

"What was the count?"

"Eighty-two percent for us," Trotsky said, adjusting his wire-rimmed spectacles. The two tiny ovals of glass reflected light from the overhead fixtures so that Alex could not see his eyes.

"Where can we claim 82 percent?" asked Lenin.

"Well, mainly in Petersburg and Moscow," Trotsky explained.

"And what, over all?" Lenin persisted.

Cautiously, Trotsky continued, "Thirteen percent to the middle-class liberal parties, 62 percent to all the moderate socialists . . . mainly the socialist revolutionaries, and 25 percent to us."

"Only one quarter of the popular vote went to our representatives in the Constituent Assembly?" Lenin asked rhetorically. "So what did you do?"

Masaryk whispered into Alex's ear. "This is a technique to control by embarrassment. You may or may not want to use it — but at least recognize it, to know when others use it on you."

Trotsky licked his lips. Another droplet fell onto the blotter. "Well, after their first meeting on January 5, 1918, I sent a sailor into the hall with a machine gun slung over his shoulder . . . and he dissolved it . . . as being counter-revolutionary."

At this answer there was the sound of low chuckling around the table, and Alex noticed that Trotsky immediately looked slightly more at ease.

"And has anyone complained?" the chairman asked.

"No, comrade. You convinced them that the Council of the People's Commissars is a purer form of democracy."

"What else?" Lenin persisted, leaning back in the chair. He played with a pencil while Trotsky wiped his glasses dry. Then Lenin held the pencil up to the tip of his nose, staring — an eye on each side of the vertical stick. The effect was hypnotic. And Alex could see from the reaction of the men around the table that the effect this grilling was having on the rest was sobering, to say the least.

"We passed the Land Decree, which states that all land goes to those who work it."

"Any complaints?"

"Only from land owners."

"And what did you say to that?"

"Death to the aristocracy!"

"What else have we done?"

Trotsky paused, looked into the darkened rafters, and spoke as if reading a grocery list. "We abolished banks and bank credit. All land is national property. Church property has been confiscated. And we endorsed Marx's view that religion is but an opiate for the masses. Factories were handed over to the control of worker soviets."

When the list ended, Lenin rose and motioned Trotsky to sit.

Masaryk nudged Alex again, whispering, "Who's the master here?"

Lenin turned on Trotsky with a nasty look. "What about peace? All these other points are commendable, but without peace — worthless! You were sent to Brest-Litovsk to negotiate a settlement with those Prussian aristocrats. And what do you do? You treat them like nobility and bring back a castrated formula of: No war. No peace. Neither! Which is to say . . . you accomplished nothing!"

Masaryk nodded knowingly. "First he frightens, then he chastises. Now will come the praise, and the master has another obedient servant, you'll see. He is relentless."

Alex listened as Lenin continued. "This is not like you, comrade. I can only conclude that diplomacy and compromise is not your forté. To your credit, action is. Therefore I am assigning you to security. We need to develop the Cheka as a national police force for internal security. Also, we need an army for external security. Germany ignores the truce and now advances with little to stop them. Increase the Red Guard! We must have an army. You," he emphasized with a pointed finger, "are good at these things. Do you agree?"

Alex looked askance, his hopes sinking. These leaders are as much ensnared by chaos as their countrymen! We'll never get out of this jumble, he thought, and was perplexed to see Trotsky brighten under the compliment, vigorously nodding yes while Lenin watched over the upturned lip of a drinking glass.

Lenin put down the glass. "I'm nominating Comrade Sokolnikov as the new commissar, and I want him to negotiate — do whatever he has to do. Compromise. Lie. Cheat. Sell his soul. Anything. Just get Germany out of our affairs!"

Masaryk squirmed with interest.

"Excuse me, Mr. Chairman," a slight man asked in a formal way.

"Yes, Kamenev?"

"If I might play the Devil's advocate, shouldn't we stand up to the Germans? They want too much."

There was a scoffing snarl from around the table.

"Only he and Zinoviev voted against the Putsch," a voice said.

"Faint-heart has now grown bold," another sneered.

"Silence please, gentlemen, we shall all be heard," Lenin cautioned. "Our comrade may have been wrong about the Putsch, but let him speak his view . . . so that we might focus our logic."

"Comrades," Kamenev began, now quite agitated, "Germany will suck us dry like an orange. What are their demands? Estonia, Latvia, Lithuania and Russian Poland. Plus, independence for Finland, Ukraine and Georgia. Impossible! Then to Turkey goes Kars, Ardahan and Batum . . . and after that . . . On top of that, mind you, 500 million rubles in reparation. Preposterous! . . . And it's true. Ask Leon."

Trotsky nodded when Lenin looked his way. Kemenev continued, holding up trembling fingers to count their losses: "This means we lose one third of our farmland. Almost all our coal. Petrograd will be in range of European artillery. Every gain made by Peter the Great will be lost. We'll be governing no more than the Grand Duchy of Muscovy once again!" He sat down in silence.

Alex was wide awake now as Lenin rose to face those thoughtful faces. Would this powerful little man be able to find a way out of the mess?

"Be wary when rats are in a corner," Masaryk whispered.

"What Comrade Kamenev says is true," Lenin began, standing up now at the head of the table, "but he is wrong! We can no longer fight the Germans. Time must be bought. If the purchase price is every one of Czar Peter's gains, then it must be so. The Romanovs dislocated fifteen million Russians — most of them illiterate — they'll not understand if we ask them to continue the slaughter. That's the reason I stand here instead of Kerensky. I don't want to hear you dreaming the dreams of idealism anymore. Now is the time for practical reality. Don't tell me what ought to be. Don't tell me the Germans should leave Russia. Tell me what is! And if you won't, then I'll tell you."

The little man's energy seemed to grow with his eloquence. His posture became vigorous, with the presence and poise of a dancer. Alex studied Lenin's gestures and how he riveted the attention of the listeners with a glare. This was a master at work, he realized. "Tell me what is, not what ought to be," Lenin had said. We could learn from that, Alex knew.

"Pragmatism. Pure pragmatism," came Masaryk's excited whisper once again.

Lenin hurried to finish, leaning forward, his fists in a truculent position — wide apart as if he might charge down the table: "We Bolsheviks don't control any of the territories Comrade Kamenev mentions. They don't like us! So don't try the impossible!" Lenin spat this out, then stepped back, calm again, hooking his thumbs in his vest. "Bide our time," he purred.

Alex scanned every eye around the table of power; each one was locked on Lenin. "We'll develop a strong central position that can be protected," Lenin said. "Let them live with the Germans for a while, or the Whites for that matter. What will the Ukrainians and the Latvians find? Nothing more than a return to the landlord economy — and they won't stand for it. It is as Comrade Trotsky once wrote about the peasant soldier who found himself for the first time in an upper-class railroad carriage. What did he do? He tore the purple felt from the seat to use as puttees for his boots. This was not merely an act of vandalism; it was an irreversible step forward, and he'll never again be content with rags. We've changed everything with our revolution, giving birth to a fairly robust child. But our newborn can't survive another war."

Alex became nervous when Lenin paused, afraid that a guard might make him leave while this political strategy was being discussed. But Lenin continued as if offering a spontaneous suggestion: "Let us send Commissar Sokolnikov to Brest-Litovsk to negotiate some kind of Draconian peace. Settle for whatever he can get. We'll wait for our time. Agreed?" Lenin looked up and down the long table, mentally recording the show of fluttering hands.

"Carried," he announced and sat down. "A further point . . . for those of you who still pray to icons, . . . you might put in a few words for the Western Allies. They could get the central powers out of our hair if they work well with the Americans. Any further business? It's late."

"One more thing, Chairman," Trotsky said, pointing to the gallery. "You just reminded me. Thomas Masaryk, the Czech. He's been waiting for three days."

"What does he want?" Lenin asked.

Alex felt the tension as he waited for Trotsky's answer.

"Masaryk wants permission to take the Czech Legion out of Russia via the Trans-Siberian Railroad to join the Western Allies in France."

"How many and what equipment?" Lenin asked.

Masaryk was listening breathlessly, a forefinger over his mouth.

"About forty thousand. Mostly prisoners. Poorly clothed and poorly armed."

Lenin removed his glasses to massage his forehead. "I don't think so," Lenin said. "We gave them refuge from the Austrians. They will serve this government."

Alex tilted his head back, looking into the rafters in dismay. His eyes closed when Lenin said flatly: "We need an army."

At this, Masaryk stood up beside Alex. The statesman gripped the railing with both fists, his face red, looking as if he were about to leap from the balcony down onto the table to take on Lenin. Alex reached up and put his hand firmly on Masaryk's wrist, gently pulling him back onto the bench. His mind was racing. Lenin was the one in control here — and listening to no one. Masaryk would have to keep quiet. This was not the time for blustering outrage. Wait. Just wait.

Trotsky appeared surprised. "Comrade Lenin? They have pledged their allegiance to the Czar . . . " He stopped, waiting, but Lenin said nothing, so Trotsky carried on. "The Czechs do not support our cause. They want to join the Western Front. I don't think it prudent to force them into a position of choosing between us or the White contingent near the Kiev Soviet."

Alex's throat was dry and tasting of coal dust, as Lenin pushed himself up from the table and walked around to the side for a better view of the upper gallery. The fiery leader of the Bolshevik party stroked his pointed goatee while studying Masaryk. There was no sign to give away his thoughts, but Alex wondered if Lenin was thinking of a time when he himself had spent days waiting for some politician's whim to go his way.

Lenin turned his attention to Alex. It was then that he appeared to struggle, perhaps trying to pull back a memory through fatigue and months of faces and speeches. Alex was suddenly conscious of the three-day's growth of dark whiskers on his face — no damned shaving gear. He hoped Lenin could recognize him.

Lenin stared at him for a few moments, finally saying more as a statement than a question: "I know you, Comrade. Don't I?"

Alex nodded quickly several times.

"You were the honor guard in Petersburg the night of my return. A night when it was plain that few wanted to honor me. You took me to Kshesinskaya Palace."

"Yes, sir," Alex answered. He breathed a bit easier when Lenin nodded. He was afraid to say more, as he watched Lenin focus on him watchfully, the colorless lips working quietly.

"Vladivostok across Siberia in February — what a prospect," he said, shaking his head wearily, still studying Alex. "What is it you're after, Comrade? You must not interfere with our cause."

"Never, sir. I'm taking my friends home," Alex said as calmly as he could.

Lenin turned back to the table. "Send them off," he ordered. "They pay their own way. Minimum equipment. Mr. Masaryk, you'd better leave too." He flicked one more glance at Alex. "Be careful not to interfere," he said, scooping up his papers. "Is that all, gentlemen? Meeting adjourned."

* * *

Following the long road trip from Petrograd, Katya left the American Embassy car and ran to the entrance of Ural Station in Moscow.

Ambassador Davis waved as she reached the front door. Inside, she ran down the platform when the whistle blew for the one train waiting, and as the wheels began to skid forward, she climbed the stair to a passenger car.

The car was crowded, and she looked around for a seat. A young woman holding a baby caught her eye and moved over. Gratefully, Katya sat down.

"Katya," she said quietly, and the young woman smiled.

"Svetlana . . . and my daughter, Maria," she said, looking at the sleeping child.

"She's beautiful," Katya said, surprised at the messages within her own voice.

With all that was happening to the world, she was completely taken with the importance of something as fundamental as a baby and talked contentedly with the young mother for the rest of the journey to Kazan. There she shook hands, and then, as arranged, hurried to the Treasury train at the far end of the marshalling yard.

The guards on duty greeted her with expectant faces. Katya tried to smile with confidence, even though she did not feel like it.

She was more determined with the Treasury staff, however, because she had a message. It wasn't much of a directive, but at least it came from Kerensky. They watched her closely as she entered the conference car. Katya thought Rovskoy looked surprised by her return. But before she had time to examine that possibility, Ordinov anxiously blurted out: "Did you manage to get to Petersburg?"

Katya did not know how to present a simple answer to a situation so complex. "Yes," she began, "I made it, but I must tell you . . . the city is now called Leningrad."

"Oh dear," Ordinov said, and sat down waiting for the rest of the report.

"There is not much more to say," she said quietly. She could see the apprehension in their eyes.

"So, you didn't see Kerensky, then." Rovskoy said this more as a challenge than a question.

"No, that's not true," Katya said quickly. "I saw him in his apartment with Ambassador Davis of the United States, and I explained our position . . . emphatically."

"Was there any instruction for us?" Ordinov asked in a hesitating voice.

Katya looked around at the anxious faces and stood up with a confident look on her face. "Kerensky said that we are doing the right thing, and that we are to continue with the original plan. America will help if needed. And now if you don't mind, I shall get some rest."

Katya entered her compartment, certain that the strain of the past few days showed on her face. Looking in the mirror above the sink, she could see the doubt. There was a knot in the space between her eyes. Her shoulders ached. "Alex, where are you? If you are in France, how shall I ever find you again?"

She was startled by a light knock on her door. It must be Ordinov, she thought, wanting more answers. She had none.

"Gospodin Rovskoy," she said in surprise when she opened the door. "What is it?"

Rovskoy barely whispered, "A moment, Miss Kazakova," pushing his way through the door.

He wore formal clothes and his hair was shining with pomade. She thought she smelled brandy. "What do you want?" she asked.

"Perhaps a little company," he grinned as he produced a silver flask from an inside pocket. "We might not have the opportunity for much longer."

Katya firmly put her hand on his shoulder and pulled open the door. "Yes we shall, Mr. Rovskoy. Have no doubt about that." She pushed him out the door and when he turned with a scowl, she closed it in his face before he could say anything.

With trembling hands she lit a candle at her dresser table and placed it beside a small icon of Jesus. Then she knelt on the floor. "Dear Jesus," she began. "Look after my mother and father in heaven. Please protect Alex and his comrades, wherever they are. Please help Marie . . . and send America to help end this terrible war."

CHAPTER 15

BAKHMACH TO SYZRAN
SPRING 1918

Alex hurried to the Borispol maintenance building for an emergency meeting called by General Syrovy. A stained staircase zigzagged precariously up the inside wall to the office level high above the engines waiting for repair. The cluttered office had two sets of unwashed windows; one overlooking the maintenance floor inside, the other enabling

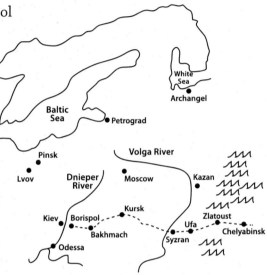

supervision across the wide marshalling yard. And on the wall was something he had never seen before in a government office: a framed picture of Lenin. Times had certainly changed.

His fellow officers saw it too. Peter, Gaida, Jan and Stefan, like him, waited impatiently for their order to leave the city. Peter, who could not stay inactive for long, seemed to suffer the most from the tension. Time was running out, and they knew that the Czech contingent was now far too cumbersome to move quickly because of their increased numbers.

After a long wait, Syrovy came clumping into the room. The door slammed behind him. He spread a map of the Dnieper River plain on a draftsman's drawing table and flattened out the corners with quick sweeping hands. "The Germans are coming at us from three sides now," he said. "They're in the outskirts of Kiev and will control the city by nightfall.

"They're moving fast, trying to snare us. So, we pull out immediately. Every available train. Get clear of Borispol, then it's two hundred kilometres east to Bakhmach. If we make it, we'll be at least equidistant from the German army in Kiev and their northern divisions coming out of Poland. I tell you this: we do not want to be cut off. It's going to be one hell of a race."

Alex looked out over the vast storage yard where sixty-four trains had been prepared for travel. They had been filing out of the yard through the night, one rumbling after another like a long line of circus elephants. Smoke filled the sky as the remaining four engines made ready. "Captain Branda, you command the last train. Your Falcons will hold the suspension bridge from the east bank 'til everyone's clear."

Alex watched Syrovy attentively. I've never seen him this focused before, he thought, which means we must be vulnerable. He could hear the thump of artillery from across the river and knew that the Falcons could hold the bridge for only so long.

Syrovy continued. "Captain Kechek. Withdraw your First Division from East Gate. You'll be the last out of Kiev on foot. The Falcons will hold the bridge open for you as long as they can. Now get us the hell out of here!"

On a high bluff on the east bank of the Dnieper River, Alex positioned his Falcons to provide fire cover for Peter's last patrol. Through binoculars he followed their running retreat from Kiev's East Gate as First Czech Division fought off German armored cars with gasoline bombs and mortars. He saw Peter running down the center of the great boulevard with a bottle of fuel in each hand. Peter suddenly ducked behind a bordering tree to put a match to each cloth wick, then he threw the last two bottles into the path of an armored car that sheltered infantry troops trotting in behind. The burning fuel spewed orange and black flame like a wall across the street. Peter took a quick look before sprinting after his men toward the bridge and safety.

Alex kept the binoculars on Peter, watching the powerful sprinter stretch out, pulling ground behind him in two-metre strides. He had lost his cap, and his long hair waved in the wind above his open collar. Peter looked for a moment as if he were playing a game of school-yard tag.

Alex shouted: "Fire!" and the Falcons laid down a withering barrage to protect the last patrol. The noise was painful, the air filled with smoke as Peter's legs pumped through the last fifty metres before pulling up in front of Alex, his smudged face red and alive with the fun of the chase.

There was a boxcar ready and filled with carpentry shavings and a box of dynamite. Alex had a stick with a rag soaked in kerosene; he lit the rag and threw it in on top of the shavings. The doors were slammed shut, and then Alex and his patrol pushed the boxcar to coast down the slight grade from the east bank. Breathing heavily, he stood watching the smoking freight car roll back over the bridge toward Kiev.

Looking past the slow rolling car, Alex tried to glimpse the Grand Hotel where he and Katya had spent the night together almost one year ago. He searched the hill trying to see the post office where only the day before yesterday he had left a letter to his father. He prayed that somehow the postal service would rise above, or ignore, the interruptions of war and find a route to his father through the Swiss address given him by Masaryk.

I should have told him to his face how much he meant to me, Alex thought, how much I valued his advice. He remembered the letter by heart.

March 15, 1918
Father,

We're in a tight spot and on the run, so it might be some time before I see you. We're taking the long way home. Across scenic Siberia by train. By tramp steamer from Vladivostok, around China, around India, around Africa (unless we can get through at Suez), across the Mediterranean to Marseilles, and to the western front. Not bad for someone who had never been out of Bohemia before. There's a girl you should meet. Her name is Katya. She's wonderful, but she's lost somewhere in the war and I have to find her. Maybe we can look together. You know, I just thought of something. My stutter. It doesn't often happen around her. I want you to know that we're doing our duty.

Alex

When the boxcar exploded on the western side of Dnieper River Bridge, black smoke rose over the flames and debris, halting German pursuit. Alex jogged beside Peter, chasing after the men of the rear-guard on their way to the waiting train. Everyone scrambled aboard, finally on their way east toward the Volga, away from the relentless pressure of their pursuers. The slow pace was excruciating.

In a car designed for meetings, Syrovy pointed to a map on the wall. "Captain Branda, as our resident scholar, tell us about Siberia."

Alex paused, unsure where to begin. "Well, General Syrovy, this is a unique undertaking. An impressive journey. The Trans-Siberian was completed by slave labor in 1902, and is, no matter how you measure it, the longest railroad on earth. Most Russians designate the Volga River as the end of Europe and the beginning of Siberia.

"There are six thousand kilometres from the Volga to the Pacific Ocean — or the Sea of Japan, to be accurate. We sit here," he said, pointing on the map just east of Kiev, "still two thousand kilometres west of the Volga. So we have close to eight thousand kilometres to travel."

Alex stopped for a moment to see if there was any comment. The officers watched him quietly as he tried to give some meaning to the distance that lay before them. Surely, he thought, it must be startling for everyone to realize just how far they were moving away from the Czech border. Once, fourteen months ago, they had advanced to within thirty kilometres of home ready to press on, and he knew that this thought disturbed his friends. Now escape was so far away — eight thousand kilometres!

"This railroad can witness temperature variations, on the Fahrenheit scale, from ninety degrees in summer, to eighty degrees below freezing in mid-winter. It has been described as: 'Two rusty streaks of iron, through the vastness of nothing, to the extremities of nowhere.'"

Alex hoped his poetic footnote would add a touch of dark humor, but the men were numbed into silence — perhaps, he supposed, because the enormity of their task was sinking in. "We can't just rattle across Siberia in a week or two."

"Quite so," Syrovy broke in. "There is only one track, so east-bound trains travel at night. Westbound trains by day. You officers will be responsible to set up a workable schedule. Major Kechek will command the rearguard. Captain Branda and the Falcons will secure the towns ahead. Our main objective? Control the flow of the trains — not every village will want to cooperate with us. If you do your job properly, you will form a gauntlet of trains and troops the full length of the line. Each train will move ahead to the next town, then pull over to allow the following train to pass. Leap-frog fashion. You will be impeded by oncoming trains, as well as Bolshevik sympathizers. Patrols will precede and protect the advance. It's up to you officers to design and coordinate this procedure. The better you do your job the safer you'll be."

In the hush that followed, Peter asked: "What are Siberians like?"

"A very hardy lot, according to what I've read," Alex began. "They like their fun, but weather conditions force them into tightly knit communities. There's a Siberian saying: A man who can't sing, dies." He flinched at his stupid choice of words. He looked at the crowd of sombre faces.

"Anyway, we won't be seeing much of their exuberant side. There's a tremendous variety of languages and tribes. Generally speaking, they're tough, fiercely independent and suspicious of strangers. The farther east you go, the wilder it gets."

"Sounds like Czechoslovakia," Syrovy's voice boomed out, bringing the room to laughter and smiles once more. The officers from Bohemia laughed, of course, but Alex was grateful to see that his comrades from Slovakia were laughing just as loudly at Syrovy's outrageous comparison. It was an in-house joke among fellow-sufferers, and Alex was content to let the meeting end on that note. He watched while men shook hands in farewell. No one knew what waited for them down the track. He allowed himself a grim smile; the journey to the Western Front had begun. It was the long way around. But they were bound for France.

* * *

On a siding beside the Volga River, Katya Kazakova stood on the carriage porch of the Treasury train looking directly south into a warming sun. It was good to feel the optimism of spring again — even though there was nowhere to go. They had made the north-south run between Kazan and Syzran countless times, it seemed.

At Syzran, President Ordinov would decide whether or not to turn onto the Trans-Siberian's southern line which labored into the Urals still full of snow, or to steam north again to Kazan along the east bank of the mighty Volga. It was dangerous being seen in one place too often. The Bolsheviks were, no doubt, desperate to recapture the Czar's Treasury and the bullion base to Russia's currency.

But now it appeared to Katya that the choice of where to go next would not be theirs. For some reason that Ordinov could not determine, the southern Siberian line was crammed with trains all heading east. "Most unusual," Ordinov had said while squinting through a telescope aimed at the never-ending line of trains crossing the Volga's Alexandrovskoy Bridge.

"Who are they?" Katya asked nervously. "Why are there so many trains?"

"I can't see. There's no insignia. Just train after train. We'd best stay here. They obviously aren't looking for us."

"Well, I wonder who is looking for us?" asked Katya thoughtfully. "We've been stuck here for three days."

"I don't know," Ordinov said unhappily.

"To whom are we to turn over the Treasury when all of this is over?" Katya asked, alarmed that no one knew.

Ordinov looked uncomfortable. "I can only tell you that I will not turn the Treasury over to the Germans, nor to the Bolsheviks," he said emphatically. "But other than that . . . I'm lost. All of us are lost. And we'll stay lost until the way becomes apparent." His left hand shook. It had been that way for the past week, and Katya did not like the morbid signal it gave.

"Perhaps we should go back up north," Katya suggested, touching his arm gently. "Everyone thinks the Czar is somewhere near Ekaterinburg. And the weather is getting warmer."

CHAPTER 16

KURSK TO PENZA
SUMMER 1918

The railroad stop at Kursk was as primitive as any of the stations Alex had seen. It was really nothing more than a platform above the mud, with a shed containing benches fashioned from rough planks. Reeking latrines and barking dogs waited down the track. The only distinction Alex could determine was that Kursk had been turned into a makeshift Bolshevik headquarters for the purpose of examining Czech trains.

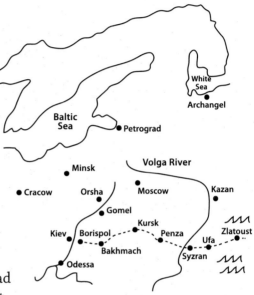

Alex saw Syrovy bristle as he walked with the Czech general through the main door. Foul language and derisive laughter barked across the waiting-room where scruffy men slouched in makeshift uniforms without signs of military distinction. The men wore red armbands, and each man was outrageously over-equipped with weapons hanging from every belt clip. Each was equal to the other, and apparently without discipline; men with power but no control.

Alex saw Syrovy's teeth clench and his barrel-chest swell when they heard the demands of the local commissar, the only man with a red star on the front of his cap. There was a terrible scar running from the corner of his mouth to his chin and the lower lip did not meet the upper lip properly. Except for this slash of pale pink skin, his face was dark from the stubble of whiskers.

It was distracting to watch the man speak. This he must have sensed because he became more irritable by the minute. "The Czech Legion will either stand with us, or return all weapons," the Bolshevik declared.

"Bloody hell!" Syrovy stormed. "You know that's impossible. And you can't take our weapons! We need them for France. We have an agreement with Moscow and you damn well know that too."

"Agreement with Moscow? What agreement? Comrade Trotsky changed his mind. He says each Soviet is to inspect every train at every stop." Pulling a telegram from his jacket, the commissar read:

"The Czech Rifle Corps will fight for our cause, or relinquish nine out of every ten rifles. Only one machine gun for every six hundred men will they be allowed to keep."

He folded the paper and pushed it back into his pocket. "We fight. We need your stolen guns." He looked contemptuously at Syrovy. "You won't miss them."

Syrovy turned toward the commander with clenched fists held at waist level. Alex unobtrusively touched Syrovy's rigid forearm, and in a matter-of-fact voice said, "Let's listen to what our comrades have to say, General. As reasonable men."

The rude laughter and coarse Russian swearing continued, but Syrovy forced a more relaxed expression and Alex felt relieved when he settled into a rough chair. Alex knew that the foul language came from a peasant's background. It was continuous filth. A form of swearing quite different from that of the educated land owner or even the arrogant police. It was a slave speaking, a slave full of fear and hostility; it was a defiant snarl with the rage from centuries of degradation at its core.

"This pus-eyed cow is getting smarter," said the sneering commander, "but needs the bull to hump some brains into her." He rubbed his hand over his crotch and then rammed his right fist into the air catching the bicep at the elbow with the flat of his left hand. His men laughed, hungry for excitement.

Alex was busy calculating how best to alert his men if Syrovy should erupt. Syrovy, however, seemed by now to be fully recovered. Alex saw him smile, patting the chair at his side saying, "Not just now, Comrade . . . let's settle some business first. And Alex," he said, momentarily silencing the aggressive commander, "have the corporal bring our host four bottles of vodka. We have some talking to do."

Alex signaled to the corporal, and the soldier hurried off.

"How many men on your train?" the Russian demanded, sitting

forward with his hands on his knees in an aggressive posture — his lower lip flopping open at the side.

Alex watched Syrovy slouch. Trying to stall for time. Trying to think of ways to protect their armament, although he had a sinking feeling that Syrovy had little chance.

"Close to two thousand. I lost five men yesterday to the Germans," Syrovy said, swallowing hard.

"We know," the Bolshevik said coldly. "My men collected their rifles."

Syrovy appeared startled, but forced himself to reply offhandedly, "Well, there you are then . . . five of our rifles. And I imagine some German firearms as well. That should help."

"One hundred and forty German guns," boasted the Bolshevik commander as he pushed himself to his feet, glowering at Syrovy. The Bolshevik looked ready to charge the Czech general, who watched closely with his one eye.

Alex could only hope that Syrovy was ready for anything. He had only just recently become aware of how difficult it was to read emotions on a face with a missing eye. Alex took the vodka from the corporal and walked across the room with two clinking bottles hanging from each hand.

"Comrade, would you be good enough to pour?" Alex asked amiably of the Russian.

"Pour?" he boomed at the top of his range. "Of course, you castrated dog." The Bolshevik snatched a bottle from Alex's hand and threw it spinning across the room to a surprised man who caught it with a laugh. He took another two bottles, one in each hand, tossing one to his right, the other to his left. The catchers were ready now to pluck the bottles from the air with ease. Then the Bolshevik commander removed the cork from the last bottle, took a long pull and slammed it down on the nearby table.

"Now," he said menacingly, pointing a finger at the silent Syrovy, "let us count rifles. Or do you decide to turn on your old comrades?"

Alex watched tensely. The Bolsheviks all stared at Syrovy's frown, waiting for his reaction. The eyebrows raised. Then Syrovy shrugged.

One hour later the train was rolling again toward Penza, but in the command car Syrovy was seething. "Nineteen hundred rifles gone! Taken without a whimper. This can't go on!" he thundered. "There must be something we can do. If this continues, we're helpless."

"Brother Syrovy, they have a point," Alex ventured. "We don't fight the Germans, or the Whites. Russia has a seasoned army on her soil. We're a threat."

"Don't be so bloody logical," Syrovy shouted. "I don't trust those bastards. There's no telling what they'll do. They've no scruples. First they pick us clean 'til we're defenseless. What then?"

Alex stood swaying with the roll of the car. He stared out the window at the sweeping farmland. "Like he says, we're castrated dogs."

"I won't take much more," Syrovy promised, getting up and going outside to stand on a ledge behind a flat-deck loaded with lumber. "How long does this go on?" he asked loudly, the wind beating against his angry face.

"Not much longer," Alex said, pointing to where farmland narrowed into a valley between low mountains. When the train curved to the right, they stood in the eastern morning sun and could look straight ahead to what had to be the town of Penza. White smoke rose from cottage chimneys, and dogs began to bark when the train whistle blew. "The Volga's not far now. We're the last train."

"So what?" Syrovy asked.

"So, the Germans will lose interest in us. We're out of reach. But . . ."

"But what?" Syrovy demanded.

Alex searched for words. "Listen . . . I, I want to go back. I've got to find Katya."

Syrovy, his face impassive, watched Alex closely before answering. After a long pause he made a gesture as if trying to express his helplessness. "Look, forget all the military nonsense for a moment, shall we? Let's say that I could let you go. Where do you start? Do you know where she is? Do you?"

Alex looked down, shaking his head.

Syrovy sighed. "If you knew where to go. Right to where she was . . . hell, I'd go with you. But the cold truth of it is, you haven't even got a place to start. Correct?"

Alex nodded, still looking down at the ties flashing below his feet in a blur.

CHAPTER 17
KANSAS CITY
SPRING 1918

The sun on this April morning was hot. Victor stood in the sweep of a fan near the window of Camp Fremont's communication hut. Dressed in a tan short-sleeved shirt, he watched idly as the troops trained on the field in front of Command Headquarters and he thought about the past few self-indulgent months. Sunday dinners with his parents in San Jose had been a singular pleasure. They seemed genuinely interested in his association with the Czech fundraising dignitaries, and for the first time he and his father had talked as equals about Europe and Czechoslovakia.

Victor had enjoyed regular visits to the Stanford campus for practices with Lefty Rogers and the rugby squad. The sprints and scrimmages had challenged him to increase his own fitness work at Camp Fremont, and General Graves had been complimentary after witnessing his determination on the obstacle course, an exercise that Victor particularly enjoyed. Here there was competition and a bit of room for inventiveness within the army's structured drills. He went daily to the obstacle run and assumed that this chase was largely responsible for the loss of six pounds. He felt much better.

The lean look certainly hadn't hurt his rating with campus women either. Miriam had long gone, but there seemed to be a parade of young women willing to engage in, or perhaps even dedicated to, experimentation with vigorous young men — and a flat belly didn't hurt.

The slam at men had always been, to Victor's memory, that men had only one thing on their minds: lust. It also seemed to him, judging from the clandestine social fervor raging just beneath

Stanford's conservative surface at campus soda shops and on fragrant grassy fields, that women too held lust high on their list of important functions to explore. In fact, Victor hypothesized, perhaps concupiscence was a more constant focus for women because of their natural, instinctive urges to make homes for babies. Whereas the male animal, speaking for his age group at least, were regularly distracted by the pull of career, or the vague but persistent urge to maybe build something . . . or to find an adventure that had meaning. Perhaps, when the finger pointing was done, lust was simply a human trait after all.

His contemplations were interrupted by the salutation click of the telegraph key, and Victor looked across the counter to the corporal on duty. This could be it, he thought. A combat assignment for General Graves would mean change, and exciting change, for Victor as well. The whole camp was one boiling pot of rumor; one wild speculation tumbling after another. This might put an end to it — no doubt they were off to France. Only a few weeks ago, fresh American infantry units had been sent to the rat-infested trenches at Chateau Thierry just forty miles east of Paris to hurl back the Germans. Then the doughboys had captured what was left of Belleau Wood, in support of the sagging French army, reversing the German offensive. There were now over one million American troops in France — or on the way — and President Wilson promised more. Victor strolled over to the corporal's desk to read the message. He planned to stick close to Major General Graves, to face opportunities as they presented themselves.

Moments later, Victor jumped down from the top stair of the communications hut and hurried through the heat of the California afternoon toward Command Headquarters. There was Graves on the broad front porch overseeing the day's drills. The general stood beside Colonel George Van Deusen, the second-in-command, while a smart-looking platoon ran through their drills. Graves looked pleased with their performance. Victor tapped him on the elbow.

"General," he said quietly. "I've just decoded this message from Washington. Figured you might want to be informed."

Graves read the paper quickly, breaking into a satisfied smile. "Guess I'm going to La Belle France sooner than I expected. George, you're in charge here for a while. Lindal and I are taking off for a few days. Secretary of War wants to meet me in Kansas City, quick as I can get to the Baltimore Hotel. Vic, call the Union Pacific office. I want the first train out. Looks like a combat command at last."

Colonel Van Deusen clasped his hand enthusiastically. "Congratulations, General. Give 'em hell. I'd love to march into Berlin with you and these boys, all spit and polish, giving Kaiser Bill the raspberry. They'll do us proud."

The colonel turned to Victor with an extended hand. "God speed, Lindal."

Victor smiled as he saluted. They were on the move again, and these were exciting, quickly changing times. "Thanks for your hospitality, Colonel. It took a bit of doing, but I'm back in shape again."

"Well, Major, you're going to need it in France. Wish I were going with you."

As he stepped off the train with Graves three weary days later, Victor looked up at the platform sign: KANSAS CITY, MISSOURI. POPULATION 304,410. Dusty and hot, he wondered why they would meet the Secretary of War in the geographic center of the country, and not in Washington, D.C. He watched a Red Cap approaching from down the platform. A Negro in his middle years, the man walked straight to Graves and from a height well over the head of either one of them asked in a slow voice: "You General Graves?"

The Red Cap watched closely through two bulging eyes yellowed at the rims — the most dominant feature of his expectant face. When Graves nodded, he picked up their two bags and began walking toward the main entrance to the station.

"Your train was late," the Red Cap continued conversationally. "So Mr. Baker wants to meet you in the station master's office. I'll go get 'im." He put the bags down and pointed to a door across the waiting room where about a dozen people lounged uncomfortably on hard-looking, high-backed benches.

Graves picked up a suitcase and began to walk across to the office, but as Victor went to follow, the Negro stopped him. "Sorry, sir. Just the general. Anyone else, he says should wait."

Victor was annoyed. He wanted to know what was going on. But he had noticed the salt-and-pepper sideburns that gave away the length of time the Red Cap had worked for the railroad. This fellow has heard every possible bluster or threat over the years, Victor reasoned, and most likely could not be swayed; so he merely nodded without complaint.

Graves gave Victor a shrug and continued toward the office.

Victor found a fifty cent piece in his change-purse — more than enough to pay for both suitcases, he hoped. "Thank you," Victor said, slipping the coin into the Red Cap's hand as he picked up his own bag. "Anywhere for me to wait?"

He saw the flicker of interest in the man's eyes and concluded that he had tipped above the average for Kansas. It had occurred to him that the Red Cap was not entirely comfortable in telling Victor that he was barred from the station master's office.

"You can wait in here," the Red Cap said, opening the door adjacent to the station master's. "My office. You won't feel so left out in here." The man said this with a wink and in a tone that Victor took to be laced with considerable pride.

Victor stepped into a cramped room permeated with the sharp smell of sweet tobacco. The Red Cap came in behind him, fishing a small round box from his vest pocket. He snuffed a quick pinch of powder into each wide nostril, blackened by years of nicotine dust. "No smokin' on the job," he explained.

There was a space underneath the door to the station master's office, so Victor could easily hear Graves enter the adjoining room. "Hello, Newton. Good to see you," the general began. "Why so serious? And all this cloak-and-dagger . . . I thought I would meet you at the hotel. I need a bath."

There was no quick response, and in that space the Red Cap whispered, "Gotta go. Close the door when you' done."

Victor sat down carefully on a creaking bamboo chair. There was a brass spittoon in the corner. The bare floor was darkened with preserving oil, but swept clean. Nailed to the wall was a photograph of the Red Cap in a baseball uniform, standing on a pitcher's mound.

After a long silence the Secretary of War began with what Victor took to be an apologetic tone. "The calendar's a bit hectic right now. My train's leaving shortly . . . but I couldn't drop this on you without some explanation. Bill, you're a square shooter. I admire that — and I'll give you no less."

Graves spoke again. "Newton, what the devil are you talking about?"

Victor waited out the silence in his windowless room. He was more than curious now. What was going on? Something wasn't right. He waited impatiently, looking up at the Regulator clock high on the wall. "I'm sending you to Siberia, Bill. And if in the future you want to cuss somebody for sending you, I'm the man to cuss."

Victor could only imagine the look on the Graves' face; it would be that careful, critical watchfulness of the academic, he guessed. During the long pause, Victor strained to hear, careful not to make a noise as Graves finally replied in a troubled voice. "I was promised a combat assignment in France. Now you're sending me to Siberia?"

"Bill, we've come to the conclusion that you're about the only man we've got with enough tact to perform an extremely delicate function. Extremely delicate."

Footsteps crossed the floor. "It's all in this envelope," Victor heard Newton Baker say. "But you will not tell your staff, or anybody else, the contents of this message." The footsteps moved again. There was no comment from Graves.

"It isn't going to be easy," Baker said apologetically. "Those sealed orders are from President Woodrow Wilson himself. The packet contains the policy of the United States for Russia — which you must follow."

The conductor's whistle blew a shrill warning outside, startling Victor. Baker hurried to finish. "I'd hang on to those papers if I were you, Bill. You might need them when all this is over. I'll vouch for their authenticity. That's the least I can do, considering what your men will be walking into. You can count on that."

Still silence from the general. He must be in shock.

"Watch your step," the Secretary warned. "You'll be walking on eggs loaded with dynamite. God bless you, Bill. Goodbye." The footsteps sounded again, heading out into the waiting room, and the door closed.

Victor could hear train doors slamming in a series of muffled thumps. He rapped quickly twice on the door and stepped into the office. General Graves was over by the window looking out through the empty waiting room with a glazed stare. He turned slowly to look at Victor.

"Look, General, I don't want you to think I was eavesdropping," Vic began apologetically. "The Red Cap put me into that little room . . ."

"You heard?" Graves asked.

"Yes, sir, I did. Didn't mean to, but I did."

Graves stood, frowned thoughtfully and tugged his jacket straight. "Oh well, that's your job," he said with a sigh. "If we can't trust our Intelligence Service, where the hell are we? Just keep a lid on this until I find out more about it, will you? I'm a little flustered right now."

"Yes, sir. Of course."

• • •

In Yokohama Harbor, Victor went to the bridge of the US Navy frigate *Brooklyn* to face an astounded officer. "They've cut your orders, Colonel. We're taking you into Vladivostok," the officer explained. "The Twenty-Seventh and Thirty-First Infantry regiments are on their way. I can't believe it."

"So, join the army and see the world," Victor said. "My papers?"

"Here," he said, handing Victor a decoded page of instructions.

"Who is the area commander?" Victor asked.

"For you — Major General Bill Graves. For the whole show — don't know yet. France's Brigadier Janin, maybe. There's supposedly seven thousand Japanese troops in place, but by our reckoning it's more than sixty thousand so the Japanese are making noises like their General Otani will be in charge. They'd love to carve up that whole maritime region. But of course that's why Graves is there. He'll keep 'em in line. By the way, good luck."

Victor stared at the officer for a moment before giving a half-hearted grin. "I guess you're right. Anyone who sneaks in the back door to invade Siberia might need a little luck."

Victor walked away from the sticky air of the wheelhouse into a cool draft off the ocean. He could feel the engine's slow buzz beneath his feet. Suddenly three sharp blasts on the whistle blew seagulls off the superstructure, and the underfoot vibrations surged with new strength. The stern swung away from the dock and soon they were heading out to sea.

He leaned on the rail in the fresh salt air. How did I get into this mess? Siberia! Sixty thousand Japanese! He felt as if he were being pulled along by an unseen current quietly taking control — he had to get off! The War Department has gone mad. Is one little Bolshevik like Lenin worth it? Are American factory owners really that afraid of their workers and unions?

Three days later a fog horn barked its low note as the frigate crept her way through the morning mist. She slid past an island just outside the harbor, and there through the melting fog he could make out the features of Vladivostok. There were steep hills above the gleaming white and gold turrets of a church. With the ship gliding closer to the docks he could make out buildings three and four stories high, their plastered arches gleaming in the morning sun. And there was General Graves waiting on the pier.

"Vic, glad you made it," the general said enthusiastically as Victor walked down the steep gangway. "We've got a few problems that I'll need you to get onto right away." The general walked Victor over to a waiting car and gave the driver Victor's kit bag to stow in the trunk. "Directly to the railroad station," he ordered, then climbed in the back with Victor.

"I want you to get to Omsk," Graves continued. "Much better position to give me the true military situation. Don't forget. You're there to help the Czechs get to Vladivostok. I'll get the transportation ready — that is, if we can clear the railroad between here and Chita."

Victor grasped the hand strap as the car bounced along a pockmarked road. "What's the trouble at Chita?"

"Bandits." Graves shook his head. "The most brazen sons of bitches you ever heard of: Skipetrov and Semyonov. It's my belief that our Japanese 'friends' encourage them to create a climate of terror just so there's some excuse for Japan's presence. And the Japanese become more aggressive every day."

The car pulled up at the railroad station and the driver got out to get Alex's ticket.

Graves put a hand on his arm. "I've assigned you a couple of communications specialists. Two boys from the Fifty-Third Telegraph Battalion — reliable. Set up an office in Harbin. Then make your way to Omsk. And keep me informed."

Victor got out of the car to collect his bag. Looking in through the open window he saluted and said, "Yes, sir. I'll check in from Harbin."

Graves nodded. "Keep a sharp eye out. Harbin is the most sinful city in the world they tell me . . . and I'm depending on you and your information."

"Yes, sir. Not to worry. I'm on my way."

CHAPTER 18

PENZA TO CHELYABINSK
SUMMER 1918

There was an unusually large assembly waiting on the platform as Alex's train slid to a squealing stop at Penza. Four unsmiling men with the red star above the peak of their caps stood beside the unpainted station house, its planks split and weathered. Up and

down the track dozens of armed soldiers were positioned for battle. Behind them, misty hills pressed in, giving an eerie sense of isolation. The atmosphere was tense, and no one seemed at all interested in diplomacy. Alex followed General Syrovy as he stepped down from the headquarters car to receive the local commissar.

"Would you like to talk in my car?" Syrovy asked of a thin, cheerless man who supported his stiff right leg with a cane.

"Of course," came the clipped response, and Alex watched as the commissar dragged himself up the stair of the command car, followed by three stony-faced cohorts.

"There's an offer from Moscow," the commissar began when all were seated. He looked to be in considerable pain, Alex thought. The leg, no doubt. "Comrade Lenin has arranged transport for the Czech Legionnaires to Archangel. From there, passage to France."

Alex felt a great sense of relief. At last, a way out, he thought, turning to Syrovy.

But Syrovy said nothing. The Bolshevik crossed his hands over the curved handle of the cane, peered at the Czech general, and said a little more seriously, "You will transfer all weapons to me to begin the journey north immediately." His eyes seemed to glow behind transparent white skin.

Alex tensed in the painful hush.

Still Syrovy said nothing.

The sharp features of the Bolshevik's face grew stern as he continued, "I will also put under your command eighteen thousand Czech prisoners of war to accompany you to Archangel."

Unexpectedly, Syrovy interrupted. "Where are they now?"

"Outside, in railway cars, waiting to be attached to this train," came the calm reply.

"All right," Syrovy said. "Hook them up."

Alex saw the hand on top of the cane give a flick, and a Red Guard left to carry out the order. "But," he heard Syrovy continue, "we're not going to Archangel."

Alex was not surprised. It was inevitable that Syrovy would draw the line somewhere, but he could feel his shoulders tighten in anticipation of a coming tirade.

"And why not?" asked the commissar of the Penza Soviet in a menacing voice.

"Because we have an agreement between our leader and yours that we have free passage to Vladivostok. Our soldiers are spread out along the railway, so we're not changing plans now."

"Very well," said the commissar, wincing as he stood up. "Stay with the old agreement if you will. In that case — unless you are considering declaring war on us — I must insist that the guns issued to you by Russia be returned immediately."

"That will leave us defenseless," Syrovy protested.

"You can keep your side-arms."

Alex stiffened. He felt trapped, powerless. It was against his nature to give up without a fight. However, in this instance, there was little else they could do. Both he and Syrovy knew it. And obviously the commissar knew it too, judging from the smirk as his guards unloaded the remaining Czech weapons.

The commissar became quite brusque. "We have completed the search. Leave now. If you think you can succeed in the attempt to overthrow the revolution, you are quite mad."

Syrovy was puzzled. "What do you mean by that remark?" he asked. "We have no wish to interfere with Russian politics. We're leaving Russia as quickly as possible."

"Is that so?" came the biting retort. "And you expect me to believe that?"

Alex could see the smoldering anger in the man now. His taut white skin stretched over sharp cheekbones. His eyes bulged wide. Threads of blue veins fed his brittle face with what little color there was, and the cane shook as he continued. "You think you can invade Russia and get away with it? We're not fools. You and your allies will be driven off. You will never foil the Revolution."

"Just a moment," said Syrovy. "What allies? Nobody wants to interfere in Russia's internal problems."

"Then why have the Western Allies invaded?" hissed the commissar, now trembling with rage, his eyes mere slits cutting across an ashen face.

"What the devil are you talking about?" Syrovy asked slowly and quietly.

"You syphilitic fool," the man scoffed. "You pretend you don't know what's going on? The British and Canadians have invaded the Murmansk Peninsula. That's why you asked to go to Archangel — so you could link up, join them and return the Czar to power."

Alex stood in stunned silence. Syrovy looked his way for help, but all he could do was shrug, shaking his head.

"Then there's the French," the tirade continued. "On the shores of the Black Sea . . . to bolster White forces. And the sanctimonious British . . . with their love of monarchy, coming at us out of Persia. While the United States and Japan invade the maritime territories. This intervention is evil, and will be burned out of Russia!"

Syrovy turned as if to speak, but merely gestured with his hands as his lips opened noiselessly.

"Comrade Commissar," Alex began haltingly. "We had no idea . . . We would never turn on Russia. We want to go home . . . that's all."

"Precisely what the Germans and Austrians say, and yet, like you, they remain scattered across half of Russia. Well you can all leave, but you'll leave without weapons."

With his lips pulled tight, the commissar stomped out of the car and climbed down to the wooden platform into the sticky heat. He waved his cane toward the front of the train, stepping back as the whistle pierced through a cloud of steam.

"Now go," he commanded. "Leave my country. And when you're out, stay out."

As their train achieved normal running speed, conversation came once again to the stunned officers in the headquarters car.

"I can't believe it," Alex said. "Six Allied nations invade Russia? Unheard of. No wonder he's furious."

"If it is true," cautioned Syrovy. "And yet . . . why would he lie? To get more weapons? He's got them all. So if it is true, they're surrounded . . . Their revolution could be finished by summer's end."

All were deep in thought. Alex finally spoke. "The Allies still have to defeat Germany. If the Reds can hold on through autumn, nobody can beat the Russian in winter."

"Except other Russians," said Syrovy perking up. "White Russians."

"Who will the people choose?" Alex asked.

"We'll see," Syrovy said. "Alex, telegraph back down the line to Peter. Let him know what's waiting at Kursk. Tell him to catch us."

But Syrovy wasn't finished. "We're sitting ducks here. I want the two of you to take some horses and a platoon. Catch Gaida at Chelyabinsk. It's only twenty kilometres. Tell him not to do anything flamboyant, but we're going to try to stay together. We'll at least have strength in numbers, and we need to talk."

• • •

Chelyabinsk had the atmosphere of a fairground as Alex and his patrol arrived at the end of a long day's ride. There was still plenty of light left for a summer's evening in this town at fifty-five degrees north latitude. The sun was pink on the Ural peaks to the west. Happy friends crowded the school grounds near the tracks close to the center of a cluster of dried-out clapboard buildings. They visited; talking, laughing, philosophizing and debating in the warm twilight. Surrounded by trusted comrades, they waited, hoping for a fast trip to the Pacific.

Alex and his small troop of Falcons strolled through this happy assemblage, waving toward calls from old friends, pausing occasionally for tea and gossip. Eventually Peter found a patch of ground large enough to hold their bedrolls, and they made camp there. They would meet with Gaida in the morning.

Alex dozed, fretting over the situation they were in. *We're far too vulnerable without weapons*, he considered. *Wide open to attack if* the Bolsheviks want to. Is there another way out? My father would have a plan. Make us discuss strategy. "What if?" he would ask. Always the coach, with ideas. Knowing what to do . . . perhaps the meeting will pull us together.

By eight o'clock the Legionnaires were busy preparing the evening meal around several small fires. An east-bound train came into view, moving slowly along the through-track, its bell ringing a doleful warning to pedestrians. Alex watched the brass bell-casing tumble backward on its supporting frame to produce one droning note. The shell then tumbled forward to produce another. Dong . . . dong . . . . After sixty metres and a dozen slow bells, the train pulled up at the water pipe and the ringing stopped.

Inside a filthy, crowded railroad car, Major Markus Adler slid back a window-board to look out. He quickly analysed the scene and spoke in a harsh whisper, "We are surrounded by Czechs. This is not our moment. Remain unobtrusive."

Listening, a disheveled Schumann looked up with hatred on his face.

It was then Alex saw that the train was filled with refugees. In the last four prison cars, when the wide center doors slid open behind bars secured from floor to roof, he recognized the uniforms of Austrian prisoners of war. They appeared extremely apprehensive; some even tried to hide back in the crowded car — until some Czechs offered them food through the metal bars. Then Alex could hear fragments of normal conversation, and he felt optimistic for the first time in a long while; it was an old feeling, almost forgotten, and it made him feel good. Maybe with time enemies can be friends again, he thought, smiling at how things change.

Peter was disgusted. "I wouldn't waste food on them. It's their damned train that's holding us up."

Alex shrugged. "They're on their way to a prison camp somewhere in Siberia. Could be the end for all of them."

As the train blew its whistle to move east once again, the Czechs nearest the track waved and called out in a friendly way, while a few men walked over to the carriage doors to hand up small bits of their meal in parting. Without warning, someone in the first prison car hurled an iron spike. There was a strangled cry, and Alex watched aghast as a corporal named Malik fell. He bled from the left temple, his hands and feet twitching in jerky spasm as Alex ran up to help. Before anything could be done, the corporal stopped moving altogether.

Three Czech soldiers leapt aboard the engine to stop the train. Others tore open the prison-car door from where the spike had been thrown, forcing the terrified Austrians out into the daylight. They pulled and shoved the Austrians roughly against the side of the car to search them. The prisoners stretched their hands high in the air, eyes wide with fright, as the cursing Czechs shook with rage.

Peter drew his side-arm, calling, "Stand back! I'll shoot the lot."

There was an immediate noise of holsters unsnapping and hammers clicking into place, and there quickly formed a long row of arms holding pistols in an unwavering line parallel to the ground. In the crackling silence, a drill sergeant's voice called out in German: "Put your hands on top of your heads! Everyone! Stand steady!"

Alex was surprised to recognize the speaker as Markus.

Looking directly at him, Markus announced to all: "These men have surrendered and are unarmed."

"Steady!" Alex called, standing up after examining Corporal Malik. "Not too hasty, Brothers. There's only one man we want. Sergeant, tell them to identify the murderer at once."

As a sergeant stepped forward, Markus turned toward Schumann. "Oberleutnant. Identify yourself."

Schumann stood in shock, shaking his head. "But why . . . ?"

Markus spoke calmly in an instructive way. "You've jeopardized the safety of your men. That is the reality to be faced."

Alex froze, as he slowly came to recognize the unshaven face of Oberleutnant Manfred Schumann.

Schumann opened his eyes wide. He looked around frantically. His cap was missing; his hair long and tangled. The Czechs had him hemmed in against the boxcar. There was nowhere to run. He tried nevertheless, but the snarling crowd drove him into the ground. The burly, unsmiling sergeant pointed a gun to the back of Schumann's head, but Alex shouted, "No!"

Schumann looked up in disbelief as Alex forced his way through the crowd.

"We haven't sunk that low yet," Alex said.

He watched Schumann peer into his face and hoped that Schumann saw outrage there. But despite Alex's glowering dark eyes and black eyebrows, Schumann brightened; perhaps he saw only the young idealist he had conscripted years before, a student who possibly still followed a strict adherence to rules. Alex's fear was confirmed by Schumann's truculent response. "Thank God there's some sanity left among you dregs. I demand a proper military trial."

Alex's arms were bare to the elbow. He held the back of Schumann's collar in one hand and asked in a low voice, "Why did you do this?"

"I'm a soldier. I demand a trial," Schumann said loudly. Now he seemed concerned by Alex's manner, although still defiant.

Alex looked at him coldly. "This is your trial. If guilty, you'll face a firing squad."

"A firing squad. How fitting." Schumann sighed, slumping a little in his grasp. It was the action of a man who had given up hope. "So be it," he continued in a vicious tone. "At least I had the pleasure of standing your father in front of one."

Alex felt the blood drain from his face. For a moment he thought he would lose his balance. He stared at Schumann as the Austrian ranted on. "That traitorous swine didn't deserve a military death. At least I'll die like a soldier, in front of a firing squad, with honor."

Alex could see that Schumann was closely studying his stricken face. No doubt the Austrian could see anguish and panic there. Then Schumann laughed.

"Yes, that's right. A firing squad. In Prague, over two years ago," Schumann said. "You and that grandstand show. Taking the Twenty-Eighth Prague out of action. He paid the price for that."

Markus gave Schumann a look of disgust as another lie was brought to light.

Alex was ready to explode. He felt the cords on his neck pull tight. His left hand began to shake until he reached up and seized a handful of hair at the back of Schumann's head. His eyes squinted almost shut, looking to the distant peaks, trying to hold in a lifetime of memories. He heard his own rasping whisper: "You had my fa-father shot?"

"Y-yes, you f-fool." Schumann laughed sarcastically until Alex reached up and grasped Schumann's chin with his other hand. Then Schumann's voice was partially muffled. "I want a proper trial," he yelled, perhaps nervous with the strength of Alex's grip.

Markus stepped forward. "I'll take over if you like."

Alex shook his head, then cleared his throat, almost choking. "I, I asked you once before . . . wh-why did you throw the spike?"

Schumann twisted uncomfortably in his grip, trying to look at the crowd. "Because each and every one of you is a traitor to Austria. You'll all pay the price for that!" came the contemptuous answer.

A strange feeling came over Alex. It was as if he were sinking slowly into a deep hole. *What is happening to me?* He thought of the day he held his rifle at Schumann's throat. Now he had no rifle. He thought about the reasons he hadn't pulled the trigger then. *A coward? Or just the stiff idealist that Gaida sees?* He thought of his father. Always there. Always ready. The man who trained patriots. *I should have pulled the damned trigger, back then . . .*

Markus recognized the strange look that came over the young Czech's face. It was a look of determination that one sees in high-level athletic contests.

Alex set his shoulders. He could feel the shirt tighten across his back. His lips pulled thin over clenched teeth while he raised Schumann's jaw high and still. "We find you guilty," he said, his eyes fixed, staring out over the silent crowd without a blink. When his forearms made a sudden twisting movement, he heard a hollow noise from Schumann's neck. Then he slowly released his grip, letting Schumann crumple to the dirt in a flaccid heap.

Alex looked down impassively at Oberleutnant Schumann's corpse before turning to wave the train away.

Markus turned to the Austrian prisoners and shouted, "Get aboard! All of you!" Then he took three quick steps over to Alex. "Where are you going?" he asked hurriedly in a low voice.

Alex looked detached from the scene but answered quickly enough, "Vladivostok. It's the only way out. I have to get my men away from here."

As the Austrian and German POWs scrambled aboard the train, Markus locked eyes with Alex and gave him an understanding nod before climbing aboard himself. The crowd of Czechs stood quietly by.

On board, Markus went to the sliding board and stared out at Alex as the train began to move eastward. Once again they were prisoners of war going deeper into Siberia, and farther from home. But what was that the Czech had just said? "Vladivostok. It's the only way." What did that mean? And surely the codes of war from the Hague Convention in 1907 were still in place . . . and would be observed. It was just then that Markus realized with an empty feeling that this was the lowest point of his life.

As a villager ran up the main road, Alex stood in a trance. The crowd turned away now, apparently satisfied with his swift action. They talked in low voices, some patting his slumped shoulders as they returned to the campfires. Some stopped to watch the local commissar coming down the main road with two police constables.

Alex was in a fog as the police escorted him toward the town centre and the local jail about five hundred metres from the station. He supposed this action to be routine, as no one was overly concerned — no one, it appeared, except the Falcon troopers who had accompanied him to Chelyabinsk. Whenever he glanced back over his shoulder, he couldn't help but notice how grim they looked while following Peter who marched just behind him.

His chest was numb. He offered no resistance to the arrest, walking in a daze down the packed dirt road and cursing himself for bringing on the death of his father. If only he had taken Peter's suggestion to finish Schumann off in the marshes . . . he might have . . .

At the end of the main street stood the jail, with a wooden sidewalk in front. He stumbled once before realizing his eyes were clouded with tears; his teeth hurt from the clenching of his jaw. My father's gone, he told himself. He's been gone for two years . . . I didn't even know.

As they arrived he heard the commissar say to Peter: "The captain and his accomplices must remain in jail for trial. I'll send for a judge. This is a difficult matter."

Alex followed him into the front office, shaking his head vigorously. "It's a simple matter," he said, breaking in, trying to control his voice. "It was an execution after a fair trial. Not once did the man deny his act. Furthermore, he was pointed out by his own unit. Justice was done, in public. We should all get on with our jobs."

"No! There must be a regular trial," the commissar insisted. A short man with a nervous cough, he closed the door and made notes while he spoke.

Alex supposed that he did not have much experience with the war because he bit nervously on his lower lip while he studied Alex's face. "You should be crying for what you've done."

"Don't be a fool," Alex said, suddenly aware that his face was wet with tears and feeling anger at this show of emotion. "There might have been a riot out there. All those prisoners could have died and not just one murderer. It's not your concern. This is a military matter."

"Don't you get out of hand," the flustered commissar shot back. "You are my prisoner. I'm in charge here."

"The hell you are," Alex said, and beckoned Peter who stood outside the window, looking in.

In an instant the door burst open. Peter, his face flushed with emotion, came in with the Falcon troopers behind. They filed quickly into the room with pistols drawn. "Move, and you die in your own jail," Peter said to the policemen.

Alex turned toward Peter's burning blue eyes. "Send someone to get Gaida over here. Let's find their armory. I've had enough of this. We're going to move like an army, not a bunch of eunuchs."

● ● ●

From the far end of the main street Gaida could see the jail. The last glow of sunset was fading over a purple outline of the Urals. Campfires lit the way from the train, across the schoolyard and into town. Through a dirty window in a light cast by kerosene lanterns, Gaida could see Alex slumped in a chair, head down.

Gaida had listened to Peter describe the execution incident back at the train. He had tried not to appear too pleased about these events, but he was. So the general's favorite has finally put a foot wrong. Branda's been a bit of a spellbinder, it seems. First Katherine falls under his boyish charm. Then Syrovy, and the men. And now he's got himself thrown in jail. Well, Gaida thought, it was time to accelerate this impossibly slow withdrawal anyway. It's time for action.

"I want you to go back to the jail as naturally as possible," he said to Peter. "Don't want to tip our hand."

When Peter left, Gaida gave the orders to the officers in charge of three hundred men he had mobilized. He watched with satisfaction the trained efficiency with which his officers commandeered all key buildings including the telegraph office, as well as both ends of every road into town.

Next he went to the armory, where they found a good supply of rifles and ammunition; he ordered these carried back to his train for storage. With the town under his control, Gaida marched up to the jailhouse door with an armed patrol.

"Put those men under lock and key," he snapped, gesturing toward the three distraught Russians.

Alex looked up with a grateful smile.

"Perhaps there's been a mistake," pleaded the commissar. "We can forget all this. Why don't you just leave . . . continue your journey. You won't be bothered anymore."

"How can we leave?" Gaida demanded. "I've been sitting here for two weeks while you tell me there aren't any engines for our use, and no room on the track. Then you take all my armament. Well, that's all over with."

"We were trying to return the Austrians," the commissar whined. "It's in the treaty. You'll get your engines."

"When? Where?" Gaida persisted.

"Immediately," the Bolshevik answered in a soothing voice. "There are six serviced locomotives in the maintenance sheds."

Gaida looked at his lieutenant and jerked his head toward the tracks; the young man left the room. Gaida turned slowly back to the commissar. At last a chance to get back some control from these peasants. "You will remain under custody until our meetings are done. It's out of your hands from here on. Captain Branda, see that your delegates are ready. Tomorrow. Eight o'clock at the depot."

"We're ready," Gaida heard Alex reply in a lifeless voice, and he saw that Alex offered his hand in thanks saying: "At least my incident has triggered some action."

The commissar looked on, horrified.

Gaida felt in complete control. This was where he belonged — at the helm.

* * *

The next morning in the school building, Alex's head ached. He listened absently to the chairman's words: "Be it resolved that the Czech Legion shall not be diverted from their goal of reaching Vladivostok . . . All in favor?" A forest of hands was raised. "Unanimous," he concluded, while the delegates applauded.

The happy noise seemed to act like a tonic for Gaida. Alex watched him hurry to the head table to put forward a vigorous motion resisting all attempts to further disarm their party. "My men hid half their weapons. We'll fight our way across Siberia if we have to." Alex heard the strong applause from the men crammed into the schoolroom, most standing behind those men sitting at desks.

Alex watched the energy of Gaida's presentation, pleased that after so many stagnant months in this political snare, they were at last determined to claw their way out. Just then, for the first time, he noticed that Gaida was wearing the insignia of a colonel. Incredible, he thought. Where did this promotion come from? The man has no shame. Alex silently determined to inquire about this new promotion at a more appropriate time. Right now he still felt physically weak from the turmoil of the day before.

Last night at the fire, his friends had made supper while he tried to come to terms with the loss of his father. Peter looked worried, attentively pouring vodka into Alex's tea, concern showing on his boyish face while they talked of their time back home; the good days, the good times, and they told the old stories once again, and sang the old songs, until Alex felt himself slip into a deep and dreamless sleep.

Alex had rationalized Schumann's execution, but remained haunted by the thought that his father would be alive if only he had shot the Austrian back in the Pinsk marshes. He realized this was not necessarily true. Anton Branda's fate had been sealed before Alex took the Twenty-Eighth out of battle. Hell, he argued with himself, it was probably sealed from the time Peter and I mutinied. More likely, my father was doomed by his own work. With this realization, as if shedding a burden, he gradually began to feel a bit better. My father knew he was being watched. And he knows I kept my word. I did my duty . . . and he's gone. Alex sighed, knowing he had finished crying for his father, and with the grieving about to end, he forced his mind onto the meeting.

Gaida pulled a telegram from his breast pocket and when he asked to read it, the responding crescendo of noise brought Alex back into focus.

"This telegram, originally intended for the commissar now locked in his own jail, came from Moscow," Gaida shouted dramatically, waving a slip of yellow paper above his head to the delegates representing each Czech division. "Hold up, disarm and dissolve the Czechoslovak Army Corps — the last remaining segment of the Czar's Regular Army. Form them as troops and working detachments for the Red army," he shouted as the din rose to an ugly roar. "I say, enough!"

His eyes shone with excitement as the clamor rose. "Are you with me?"

A sea of faces crowded into the school room shouted back, "Yes!"

"Right. We take back our weapons and move like an army. What do you say?"

The delegates erupted again, brandishing fists and shouting: "Like an army!"

"All right then," Gaida continued. "The First Division has reached Vladivostok and set up a tent city. Let me take the rest of the Second Division with the Falcon Regiment. We'll drive east and clear the track and control the railroad from the Volga to Lake Baikal." He paused to search the silent room. "We re-arm wherever we can find weapons. The telegraph and telephone systems will be ours, and that will put us in control while moving eastward. That is my suggestion," he said.

Alex smiled at the audacity. He would certainly have made a good footballer.

CHAPTER 19

CHELYABINSK TO BARABINSK
SUMMER 1918

Alex hurried over to the Chelyabinsk station house by cutting through the old side of town past the sprawl of drab huts clumsily fashioned from logs dragged from the surrounding forest years before. There was little culture here among the river-stone chimneys or the sidewalks made from hand-sawn planks, and he realized just how much he missed the splendor of Prague. He tried not to notice the foul stench of privies, taking instead a small amount of satisfaction in the fact that the guards on the platform were now Czech guards, and these men were his friends, armed and in control of any communication in and out of Chelyabinsk. He gave them a wave.

In a small back office he telephoned Syrovy fifteen kilometres back down the line toward the Urals, still visible to the west and beautiful in the morning sun. Over a crackling telephone line, Alex reported the conference decisions to the general, who listened without comment other than to say, "Repeat, please" when the static become too harsh.

There was nothing really to debate, Alex knew. The conclusions at the meeting had been supported with a strong vote, and the new path was clear, so Syrovy's only reflection concerned Gaida's conscription of the Falcon Regiment. "The Falcons are on their way. I'll be sorry to see you all go. You gave me good advice . . . ."

Alex listened carefully. It sounded as if Syrovy wanted to say more, and Alex certainly wanted to hear more, but perhaps it didn't feel right, over an open line, so Syrovy merely added, "Take your patrol with Gaida then. But stay in touch."

"Right," Alex said, "I'd prefer to stay, but there's not much choice. We're here now. I . . . we'll miss your command." Alex was just now realizing how much he would miss the extroverted general, hoping privately that Syrovy felt the same about him.

There was a pause before Syrovy answered, and his voice seemed strained. "All that I'll miss are the five horses you've taken. You've left us short."

Alex laughed, but could think of nothing more to say. He recalled how close Syrovy had been these past two years — almost like a father. Then Alex remembered: "Say, did I tell you that Acting Captain Gaida is now Acting Colonel?"

"A self-made man," came the knowing retort, "but don't let that bother you. He'll get things done. It's all horseshit, as you'll remember from Petrograd."

"Yes, but on the ride to Chelyabinsk I finally thought of something that's not."

"Not? Repeat please."

"Not horseshit."

"And what might that be?"

"Art," said Alex proudly. "Great art."

"Good God, man. You're not even close," General Syrovy scoffed. "Art is pure, unadulterated horseshit piled upon us by the best purveyors of manure in Europe: fashion designers and architects — and I should know, because I am one. Art is nothing more than fantasy and escape. Its most significant use is to break the monotony of a blank wall. You'll have to do better than that."

"I'll work on it and I shall telephone when I solve your riddle. Goodbye, Brother Syrovy."

"Au revoir, Brother Branda. It's nicer than goodbye."

"Au revoir," Alex said, surprised at a sudden surge of emptiness. "Let's be sure to meet again."

"Of course," Syrovy said simply.

● ● ●

"A little more tea perhaps, Katherine Kazakova?" Mrs. Ordinov asked in an anxious voice, her fingers tapping lightly on the handle of an elegantly carved English-style teapot. It was sterling silver and sat on a heavy ornate tray.

"No thank you, my dear Mrs. Ordinov. This has been just enough," Katya answered softly. "I've so enjoyed our visit, and your lovely things." She carefully placed a delicate china cup and saucer on the side table. The cup was purple on the outside; a golden band around the rim spilled down the inside of the cup in a gaudy sheen. The matching saucer rattled slightly as their train swayed around a curve. Katya looked up to the majestic Ural peaks. Snow caps glowed orange toward the end of a long Siberian twilight.

"Please stay for a moment or two longer, Katya. I must somehow make some sense of all this. Why do they keep moving us around all the time? It was so much better at the Treasury Building in St. Petersburg. We all knew where everything was."

We knew where our lives were as well, Katya thought, as she watched the distraught woman wringing her hands on the lap of a lavender dress. Suddenly, Mrs. Ordinov brought one clenched hand up to press against her lips. "I'm so frightened," she confessed, looking as if she might collapse.

"Mrs. Ordinov," Katya said soothingly as she took the older woman's hand. "It's just the unknown that has you edgy. Everything is quite normal . . . for a war."

"That's what I mean," said the older woman, clutching Katya's hands. "You're so good at logical deduction. Please tell me what you think is happening. My husband tells me nothing." She put her hands in her lap to stare at them again saying, "I know that he's under a very great strain . . . and it is affecting him." She raised her gray head, looking at Katya with eyes ready to overflow.

"Well of course," said Katya, trying to sound confident. "Let's talk about it. Things are quite straightforward, really. The new Bolshevik government could never risk losing the precious metal base to its paper money. Now you and I know very well what would happen if someone, say a banker in England, suspected that the amount of gold available to Lenin did not equal the certificates issued. Financial ruin. The notes say right on them 'redeemable in gold upon demand.' Don't they?" She watched the woman brighten.

"Now Mr. Lenin is quite concerned about the Czecho-Slovak Legion," Katya continued while looking out at the mountains again. The pink on the snow had mixed with creeping shadows and was turning blue. "He claims the Czechs might try to steal the gold to give to Russia's enemies. Although I can't see them doing that."

She allowed herself to think briefly of Alex, even though it was a luxury in which she scarcely indulged, for fear she might lose control. Alex is quite right, she reminded herself. War has no place for a serious love affair. The losses are far too prevalent; the pain for unrealized dreams, too severe. And certainly she hadn't heard from him for so long. The chilling thing was that Rad Gaida had been writing, but he never mentioned Alex . . .

"Oh that wretched Lenin," Mrs. Ordinov broke in. "He has ruined everything."

Katya was inclined to agree, but as a member of a privileged class of people who were oblivious to the hardship of their workers, she kept wondering how much of this chaos was our own fault.

Mrs. Ordinov continued. "I wish we could have stayed near the Czar's country-house in Ekaterinburg. Even though we could never visit, it was comforting to know that he and his family were there."

"That's probably why your husband ordered our train west again. Lenin might be afraid the Czechs will try to liberate the royal family and would have the town heavily guarded."

"Oh, Katya," cried the older woman excitedly. "Do you really think that is possible? What a wonderful idea! Everything could return to normal again."

Katya frowned, hiding her pain so as not to upset the woman. "Perhaps not, I'm sorry to say. Things like the royal family will never be normal again . . ." The people won't permit it, she thought, remembering the poverty and the suffering. "I wish it could be, with all my heart," she added. "Then perhaps we could correct some of the mistakes."

While Mrs. Ordinov reflected on her words, Katya turned again to her own thoughts. I hate this damnable war. It has spoiled everything. Marie gone . . . and now, Alex. I'm a prisoner on this train, in these mountains . . . in Russia itself . . . "I wonder where Marie is?" she asked aloud.

"Marie?" Mrs. Ordinov looked up, puzzled.

"Grand Duchess Marie . . . People at the market said the immediate royal family live in a country dacha in Ekaterinburg. They said more of the Romanov family is living farther north at Alapayevsk. Safe from harm, I hope."

● ● ●

Alex stood at the western edge of Chelyabinsk waiting for the arrival of the Falcon Regiment. It would be good to see them again. He had been called by a sentry, and Alex could now see them on the dirt road far down the railroad track on their hike from Syrovy's train back near Zlatoust. He ran forward, greeting them by their first names, and then marched with them to the train that was to carry them east into Siberia. Rad Gaida came out from his staff car ready to meet his new combat troops.

"Brothers, how good to see you," he called loudly with great charm and enthusiasm.

Alex called, "Colonel Gaida . . . may I present the Falcons?"

"Never mind the formalities with me; we're all of us old friends here." Then, turning to the Falcons, he said in a louder voice, "Brothers, we are the originals from the old days. Captain Branda is your commanding officer. We'll be together on the first train. I want the Falcons to clear the track for those behind. It's up to us to get our trains to Vladivostok — the sooner the better. What do you say?"

The response from the weary Falcons took Alex by surprise. His men shouted their approval, and continued laughing and whistling as they moved off to find their three dormitory cars. They wanted action. Action to move them home.

Alex followed Gaida to staff headquarters. "I want direct responsibility for the tactics used by my bunch," Alex said, still leery about Gaida and determined not to give up close control of the fate of his friends from university days. "We work best at night."

Gaida looked up. "Of course. Didn't I mention that? No need for worry," he said in a soothing tone.

Alex studied the self-assured face. The man has flair, of that there was no doubt, and Alex found himself smiling at this model of unswerving confidence. In spite of the self-promotion, Alex thought to himself: I like him, Acting Colonel or not.

Later that day, sitting with his old friend Lieutenant Pavel, Alex watched the landscape glide by as Gaida's train uncoiled smoothly from the foothills of the Urals. In the wetlands, swarms of birds blinked warily at the caravan surging eastward as the tracks straightened out across the steppes — a long straight slash through endless farmland. The gently rolling fields on either side looked alive. Soft winds blew over chest-high wheat, causing each field to roll and heave like a golden ocean washing back and forth, hypnotizing the men who watched the unrelenting enormity of Siberia from their train.

"This is more like it," Pavel said when they reached the next village. They stepped down from their car and walked over to Gaida. "No holdups."

"Now they're doing their best to get rid of us," Gaida said, watching a fat little station-master trotting back and forth from engine to station. "Something's not right here," Gaida said frowning. "Why is it so easy all of a sudden?"

"Maybe your, shall we say, diplomacy back at Chelyabinsk scared the hell out of them," Alex suggested.

"Could be," Gaida said, deep in thought. He squinted over a sharp nose while slowly stroking his soft moustache. "What if they're trying to split us up? String us out like pearls on a thread." He bit his lower lip. "Yes, that would be the ploy. Separate us. We're already a long way from Syrovy and your friend Peter, . . . and Novosibirsk is another hundred kilometres farther on!"

"No need to be hasty," Alex said. "They're probably afraid of us turning on them." He was trying to divert Gaida from the hard line. They needed time to think of a diplomatic approach. "Why create unnecessary conflict? If we push too hard, we'll have every village against us."

"Nonsense," said Gaida confidently. "Are you going to allow some Siberian train dispatcher to determine when, and if, we make it across this wilderness? Our trains aren't in Vladivostok harbor yet because it's the bloody Bolsheviks who decide when our trains can run. More trains go west than east — and they're full of German prisoners being shipped back to the war. Or is it to surround us? If we had control of the railroad, our trains could move throughout the day. Westbound traffic and freight would move at night. There's no telling when they might attack us — or which train. So . . . we have to secure every village along the line. Consolidate." He nodded as if talking to himself. "Take control. Yes, that's it. Take control."

● ● ●

Sitting at a long table in the Treasury train office, Katya made notes while looking over a heavy ledger marked "Platinum." She looked up as Ordinov entered the room.

"Good morning, Katherine. How do things look?"

"Good morning, Mr. Ordinov. The price on platinum has gone mad. Europe doubts Russia will produce any more under Lenin. They say that we have the last of it, and so the ruble is depressed on every market. I have no good news."

Ordinov smiled softly as he pulled a letter from his inside pocket. "Well, perhaps I do," he said. He placed it on the table beside her. "I'm going for breakfast."

Katya seized the letter and opened it quickly. It was from Alex:

Katya,

I don't know where you are. Grand Duchess Marie said you were incommunicado without saying why. We are trying to get to Vladivostok via the Trans-Siberian Railroad. From there an American navy ship will take us to the Western Front. We will accept nothing less than Germany's total surrender and freedom for Czechoslovakia. I can tell you, it hasn't been easy. You are constantly in my thoughts.

Alex

• • •

In the mountains near Zlatoust with Peter and the rearguard, Alex lounged on a blanket, enjoying a quiet Sunday afternoon at the side of the rail yard. His head rested on a log, face to the sun.

Summer in the Urals was a joy, and he listened to the regimental band practising for a concert they planned to give that night in town. There was washing to be done, and a diverse array of men's clothing hung on makeshift clotheslines strung from telegraph poles to the train. A bare-chested man with suspenders dangling down by his knees strolled toward a small shed providing hot water for the ever-present pots of tea. The pace was leisurely.

Then, without any warning, there was the sharp pop of a rifle, the sound barely noticeable in the open air. The man fell. Then more rifles were fired, interspersing with the spasmodic chatter of machine guns in the trees on the ridge above them.

Alex rolled from the blanket and sprinted across the thirty flat metres stretching from the track to a steep bank of grass clumps and gravel which ran up to the edge of a thin pine-grove. From here he could see white and blue puffs of smoke blowing out past the edge of the bank to hang in clouds over the turmoil below. The noise was unbearable with shouts and cries of pain, rifle-fire and machine guns.

At the first shot, Alex could see experienced troopers instinctively running for the nearest shelter from the deadly commotion. Those near the train were under it in a scramble. Others, like himself, who were separated from the train raced to the shelter of the bank under the line of fire. Those who hesitated in the confusion were cut down.

During the first few driving strides to the bank, Alex experienced the acuity of mind that only fear and adrenaline can provide. His world became focused as never before. Time and vision expanded; a second became a minute, he saw everything in sharp detail. Although his movements were at full effort, the result felt like a dream-like crawl. Within this eternity of seconds, and the slow-motion sprint of just a few yards, he and Peter and the men near them made their decision: they charged up the ridge without weapons.

Clawing his way up the bank in a frenzy, Alex threw dirt, sticks, gravel — anything his hands grasped as they clambered up the hill under the angle of fire from the deadly machine guns concentrated on the train below. Alex heard his men shouting, screaming, cursing. The Bolsheviks appeared shocked, then horrified, as they were showered with rocks and dirt by the desperate men charging their guns.

Alex saw that some of Peter's men had taken the bayonet hanging from their belt to use as a sword. Someone from below lobbed a grenade in a long arching parabola and he watched it destroy a machine-gun emplacement. Another machine gun was silenced when a half-naked man hurled a large rock with two hands, crushing the chest of a young Russian gunner. When more Czechs swarmed over the crest, the Bolsheviks dropped their rifles and fled, but the aroused Czechs did not stop. Peter called over to Alex. "We're going after them."

Alex stopped to check for survivors near the gun emplacements. "Sergeant," he shouted from the ridge, "get a medical squad up here."

Alex scooped up a rifle and took several sliding steps down the gravel bank to track level, stepping over men who lay where they had fallen. He called to three men still under the train, "Gather up any weapons you can find."

Alex waited as one of his medical officers came up.

"Bad news I'm afraid," the physician reported. "Eleven dead and thirteen badly wounded up on the ridge. Things are worse down here. Perhaps one hundred dead. Twice that, wounded."

"Can you handle that many casualties in the hospital car?" Alex asked.

"Only if we must. There's not that much room. Most need a hospital."

"Stay with me, Doctor," Alex said, and then he turned and bellowed, "Officers! Meeting!" The Falcon officers came on the double from across the rail yard.

He pointed to a young lieutenant without a cap. "I want you to organize the litter bearers and burial party. Follow instructions from the doctors. No one acts without their direction. When you're done, help the medical staff prepare a second hospital car." The young man nodded solemnly.

Alex turned to another silent man soiled with sweat and dust. "Secure our position. Keep that line open." Again a head nodded. It became apparent to Alex that these men realized what had to be done. It was just that someone had to say it out loud and in public, so all knew that order had been restored. "We're going to link with the trains ahead. We'll pull everyone away from the Volga with every weapon we can carry."

"Come on, Doctor. We're going over to the hospital with one hundred pairs of boots and provisions. If gifts will guarantee their safe sojourn, you can promise them that I won't come back and burn their goddamned hospital to the ground."

Alex looked around the circle of serious faces. Bathed in sweat, he spoke quietly: "We were lucky, you know. Permanent patrols, starting today, that's what we need. I'll tell Syrovy. Things are getting nasty."

* * *

Katya was at last getting a holiday from the train, which more and more each day felt like a prison and not the temporary quarters of the Royal Treasury. The staff was nervous. They knew that many of the bored guards had deserted; as a result, everyone else suffered feelings of isolation under these towering mountains, as well as the fear of discovery and, God forbid, capture. But for today I'm visiting the real world, Katya remembered happily, where even shopping for spice deep in the Urals is considered an outing. She felt a familiar satisfaction knowing that they were at a village only ten kilometres from Ekaterinburg where it was rumored that their beloved Czar was waiting with his family for the end to this nightmare.

When Ordinov gave orders for the train to move closer to Ekaterinburg, Katya had thought this odd. Previously they had pointedly avoided larger towns, trying as much as possible to remain on the move. They all realized it was not wise to allow people of a village, however isolated, to discover the importance of this train, and therefore they felt quite vulnerable when several of Kerensky's so-called trusted guards disappeared. Where had they gone? To Moscow? To Ekaterinburg? For what purpose? To find the Czar? It was maddening. Still, in keeping with her training, and with the prospect of an outing, she decided to dress accordingly.

Shortly after, Katya laughed as she took the cook's arm for the walk to market. The cook looks wonderful, she thought, carrying a wicker basket and dressed in his white smock. He even had a chef's hat on above his wide face. Constantine, the young guard with the moustache and boyish complexion, who she thought might be unsuccessfully fighting a severe case of puppy-love, came along for a change of scene and perhaps the opportunity to bask in the glow of her smile. "I'll carry your basket," he offered, his spaniel eyes watching her for any sign of appreciation.

By the time they arrived at the market, Katya had stopped smiling. She saw the stares from these mountain people standing behind their carts and wagons heaped with potatoes, cabbages and mushrooms, and realized that she had made a terrible mistake. Her Petersburg clothes must scream of social status, she realized too late. The chef in costume, plus a guard. What a fool I am! We must look the epitome of ostentation. She berated herself and began immediately to shop without wasting time, wanting to get back to the train. She could see scowling women staring. She could hear their whispers. Her fear grew with each cutting remark.

"Who does she think she is?" said one, in a voice purposefully loud enough for Katya to hear.

"A society bitch," said another one. "She should be with the Czar's bitch."

"Or at Alapayevsk. With the rest of the Romanov scum."

Katya could feel the blood drain from her face. Good God, she thought, the Czar really is in Ekaterinburg. Kerensky had sent the family somewhere for safety, but was it safe in there? Is anywhere in Russia safe for those of the upper class?

The cook began shopping faster. Young Constantine looked upset, nervously looking toward the train. "I have no weapon," he whispered to her.

She turned to the cook. "Phillipe, pay them. We're going now." She could hear the catch in her own voice. Her heart pounded in her chest. What was all that about Romanov scum? We must get back to the train.

The chef hurried to finish his business with the grocer and then slung the basket-handle over his arm. Katya fell in by his side for the walk back to the train. The guard kept his eye on a woman who ran away from the rest calling back, "I'll fetch Dimitri."

There seemed to be more of them now, Katya thought. "We'll just stay calm," she said quietly to the perspiring chef, but they walked faster. When they were almost to the train, loud voices made her look back. A crowd of men and women had caught up to the guard and were arguing with him.

A large woman with eyes like a raven called out to her, "Stop, bitch!" But Katya hurried to the train to call the sentries. A shout went up when the crowd suddenly surrounded the guard Constantine, pulling him down out of sight.

She heard him cry out with a scream that went through her like a knife, so she ran.

Ordinov came to the door just as Katya and the frightened chef climbed aboard. She saw him grabbing for the signal cord as the crowd broke away from the guard, who was now lying on the street, and they began a run at the train. Several guards dropped to one knee and leveled their rifles at the crowd, which stopped. The train began to roll and the guards stood up again to trot alongside, checking the crowd until it was time to jump aboard themselves. When they were all on, the crowd ran forward again, throwing rocks and curses after them.

Katya was aghast. "There's no hope. Constantine, that poor boy. He seemed so full of hope. It's all my fault," she said to Ordinov, holding her hands to her cheeks as if for protection from blows. "Alex was right. They hate us," she admitted with a sob.

CHAPTER 20

NOVOSIBIRSK
SUMMER 1918

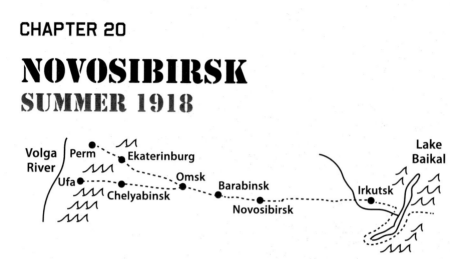

Although a wind-driven rain drummed noisily against the windows of his conference car, Colonel Gaida remained in high spirits. "Come in, brothers," he called happily, stepping aside to watch his staff officers hang their wet coats and caps on wall hooks. "I've good news for you all. Please sit."

On the long table made from shellacked planks, a cup of steaming tea waited at each place. Most of the men wrapped stiffened fingers carefully around the white metal, looking past the warm mist into the clear amber brew. They were tired; Gaida could see it in their lackluster eyes, although some were distracted enough to study the murals depicting the valleys and mountains of old Bohemia that covered every wall.

"We've come a long way in a month," Gaida began while circling their table. "Colonel Kechek left the Alexandrovski Bridge and the east bank of the Volga in good hands. Yesterday he linked up with Syrovy at Chelyabinsk."

"Excuse me, Brother Gaida, but in what 'good hands' did Peter leave the east bank of the Volga?"

"Not right now if you don't mind, Captain Branda," Gaida said, forcing his voice to stifle any trace of annoyance. "I would like to develop the situation first. And I'll tell you the best part right away. Pavel has captured four artillery pieces and three hundred shells." He was glad to hear table-thumping and some laughter. Gaida laughed too. "Three hundred shells . . . I had only four shells for one gun . . . and I had to lend him two to capture all of that. He owes me at least half, don't you think?"

There was laughter at this remark, but it died down when the driving rain rattled against the windows. Gaida was startled by lightning crashing into the forest outside. Rain fell in silver sheets, and treetops thrashed about in the bright white light. The rain drummed loudly on the roof, lashing everything in its path with a torrent of cold and damp which threatened to seep into the spirit of everyone near this hostile ground.

"Finally," he added, "we have twelve thousand men in a tent city on the hills outside Vladivostok. The French and Americans are organizing navy transport for us to the western front. What do you think?" he asked. "Can we make it this summer?"

His question was answered by more table thumping until Alex broke in.

"Not wishing to put a damper on all this good news, but we've been fighting every day for the last four weeks. If the Bolsheviki pull together, it could take months."

"The resistance will end soon," Gaida said confidently. "Trotsky himself says that we can leave peacefully. There shouldn't be much more trouble. I'm issuing a proclamation to be posted in Novosibirsk tomorrow, announcing our peaceful intentions."

Alex, he noted, nodded agreeably to this announcement, and Gaida felt somewhat relieved. "So now," he continued, "let's look at what has to be done. There are two main problems." He jabbed the pointer into the center of the map of Siberia. "Omsk is a well-organized city sitting here, like an awkward porcupine. From Omsk the northern rail-line travels northwest through Ekaterinburg to Kazan. This supply line must be cut to isolate Omsk, if Syrovy is to capture it," he said in a matter-of-fact voice.

"The main tactic will be to hit the enemy with the armored cars while flanking them with the Falcons." As an aside he added: "Apparently that's the way Captain Branda likes to do it."

He started to continue but Alex interrupted, using the more familiar form of address. "Brother Gaida, it seems to me that these plans clash with tomorrow's proclamation of our peaceful intentions."

Gaida suppressed his annoyance. "Precautions, my dear captain, only precautions. No one wants to fight unless we have to," he said in as reassuring a tone as he could muster. "Now let me see, was there anything else? Oh yes, I'm sending three thousand men north to Ekaterinburg. They are to cut the line."

"Rad," Alex blurted out in astonishment. "Is this wise? It seems far too aggressive."

"At staff meetings, please address me as Colonel," Gaida replied as calmly as he could. "Aggressive it may well be, but that's why I'm in charge. Captain."

Alex spoke again. "And who put you in charge of strategy running counter to our agreement with Moscow?" The question held no tinge of impudence, Gaida was disappointed to note. It was ice cold, without passion, and Gaida was determined to answer in kind.

He looked at Alex squarely, and without hesitation said: "The Czech Legionnaires Conference at Chelyabinsk. And they gave you to me as well."

He was surprised to see that this remark did not put Alex in his place. "What 'friends' are guarding the Volga Bridge?" Alex asked. "The Volga is the end of Europe. We want to leave Europe, don't we? Come on. We might as well know it all."

Gaida dropped his eyes for a moment before looking up defiantly, his eyes flicking from face to face. "Peter Kechek turned our position over to Major Galikan of the White Guard."

Gaida felt rather than heard the room fall silent just before a new roll of thunder crashed above the train. Every man watched him without a sound or a blink.

"I know what you're thinking," Gaida shouted. "That this is interference with the affairs of Russia's Civil War. Well it's not! Every time we move, we create a vacuum. Someone has to take over. Who do you want to move in? The Bolsheviks and their Red Guard? We can't trust that scum. You know that." He had not wanted to shout, but there was thunder. Now it was quiet.

"We gave our word," Alex said. "Major Galikan is a Czarist officer. The Reds, and certainly Lenin, will never believe us again."

That was too much for Gaida. He could not tolerate the advice of the weak-minded. "They don't believe us now, you idealistic fool!" He realized that he was shouting again. "The Reds hate us! The Whites want us!"

Gaida saw Alex stand up with angry dark eyes, but saw too that most of the officers had returned their attention to him, their colonel. Thus encouraged, Gaida continued before Alex could speak again. "You want to reason with the Bolsheviks? Well, I have different plans. Tomorrow we begin. Now see to your duties!"

Gaida noticed that Alex held the door open for the other officers until all were out. Then he pulled the door inwards, leaving just the two of them. Gaida watched him warily.

Alex's face was white. "That's the last time you degrade me in front of our colleagues, Acting-Colonel Gaida. If ever you feel the urge again . . . talk to me privately, then face the consequences. Is it understood?"

Gaida stood rigid, studying Captain Branda cautiously. There was something different about Alex, and it puzzled him. What was it, he pondered. A new confidence? Wait . . . he no longer stutters. That was it. But why?

Gaida slowly relaxed. This was not the time for a showdown. He did not want a confrontation with this fellow just yet. The Falcons were devoted to their leader, and as such he was key to Gaida's strategy. Besides, he had other plans for Alex.

When passing through Omsk, Gaida had taken on more Czech prisoners sent from Ekaterinburg. With them was a deserter who claimed he had served as a guard for a special train; when Gaida interviewed him privately, he was delighted to hear the accurate description of Katherine Kazakova, which proved that this deserter knew what he was talking about. The crowning touch was that the guard revealed the coded address at Kazan where President Ordinov picked up the mail.

Gaida stayed calm in the face of Alex's challenge. He knew that sometime later there would be an opportunity to punish this persistent idealist who had dared to steal Katherine from him. So for now he gave a shrug of his shoulders. "Agreed," he said.

He watched Alex step out into the rain. Then he went to his desk and picked up his pen with a smile. "My dearest Katherine," he wrote, "I will soon be able to get you out of Russia safely . . . ."

• • •

Alex left Colonel Gaida's command car and walked to his bunk at the end of the Falcons' car. On the pillow lay an ivory-colored envelope with a golden eagle on the upper corner. It had to be from Katya — mailed before the postal bureaucracy learned to isolate the Czech Legion. He quickly lay down, tore it open and read:

My dearest Alexander,

I don't know where you are. Neither do I know where I am, although it is safe here for the time being. How I miss you. I've not had a letter for so long now. You might not get this one. I've not heard from Marie either, and pray she has not been captured; a fate, I hear, that has most unhappily befallen a great majority of the Romanov family. They are in Ekaterinburg and we are trying to make contact without being caught ourselves. This really is an unspeakable nightmare, and sometimes I wonder how I can continue, but then I think of meeting you one day in Prague, on the bridge any day at noon, and I'm all right for a little while.

Yours, Katya

Alex lay back to stare at the low ceiling and listen to the drumming rain. I'm moving farther and farther away from her. How do I get back? How can I find her? If the Reds win, what then? They can't win, can they? They're surrounded.

● ● ●

In Moscow, three thousand kilometres away, Lenin stood with one hand leaning on the back of his chair. Sombre men around a massive oval table listened to rain beating against the leaded windows of the Kremlin. He could tell that they also kept a close eye on their angry leader. When had he become so weary of his task? He dabbed a handkerchief to his forehead. His shirt sleeves were rolled up to the elbow and he could feel the vein at his temple throbbing. They could probably check his pulse from the far end of the room. "Find that damned Treasury train! Someone must have seen it."

Lenin watched Trotsky get up from his chair and walk to the rattling windows. Trotsky pulled a cord for the floor-to-ceiling burgundy drapes; he reeled them across to lock out the elements. Well, they couldn't hide from the Bolshevik's predicament so easily. "I cannot understand how the situation got so completely out of our control," Lenin muttered into the handkerchief. "The Czechs have our jugular vein running through their fingers. If they pinch . . . twenty years of work, shot to hell. What irony, the Czechs can't get out, so we have a trained army in control of our backyard." He swept his palm back over his bald pate a few times. He was sweating again. "Increase the propaganda campaign condemning the Czechs, but let them pass. Get them the hell out of here!"

Lenin paused as Trotsky slipped back into his seat, and his face clouded. "Leon, if the Czechs show any sign of looking north, it's to rescue the Czar. You know what has to be done." He looked deep into Trotsky's eyes before continuing. "There must not be a single symbol for the Whites to rally round. That is their only power with the people." Lenin looked distracted for a moment. "And that Jewess? What's her name? Kaplan. Trying to kill me, right here in Moscow. I never knew there could be so much pain from two small bullets."

He looked up at his own portrait hanging larger than life above the empty fireplace. A square white brow dominated his image above the hypnotic stare and jutting goatee. He appeared so energetic in the painting. "Hmpff . . . she might have done me a favor."

Lenin finished mopping his face and stuffed the handkerchief into a back pocket before he sat down on the hard chair to read the list before him.

"I want these things attended to immediately," he stated without further passion. The others sitting before him began taking notes.

"Russia declares war on the United States of America, France, Great Britain and the rest of the Interventionists. See to the documentation. Find out the organizational strength behind Kaplan's assassination attempt and then eliminate it." He licked his lips. He did not want to appear frightened by the inevitable occurrence of enemies. "I hope we gave her time to think before she died."

Lenin picked up his papers as if ready to leave. "One last morbid thought: can you imagine if the Whites recruit the bandits Semyonov and Skipetrov against us? We'll be facing the Mongol hordes once again and the return to the Dark Ages."

• • •

As his head cleared, Colonel Victor Lindal found himself on all fours staring at parched ground just a step or two away from the railroad tracks. Tasting blood on his lip, he carefully reached up to touch the cheek now burning and swelling after a slap from the stock of a rifle. How long have I been here?

Still on his knees, he swung his head drunkenly to watch a Mongol in cavalry boots walking toward him. Victor shaded his eyes blinking into the sun, trying to focus on the man who now walked imperiously from the train's engine and coal-car toward the first passenger carriage. Neat printing on the side of the car proclaimed it as property of the Chinese Eastern Railroad. Now he remembered! Igor Skipetrov! All the warnings had been of little use. Here was the vicious bastard in the flesh.

As Skipetrov approached, Victor saw that the notorious bandit slowed his walk to a swagger. The Mongol looked up with some interest at one of many broken windows. A lifeless arm hung out through the broken pane and dripping blood ran down the wall of the carriage staining the gold letters: **HARBIN EXPRESS**.

Victor dropped his head as Skipetrov crunched down the gravel path in front of him. He did not want another beating, nor did he want to see the two companions who lay beside him humiliated by more kicks and curses. He would have to contain his rage and the impulse to lash out at this infamous murderer.

Feet planted wide apart, Skipetrov posed before them with closed fists on his hips. Behind him ranged an endless stretch of sandy plateau and scrub vegetation. It was not a landscape conducive to escape.

Victor watched the Mongol's hooded eyes study each man, examining their military uniforms, perhaps measuring the anger on each sweating face.

One soldier was bleeding from a nasty cut on his forehead. Skipetrov watched this man with a dull expression, as if not understanding the shoulder patch that read: **AEF, SIBERIA**.

Victor hoped that he would not have to explain to this debased brute what was meant by "American Expeditionary Force" and why they were in Mongolia on their way to Lake Baikal. It would be even more difficult to explain why an intelligence officer from the War Department was going into Russia.

Victor could hear a woman sobbing out of sight on the other side of the train. When another screamed, Vic jerked his head around, swearing in protest. Skipetrov whirled, kicking him hard. He felt a rib go, then heard himself moan as he collapsed face down in the sandy soil while Skipetrov began kicking them all, shouting, "Kow-tau, kow-tau."

With rifle muzzles lowered, Skipetrov's men rushed forward, jabbing at the prisoners until they moved into a position of supplication with hands on the ground near their forehead.

Victor heard Skipetrov shout an order which was followed by the sound of men running from inside the five-car train — presumably hurrying to their horses. Victor stole a sideways glance. Most of them carried at least one prize from their raid — a watch, or luggage, or clothing. Skipetrov jumped onto his waiting horse.

Skipetrov shouted tersely once again, and the nearest Mongols began to strip their kneeling prisoners of boots and uniforms. Victor gritted his teeth as his tunic was wrenched away, but he could not prevent the exhalation of air that escaped as a groan. His hands were pulled behind him and he was tied at the waist to his two companions. They were jabbed until the three stood unsteadily in a single line.

Victor watched Skipetrov ride up to inspect his sullen prisoners before returning to the head of his horsemen. Then he waved the Mongols forward across the plateau toward low hills in the distance. Where is this son-of-a-bitch taking us? Victor wondered. And who in hell is going to come looking for us when no one knows where we are?

His mouth was full of cotton — like the days of wind sprints back on Stanford's rugby field. He licked his lips, tasting blood again. His rib shot daggers of pain with every movement, so he stood unsteadily, breathing in short puffs while he searched for some way out. The reality of the situation was hitting him hard now and he saw confusion distort the faces of his companions.

They, like him, had been stripped down to their long underwear and bare feet. Anger had been replaced by fear. He wanted to say something encouraging to these young telegraphers who did not even know why they were out in this wilderness in the first place, but he couldn't think of anything.

Without warning he was jerked forward by the tug of rope around his waist. He lurched to the right, trying to keep his balance as they were pulled over the rough ground behind a pack horse.

One of the young soldiers turned back, looking at Victor with a tight face. "Colonel, will H.Q. be able to find us? Do they know where we are?" he whispered.

Victor stumbled, trying to keep in rhythm with the tethered men who marched awkwardly in front of him, sensitive to the fact that they looked back every few steps, waiting for his response.

He searched for the right words, the careful words, but finally decided on the truth. "No one knows. We're screwed."

• • •

Katya sat nervously in the chief accountant's conference car. Everyone had been sitting in the heat for over an hour waiting for Mr. Ordinov to come back from the village with news. Her thoughts wandered, and she absently noticed that the calendar on the desk was incorrect, so she went over to tear off a page, dropping it in a wicker waste basket. There, she thought, July 15, 1918. It was eleven o'clock with still no sign of President Ordinov. But just then she could see him coming along the trail through the pines between the track and the village. "Here he is," she said.

The rail inspector walked with Ordinov. Katya had seen him before. He had been a dependable friend to those on the secret Treasury train and a reliable source of news. A frail man, he walked with a stoop — and now it looked as if Ordinov was mimicking him. They would stop every few paces. The rail inspector kept raising his hands and shrugging his shoulders in what could only be taken as gestures of futility. Ordinov slumped, his chin drooping to his chest.

Katya felt a cold shiver across her shoulders. Something was very wrong.

The Treasury staff had stopped breathing, it seemed. Their faces showed the strain of waiting in this silent room and all heads turned toward Ordinov as he entered.

The man looked as if he was going to be ill. His hands trembled.

"I have terrible news," he said in a cracking voice. "The rail inspector has confirmed rumors from a fellow worker who was an eye witness."

Katya clenched her fists in her lap.

"Sadly I must report . . . this morning, Czar Nicholas Romanov, his wife Alexandra and family were taken to the cellars of their mansion in Ekaterinburg . . ." He sucked in quick gulps of air. "which has been their prison for several months — and there . . . and there, they were shot."

Katya cried out. "All shot? The children too?"

Ordinov closed his eyes, bowing his head. "Everyone gone. Every last one of them. Gone forever."

A strangled wail from his staff interrupted the shaken man.

Katya's hands went to her face, her eyes wide, watching Ordinov for some sign of hope.

He looked up, forcing himself to continue in a rasping voice: "The executions were carried out by a committee of the commissar, chosen by lot. The witness said that two of the princesses did not die with the first volley." Ordinov choked.

Katya could feel tears falling onto her hands held rigidly in her lap while she listened. I used to dance with them, she thought.

"There were jewels sewn into their clothes . . . bullets deflected . . . The commissar dispatched them with his pistol. The Czarievitch died clinging to his father."

Katya looked around the room. Her colleagues were in shock, many sobbing into cupped hands. Her own eyes were filled with tears and there had been enough hurtful news but she could not stop, she must know. "What about the Czar's relatives? What about Grand Duchess Marie?"

Ordinov stood stiffly silent. His glazed eyes stared back toward Katya as if he were watching a faraway scene. "Last Sunday the rest of the Romanov family at Alapayevsk were forced over the edge of an abandoned mine shaft."

He coughed, trying to clear his throat, but began to gag. He finally managed to catch enough breath to gasp out his last sentence: "Some villagers listened from the edge . . . on the third day the moaning stopped."

It was only then that he allowed himself to collapse.

CHAPTER 21

OMSK TO IRKUTSK
SUMMER 1918

Sitting in their railcar, Alex and Peter were studying the problems involved with the Czech journey across Siberia when they were unexpectedly distracted by the clip-clop of approaching horses. Packed dirt on the road outside muffled the sound, but as the mounted troop grew nearer, they could hear heavy footsteps on the metal stairs.

"What's this?" Peter asked.

"I'll see," Alex offered, but before he could walk the length of the room, a large figure stepped into the car filling the space from ceiling to floor. A giant stood in a gray Astrakhan hat; his flared coat reached to the ankles. Black piping curled across a wide chest toward black buttons. A fist as big as two normal hands began opening the top button just below a beard the color of coal.

"Good evening comrades," a voice rumbled from under the whiskers. "I am Major Zotov, Third Cossack Horse Guards. May I remove my coat and hat? It is warm."

"Of course, Major," Alex said, coming forward. "Here, let me hang up your things." He took the belt and saber the Cossack passed him, hefting the weapon in one hand to feel its weight. "Look at the size of this," he said to Peter who brought vodka and glasses from a side board. Alex hung up the cap and heavy coat. "Join us for a drink, Major, then we'll hear your business."

"Good man," the voice rumbled once more — a full octave lower than most. He picked up the glass and held it in salute. "To the success of your journey," he said, taking a large swallow before settling onto a chair with a sigh.

Alex felt a wave of relief. No hidden meaning there. "We'll certainly drink to that." He raised his glass then tipped his head quickly back, recalling for a moment the time he had been called to the Winter Palace to receive the Cross of St. George. He remembered the Cossacks in the great hall where the Czar had shaken his hand, and where Katya had kissed his cheek. He felt a rush of pride return. "Once, I toasted the Czar in Petersburg," he said.

"We might again," suggested the Cossack, who now sat in a brown tunic similar to the cavalry issue Peter wore. Zotov unfastened his collar at the side of the neck and looked quite at ease, stretching his legs across to an empty chair.

"Personally, I'd like to see that, Major Zotov," Alex said easily, "but we're not permitted to help you."

"Your comrade here helped us at the Volga," the Cossack said with a casual gesture, studying Alex carefully and sipping vodka with an air of someone biding time.

"Different situation," Peter said off-handedly. "We merely turned over a position. We didn't actually do anything . . . actively, in a fighting way . . . to assist the White Guard." He struggled a bit with the logic.

"Don't do anything again," came the friendly invitation. "Stay at your job. Tomorrow we might help you. Lenin is determined to stop you at Omsk, as you might have guessed." Zotov said this more as a statement than a suggestion.

Alex smiled, shaking his head. It was tempting, this offer of assistance by the world's most skilled and feared cavalry unit, but he knew they could not accept. The villagers were watching closely, full of threats and demanding proper payment for food and coal. Isolated groups put up occasional obstacles to the passage of their trains — to test their territorial rights, he supposed. But he knew that as travelers in a foreign land they had to work through this situation in an organized, military way. No panic, no incidents. And certainly nothing that might turn the whole country against them as foreign intruders.

We can handle the Red Guard, he thought. They represent only a fraction of the local population, and they are taken, this far into Siberia, as isolated packs of wolves rather than a military force. He'd heard no more rumors beyond the fact that the Western Allies had actually invaded Russia. Impossible, he thought, but the rumors were persistent. The Japanese and the Americans were in Vladivostok; the British and Canadians are at Archangel in the north; and the French occupy Odessa. It just didn't seem possible. Bolshevism wouldn't stand a chance if the interventionists were to move in concert. But there was no local panic — just the Red Guard, watching from the hills — and the local citizenry did not trust Trotsky's radicals any more than any other outsider.

As he reviewed his worries, Alex idly swatted the mosquitoes which lunged at them night and day. His friend Peter also silently waved away the insects nurtured in the swamps of the tundra. The Cossack officer simply lounged back in his chair, curiously unaffected, watching their futile and never-ending contest.

"Did you come to Siberia to fight flies or Bolsheviks?" Zotov asked good-naturedly.

"Neither," Alex said, shaking his head vigorously. "We can't get involved in your civil war. We're traveling to Vladivostok. Nothing more. Why don't the mosquitoes bother you?"

The giant heaved himself out of the creaking chair and walked to where his greatcoat hung. "Here, use this." He held out a small glass cylinder containing a brown sludge stopped up with a cork. "My men will teach yours how to make it."

"My Lord!" Peter said, sniffing the muck and making a face. "What a smell."

The Cossack poured himself another vodka, and responded without apology: "Do you want to smell good, or be eaten by flies?" Then a sudden thought seemed to brighten his dark face. "Are there women on this train?"

Peter laughed. "You think because we don't smell like creosote we have women here?" He laughed again and got up to make tea.

"I have not seen a woman since, well, it feels like fifty years. Damn! Those Bolsheviks are going to catch hell tomorrow." They all laughed at that.

Within two days, Alex and Peter — still refusing to accept aid from the fearsome Cossacks — rolled cautiously into Ufa with a show of force by advanced infantry to link successfully once again with General Syrovy. The Czar's Cossacks watched from a distance, eager for the respected Czechs to join their White cause.

Syrovy was elated by their progress and slapped Alex on the shoulder. "Good! Things are looking up. The railroad, the telephone and the telegraph — through the Urals, right across the steppes — they're ours. Now for Lake Baikal."

The push toward Lake Baikal was not so simple, Alex discovered. It required Herculean effort on the part of the Falcon Regiment. They marched on continuous sorties through the dwarfed trees and marshy ground that Russians called the taiga. They surrounded villages ahead of the train to avoid confrontation, and protected the tracks from sabotage. Heat, mosquitoes and leeches ate away at their patience. Long, rocky climbs sapped their strength. At every turn in the track they could expect an attack, but Alex was relieved to find that the strategy worked.

Alex supervised almost all the patrols. He was not sure why he took so much upon himself; certainly he trusted his men, and did not mind delegating responsibility. But it looked as if they were succeeding, and he did not want any slip-ups. It's too boring just waiting for the boys, he told himself. I'd rather be there.

Looking inward, Alex had to admit a twinge of jealousy watching Gaida's continuous and energetic presence with the infantry.

Gaida was up and down the line, snapping at their heels like an ambitious herding dog. He often said that the hope of escape would vanish when cruel winds howling down from Barents Sea brought the first snow. "God help us if we're not out of here by winter," Gaida reminded his officers, and Alex believed him.

Once, after three days of a sustained chase near Krasnoyarsk, Alex's Falcons met Gaida's men just after they had caught the Bolsheviks at camp cooking their evening meal. Gaida's troops ran them off into the north woods away from the trains. When they returned to the Reds' campsite exhausted, hoping to scoop up the purple borscht left simmering in steaming tubs, Gaida gave them only fifteen minutes. "Get up and get on with it," he demanded. His tone made Alex uncomfortable. It was not the way to speak to a comrade-in-arms. "Don't let your enemy rest or re-group. Push them off this railroad — it's all you've got. I'll send the train after you."

"He's getting worse, I tell you," a trooper snarled as Gaida strode away.

"Stopping to fight is our only ruddy way to rest," his mate agreed, crunching off down the line.

He's good, I have to admit, Alex said to himself one day during the break. But I'm not putting myself into an early grave proving myself to him. No . . . I don't think that's why I take so many patrols. I want to speed things up. I want to get out of here. Find Katya . . . that's all. I'd give anything to hear her laugh again . . . .

This latest flanking patrol had been particularly strenuous, and it was not until three in the morning that Alex led eighty numbed men stumbling into their dormitory cars.

"Lieutenant Marek, I want you to take fifty troopers to Seberta tomorrow — early. My boys will catch some sleep." Alex took off his leather belts and equipment, dropping them on the floor behind him. "Take your time. It's twenty kilometres. Wide sweep from the south. Then pinch in on the station — two days at the most." He kicked off his boots and rolled heavily onto the bed, lying on a dark gray army blanket highlighted by two black stripes; one passed under his shoulders, the other under his knees. A second blanket was folded under his damp hair as a pillow. "Be careful," Alex warned.

"I will. Now get some rest. I hear the Cossacks are still tracking us from the north."

Alex's eyes were heavy. The voice was a drone. He felt Marek drape a blanket over him and he lay like a stone.

He liked Marek, having known him since their football days at the university. Marek had been reluctant to leave school, but finances were such that he accepted a waiter's job at eighteen, in order to marry. Now twenty-two, he often complained about being a long way from his family.

Two days later, Alex looked out from the shelter of the taiga across a field of barley. He saw Lieutenant Marek leading a skirmish line across the hip-high grass toward the Seberta station house. "I can't see anyone," Alex said, anxiously scanning the station with his binoculars. "No trains either."

At that moment a murderous fire exploded from well-concealed rifle placements on the far side of the rail bed waiting for Marek's advance. "Good Lord, a trap!"

Those Czechs hit by the first fusillade fell. The rest hurled themselves to the grass for what little protection it provided. Now the guns began the leisurely chore of picking away at them, one by one.

Alex waved Pavel forward. "Get to that station. Stay in the trees."

Through the binoculars he could still see Marek, his face turned around looking at his patrol. Alex saw that Marek yelled instructions, then Marek waved his arm to signal a charge. Alex shouted: "Stay down!" But it was too late. Marek gathered himself and then sprang forward. Instantly he was knocked down by a bullet through his forehead. Marek's head snapped back; his arms flung to the side. His body went slack and he fell limply, almost gracefully, like a swimmer diving into a deep, dark pool.

The Czechs were pinned down, and Alex heard the frustrated curses of those who had been hit. It was terrible to hear the cries of badly wounded friends. They could do nothing but lie in the unsympathetic sun, tortured by fear and pain and thirst. For the Bolsheviks, it would be a summer afternoon's shooting practice at any target showing itself — at least until Pavel could get through to the station. Alex stood in suspense listening to the echo of gunfire blend into silence until at last a grateful voice called out, "Cossacks!" And soon, triumphant shouts from all over that bloodied field answered back: "Cossacks."

Alex looked up a grassy slope on the other side of the tracks. Sweeping down the hill out of the taiga to the north came the rumble of one hundred ponies. Their hooves drummed out a muffled tattoo as a strong canter accelerated down the length of the grassy slope. He swung his binoculars across a line of the charging horses until he could focus on Zotov and his black beard. The noise became a thunder-roll when a deep-throated roar from one hundred horse-soldiers greeted his cry: "Full gallop!"

Then Alex swung his binoculars slowly down the front rank of wild-eyed horses. Each rider showed the teeth of a charging lion, mouth wide open, emitting a fearsome roar. Alex watched them charge in the classic mold of fighting cavalry; a charge that had become Cossack tradition across centuries of desperate times. As young boys, these horsemen's minds had been etched with repeated stories of similar rushes against Mongols, Turks, Persians and Poles, and they rallied to the calling of their clan. To die fulfilling this art-form was not distasteful, Alex knew. Legend had cemented the belief that each saber-wielding giant was fulfilling a destiny — and doing that for which a Cossack is born.

Down by the track Alex could see the Red Guard turn in confusion, scrambling to re-establish a fighting position from their concealment which was protected only to the south. It was then that they saw the glittering sparks flashing from a hundred sabers swinging through high circles in the sun, because the Bolsheviki stood, strangely enfeebled, like forest deer mesmerized by a hunter's lamp. Then Alex watched them fall, while the Czechs exalted, tears of relief streaking each dusty face.

Later, as Alex supervised the clean-up, he met General Syrovy walking across the field from the train in front of the station house. Syrovy was concerned but clinical: "The Red Guard will get better, you must realize. We can never ease off."

Syrovy looked up above them where the Cossacks were camped. Zotov's men lounged about, cleaning their weapons and no doubt recalling their dash down the grassy slope. The sound of easy laughter drifted down the hill. "I'm sure we're all very grateful," Syrovy said. He adjusted his eye-patch. "Someone will want to be paid for this rescue — of that you can be quite certain."

"I know," Alex agreed. "But we can't be pulled into a civil war. We'd never get out. Interventionists, Lenin calls us. They must be furious."

Syrovy sat down, thoughtfully scanning the battle scene. "What next then? The Romanov dynasty wiped out, yet the White Guard want to revive the old days of groveling. Impossible! There are no more symbols. But then . . . perhaps that is to be Lenin's legacy: if the Bolsheviks are defeated, not one Romanov remains."

• • •

Katya could not believe her eyes. There was a letter from the hospital in Moscow where Marie had been a nurse. The envelope carried no name. It could have been the hospital writing to the family of a deceased soldier, but the penmanship shouted out to Katya. "It's Marie!" she called to the staff, and their heads turned to her. "The Grand Duchess is alive!"

Katya pulled the letter open. Where was she? At least not in Ekaterinburg — thank God! Or worse, the tomb in Alapayevsk. Anxious eyes watched. The staff hung on every word, while Katya read quickly.

My Dearest Katya.

I pray that you are safe. I am on the river Dnieper at Orsha, only six hundred kilometres north from Kiev where I wait as the unrelenting August sun beats down on this parched field. Over the hills as far as I can see, German barbed wire stretches in a tight line, keeping out of White Russia and Ukraine the petite-bourgeoisie, who know they must flee Russia and the coming bloodbath. Only fifty metres to the east, there is a parallel Bolshevik fence, to prevent our escape. Refugees wait beside their carts looking as tired as the horses that stand with drooping heads staring dully at the baked grass.

Whole families watch the rough wooden hut which serves as a documents checkpoint for those who would leave Russia for the German-occupied Ukraine. Almost no one has the necessary travel papers, so they sit close to their suitcases, or hug their carry-sacks as though they might be clinging to a lifetime of memories; and we wait.

I watched my husband pull a rolled banknote from his fountain pen to pass over to me. "Wait for me, Sergei," I said, "and pray. Today is my All Saints' day — we could be in luck." I walked directly to the Bolshevik guard on the steps of the hut, and I could feel his hostile glare. "You can't get through," he said. "We're closed."

"But I must," I pleaded, and surreptitiously passed him the folded banknote. "My family are over there," I said, pointing to a cluster of people near the German gate. The soldier looked around cautiously. "Where are your documents?"

"That's just it. They have my papers. I must retrieve them or I'll have to start all over again in Petrograd."

"Your troubles don't concern me. I can't let you through without a proper documentation."

At first I was panic-stricken, but I saw him pocket the banknote and so, decided to press the point. "Look. There's my husband with our luggage. Let me fetch our papers, I beg you. I'll be right back." Again he looked to see who might be watching. "Go now, or it's never," he said.

• • •

Major Markus Adler walked slowly in the summer heat and paused near the two guards on duty at the gate. Turning away for a moment, he stopped when the guard said, "sir, someone coming." He watched as a woman hurried across the strip of neutral land between two incompatible nations. Markus understood a lot about old Russia, but Lenin and his discordant political philosophy were contrary to all that he had seen.

He watched as this obviously agitated refugee hurried to his gate. What would she say?

"Entschuldigen Sie bitte, Major. May I have a few words?"

Taken aback at her speaking in German, Markus was slow to respond. "Fräulein, you are correct with my rank . . . and speak my tongue. Do I know you?"

The woman held onto a line of the barbed wire at the German gate. "I pray to God that you do." Then she reached into the pocket of the coat she was wearing — despite the pressing heat.

She showed him a used bar of soap, holding it like a magician about to do a slight-of-hand trick. She broke the bar open and removed a card announcing: THE GRAND DUCHESS MARIE PAVLOVNA. SWEDISH EMBASSY.

Markus read the gold print carefully, then with worried eyes, studied her face. He held up his hand to the guard and pointed to the gate. The bolt was pulled back and the gate opened just enough for Marie to come through.

Beyond the far fence, some in the crowd stood to watch, but sat again when the guard pulled the bolt into place.

Unexpectedly, Marie grabbed the guard. "No stop . . . please wait."

"Your Highness, enough! Do you want to start a riot?" Markus said forcefully.

Marie was agitated. "You don't understand. My husband . . . he's a soldier like you . . . but a palace guard who will surely be shot, as were the others."

Markus checked the fence again.

"In a world gone mad, is there any honor left?" she pleaded.

"Which one," said Markus relenting.

Marie pointed to a man standing near the Bolshevik gatehouse and Markus spoke quietly to the guards, "The tall one with the brown jacket."

"We require visas," she interrupted.

Markus looked at Marie, then said to the guards, "Keep your eye on him."

He turned to Marie, "You seem determined to complicate this day . . . please come with me." Taking her arm he led her back to his office, where he stopped by the aide and instructed him, "We need two diplomatic visas — quickly. The uncomplicated ones."

After a short wait in the office, Markus and Marie returned to the gate where Markus handed two visas to one of the guards. "Say nothing. Show the visas to the attendant. Get them back, stamped. Then escort the gentleman back here."

Markus opened the gate and watched the guards enter the Bolshevik hut. Minutes later they emerged with Prince Putiatin carrying two suitcases.

With a trooper at each shoulder, he marched quickly back to the German fence. Markus held the gate open as they came through, then slid the bolt firmly in place.

He saw Marie touch Putiatin's hand and her anxiety seemed to melt. She turned to Markus to say with intensity, "In a brutal world overrun by brutes, I'm glad to see a code of honor still exists. Thank you for your civility."

Markus smiled warmly and kissed her hand. "My privilege, Your Highness." He shook hands with Prince Putiatin before indicating to a guard to bring the suitcases, then said to the royal couple, "Please follow me," and led them to his office.

The aide spoke briefly to Markus as his guests sat down. "I have a car, sir, and there's a train in four hours."

Markus put a hand on the aide's shoulder. "Bring our guests some tea and lunch." Then he closed the door behind him. "Citizen and Citizenness Putiatin, welcome to our humble office . . . I must say, I don't know how to address you . . . but I am happy to see you together, and safe."

Marie sat holding both Prince Putiatin's hands and Markus thought that the strain of her adrenaline-charged day was taking hold. "That appellation will be satisfactory for the present situation, Major. And now I must say that I am at a loss to know how to carry on a conversation with one of our enemy's officers."

Markus was taken aback for a moment, and noted that Prince Putiatin was uneasy, most likely from being out of the communication. "Perhaps we should speak Russian, Your Highness. For your husband's sake." Markus could see that now it was the Grand Duchess Marie who was surprised as he spoke in her native tongue.

"War is strange, don't you think?" he continued. "It is most often an insane reaction of governments to problems . . . economic problems. Ordinary people like us are swept along in the wayward currents." He watched the faces of his guests change with surprise, but he saw that they listened to his words.

"Germany wanted to be Russia's good neighbor. However, this wish somehow became twisted, and my country was surrounded by fear and suspicion . . . and so began this 'war to end all wars.' In the middle of all this, I come upon two desperate 'citizens' who need a Samaritan's hand . . . and I am called the enemy."

Marie's face showed anger. "I did not intend to give that message," she said curtly, "and I've never been called 'ordinary' before."

Putiatin broke in, "Major . . . you are full of surprises. All of them so far beneficial to us. Please forgive our oversights. This past week has been extraordinarily perilous. I wish there were some way of repaying your timely intervention. I have nothing to give to you other than my lasting gratitude."

There was a silence as the Putiatins watched Markus closely for a response. He took his time. "There is one way you could repay me," he said. "When your children are old enough . . . let them know that Germans have their good points. We hold honor, allegiance and determination in high regard . . . as do you two, I've noticed."

The Grand Duchess Marie stared at Markus as if embarrassed. But before she could say anything, Prince Putiatin laughed loudly, got to his feet and offered Markus his hand. "Done!" he said enthusiastically. "That prize is well deserved." He drove his emotion home with a vigorous handshake.

Markus smiled and nodded. A lunch of tea and sandwiches was brought in. Marie began to serve while looking very comfortable in her un-royal role. "You seem rather young to be a major. Are you married?" she asked while pouring tea.

"I am hopeful," Markus replied.

"Will she wait for you?"

"So I'm told . . . but time will tell."

As the lunch dishes were being cleared away, Markus picked up the telephone answering a call from his aide. "Sir, Leutnant Schumann is here."

"All right. That means that you'll be taking the Putiatins to the station . . . make sure to bring back a receipt for the tickets . . . tell Schumann to wait in the barracks. There's no need to let him know who our guests are. He'd probably want them as prisoners of war."

"Yes, sir. The car's at the motor pool. I'll have it brought around."

Markus escorted the Putiatins out to the car. Both men carried a suitcase. As Markus stowed them into the trunk he turned to the couple. "My aide will take you to the station for the two o'clock train. The German government has taken care of the tickets . . . I wish you Godspeed."

Grand Duchess Marie was strangely silent. She became very serious as she approached Markus and opened her hand. "We want you to have this ring, a ruby set in platinum. May I suggest that you present it to your chosen lady, and that you tell her how you helped the last Romanov to safety . . . like a true Knight. Major Markus Ritter von Adler. Take with you my deepest wish for your happiness."

Markus bowed over her hand. "Again my privilege, Your Highness," he said. "Indeed there is nothing 'ordinary' about you."

Stepping back, he watched them wave as the staff car drove away. He studied the ring with a smile. Perhaps it would be a perfect way to charm Erika.

• • •

Katya wiped tears from her eyes before turning the page to continue reading Marie's letter.

One month later in Odessa, White Guards escorted me to the train where every light had been extinguished for secrecy. Only dull lamps along the platform lit our way as four officers followed me into my unlit compartment, bringing with them the smell of campfire-smoke and leather. Their equipment jingled in the dark.

I lit a single candle before turning to the officers, my eyes streaming tears. I lifted the yellow flame up to each face trying to memorize those who had arranged our escape; the men who would deny the reign of Bolshevism. I shook each hand as they left.

Then, as the carriage began to move, I positioned myself in the center of the compartment window, looking out, with the candle held near my waist. There was a faraway command that called the line of soldiers on the platform to the present-arms salute. They stood perfectly still as if frozen by the first frost of October. Soldier after soldier formed that rigid line, eager to glimpse what I tried to be: an image of hope standing behind candlelight in the

Royal Coach. I watched their determined faces slide across the window in front of me, slowly at first, but then faster and faster like a mad dream — until abruptly they were gone, and I was left looking out onto the black fields of Ukraine.

Katya saw that most of the staff wiped tears of relief from their faces, but Rovskoy was frowning as she read the letter's closing:

One day, Katya. One day. Until then, I pray for you.

Marie Romanova Putiatin

● ● ●

Katya dried her eyes, smiling triumphantly as she looked around the room. "Now we carry on," she said with conviction.

But Rovskoy stood up. "Just a minute. This doesn't help us at all."

Katya ignored him, and turned to face Ordinov. "How many guards do we have left?"

Rovskoy approached aggressively. "There is no sense carrying on with this futile game of hide and seek. We must turn the Treasury over to Lenin."

Katya turned on Rovskoy angrily and stared him down. "We will not! We are going to do our duty and nothing less. Would you let a guttersnipe take over your country? Mr. Ordinov, how many guards are left?"

Ordinov looked down to the floor. The fight had gone out of him, and he slumped against the back of his chair. "Forty-three."

This number shocked Katya. "Out of one hundred?" she managed to ask. The downcast Ordinov could only nod. Nevertheless, Katya made up her mind, and with a determined look she left the conference car. Hurrying outside, Katya strode away from the train over to where four sentries stood near the edge of the forest. They looked up apprehensively as she approached. "I must talk to you. All of you — right away."

They looked at one another in surprise, before one hurried back to their dormitory car. With a glance toward the conference car, Katya could see that Treasury staff members peeked out from behind the metal blinds to see what was going on.

Guards came running from the dormitory car in various stages of dress. When the last few arrived, pulling on their jackets, Katya took out Marie's letter. "There is something you should hear," she said.

She could tell that the guards were puzzled at first, just standing casually while she began to read. But as they listened, they pulled closer — and stood taller, she thought. By the time she had finished, they were applauding. "It was important information that I thought would help you in the performance of your duty," she said. Then Katya turned and walked back to the train.

CHAPTER 22

LAKE BAIKAL TO SLUDYANKA
AUGUST 1918

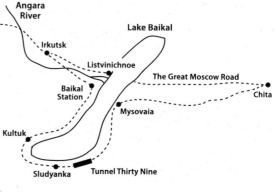

Gaida had learned from one of Captain Alex Branda's discourses on the history of the Great Siberian Railroad from its beginnings in 1893, that the steep granite hills on Lake Baikal's west side had prevented travel around the lake, forcing trains onto barges at Listvinichnoe on the Great Moscow Road. During winter, with the deepest lake on earth stiffened by an ice-cover several metres thick, train tracks were simply laid down on the frozen surface. But by 1905, forced labor had completed an engineering triumph. A system of tunnels had been bored through thirty-nine mist-covered mountains around the lake.

If they could secure this tunnel system, Gaida believed that he would have a good chance of linking with the advance group of Czechs waiting at Vladivostok. If he could just get around the formidable natural obstacle of Lake Baikal the dream of escape by train might be realized. And if the impossible trek were to be successful, it would mean international fame for him as the man at the forefront leading over seventy thousand of his countrymen out of danger.

On the other hand, should the tunnels be destroyed, the Bolsheviks could prevent their escape. He might be disgraced. Worse, the forces under his command could easily be surrounded during winter and eradicated.

It was this fearsome possibility that had driven him to send Captain Branda and the Falcons on their exhausting trip south to Kultuk. It had to be done, he was certain. If I'm successful . . . one day even Branda will understand that, Gaida thought to himself. Alex can't be manipulated . . . This young idealist from Prague has some unexplained sense of discipline and determination. But he'll do the job for me. Still, I must keep watch, he reminded himself. He could turn against me any moment. I can't trust him — or anyone, really.

In the poor light, Gaida led a unit of engineers creeping down the side of a slippery rock-face with barely enough trees for a foot-hold, to within four hundred metres of the station. He whispered to his men. "Quietly, all of you."

Sprinting into the marshalling yard, the engineers set long fuses to a munitions car loaded with dynamite which was standing by itself.

The engineers hiked back to Gaida's position with sweating faces and anxious eyes. Gaida knew they wanted to get farther away before blowing the charges, but he could hear the Bolsheviks coming back down the track. Damn! He needed more time. What if the charges failed? What if they had been duped into mining the wrong car? The Bolsheviks must not have a chance of saving the dynamite car. He could see them coming down the track toward Baikal Station.

"Now," he ordered in a harsh whisper. "Now!"

The engineer pushed the plunger. Nothing happened for a moment. Then Gaida heard a sharp bang, followed abruptly by a thundering roar. Stupefied Bolshevik soldiers threw themselves to the ground. The din bounced from mountain to mountain until rocks broke loose, falling hundreds of feet down into the churning lake. Smoke and planks torn apart by the blast spun through the air. Gaida watched with satisfaction as the noise rebounded, back and forth, until at last it rolled away far across the lake — leaving only screeching birds and the shattered remains of Baikal Station.

Gaida strained to see down the track toward the dark opening of tunnel number one. "Get those wheels off the track. Hurry up."

"You mean we're not going to pause here?" an astonished officer asked.

"No," snapped Gaida. "God damn it, no! When do any of you realize we have to press on? This is only one of thirty-nine obstacles that could ruin us. They can't be allowed to find more explosives, or to counter-attack."

He turned, shouting to the men. "Move! Tell the men in the mountains to follow. The rest of you, come with me!"

When the tracks were cleared of debris, Gaida's war train steamed ahead as troops walked uneasily on both sides of the engine, feeling their way along the long, dank holes bored through the mountains.

He looked back at them closely, noting the ones who appeared uncomfortable in confined spaces. Fear showed in their eyes as they first approached the tunnel entrance hacked out of gray rock, each piece split painstakingly with chisel and sledge. The eyes grew wide, the mouth rigid, as their mind told them of all the dangers involved with chasing any desperate animal into a hole. "Stop acting like cowards," Gaida called. "Move on!"

They pushed the Bolsheviks ahead of them through the first unlit tunnel and came almost immediately to the second. The faces tensed again.

"Branda and the Falcons are marching toward us from tunnel nineteen. Be careful who you shoot at," Gaida shouted as he rolled the armored train slowly forward. He looked down the shaft of yellow light from the headlight, now sharply aware of how close they were to the low ceiling and how smoke had stained those chipped walls with a thick layer of soot.

There was very little space in the dripping tunnel and Gaida felt a sudden chilling image: How long would it take to dig them out if things went badly? He thought of the men somewhere high above them scrambling across the misty granite knobs, and hoped that they could keep up, so that no Bolshevik dynamite party could crush his plan. He looked down the black tube in front of him, hoping that Branda would hurry.

Alex met Gaida at tunnel thirteen, and following a brief and noisy encounter with the enemy trapped inside, Gaida controlled all of those stark granite tubes except for one: number thirty-nine south of the village of Sludyanka.

There was nowhere to bury the dead, and Gaida had made sure there would be no survivors — certainly there was no room for prisoners. Gaida had the bodies taken to the end of the tunnel into the light of day where the railroad swung close to Lake Baikal near the piles of rock dumped off the side of the track. The dead were weighted down with chunks of granite in their kit bags and clothes, and then slung into deep water. He could see that Alex and Zotov watched with sombre expressions.

Their faces changed to frowns when he called out: "Everyone on board. We're pushing ahead. Falcons into the hills on our right."

Gaida braced himself for a reaction from Alex and Zotov. Zotov took commands well, but Alex was forever correcting his judgment and was glaring at him now. "Colonel Gaida, let's think this through," Alex warned. "The flanking tactic's old hat. We could be punished for it one day."

"Would you mind telling me what the hell else I can do?" Gaida shot back. He was tired of discussion. "Get on with it."

He watched Alex's serious face — as if sincerity meant anything at a time like this.

"How about negotiation?" Alex asked. "Syrovy thinks it best. They probably won't want to damage their own tunnels. The locals let our first trains through. Besides, I'm sick of burying good friends in places their families can never find. Talk to the Reds. We just want out. Tell them that."

"No, damn it! No!" Gaida shouted in response to that nonsense. "We won't negotiate with those cut-throats. Kick the buggers out of Russia."

He saw Alex's surprise. "You want the Whites back in control, don't you? And you're doing all you can to help."

"Of course," Gaida said with a sneer. "These people weren't meant to rule. They're not educated for it. A monarchy will be returned. There must be someone left to reign."

"A grateful monarchy," Alex suggested. "One which would reward you with the power you deserve."

"For that, I would march back to Moscow tomorrow," Gaida responded defiantly. "But for now, you're going to circle Sludyanka. Pinch that properly, and we'll have pulled it off. There's only one tunnel after that. Get going."

He watched Alex swallow his anger and wave his men on.

The going would be hard. The fighting would be fierce. There were long hikes ahead over steep and treacherous rocky trails, and still the Bolsheviks could fight them off. But Gaida promised himself he was not going to let fatigue stop his plan. He was unrelenting. "Move ahead. Make them run," he called, until at last Sludyanka fell.

• • •

The next day, from high on a bald ridge, Alex watched Gaida's armored train move cautiously eastward from the old town of Sludyanka. Four kilometres down the track, their last hurdle waited: tunnel number thirty-nine. Infantry walked beside the train. Patrols marched ahead probing both sides of the track. The troop train followed at a distance. There was no sign of the enemy.

Alex and his ten-man patrol had just climbed a steep hill south of the last tunnel when a trooper tapped his shoulder.

"Sir. Down there. Infantry on the move."

"Heading south?" Alex reached for his binoculars. "But there's no railroad that way — only the Mongolian border."

He searched the long lines of fast-moving troops. They wore a strange mix of gray uniforms, and in the dry heat of August they kicked up a trail of dust in their wake. "Where did they come from?" he began. "I wonder why–" He was interrupted by a muted explosion. A dirty fog boiled up from the railroad tracks, as black cordite smoke mixed with granite dust. Alex shuddered. He knew that tunnel thirty-nine was gone.

Alex scrambled back down from the hill to find a crowd of Czechs examining a pile of broken rock at the entrance to the last tunnel. In front of Gaida's engine, the rails disappeared under the rubble. Soldiers stared as if they had come to the end of the earth. All were silent except Colonel Gaida who shouted angry questions.

As Alex approached, Gaida called to him, "Did you see anything?"

"Yes, Colonel," Alex replied, pointing toward a gap in the low hills to the southeast.

"Between two and three thousand troops on a hasty withdrawal down that pass — I think they're German and Austrian prisoners of war, heading for the Outer Mongolian border."

"Well, after them!" Gaida shouted. "Take Major Zotov and cut them down."

Alex watched Gaida for a moment. He began to form some sort of an answer but stopped. The man's cracking, he thought. We're all wound too tight. I'll take the Falcons for a ride. We have nowhere to go anyway.

Alex saluted before going back to Sludyanka for horses and Cossacks. Within an hour they were ready to ride south. He stopped to report to Gaida who stood with slumped shoulders. With an angry look he passed Alex the telegram:

Troopships waiting Vladivostok (stop) When can we expect your arrival (stop) General Dieterichs (end)

Alex read the telegram, shaking his head. His lips clamped shut. We'll never know, he thought. We'll never know if we were too aggressive. Certainly we shouldn't behave like sheep herded to slaughter — a middle position maybe. But now . . . what the hell happens now?

• • •

At the Ekaterinburg railroad station on the northern Siberian line, a soldier wearing a red star on his cap watched through the office window. Leon Trotsky was inside talking to the station master who was nodding and pointing. Trotsky followed him to a wall map and the station master traced his finger in a triangle across the north section of the Ural Mountains.

Trotsky saluted the man and then burst through the doors back out onto the platform. "They've been here before. There's only one direction they can go."

Trotsky and the soldier hurried to a train with a large red star painted on the front. Trotsky waved to the engineer before climbing on board as the train pulled away.

CHAPTER 23

MUKTUI
AUGUST 1918

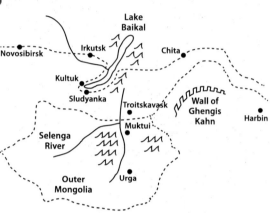

It was not difficult for Alex and his Falcon patrol to track the fleeing troop. A natural path climbed a steady slope through the mountains until it opened out onto a high plateau. Here the landscape changed. Dry dirt was commonplace, and the footprints upon it swung eastward toward Troitskavask on the northern border of Outer Mongolia. Little more grew here than hardy scrub vegetation, the odd tree and some grass. The scouts could see to every horizon; the way was easy.

Pavel trotted up to ride beside Alex. "Alex, a word?"

"Of course," Alex replied. "What's bothering you?"

"Nothing. Some of us wonder why we aren't pursuing with more speed, that's all."

"Fair question," Alex replied easily, his relaxed body rocking back and forth with the natural motion of the walking horse. "I've been trying to answer another question — one I'll pass on to you. What will we do when we catch up with three thousand fleeing troops? Fight, watch, or run away?"

"Fight of course," was the confident response. "Wipe them out!"

"Why?" Alex asked.

"Why? They're the enemy."

"Are they interfering with our purpose? And just what is our purpose anyway?" Alex persisted.

"Traveling to Vladivostok. And these fellows are preventing us."

"Were . . . hampering us," Alex interjected. "What's preventing us is a tunnel full of rock. These fellows seem to be quitting the whole expedition for some reason. Let's find out where they're going.

Or would you rather be heaving boulders out of the hole in that mountain back there?"

"Not at all," the lieutenant admitted. "It's not so bad out here." Pavel looked across the plain. Tough little bushes dotted the dry plateau and skittish rabbits kept darting past. "I just wondered why we weren't trying to catch up."

"Look around. Some of our boys are almost asleep in the saddle. They're worn thin. The Cossacks have little left. This trip could be as good as a holiday."

Late in the afternoon, a picnic-like atmosphere developed when Alex stopped them for the night. He watched the men snare rabbits, so abundant on the plain. He saw the happy attention given to the roasting spits rigged over dozens of open fires. Every scrap of meat was devoured, bones chewed and sucked clean.

His troopers lay back on their blankets contemplating the endless black sky filled with stars. Everyone had much to think about, but their tension eased away as they listened to the rumbling Cossack voices sing of manly bravado and passion for duty. In one last reflex of military vigilance Alex set sentries in a half-mile picket around the camp. Then, knowing their quarry was at least an hour's hard ride to the south, he slept.

He continued this easy routine for two days, walking the horse across the plateau toward low hills to the south. They covered eighty kilometres before arriving at the Selenga River which poured out of the Mongolian highlands to find its course back toward Lake Baikal. Knee-deep, crystalline water had rounded and smoothed its riverbed stones with a thousand years of gentle washing.

His horse walked determinedly to the edge of the flowing water, and Alex let the reins hang loose. Listening to the horses sucking in the pure water, he looked up at the empty violet sky. The sun was warm on his face. "This glorious day shall not go unnoticed," he said to Pavel beside him. "How do the men appear to you?"

"First-rate. Rested."

"And in need of a wash. Tell them to finish watering the horses and then scrub everything. Blankets, utensils, clothing, themselves. Cossacks too. Clean every piece of harness."

Alex moved back from the river and the long line of horses. He found a boulder upon which to place his saddle and his clothes. Then he walked naked into the river.

Soon, in this far-flung meadow on the Selenga River, a great communal bath took place. Two hundred and thirty men found their way into the bracing water, awkward at first on the slimy rocks as friends splashed them with handfuls of the frigid stream. Exotic curses, shouts of anguish and half-joking threats of unparalleled violence filled the desert air; and laughter — Alex noticed that — plenty of laughter.

As his skin adjusted to the mountain water, Alex lay contentedly soaking, hanging onto a rock, balancing in the pull of the current.

He watched his men as they spread their washed clothes on boulders or bushes in the sun. They cut their hair and shaved. Each brisk stroke of the razor took time to plan, seeming to hold the attention that a painter's palette-knife might receive.

It was an afternoon well spent, for a far different group of soldiers entered Troitskavask than left Sludyanka. And as Alex surveyed the faces lining the main road of this wild frontier town, he saw respect, as clean, strong-looking men rode in formation down the dirt road.

● ● ●

"Not Russians, Excellency," the headman of Troitskavask emphasized in answer to Alex's question. The southern extremities of Siberia were not civilized sufficiently to call this nervous man a mayor, and Alex saw his worried glances at the looming figure of Major Zotov striding across the road toward them.

The headman's features carried the distinct stamp of Mongolia: hooded eyes and a deeply tanned face with the look of leather. His hat was orange fur. Neither could he be called a commissar, so far was he from Moscow's influence. He was a simple herdsman, and there was little guile to his story.

"My people count three thousand soldiers. No Russians. They buy food and pack animals."

Alex was surprised. He hadn't imagined that German forces could be this far from the war back on the Volga. They must have been prisoners who negotiated some kind of agreement with the Bolsheviks. That makes more sense, he thought to himself. I can't imagine a Siberian blowing up his own tunnel.

"Going where?" Zotov growled, fully aware of the effect the giant Cossacks had upon this small community.

"To China. Yellow Sea," the headman offered matter-of-factly, pointing his arm due south. "My son guides soldiers to Urga." Then with casual conviction he added, "Four days," as he gestured with his hands that he was prepared to drop the subject.

Alex nodded his thanks, and strolled back with Zotov to the paddock where fretting horses milled around on the unfamiliar field. Lieutenant Pavel was waiting by the gate. "What do your patrols report?"

"Nothing, Brother," Pavel answered quickly. "Absolutely nothing."

"Well then," Alex shrugged, "there's no reason not to believe the headman. Why don't Major Zotov and I take ten fast riders to check their route? There's no need to commit the full company, if they are German prisoners running for China. What do you say, Comrade?"

"Agreed," came Zotov's laconic rumble.

"I shall wait for you here, then," Pavel said.

For the rest of the day Alex rode with the Cossacks at a pace for which he was ill prepared. On firm, level ground they would trot. Down hills they would canter. On long hills, riders would dismount and walk the horses. The terrain was numbing in its arid consistency, but in the distance he could see the mountains of Mongolia. Alex wondered how long he could keep up the pace, so when he spotted the dust cloud that marked the tail-end of the marching column he slid down from his lathered horse with a groan. He alternately massaged and squeezed his aching thighs while peering after the unswerving southward trail of the German prisoners of war.

Alex took out his binoculars and swept down the ranks until he came to the man in front. He focused in on their leader and smiled. It was Major Markus Adler . . . that stubborn bugger had somehow made it out of a Siberian POW camp.

Alex saw Markus stop. The German officer stepped off the trail to look back, undoubtedly to check the intentions of the Cossack platoon coming up on his left flank.

Alex watched with interest as Markus pulled out a single tube telescope to scan the hill occupied by Alex and his patrol.

It was a strange feeling . . . Alex could see Markus looking back at him — at least he thought that might be the case — so he lowered his binoculars, stood up in the saddle and waved.

He waited for a moment, then broke out into a grin as Markus waved back.

When Alex waved once more, Markus saluted, turned and trudged off in front of his men.

"Good luck, Major," Alex whispered. "You'll need some."

Zotov was puzzled. "What are you thinking?" he asked.

"I don't think we'll ever see those fellows again," he suggested.

Zotov shook his head eloquently. "They are warriors no longer."

Alex wanted to make sure though, and followed the retreating squadron to watch them clear the village of Muktui and continue on to the south.

"My men want cooked food, and women," Major Zotov announced without apology when Alex suggested that their patrol could now return to the collapsed tunnel at Sludyanka.

"I see . . . could they wait until we get back to Troitskavask?"

"Women are gone now," was the simple prediction.

"Well I'm sorry, but there are not enough of us to play it safe with a long stay. We have to get back to the tunnel."

Zotov looked so dejected that Alex felt obliged to bend a little. "Perhaps the men deserve a hot meal at least. Does curried lamb and rice sound all right?"

"Good man, Comrade," Zotov said, apparently happy with the face-saving compromise. "With raisins."

● ● ●

Katya sat with Mr. and Mrs. Ordinov in the dining car being served by a waiter in a white jacket. Another waiter turned the wheel which tilted the metal window shutters to the open position. It was a small luxury not enjoyed very often these days. Katya watched Ordinov. He did not look hungry, or even interested in lunch, she noticed. She took a mouthful and casually looked out the window. But what was that? A flash of light in the trees, and then she saw the mounted horsemen waiting in the shadows just before they charged the train.

The roar of gunfire shook the car as the Treasury guards opened fire on the mounted troop charging with swords drawn or pistols blazing. A bullet crashed through a window and a waiter ran forward to spin the wheel closed. Katya dropped to her knees and helped Mrs. Ordinov to the floor as the shooting continued. She could feel the vibration of the turning wheels as the train began to roll away from the charging Red Guard.

When the train was rolling steadily, Katya peeked out of the window. The horse soldiers were falling back. She could see a man with spectacles and a goatee shake his fist at the train as the dining car swung round a turn in the track. Katya put her hand over her heart and tried to calm her breath. "That was too close," she said.

● ● ●

To Alex, Muktui seemed to be just a small pastoral village, not large enough to be menacing even to his small patrol of a dozen men — especially when the patrol was obviously well trained and cohesive. Alex felt privileged to be with the Cossacks, and was continually amazed by the instantaneous recognition and respect this renowned regiment commanded, however far afield they ranged. It was a respect that each horseman seemed to expect as nature's mantle, so nonchalantly did he receive it. There was no bullying nor braggadocio, only a simple, confident acceptance of the homage which was their due.

Nevertheless, Alex insisted that Zotov limit the drinking. "No fighting. No incidents. Do I have your word?" he asked.

"Of course, Captain Branda," was the ready answer. "You are in command." The welcome words not only satisfied Alex's requirements, but also banished the corrosion of self-doubt from the darkest corners of his mind.

They took their mounts to a barn where three nervously grinning boys took charge. The Cossacks dismounted, watching critically as the youngsters led the horses into separate stalls. Dusty streaks of sunlight pierced the relaxing gloom through knotholes in the wall planks. Two horse soldiers were slow to follow their comrades, calling out unintelligible commands to the boys who nodded and waved with deference, being keenly aware of their place in the hierarchy of men — especially fighting men. Perhaps it was this ready acquiescence from the boys or the sight of fresh hay and water for their mounts which satisfied the Cossacks, Alex thought. More likely, however, it was the contentment of the ponies themselves that reduced their suspicion. The beasts settled down to feed immediately, quietly accepting the annoyance of boys removing harness and tolerating the abrasive scratch of a stiff-bristled brush.

Alex's patrol left their bedrolls with their mounts and then followed him to an ancient inn adjoining the barn. The ceiling beams were rough-hewn and nearly petrified, having been torn from life-giving soil centuries before. Each had been stained to the color of coal by the smoke from countless grease lamps and candles; the benches worn smooth by a thousand years of visiting caravans. And yet, despite its physical state, in the tradition of great hotels everywhere, this aged hostelry remained an oasis of rest and hospitality to strangers. Smells of spiced meat hung sweetly in the air, and when an oversized, black-iron kettle was swung above the glowing coals of a central fire, it began boiling almost immediately. Soon a metal plate heaped with curried rice and lamb was placed before each man. And soon after, each face took on that tranquil glow that accompanies contentment and warm drink.

The innkeeper hovered near Alex and Zotov, presumably having recognized earlier the source of payment for the food, and wishing to ensure that at least the leaders were well pleased. Alex imagined that the innkeeper was also hopeful of learning news of the outside world, which he, as host, would be expected to share with other guests.

"Good day, honored visitors. My name Ulan," he said to Zotov with a bow. "Where are you bound, Excellency?"

"Siberia," was the terse reply.

"And where are you come from?" he persisted, turning to Alex.

"Siberia," Alex responded with a wink to Zotov.

"I see," he said in a whimsical voice, disappointed that he was not drawing much information out of these two strangers. Suddenly brightening, perhaps with the prospect of trading knowledge, the innkeeper began anew.

"Other outlanders come here," he said in a conspiratorial tone. "Nobody understands them."

Alex exchanged a concerned glance with Zotov before he asked, "You mean three thousand foot soldiers from the north?"

"No, no," said their host emphatically. "Soldiers did not stop. They go to Urga. These are strangers. Slaves from far away. Nobody knows where."

"This is interesting news, Ulan," said Alex standing. "May we see them?"

"Yes, yes. Across the road in jail."

"Why in jail?" Alex asked as he followed the Mongol.

"So they don't run away," was the irrefutable answer. "They belong to Tsun. He owns them."

In the jail's office, Alex and Zotov were introduced to Tsun, a small man who looked like Buddha, Alex thought — except for the pistol jammed under the belt around his wide belly. Tsun stood up looking decidedly uncomfortable at the sight of uniforms, and he declined much conversation.

"We'll try to determine the language the prisoners speak," Alex offered as he was led through a heavy door into a dark and stinking hallway. From here he peered through narrow slits in a thick door set in stone and wrapped with three metal loops so that it resembled a flattened wooden barrel. On the floor lay two men asleep on some filthy straw. The third, a bearded man with hair the color of a chestnut, sat leaning back against the brick wall staring sullenly at the doorway. Alex could see that the prisoners were in bad shape, with a chain between wrist and ankle. None wore boots. Their feet looked swollen and sore. None was properly clothed, wearing only the dirty remnants of one-piece underwear.

He watched the prisoner by the wall closely for some clue as to his identity, but received only a glare in return. Alex swore quietly in Czech, not wishing to insult the Mongolians, saying to no one but himself, "Smells like a public urinal."

"Like an open sewer, you mean," an angry voice from inside the cell answered in the same language.

Alex was startled. "You're from Czechoslovakia?" he asked. "How did you get here?"

The man with chestnut hair pushed himself away from the wall and walked unsteadily to the door. The Mongolians stared in amazement. "My name is Victor Lindal, Colonel, United States Army. Some vicious son-of-a-bitch called Skipetrov held up our train from Harbin on the way to Chita. He sold the three of us like cattle."

Alex was embarrassed to see tears in the prisoner's reddened eyes. "How do you come to speak Czech?"

"Parents," he managed to blurt out, obviously in a very emotional state. "Can you help us?"

"Yes, of course," Alex said in a confident tone. "Just give me a few minutes."

He reached in through the barred window to shake the man's hand. Colonel Victor Lindal, the prisoner had said. Alex felt the desperation in the grip of two filthy hands and could see the panic in the swollen red eyes. "We'll be right back, don't worry," he said, trying to reassure the man before leaving the doleful hallway for fresher air in the outer office.

Alex had to get some air. He walked to the door which stood open to the street, coughed, spat, then took in some deep breaths before turning to Tsun, who watched him suspiciously, out of the sun, under a roof made from bamboo poles with bundles of straw laid on top. What the hell were American soldiers doing here? From Peking? Harbin? He saw that Tsun's stare wavered — fear, perhaps.

"Someone has tricked you, Tsun. This will cause big trouble."

Tsun merely shrugged, but Alex could see that he was paying attention. "Soldiers in a foreign army — friends will come," Alex said in a warning tone.

"Soldiers forgotten," the slave owner said with a shrug before turning back into the cramped office.

Alex stood outside the doorway in the clean air, struggling to think of a way to unsettle Tsun. The fact that these prisoners were Americans would likely have little effect, if any, but something Mongolians understood would have a better chance.

"They work for China," Alex said. "Do you want Chinese soldiers here?" He noted the apprehensive looks at this new suggestion and drove the point home with an offer: "How much are they worth? I could take them with me to Siberia . . . but they must have boots."

Tsun pulled at his long chin whiskers before asking, "What do you trade?"

"Repeating rifles."

Tsun got to his feet, watching Alex intently as he came outside under the bamboo roof. He stared again, then finally nodded his agreement.

"Good," Alex said, ignoring Zotov's concerned glances. Then he turned to the innkeeper. "Here's money for our meal," and emptied his pocket of coins, passing Ulan all but six. As the hotelier stood in the jail doorway counting the money with satisfaction, Alex began dropping the remaining coins into his upturned hand one by one. The metallic ring of the currency echoed in the hollow stillness of the stone-walled room. Alex wanted to make certain that he held every man's attention. He did not want anyone to think that he had money enough left to risk fighting for. "Will this pay for hot baths and three more meals?" he asked as the first piece dropped.

"Yes, generous, Excellency," Ulan said with a hungry smile.

"And will these buy three horses?" Alex asked, continuing to drop coins.

"Of course, Excellency, the best!"

"Done then. Get them washed and fed. I need a bottle for Tsun and myself, while we talk business. I have no more money," he said trying to decrease the reasons for ambush.

Alex noticed that the Mongol slave-owner stayed two of his men with a slight motion of his hand as Zotov went back down the evil-smelling hallway to release the Americans from their cell.

Tsun followed Alex across the road to the inn where they sat down to drink a sweet and powerful brew made from mare's milk.

By the time the three Americans had washed and shaved and been given bits and pieces of clothing by the Cossacks, Alex and Tsun were speaking with more volume and repetition than anyone else in the tavern.

"I will give one rifle for each man," Alex stated loudly.

"Three for each man," Tsun answered, his eyes mere slits and his jaw thrust forward defiantly.

"For these amazing rifles — one man, one gun," Alex said firmly, looking up as the Americans entered the room with Zotov. Two of the prisoners sat down at a long table that Zotov had indicated, but the colonel did not. Alex saw that he was looking at Tsun with glaring eyes full of hate. Good God! He's going to come over. Alex stood up quickly, speaking in Czech: "Sit down with your men, Colonel Lindal. Tell them to stay close to Major Zotov. He and his Cossacks can get you out of here if there are no incidents. Tell your men that I am negotiating your release, and that you should all behave. Please sit."

Alex watched the indecision on the American's face. Colonel Lindal may want a settlement with Tsun, but this was not the time. He could see that the colonel must have realized this too, because he adjusted his angry expression and sat down beside his men, glancing over toward Tsun periodically. And when a kitchen girl put heaping plates of lamb and rice in front of the Americans, they turned their attention at once to the meal, eating like wild men — much to the amusement of the Cossacks at their table.

Alex sat down again and the haggling continued while he watched the released prisoners washing their food down with green tea. When they had finished, he called loudly to Zotov in a drunken voice, "Bring me one of those amazing new rifles."

With Tsun and three of his men following, Alex strolled a wavering path down the street away from the barn. He gave a lengthy description of the attributes of the rifle, finally slapping a spring clip holding six shells into place.

His attention turned to a gathering of watchful ravens, and he suddenly began firing. One raven collapsed in an awkward heap on the ground while the rest labored aloft. Two more exploded in a shower of black feathers as they reached eye level. The fourth and fifth birds went down from a higher altitude in limp arcs carried forward by the momentum of their last few seconds of flight. The final shot scattered the survivors into soaring retreat.

"I'll give you three of these rifles," Alex said, suddenly dropping the pretence of intoxication now that they were ready to go. "One man — one rifle."

"Not enough," the Mongol protested, thrusting his chin toward Alex with a menacing scowl. "Nine guns."

"Three is my last offer," Alex said, stepping past Tsun and his companions. "One of you must accompany us to the border to receive them. You know I have no more money. We leave now."

Scowling fiercely, Tsun turned toward Alex with a curse, but stopped short when he saw the Cossack patrol drawn up behind him in three columns of four. The men were mounted, with their bedrolls lashed to the saddles and their rifles at the ready, with the three Americans in the center column. Tsun now looked uncertain.

Alex strode to the lead pony held by a boy from the barn and swung easily into the saddle.

"One of you may follow us to the frontier if you want your three rifles," he said, wheeling his horse in a turn before nudging it into a canter north toward Troitskavask.

When they had ridden the easy climb to the plateau he looked back on Muktui a kilometre or so away and signaled the patrol to a walk.

He watched as Zotov searched the trail behind them for followers. "Well done, Comrade," the Cossack said enthusiastically. "Five out of six ravens. Good for a Czech who wanted no drinking and no incidents."

Alex listened politely to the laughter from the Cossacks and waited with an innocent smile. "What ravens?" he asked. And the Cossacks laughed again.

As soon as it was dark, Alex stopped the patrol so that the weakened prisoners could rest. "All Americans are not cowboys," Zotov commented, watching the three Americans asleep in borrowed bedrolls. He sent two Cossacks back to see if they were being followed, and would not permit a fire to be lit until they reported to him.

"No one, Major," said a scout with a touch to his Astrakhan. So they were soon able to relax over dried beef and tea. It wasn't much, but it tasted all right to Alex. They might have done something useful today.

● ● ●

Victor woke with the sun in his face. He rubbed his shoulder and rolled over on the blanket, carefully stretching his back. In spite of the stiffness, he smiled. He was alive and free again — and by God it felt good. He got up and walked over to his two signal specialists who were already up and chewing on hard tack biscuits and bacon. They looked quite different in their borrowed Cossack clothes. He supposed he did too. Victor gave each man a gentle smack on the back trying to think of something clever to say, but he could see in their eyes their fragile state, so he left it alone. This was not a time for emotion. They were out, that's all that mattered, so he greedily accepted some of the rough, salty breakfast food, grinning around a mouthful at his two countrymen.

Victor looked up to see Captain Branda coming over. The young Czech was well built and energetic, moving like a sportsman. He had been a godsend of course, but Victor wondered now what kind of a man he really was. He appeared likely to be right at home in the locker room back at Stanford. Lefty would no doubt have deputized Victor to sign this fellow to play rugby.

"Good morning, gentlemen," Captain Branda said offering his hand. "Are you ready to ride?" Victor took the strong hand and shook it vigorously, but again he found that he had difficulty knowing what to say as he watched his men greet the Czech captain. They stumbled with their words of gratitude in English — which neither Branda nor any of the patrol seemed to understand, even though they nodded and smiled enthusiastically. Victor tried to translate their appreciation into Czech, but it seemed awkward. He swung stiffly up onto his saddle ready to move on.

He rode beside Captain Branda with his two fellow captives behind. "You got us out of a real bad situation back there, Captain. I don't know how we can ever repay you."

Branda smiled easily. "Please don't worry about it. And tell your men the same. We're all in a peculiar situation. Everyone will feel better when we're out."

The man seemed sincere but Victor pressed on. "What did they charge for us?"

"Far too much." Branda said this with a friendly smile, his dark eyes looking back down the long flat trail through the scrub brush, probably checking for followers and their telltale cloud of dust. "But don't worry. They haven't collected yet."

"We owe you, anyway," Victor said, remembering that he had no money, no equipment — nothing.

He would have to find something to even things up. Maybe when he contacted General Graves — who must be wondering where he was. "I'll find something."

"You don't have to," Captain Branda insisted. "You would have done the same for me. By the way, just how did you get into that predicament anyway?"

Victor felt suddenly uneasy. He did not have control of his emotions yet, and he had not instructed his intelligence colleagues on an explanation that would pass public scrutiny. It was not possible to disclose that they were, after all, on what would be considered by most to be a spy mission.

"Bandits," Victor replied quickly.

"I see," Branda said. "But where were you heading?"

Victor felt foolish. Of course Captain Branda wouldn't understand about his role as an intelligence officer for the War Department; nor should he try to explain. And what about his mission in Siberia? After all, he was, according to military law, a spy ducking in the back door of an allied country. How would he explain that?

"Peking," he said, and at once regretted the lie. He saw Branda glance down, dark eyebrows shielding his eyes from Victor's face. "Just a minute," Victor added quickly. "Give me a little time. I'll get back to you on this one. OK?"

The Czech gave a quiet nod while looking Victor square in the eye.

"Thanks," Victor replied quickly. "You see . . . our goose was cooked. And I guess Americans aren't so good at being in debt."

His two companions drifted back in the line, tired of the translated conversation, he supposed, leaving Victor alone with the Czech captain.

Branda glanced over. "I didn't want to seem nosy."

Victor watched Branda closely. The Czech seemed to be genuinely embarrassed, and so, to lighten the mood, Victor said, "Really. How can we repay you? Humor me."

He saw Branda hesitate. "It really isn't necessary, but there is a way — if you insist."

"Name it."

"You could teach me some English."

"Of course," Victor laughed easily. "When do you want to begin?"

"Now. It would pass the time. What does 'O.K.' mean?"

"Ha," Victor laughed again. "That's some beginning. But OK, here we go. It means 'all right.' It could come from the Scottish 'Och aye.' But I don't think so. I believe it comes from the Navajo word 'okeh.'"

"What is a Navajo?" Branda continued.

"Well, the Navajo is an Indian tribe living in the state of Arizona. Look here," he said, removing a ring from his left hand. It had a large piece of turquoise jade held firmly in a broad band of silver. "The Navajo make jewelry with this stone. I kept it in my mouth when those bastards back there stole everything else."

"It's lovely." Captain Branda reached for the ring. "What a wonderful color. It reminds me of someone's eyes," he said, then abruptly fell silent.

Victor raised an eyebrow quizzically but did not break into the Czech's reverie as he gazed into the blue stone.

There's a story here, Victor thought before continuing: "Where was I? Oh yeah, well, the Navajo, as you see, are quite artistic as well as great warriors. They dance. They sing. Fiercely independent. They are truly free spirits," he added thoughtfully, worried that he had confused Branda.

"Are they like the Cossacks then?"

"Why sure," Victor agreed. "That would be about right. Like Cossacks."

"So, I think I'd like them," Branda said with a satisfied smile, handing back the ring.

"No, Captain Branda, please," he protested. "It would mean a great deal to me if you'd keep the ring. I can get another."

Victor watched the captain search his face while he examined the ring. Branda put it on, smiled and then offered Victor another firm handshake. "Call me Alex," he said.

Victor felt better the rest of that day, even though riding was an unfamiliar strain. He found the Cossacks a puzzle. They kept to themselves. They've had a rough four years, he knew, and there was no way of knowing what they were thinking. It was enough that he was beginning to understand his new friend, Alex.

● ● ●

Just at dusk, Alex could see Lieutenant Pavel riding toward them four kilometres outside of Troitskavask.

"Brother Branda. Major Zotov," Pavel called swinging his horse around and falling in beside him. "Glad to see you. I was getting really worried."

Alex frowned. "We've been only four days. I told you we weren't going to engage the enemy. Why the bother?"

"It's not that. I don't know how much more degradation Troitskavask can take!" Pavel complained.

"What do you mean?" Zotov broke in, suddenly interested.

Pavel turned to Zotov explaining in a concerned tone. "It's been one depraved frolic since you left. Carousal every night. There's not a brothel in town that hasn't been in a mad revel 'round the clock."

"And what about my men?" Zotov persisted.

"Well, frankly, Major, I didn't want to bring that up, but the Cossacks have not been behaving well at all," Pavel said, with all the indignation a young man can muster. "They act like a raving bunch of debauched fornicators! I hope you'll discipline them. They wouldn't listen to me."

"I'll try," Zotov promised. He barked a guttural command to his men, who followed as he galloped away.

"You'd better stay with us, Lieutenant Pavel," Alex said. "Meet our American friends. I wouldn't want to be around when Major Zotov disciplines his men." Alex laughed. "Besides, we leave for tunnel thirty-nine in the morning. He'll need a little time."

● ● ●

The next morning, the company of five hundred horse soldiers turned their mounts toward the Trans-Siberian Railroad in the northwest. Alex had Victor ride beside him at the head of two long columns so they could practise English.

On the second day Victor asked, "What's all this noise about tunnel thirty-nine?"

Alex pointed in the distance to the low mountains of Lake Baikal. "The last obstacle to our mission," he began. "We have to transport sixty thousand troops to Vladivostok and then travel to France and the western front. But those Germans we saw — probably recruited by the Reds — blew up the last tunnel. Now we're stuck."

Victor did not answer. Perhaps he is searching for a diplomatic opening, Alex thought, so he waited.

"Look, Alex," the American said finally. "I didn't want to interfere until I knew you better, and yet, how long does one wait? You saved my life . . . ." Victor shrugged apologetically. "I'm afraid your plan is not going to be that simple. Haven't you heard? You Czechs have been ordered to return."

Alex felt a cold shiver run across his neck; his hair bristled. He looked back at Victor darkly. "You had better explain that," he demanded.

Before Victor could reply, Alex glanced at the horsemen behind, holding up his hand to restrain them. Then he cantered ahead with Victor. After fifty metres he reduced the pace to a walk once again. "What do you mean, return?" Alex asked intensely. "Return where, for God's sake? Under whose orders?"

He could see that Victor did not look comfortable. There were deep creases between his eyebrows, but he finally spoke. "I thought as a regimental commander you'd have been told. This information, I must point out, is . . . um . . . politically sensitive. For your use only. I'm sorry to be the one to tell you, but the Western Allied Command has said it's back to the Urals for the Czechs."

Alex was getting angry. "The Urals?" he repeated. "What the hell for? We just spent five bloody months fighting our way out of there! Vladivostok's within reach, if we can breach that goddamned tunnel."

"Easy. I had no idea Vladivostok symbolized so much for you."

At that statement Alex changed slightly, to sit erect once more. 'Symbolized,' he thought to himself. This American doesn't know what we've been through — but he's right. Vladivostok is just a symbol — a sort of grand solution to all our problems and fears. We concentrated on that goal to overcome the impossible . . . but all the way back? . . . God! I couldn't ask the boys. They've done their bit. Four bloody years, and we're still trying to get out of Russia. Now to go back! It's too much to ask.

He wrestled with the enormity of this new idea, trying to fight back his rage. I suppose I was always going back anyway, he admitted to himself. Katya's still back there . . . somewhere. He felt a little calmer with this thought, and so returned to business.

"Why go back?" he asked in a new tone which he could see allowed Victor to relax. But he noted that the American still seemed reluctant to confide the source of his information. Victor looked ahead toward Lake Baikal, shaking his head.

"OK," he began. "This is not general knowledge. So, for now, just between you and me, the Czechs are officially part of the French army. General Janin is working his way west toward Lake Baikal. He's got fresh troops, fresh supplies and even new blue uniforms for you. By the way, I think you're all ready for some new stuff."

Alex looked down at his worn clothing, stained with the record of four years of struggle. Victor continued: "The Allies want to get this god-awful war over with. They're calling it 'The war to end all wars.' France is a slaughterhouse. Russia's lost ten million men."

"And still fighting," Alex said.

"That's the problem. General Dieterichs has been waiting three months in Vladivostok now, living in tents outside the city. Then last month he notices the Bolsheviks sending trainloads of troops to prevent your trains from reaching the Pacific. He told them to stop. They agreed. But the general caught them up to their old tricks at night, so wham! He attacks. Takes over the port with the help of the Japanese navy, and the fat's in the fire."

"So the rules change," Alex replied.

"Yeah, well . . . ." Again Alex heard that pause. Where was Victor getting his information?

"General Graves and the American force are here to help the Czechs, and that's all. They have orders not to go beyond that. But there are huge supply depots at Murmansk and Archangel in the north, owned by the Western Allies. The British and Canadians are there now, with the USS *Olympia*. The Allies don't want to lose these supplies to the Reds . . . or to the Germans. They especially don't want almost four hundred thousand German and Austrian prisoners released on the western front. So . . . they want you Czechs back to the Urals, to contain these prisoners and then open an eastern front of your own. You're going to fight Germany from inside Russia."

"Vic, where did you hear this?"

Again Victor was guarded. "It's my job," was all he would say.

"Well, what if the Bolsheviks get in the way?" Alex asked with a knowing look. He watched Victor's face closely.

"I don't believe the monarchists of Europe would mind if Bolshevism was eliminated in the process," Victor replied cryptically.

"All right. Let's play along with your idea for a moment," Alex said. "Why not move in themselves? Why are we the hatchet men?"

"Hey, Alex, you know the answer to that," Victor said. "You've got unbelievable strategic position. You Czechs control the transportation and communications through most of the country. Besides, my friend," he said lowering his voice and laying a friendly hand on his shoulder, "it's much tidier when hired assassins do the dirty work."

Alex flinched. "Hired assassins?"

"Come on, Alex. You do what the Western Allies want, and Czechoslovakia gets what she needs. Quid pro quo. As old as politics."

Alex tightened his lips. "I just hoped we could get out clean, that's all."

"Well, Masaryk didn't like the deal, but he had to go for it. You all do. It's your future," Victor concluded simply.

Alex felt the rage begin again. There was a sour taste in his mouth. Victor sounded as if he knew what he was talking about. "How long has this policy been known?"

"Well, in political circles, about two months. The commanding officers were told by coded radio one month ago," Victor said matter-of-factly.

"Would Colonel Gaida have known last month about us returning to the Urals?"

"Certainly," Victor said, nodding solemnly.

Alex was unusually quiet as his Mongolian expedition arrived back at the blocked tunnel where their journey had begun. There was much to consider. The entrance to the railroad track, so vital in their connection with Vladivostok, was swarming with long lines of infantrymen laboring to clear away the rock from inside. They worked like ants at the base of a collapsed colony. In the nine days Alex and Zotov had been away, the Czechs had cleared the entrance archway from the ten-metre ceiling of the granite corridor to the rail-bed.

Colonel Lindal was immediately energized. Alex watched as Victor jumped down from his horse, and as quickly as numbed legs could carry him, hurried over to the opening to peer in.

"Who's in charge here?" he called in Czech, until one of the Bernaul Engineers came out to stare at this strange traveler dressed in bits and pieces of borrowed clothing. Alex noted that the engineer paid more attention when Victor came to the point without ceremony: "Vic Lindal, with American railroad experience. I think I can cut your work in half. Interested?"

The Czech engineer looked at the newcomer skeptically, but Alex gave him a nod and so he asked, "What did you have in mind?"

"Well, we get this situation quite often back home, with snow slides or spilled grain and stuff. What we used to do, if there was a hurry — are you in a hurry?" Victor paused long enough to receive assent from his now attentive engineer colleague. "What we'd do is simply lay new tracks on top of the debris. There's a bit of a grade for a short haul . . . but you can be rolling again on a temporary track in half the time."

The two men turned into the tunnel, absorbed with the challenge. The last thing Alex could hear was Victor pointing out, "Look, your ceiling's thirty feet high . . . the engine's under fifteen. Scrape the stuff out until she can just clear the ceiling . . . then you've got mobility. You can leave a crew here to pick away at it with all the time in the world, plus they can take ore cars right into the tunnel. What do you think?"

Satisfied that Victor could look after himself, Alex reined his horse toward Colonel Gaida's command car to report on his mission. He felt drained physically, but his mind was in a rage. "That bastard drove us relentlessly. He knew we didn't have to take those risks . . . "

As soon as he stepped into Gaida's headquarters car Gaida jumped up from his chair. "I told you to cut them down, but you let them get away — like a coward."

"Let's not get silly," said Alex coldly. "Germans wandering across the Gobi Desert won't bother anyone. And bringing back an American who'll have us through the tunnel in a matter of days, I should think you'd want to compliment us."

"Don't patronize me," said Gaida angrily. "I am your commanding officer."

"So I hear," interrupted Alex, an edge to his voice. "And how long have you known that our new destination was the Ural front?"

"Where did you hear that?" Gaida demanded, his flushed cheeks draining white.

"A Colonel Lindal, United States Department of War, just out of Harbin."

"Well, it doesn't matter really," Gaida said, now calmer but still trying to regain control. "I was going to tell you, of course," he continued smoothly. "Perhaps now is a good time to tell the men. You can attend to that tonight."

"No," Alex said. "That's your job. You tell them. You want the command; you take the responsibility. I've been used for the last time."

Gaida's face drew in so tightly it seemed to shrink. His eyes grew cold and distant. His voice was barely a whisper. "What do you mean by that?"

"I mean you drove us to the breaking point, all the time knowing we'd have to go back. You had us fighting people who could have been cajoled. I mean, you can go straight to hell!"

"As you wish, Captain Branda. So be it. I shall inform personally every man who must return, but only after we break through the tunnel and link up with General Dieterichs. Then and only then will I tell them. But today," he said contemptuously, "I'm telling you! You leave for Chelyabinsk tonight. There you can report to your precious friend Syrovy, whom the French have seen fit to make the Supreme Commander of the Czechs in Siberia," Gaida said with a snort. "He's half blind and half drunk, yet they chose him over me."

"Because men will follow him," Alex said, angry but still under control. "My God, your infatuation with power is unbelievable."

"Get out, you stupid ass," shouted Gaida. "Go back to the Urals! If you see me again you'll call me General, because I," he said jerking a thumb toward his chest, "I brought you all across Siberia."

"A shame," Alex said, turning to leave. "I had hoped to call you Brother."

Gaida stopped him with what seemed to be an afterthought. "Before you go," he said reaching into his desk drawer, "take this with you."

Alex thought Gaida's hand seemed to pause, hovering over a package of letters tied with string, but Gaida picked up only one letter off to the side of the package, and threw it onto the desk. "Masaryk sent this. Now get out!"

Still angry, Alex picked up the letter without much focus. He knew it wasn't from Katya because of the heavy lettering printed in pencil. An aching feeling overcame him. He could not understand why she had not written him.

With the letter in one hand, and feeling lower than he had ever been before, Alex led his horse to the livestock area. Dejectedly he patted the beast's neck in silent farewell. His depression sucked the energy from his chest, reducing his mind to a blur of pain.

He found his way to the officer's dormitory car where he sat strained and brooding on his bunk. They had been so close to opening the line to Vladivostok and a ship to freedom. *That Gaida is an idiot! I should have put him in his place a long time ago.* Alex put his face in his hands with a silent scream. *I'm trapped.*

Alex opened the letter with little interest at first, but froze when he realized it was from his father. Fighting to control himself, he unfolded the single page with trembling fingers.

My Dear Son Alex,

It is hard for me to realize that I shall never see you play football again. Or even see you at all. This is my only real regret. Your courage and determination were inspirational to your friends, and I must tell you before it is too late, you were an inspiration to me as well. That is how you led, by example. What I did — what you and your friends did — had to be done. I am content whatever the cost. Sometimes I worry that we won't have the determination to complete this work. It's a lot to ask. But then I remember what you and your friends have already accomplished, and I feel confident again. I was so proud of your work, and the medal. Very proud. It was even better than the University Cup. Freedom will be the best prize of all. And this is my wish for you. Never give up. I shan't.

They've taken our house. So my watch is all I have left to give you. It has a picture of your mother in it. You will find it at the office in the armory. Maybe one day, after this war is done, you will find a good lady. If you do, don't neglect her. Because if she is not part of your dreams, she will feel too much alone. I don't know how to say goodbye, but I hope you know that you mean everything to me. Farewell. Your Father.

Alex slumped onto the edge of the bed. His head drooped between sagging shoulders and he squeezed his eyes tightly shut to hold in the pain. Suddenly he sat upright realizing that tears were dropping onto the letter and staining his father's last words. He blotted the page with the sleeve of his tunic so that he could read it again later. For now he wanted to ponder his father's message. What was it: Determination and freedom? Yes, that was it. The goals were still the same — never give them up!

He walked over to the basin to pour water over half a towel. He sat down again on the bunk, rubbing away the tears. By the time he had dried his face he somehow felt a little stronger.

I meant everything to him . . . as he was everything to me. But now I'm alone; alone on Gaida's train; alone in Siberia. He sat up and threw the towel across the car. "Well, to hell with that," he said out loud, standing up. "And to hell with Gaida, too!"

Alex hurried to clean out his foot locker, stuffing his few possessions into a kit bag. Then he hiked down the track to the car they used as an armory. After signing out a new rifle, his next stop was three cars along to the supplies car for a new pair of winter boots. Preoccupied, he paid little attention to the growing number of Falcon troopers who began following him. There was Pavel, looking concerned as usual, and Jan and the others.

By the time he arrived at the supply-car storing the Kiev sheepskin coats, there was a crowd that could not be overlooked. Alex felt his confidence growing enough to allow himself a grin when he heard the flustered supplies-sergeant complain: "Is there authorization for this?"

"You'll get your paperwork in the morning," Pavel said soothingly.

"But why are you leaving?" the sergeant insisted.

Alex liked Pavel's simple answer: "He looks after us — we look after him."

By the time the night train pulled out of Sludyanka Station westbound for Omsk, two hundred and twenty men of the Falcon Regiment were on board with their winter coats. Alex felt a curious contentment. "I'm going with my friends to find Katya," he promised himself. "I won't be separated from her again. Gaida can rot in hell."

CHAPTER 24

LAKE BAIKAL TO OMSK
AUGUST 1918

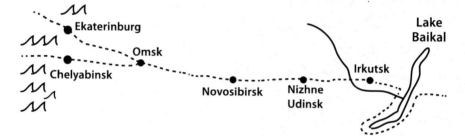

Alex sat up late looking through the window of an ordinary passenger car. There were no special modifications to accommodate the two hundred men of the Falcon Regiment, so three dimly lit cars were littered with sleeping men. The only glow, coming from a soft light in the vestibule, showed them lying across seats or sprawled on the floor. Equipment was stacked everywhere.

Because he was grieving for his father, Alex supposed that the Falcons had left him two seats facing each other at the end of the car by the door. With everyone else asleep or dozing, he stretched his legs across the facing seat and watched the moon over Lake Baikal gliding beside him on the right. The silver water disappeared suddenly as the train was swallowed by one of the tunnels lining its shore — a tunnel he had hiked through a fortnight ago, sobered by the thought that he might be buried alive or ambushed. Now he was just a passenger to Omsk. It would be good to see General Syrovy again. The Falcons would serve with him, as they went back to bloody war . . . .

His thoughts were as dark as the tunnel and unusually dark for him. How can I find Katya? What if something's happened to her? He brooded, wondering where she might be . . . Suddenly he was jerked back to wakefulness by someone opening the vestibule door and sitting down across from him.

"Vic!" Alex said, coming out of his fog but quickly lowering his voice to a whisper. "What are you doing here? I'd forgotten all about you," he confessed happily.

"You forgot about everything," Victor said, looking concerned. "You haven't even been to the dining car. What's going on?"

"Not much," Alex said. "You seemed pretty occupied with the tunnel. I was in danger of losing my temper back there and doing something crazy. Gaida banished me to Chelyabinsk."

"He's quite a guy, from what I've seen of him. Those little men are all the same, like the bandit Skipetrov. One day I'll take some time-out and find that son-of-a-bitch." He said this more to himself than to Alex. "But first, I've got to get to Omsk, and if I have to travel twenty-five hundred miles . . . I thought I'd ride it with you."

"Good idea. I'll need some company. They tell me it'll take five or six days even with this small a train. What's your assignment?"

"Omsk. That's where Allied headquarters in Russia is located. I'm representing the United States until some big brass comes . . . if they come."

"What do you mean if?"

"I told you before, old buddy . . . I think there's a lot of people just a little embarrassed about being here. So until things start looking successful, they might not make an appearance at all. Graves flat out refuses to interfere. Says the Americans are here to get the Czechs out safely — period. President Wilson committed to that, and Graves is determined to live up to his word."

Alex paused. "These aren't just rumors you're giving me, are they?"

Victor appeared to be wrestling with a decision. "No they're not," he said finally. "No rumors. Straight goods. But just for your use, ok?"

Alex looked at Victor for a moment, then nodded slowly before continuing. "So for now, the Czechs will join the Whites in their civil war, and the Western Allies will watch how it goes. Correct?"

"You got it. Do your men have any idea of where they're headed?" Victor asked.

Alex chewed his lower lip. "No, not yet. I was the only one ordered away."

In the half-light he saw Victor staring at him with what seemed to be a tender look. "If you didn't tell them to come," Victor said, "then they came on their own. Very nice. Lieutenant Pavel made up the train — I know that because he made room for me — but I don't think Gaida knows the Falcons are gone. That guy is a loose cannon. Hope he doesn't make any trouble."

"I'd like to think not," Alex said. "Technically, they came with me from General Syrovy anyway. We're simply going back . . . but I'll watch it, thanks."

The next six days passed as a leisurely parade for Alex and Victor. Alex pointed out scenes from the recent Czech odyssey across Siberia: the demolished Baikal Station; the railroad bridge outside Irkutsk; the bloody field at Seberta where Zotov had led the Cossack charge; and Novosibirsk where Gaida showed first signs of his hunger for power. There were peculiar sensations for Alex when he came to these sites. He was enthused at showing them to an interested friend, but disturbed by the fact that the events were no longer in the historical past — instead they loomed on the horizon for his future. Would they have to go through this all over again? Or were they expected to march to Moscow and throw Lenin out with the German army. He was grateful for the English lessons which distracted him from the unfinished task of getting out of Russia and getting home.

Regarding their new assignment, Alex briefed his men as much as he could before speaking to Syrovy in Chelyabinsk, as the field commander for the Ural region. His men were not happy, but they knew Syrovy and trusted him. Alex could tell by the easy way they spoke their mind that they trusted him, too. And this only heightened his resolve to keep them out of politics and get them out of the country. At last the train pulled into Omsk.

While the train re-fueled and took on water, Alex took the American colonel to headquarters with a first stop at Supplies. Alex was not only reluctant to part company, but was also suddenly aware that Victor was far from his own unit, in a war zone and still without proper uniform or identification.

"I can look after identity cards later," Victor said. "Right now I need a clean uniform that fits."

"Brother," Alex called to the supply-sergeant, "can you do me a favor? Kindly dress Colonel Lindal here, properly. If necessary, give him a Czech uniform. He's a good friend and half Czech anyway."

"No trouble at all, sir."

Alex noted, with a little surprise, how willingly and quickly the sergeant hurried to the task. Interesting, he thought to himself, no trouble at all. "You know," he said, "I'd forgotten your proper rank, meeting you first in your long underwear. A new uniform will set things right again, Colonel Lindal."

"Hey, to you I'm Vic," said the man still dressed in his collection of Cossack hand-me-downs. "I hope it'll never be formal between us . . . we had an auspicious beginning."

"Of course," Alex said, taking the offered hand. "Goodbye, good friend. Stay well."

"No, no. In America we say: so long."

"And what does that mean?"

"So long means we'll meet again soon."

"Right then," Alex said with a smile and a Slavic embrace. "So long, Vic."

● ● ●

The Treasury staff in the lounge car rocked to the sway of their train as it sped south on the northern line toward Kazan. It was a quiet atmosphere, as most were reading. They could not see out on this dark night because the metal window shutters were closed permanently after the last attempt to capture them outside of Ekaterinburg.

Without warning, the train squealed to a grinding stop. Katya grabbed for a handhold too late to help Mrs. Ordinov, who fell with a cry of fear.

The cars shuddered and lurched as if the tracks had come to an end. Her mind raced. What was the matter? They were somewhere near Kazan to pick up their mail.

Outside in the dark, she could see burning torches. People in the marshalling yard held them high in the air yelling and cheering. Katya could not make sense of the words, but there was anger in their shouts and triumph in their wild eyes. Shadow and light danced across the excited faces as flames blew in the wind. When the cars stopped shaking, several Treasury staff members burst into the conference car uncertain as to what was happening.

From down the corridor she could hear voices bawling terse orders. The door, usually locked, must now be open because the harsh voices and footsteps approached from the neighboring car. When the president of Russia's National Treasury stepped inside, it was with eyes cast down to the floor. Right behind Ordinov came a stern-looking soldier, a blood red star centered on his cap.

While Ordinov seated himself, the soldier looked around the room warily, trying to estimate the potential for resistance. Apparently finding none among their frightened faces, he said in a contemptuous tone: "This train has been seized as the property of the Moscow Soviet. You are all under the direction of Comrade

Leon Trotsky, President of the Supreme War Council for the Soviet Socialist Republic."

Trotsky entered the room with a triumphant look. "Which one of you is Ordinov?"

Ordinov stood up slowly. Trotsky looked him up and down, then lashed out with the back of his hand. "Traitor!"

Ordinov fell back into his chair and Katya rushed over to hold him protectively.

"This man is no traitor," she cried. "He loves Russia!"

"He loves the past, and that is his blasphemy."

Katya sagged to the chair behind her. All the secrecy and hiding — and the fear — all over now. They had lost the Treasury. Dejectedly she looked out to the Ural Mountains, their hiding place for so long. This was the end. She should have considered more seriously Rad Gaida's promise to rescue her, but she had had faith that they could continue to hide in the mountains waiting for . . . waiting for what? The end to the war? That would have helped. She could have made it to Prague, to wait for Alex. She could have found a job in a bank perhaps. Going to the Charles Bridge every day to wait for Alex. How long would she wait: A month? A year? Forever?

She felt ill, and covered her face with one hand. Why had she heard nothing from Alex? Nothing! All those letters she had sent to the Czech train. Gaida never mentioned him once. Alex must be dead. And now the Bolsheviks had denounced the Treasury staff as traitors. This could be the end.

Katya was startled by the sound of gunfire. It was all around them. The Kazan commissar cursed and ran from the conference room with Trotsky.

"Everyone stay down," Ordinov called. "Lock the doors!"

* * *

At Chelyabinsk Alex left his passenger train at the platform and went searching for Syrovy's troop train. The general's railcar was pointed out to him on a nearby siding. Alex entered with some apprehension, wondering what his reception would be.

"General Syrovy," he said saluting. "I am reporting as directed."

"Alex, good to see you," Syrovy called out loudly, getting out of his chair to bear-hug Alex, casting away any doubts about welcome.

"You're just in time. Sit down, young man. Tell me all about Siberia . . . I leave for the Volga in ten minutes."

"It's big," said Alex smiling now. "But getting crowded."

"How many men with you?" asked Syrovy, watching as intently as a man with only one eye could. "Gaida was prattling on about you leaving with some of the Falcon Guards."

Alex shrugged. "Four officers including myself, and two hundred and eighteen troopers. Full complement, two hundred and twenty-two."

"Impressive," nodded Syrovy quietly. "Why'd they come with you?"

"I've no idea, General. Didn't ask."

"Do you have anything to tell me about Colonel Gaida?" he asked.

"No, sir. Nothing to report."

Alex watched Syrovy. The colonel glanced his way and then fingered some paper on the desk as if waiting for more. Syrovy glanced up again. "Nothing?"

"Nothing," Alex repeated.

Syrovy became animated once more. "Excellent," enthused the rejuvenated commander. "You might make it yet . . . and you can't know how timely your arrival is. Come over here."

Syrovy walked to a wall map to trace with his finger the Volga River from the Caspian Sea in the south to Lake Rybinsk north of Moscow. "This is what we want," he said with feeling. "The east bank of the Volga. We meet up with General Deniken's White army from the Caspian area and the Don Cossacks in the south Urals. Then we advance west in a coordinated sweep."

"So," Alex said, "we're stepping into a civil war? And we're siding with the Whites — right out in the open."

"That's it," said Syrovy. "Just soldiers for hire. We're all of us whores, you understand. The politicians issue orders, and we perform. Now, I want you to move your regiment of, shall we say, volunteers?" he said with a smile, "north along the Ekaterinburg line to Kazan. We've had the Bolsheviks surrounded now for two days. I can't quite understand why they're so stubborn. They won't relinquish the town, or move across the Volga. They're taking considerable casualties. Uncharacteristic of this bunch," he said with a puzzled look.

"What would you like me to do?" Alex asked.

"Get up there fast as you can," Syrovy said as he scribbled a note. "Find the problem. Punch through it. You're on your own now, m'lad.

See you on the Volga." He picked up his cap and case, handed Alex the note and left.

The note was short and direct: "Issue Captain Branda any materiel required. By order: Chief of Staff." It was signed in a bold scrawl, "General Jan Syrovy."

With this permit, Alex had an engine stocked for the long haul north to Ekaterinburg. From there, the track would turn due west to Kazan, a journey of one thousand kilometres. His ten-car train was loaded hurriedly with food stores and fighting equipment, so that by late morning they were away in high spirits.

It was after midnight the next day when they arrived at the outskirts of Kazan, and Alex led two hundred and twenty fresh men down the track to a log barricade blocking the rail line to Kazan Station.

"Good morning, Lieutenant Stefan," Alex said as he came up to an officer peering intently into the gloom of Kazan's railyard. "Remember me?"

"Alex!" was the startled response from a drawn and weary face. "Do I remember the friend who saved me from that bastard Schumann? Could I ever forget? Of course not," Stefan said, hugging his old schoolmate, slapping his back with both hands. "How many with you?"

"More than two hundred. Syrovy thought you could use some fresh legs. What's the situation?" Alex looked down on the besieged railyard. There were few lights, but with the muzzle flashes from periodic gunfire, the field of combat was discernible to the trained eye. The Czechs controlled three sides of the marshalling yard. The Reds were scattered over the north side dodging behind freight cars and protected by troops well positioned in the trees between the railyard and Kazan.

"We've had them holed up for going on three days now," said the perplexed lieutenant, "but there's no let-up. I can't understand why they fight on."

"How were you able to pin them down?"

"Caught 'em by surprise. With a bit of luck we came at them from the south unexpectedly. Hiked all the way up the east bank of the Volga, from Syzran."

Alex looked impressed. "Not a bad hike, two hundred kilometres. What happened?"

"Well, confusion at first. Then rage. Wild energy and something new — this incredible determination. They didn't melt away like before. We couldn't budge 'em."

"So what are they trying to do?" Alex persisted.

"That's the confusing part. At first I thought they were trying to escape in that train," Stefan said, pointing to the back end of a darkened line of twenty cars. "But once they realized we'd blocked the track east and west, I can't imagine why they didn't break out on foot to the north. Now we've got them in a stalemate, but they keep that train ready to roll."

"Who's your commander?" Alex asked, suddenly energized.

"Peter Kechek. He has headquarters on the west edge of town."

"Well then, Brother Stefan, we'll make our way round and speak to Peter — and perhaps overcome this impasse."

Stefan sent a scout to show the way, and soon Alex was slapping a grinning Kechek on the shoulder. "Petya," Alex said with some exuberance as he entered a dreadful little hut. "What a fine office you have, and you don't look at all tired."

"I don't?" Peter asked, sagging back into his chair. "I'm glad to hear that; I was beginning to feel sorry for myself." His red-rimmed eyes blinked in the dim light.

"Why not relax? I'll try to crack the problem for you with some rested Falcons."

"And just how do you think you'll do that? The Reds have sharpshooters under the train lying between the wheels — no doubt in their own excrement — two and a half days now. Can't chase them out. Don't know how much water they have left. They must be in desperate condition."

"Well, if they're half as rundown as your bunch, we could get lucky. In Siberia we found that trains have their blind spot right under the head lamp. Besides, we've become very stealthy in our old age," he said with a grin.

"All right, let's see some of this new panache, but don't force it. We can always starve them out," Peter said.

While troops harried the defenders from both sides of the train, Alex led two lightly equipped men crawling two hundred metres down the cross-ties toward the darkened engine. They had left their caps behind and had blackened their faces, appearing only as murky shadows barely visible above the height of the rails. Undetected, they came to the front of the locomotive and soundlessly climbed its face.

They crept over the roof and sides searching for a doorway, but all were sealed. A glimmer of light gave away a single steel vent that opened into the cab. Alex pushed it open the width of his fist and looked down on two frightened faces. "Unlatch your door, comrade," he said in a low, clear voice.

The two train-men looked at each other apprehensively, but when Alex shoved a grenade into the vent with the admonition, "Now!" one of them unloosed the door and Alex swung down onto the main deck and hurried inside.

"Can anyone drive this thing?" Alex asked as an afterthought. Then, pointing his pistol at the perspiring face of the engineer, he said, "Slowly down the track, six hundred metres and then stop."

The driving wheels shuddered into action, and following a few skidding motions, the heavy train rolled toward the Czech barrier on the river side of Kazan. As the train pulled away from the gun emplacements under the carriages, Stefan's troops at the rear of the train opened fire. The Bolsheviks scrambled out from under the wheels, dodging across the marshalling yard over side tracks in a dash for the shelter of parked freight cars. Some ran in the shadow of the moving cars only to be met head-on by a devastating barrage from the advancing Falcons. Survivors had only one chance; they clambered over the couplings between cars in a frantic race for the trees where the fire-cover from their comrades gave them protection.

Alex dropped down from the engine, running across tracks and through the darkened railyard. "After them!" he called, while the Falcons gave chase. Alex jumped between two cars. He could see that the Reds were now abandoning their positions on the edge of the yard as the Falcons bore down on them, running hard and firing on the move. They ducked under freight cars, flushing out the Bolshevik troops. Alex could hear his men calling out to one another as they cleared the yard of opposition.

The Red Guard had one escape route — retreat north toward the center of Kazan. Alex urged the Falcons on, relentlessly forcing the Reds from every refuge. Like a cohesive team they jogged down the paved streets of Kazan staying close to the brick walls of buildings, checking each dark entrance and alleyway. They harassed Trotsky's Red Guard through every step of a long running retreat until they were driven across the bridge at the Volga, and Kazan belonged to the Czechs.

Alex and his men returned to inspect the abandoned train, standing where they had left it. The locomotive was not the traditional black, but a dark forest green, as were the cars themselves. In fact, this was a train unlike any Alex had ever seen. Each car seemed streamlined because the sides were slightly rounded, and curved steel doors conformed to a tight fit with the body of the car. There were no stairs or handrails. The vestibule at the end of each coach was covered with a flexible blind. Some cars had windows, but these were all closed and shuttered so that there was no easy entrance. Alex went to the side of one of the few cars boasting windows, then rapped insistently on the metal shutters with the muzzle of his rifle.

"I am Captain Branda of the Czecho-Slovak Rifle Corps!" he called loudly, giving their old name — not knowing who was inside. "Open up or we'll blast the door in." He turned to his men with a shrug while they waited.

Eventually, from inside, came the metallic sound of a bolt being drawn. Stairs folded down from under the blind, and a door opened.

"Please come in, Captain," said a gentleman with a cultured voice and the accent of an aristocrat. "My name is Ordinov. I am president of the Imperial Treasury."

Ordinov did not say more as Alex climbed the four steep metal stairs into the vestibule. When Ordinov held open the door to the conference car, Alex stopped short, staring dumbly into the room filled with staff but seeing only one person. There stood Katya.

Alex slowly removed his cap, his dark eyes widening under thick black brows. He stood frozen to the spot. He heard Ordinov close the door behind them and say, "I believe you know Miss Kazakova."

"Hello, Alexander," Katya said quietly, offering her hand.

In a trance, Alex kissed the fingers, sensing a slight tremble. "Katya," he whispered. "What a delightful end to a hideous summer." He wondered now whose hand was shaking as he held her in a gentle embrace. Only when the onlookers began to applaud did he realize that several more people were in the room, and he suddenly remembered his unshaven face and the jacket stained with tar and sweat. Soil had been ground into the knees of his pants from his long crawl, but really, none of this seemed to matter. They were all smiles.

He heard Katya ask, "Mr. Ordinov, I wonder if you and I could speak with our Czech friend alone, so that we can determine the details of our situation?"

"Splendid idea, Miss Kazakova. Would the rest of you mind retiring to the lounge car? We'll meet shortly."

Alex noticed that he still held her hand, and she his. He broke the silence to say simply, "I missed you."

She threw her arms around his neck and squeezed hard. She did not speak, so he held her tightly until he heard the door close. A gentle cough preceded an invitation to sit down. They both complied, but continued to gaze at each other.

Apparently concluding that his companions were not yet ready for business, Ordinov busied himself getting tea and biscuits, but so unaccustomed was he at performing this chore that the noise of cupboards and the rattling of china finally woke Katya from her spell and she rose to assist him.

"Captain," began Ordinov solemnly, "we are so very relieved to see friends of the Czar. I came to believe our situation quite hopeless."

"Sir, we're not . . . well, you're welcome to any assistance we can give you. But I'm not certain how we can give further help. What are you doing here?"

"Oh dear," said Ordinov. "I assumed you knew." He sat down, looking hesitant about continuing.

It was Alex who spoke first, after finally focusing his attention. "Good God," he began, as the situation became clear to him. "Katya here . . . the special cars . . . impregnable. This is the Treasury?"

Ordinov answered. "Quite right, Captain. This train is a wandering vault." Ordinov hesitated again, and then, as if making a critical decision, began once more. "We carry more than 500 million rubles in gold, silver and platinum." He paused as if to let that information sink in before adding: "There is that much again in jewels and coin; wealth beyond imagination."

Alex considered these circumstances for a few moments before answering, "Well this certainly changes the military viewpoint. What do you see happening?"

"I must confess," Ordinov admitted, "I am not certain any more. This train is the foundation of Russia's economy. It is the sole source of tangible capital for any international business transaction. It must be kept safe. But to whom do I turn it over? Are there any of the Czar's heirs remaining?

Katya became excited. "Marie. Grand Duchess Marie. She's in Romania. Is she the last?"

"As far as we know," Alex said. "We've been isolated, but the Bolsheviks tried to make certain of no return to the old structure. That possibility died at the bottom of a mine in Alapayevsk, and in a cellar in Ekaterinburg."

"Except for Marie," Katya said.

"Do I surrender the Treasury to a gang of revolutionaries?" Ordinov asked.

"You may have no choice."

"Right now I do have the choice, you see. But to what authority do I surrender the bullion?"

"Are you referring to the Whites?" Alex asked. "Who are they? Where are they? Where's their center? You'll have to wait 'til they battle it out."

"Kerensky and the Duma?" Katya suggested.

"Again, it's a waiting game," Alex said. "The Reds or the Whites? Now we're all caught up in civil war which itself is in the middle of an international war. Not an enviable position. You could turn the train over to the Allies, or England."

"Foreign powers?" Ordinov blurted out. "I can just see Great Britain, sizing up Russia as one more colony. No!"

The three of them sat without speaking for a while, until Alex suggested, "The civil war could be decided sooner than we think. A new front will be launched along the Volga and . . . it's official now, the Western Allies back the White forces. You might simply want to bide your time." He watched Ordinov. The men must be under tremendous pressure. They all must be worn thin. "Yes," agreed Ordinov with a sigh. "That appears to be all we can do." He fell silent again.

"Alex," Katya said. "President Ordinov mentioned earlier that the identity of this train must remain secret."

"Good Heavens, yes," Ordinov said, breaking in. "Thank you, Miss Kazakova. Can you imagine what could happen if word gets out? It must be kept secret. It simply must be kept secret!"

Alex sighed. He pushed himself up, becoming now acutely aware of his rough condition in such elegant surroundings. He tried self-consciously to straighten out his jacket; not much he could do about the need for a wash. "Keeping the train's secret will be difficult . . . not impossible, just difficult. People on the Bolshevik side of the river know for sure, so they'll come back in full force. Others in Kazan surely know."

"Then we must move this train, Alex," said Katya forcefully. "Another day like the last three would mean disaster."

"Right," Alex said, turning to Ordinov. "Any suggestions, Mr. Ordinov?"

Ordinov just shook his head wearily, so Katya spoke up. "Back into the Urals. Nylga, perhaps. It seemed safe there," she recalled. Ordinov shrugged, nodding.

"I'll see what can be done," Alex said. Then he held Katya by the elbow. "I'll be back in one hour. I promise. Don't disappear on me again. Wait for me."

Alex left guards on each side of the tracks and then hurried directly to Peter's hut.

● ● ●

"Petya, we have to talk. Got a minute?"

"Of course. Here, have some bread and cheese."

"Thanks. I need a bite. Anything to drink?" Alex said, leaning his elbows on the table and cradling his head in his hands.

Peter poured tea into two tin mugs, then laced the brew with vodka as he watched Alex. "We've come a long way from the schoolyard," he observed. "I guess I was your shadow."

Alex took a long sip of the steaming tea, looking up briefly. "You were always your own man."

"Not really. I learned a lot from you and your father," Peter said, lowering his voice. "I hear he's gone."

Alex took another swallow from the mug and bit into the sharp cheese. Without looking at his friend, he nodded, then drank again.

"I also hear you wrung Schumann's neck . . . like a chicken."

Alex stared into the bottom of his cup. "I executed a murderer," he said, tossing back the rest of the drink. As the warmth from the cup spread through his body, he began to think of his father but stopped himself, saying, "Time to start a new life."

Peter seemed mildly surprised. "I have," he said. "And I like it."

This statement seemed to revive Alex. He looked at his long-time friend who was now a full colonel, and realized just how well-suited to the military Peter was. "I'm glad. You do it well. I see you've cut your hair."

"And you've let yours grow," Peter observed.

Alex stood up and paced the length of the dingy hut. The dirt floor was littered with debris. "Petya, we've hit something big — very big. It's got to stay between the two of us until we can get hold of Syrovy." He went to the window to peer through the cracked glass. There was no one to overhear. "You should talk to him face to face, not over the telegraph. This must be kept quiet."

Peter became wary. "Who was on that train, Alex?"

"It isn't who . . . exactly," he hedged. "It's what." He lowered his voice. "That train just happens to be carrying the gold bullion reserves of Russia. All two hundred and thirty tonnes, and that's only part of it," he added slowly, watching a quizzical frown form on Peter's face. "This is between the two of us."

"And you captured it with two men?" Peter gave a soft whistle.

"I'm glad you brought that up. Didn't want to be presumptuous, but I want command of that train. There's a special passenger on board . . . one of the accountants . . . anyway, I want command of the train." Alex could see his friend's searching look, weighing all the possibilities.

"Knowing you as I do," Peter began, "it would be useless to argue, but does it have anything to do with the lady with the blond hair? From the Winter Palace?"

"With eyes this blue," Alex said, holding up his Navajo ring.

Peter smiled cautiously. "Well, that's great, my dear friend, . . . but there's a problem. A soldier can't go around looking after civilians. You know that."

Alex was surprised. When did Peter start sounding like a government official? "He can if he's on special assignment to escort a very special train. A train that could bring this war to an end."

Frowning, Peter began shaking his head from side to side. It was as if it was part of the thinking process.

"But I will have to turn the train over to Deniken, the White commander-in-chief. This isn't just some football caper. I have form to follow."

Alex stopped in disbelief. "The hell you do! Deniken's just a soldier like us. And there are no rules — you know that too. If there were, we broke every one of them with the first man killed . . . ." He looked hard at his friend. "What do you say, Field Commander? Let me pull out of here. Every Bolshevik from here to the Gulf of Finland will be after that bullion soon. It's their last hope."

He watched Peter think the proposal through. He could imagine the line of thought. Power for the Whites. Wealth that could bring back the old days. "You always lived by rules," Peter said at last.

"Then I discovered I was the only one who did! Syrovy told us it was all horseshit. You were there. So what's so important? They'd only make you a damned general."

Peter did not respond, and Alex studied his friend in the eerie silence. For the first time in his life Alex felt doubt about his childhood friend. Had Peter changed that much? Has he forgotten what we've been through? Maybe he doesn't understand how much I want to be with Katya. Or is he thinking about fame — so close at hand?

At last Peter spoke. He cleared his throat to say, "All right, you're in charge. But only until Syrovy hears about it. Just remember, this train could be the bargaining chip for all of us, not just Katya."

Alex pulled in a long breath, blowing it out slowly to let his tension escape. He walked slowly over to his friend and laid a tired hand on Peter's shoulder.

Alex had left orders at the round-house to turn the sleek locomotive toward the east and to attach the Falcon's train to the treasury cars; five in front and five behind. An infirmary car was added for Falcon casualties who did not require hospitalization.

Within the hour, Alex shook hands with Peter. "Thank you, old friend. Thank you. If we never meet again . . . I'll remember you for the chance you're giving us." He felt a surge of deep emotion, but held himself back, not knowing if he was just tired, or happy about being with Katya again. His clothes were filthy and his face still blackened from the night before, but he would be able to wash up and rest once the train pulled away. Peter, however, would soon have to face the wrath of the Red Army.

When Alex was ready to climb aboard, Peter waved ahead to the engineer to take the special train into hiding deep within the Ural Mountains. There was a frown on Peter's face and he grumbled, "I have a nagging feeling that the train was a great opportunity for me."

Alex shrugged, giving Peter a clap on the back and a kiss on the cheek. "Never mind, Petya. What's more important, really? Praise from strangers or the gratitude of a friend?"

CHAPTER 25

NYLGA
AUGUST 1918

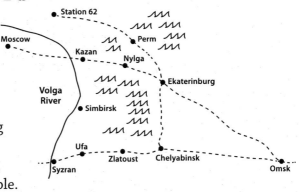

For two days the Treasury train climbed into the mountains. And yet, despite the increasing distance from the Bolshevik Red Guard, Alex still felt vulnerable. The Treasury had to be secured. He made certain that horse patrols were out in advance of the train for the entire two hundred kilometres from Kazan. In truth, he rode most of the patrols himself, despite the fact that he wanted to spend time with Katya. There was a lot he wanted to say, but duty had to be served.

Alex was on patrol when they reached the isolated hamlet of Nylga deep in the Urals. From a steep ridge on a mountain high above the railroad tracks, he looked down on the settlement with its tidy-looking homes neatly tucked between looming peaks. Sheer granite cliffs pressed in on the railroad which had been squeezed between rock faces. This difficult construction made the village quite isolated and in a location virtually out of sight of the tracks.

On the other side of the steep valley, a spur ran parallel to the main line until it disappeared into a forest around the side of the mountain, and he watched the Treasury train pull in there — a perfect hiding place. Surely there was little rail traffic in this part of the world. There wasn't room enough in the cleft of this mountain for a platform, or even a station-house. So perhaps there was little need for worry.

Feeling comfortable about their position, although drained physically, Alex turned his horse down the trail toward the spur until he came to Katya's car.

"Alexander," Katya said, "you must rest. You look terrible."

"I fight my way across Siberia to rescue you, and get criticized for a little roughness around the edges?" He said this with a weak grin, looking up the track from their siding toward the village which was out of sight. "Are you confident about Nylga?"

"Yes, I'm sure," she said. "We've been here before. The townspeople respect privacy. The spur is isolated, and joins the main line down there about one kilometre," she said pointing to the southeast. "You can relax now."

"Well, I might just do that." He stretched, trying to ease the tension in his back and neck. "First I have to set up the sentry formations to watch the entrance and exit to this spur. I can see you later, I hope."

She stopped him, holding his sleeve. "Put Pavel in charge. Get some rest. See that sports lodge up there?" She pointed to a trail winding easily up the mountain nearest the train. "Village hunters use it in winter. Meet me there in an hour and I'll make lunch. I'd like that," she said as if explaining something to herself. "I'll put a hamper together."

Some time later, Alex followed the mountain path, allowing his pony to plod steadily up the slow grade. He felt numb, lifeless, but the farther from the train he rode the freer he felt. It was not long before his mount turned off the trail to stop at a stone and timber alpine retreat. Dismounting, he swung open the door to a diminutive barn. There was a soft whinny of recognition from the mare inside. Alex led his horse into a neighboring stall and then stroked its velvet muzzle. The tissue was pliant and soft between the two flared nostrils from which warm air was gently snorted across his hand. He paused, too tired to continue, choosing to reflect on the smell of straw and hay within the snug atmosphere, noting how comfortable the horses seemed to be. For himself, he felt unwilling to move.

Making his way across the enclosure, he knocked on the door to a pine wood chalet. "There's no need to knock here, my friend," rang out a cheerful voice as Katya came to the door. "This is your home in Russia," she added. He could see the concern on her face as the door opened.

Alex looked up with a wan smile. "My dear Katya. St. Petersburg . . . when I first saw you . . . almost four years ago," and he slumped on a row of firewood stacked on the enclosed porch. "I've missed you."

"Alexander," Katya asked nervously. "Are you ill?"

"Just tired. Haven't eaten for a while."

"Come in," she ordered, hurrying to the stove to ladle a thick barley soup into a wooden bowl. "Here, try this. Then you can lie down while I prepare the entrée."

"Entrée," he repeated between spoonfuls of warm broth. "Not like our dormitory car."

He looked around the lodge which had been built by villagers for their winter hunting. He could see loving care in the construction. From the long dining table where he sat on one of a dozen hand-carved wooden chairs, Alex's gaze followed a pipe six inches in diameter, which penetrated the wall from outside. It slanted across the kitchen wall and entered a sturdy, black iron stove, then disappeared around the fire-box in five smaller pipes.

Watching from the pass-through, Katya followed his gaze with the simple comment, "Hot water."

He nodded while sipping more soup from his wooden spoon.

The main room was distinguished by a wide fireplace made from small, rounded rocks taken from the stream. The floor was constructed of straight planks with tight seams, carefully fitted by patient hands and sharp planes. Thick wooden benches lined the walls, and each arm-rest displayed the decorative carving of local artisans. The shallow roof was supported by a row of beams that looked strong enough to support a snowfall of the most severe winter. On one side of the room a wide leather couch waited, handmade and covered with an abundance of wolf pelts selected for the length and thickness of their fur.

Toward this comfortable shelf Alex trudged. With one knee on the frame he pushed his hands out through the plush hair until he was stretched full out. He exhaled into the fur and, listening to the rush of water outside in the creek, fell into a deep sleep.

The snap of a branch in the fireplace woke him. Katya was sitting on a fur mat in the glow of the fire.

"What time is it?" he asked, sitting up blinking, trying to sharpen his vision.

"Eleven o'clock," she said with a smile.

"Impossible," he said, standing. "Is it night? . . . I have to get back to the train."

"No, you don't," Katya said, looking back into the flames. "Pavel was up here several hours ago. I told him you'd been shot. When he saw you on the couch, he was prepared to believe me, and said he'd welcome being in charge for a while."

Alex laughed and sat back down.

"How do you feel now?"

"Not bad," he said, stretching. "Famished. And," he said as an afterthought, "ready to burst."

Katya laughed and pointed to the door.

The outhouse was at the far end of the lodge, built out over a cascading creek. From higher up the slope he could follow the thick pipe running from the house to the water source. "Ingenious," he said above the sound of falling water.

On the way back he could hear Katya singing, and he was happy to note how content this simple act made him feel.

"I've started your lunch again," she said over her shoulder. "You could take a little time washing up. Here's a fresh blouse. And by the way, Pavel brought your shaving things. He said you should take a few days' leave."

"Did he now?" Alex said as he went into a spacious wash-house. The floor was rough cement, peppered with gravel and fist-sized rocks. A bench over a wooden grate held five earthenware wash basins, each basin under its own brass tap. Wooden toothbrushes hung on nails beside another bowl filled with coarse salt.

Alex set down his soap, brush and razor in a neat row before peering critically into the mirror. He rubbed his hand across the stubble and then set about reclaiming his true image with the luxurious sting of hot water and strong-smelling soap.

"Well, I do believe it's my dashing captain after all," Katya said when he returned to the kitchen. "How Russian you look in that blouse." And she felt relieved to see how rested he looked as well.

"Yes, that feels much better," he said. "There's a steam-room back there. And a concrete pool set in the floor."

"I know," Katya said. "It will be very hot and ready for you after dinner. Not that you need a bath, after only three days on a horse." She kissed him on the cheek and patted his shoulder with a laugh. "If you promise not to be embarrassed, then neither shall I be. I'm really not a cook at all, but I do have a few things. Baked potato — you can't hurt those. Some boiled onion. And," she added with a flourish, "venison with blueberries!" She watched him expectantly.

"Marvelous. Absolutely marvelous. I can't wait."

"You don't have to," she said, feeling very proud as she checked the venison and savored the rich smell coming from the oven. "But first you must look here. Mr. Ordinov gave me this. A bottle of wine from his private store."

"Chateau Lafite, 1900. Bordeaux Rouge," Alex read. "Good Lord, they say that this was a banner year. Too good for us."

"Frankly, I don't care," Katya said. "President Ordinov insists one wait ten years for a good wine to become great. It could be very special by now. Let's open it."

"Where's the corkscrew?" he asked.

Katya was perplexed, then devastated. She had brought a collector's bottle of wine, but had forgotten the corkscrew. It was a fair way back down to the train . . . but Alex was quick to ease her shock.

"Don't worry," he said. She waited while he searched the kitchen, rummaging through drawers before finally holding up a heavy-bladed knife. He took measure of the intended stroke, then swiftly whacked off the neck of the bottle. "There," he said, smiling. "I hope you weren't planning on saving any."

Dinner in the soft light of a guttering candle was a delight for Katya. At last, she thought, a little normalcy. I've waited so long.

At each mouthful Alex groaned with pleasure and Katya laughed, really laughed. "Do you remember the dinner we had in St. Petersburg. And we stayed up like this in front of the fire?"

Alex nodded with a smile.

"I asked you what you wanted, after the war was over . . . have you thought about an answer?"

He nodded. "Often."

"Well, what have you chosen?" she asked softly, trying to hide the serious note in her voice.

She waited as Alex took time to sip more of the full-bodied wine. "One more summer," he said slowly. "That's what I'd settle for. Just one more summer."

Katya looked puzzled.

"I've given five years of my life for my country, and I'm tired. There are too many ugly things. I could see it through to the end . . . if I could live just one more of the good summers. No war, no bad times . . . where my friends are all working and healthy . . . when we could play games on green grass again, and victory is a score — not how many cripples are counted the next day. Time to do more of this with you. I'd give it all up for that . . . time with you." He touched his glass to hers and drank again. "We had only two days in Kiev."

"They meant so much," Katya said, remembering. "I was able to endure."

"When did I fall in love with you?" he asked, touching the tips of her fingers. "Kiev? St. Petersburg? Or was it Kazan? A little in each place, I think."

Katya became meditative. "I'd like to share a summer like that. Do you think we'll have one?"

"Let's make it happen," he invited.

Katya felt her spirits soar, but she held back. "Could we both stay with the Treasury until it's over?" she asked. "Then get away? I don't care who wins anymore — it's all so barbaric. But I want to complete my pledge to the Czar . . . to my profession."

She watched the wavering candle-flame while contemplating their chances for a future, until Alex jerked her back into the present. "I've forgotten the horses."

But Katya held his hand. "I looked after them. Why not have a Russian bath?"

"Good idea," he said. "By the way, what is a Russian bath?"

Katya's eyes were serious but her mouth stretched into a grin. She glanced to the floor then back into his face. "It's like the Ukrainian cookbook you read: First, you steal a girl from Kiev."

* * *

Alex stepped tentatively down the rough steps into the cement cauldron. Steam rose from the simmering pool and his tingling skin turned pink. He sat on a ledge up to his chest in all-embracing warmth, peering through the mist at the glow cast by a kerosene lantern on the deck.

There was a faraway voice. "Close your eyes, please."

He put a dripping hand over his eyes but stared out through a crack between two fingers. Katya's bare feet padded quietly across the coarse floor. She wore only a half-slip of simple cotton, slung low on her hips and hanging to her ankles; its length somehow accentuated her nakedness. He watched as she raised her hands to tie up her hair in a golden heap. The strands she missed fell past sculpted ears and the slender sweep of her neck. Her underarms showed the same light-colored hair.

Alex caught his breath as she passed in front of the lantern which gave him a shadowy glimpse of a veiled and secret world. He wondered if she heard his sudden inhalation, but saw no sign of this as she hung her one garment on a wall peg, and without pause moved in a flowing motion across the floor to descend the steps into the pool. Alex could hear his pulse. "Katya, this isn't wise," he whispered. "I'm too weak."

"You're far from weak, Alexander."

"You know how I feel about children in the middle of a war . . ."

"If that's what's bothering you, you can stop worrying," she said firmly, not wishing to discuss such a personal matter.

She saw Alex frown, but he said nothing.

"I'm not going to give you a physiology lesson," she said. "Leave that to me." Then she added gently, "I have a soft soap. Turn around. I'll wash your hair."

He turned his back while she worked her fingers through his tangled black hair with a mass of slippery lather. She rubbed his neck and shoulders, amazed that the sculpted muscles across his shoulders and back were like a Greek statue. "Your skin is dry," she said clinically. "I'll put some mineral oil on, later."

Alex could not speak. He was keenly sensitive to her nearness and to the light touch of her hands. He was painfully aware of his own needs, and when, while Katya was rinsing his hair, the swollen tip of her breast touched his arm, he felt an electric shock race through his body. Turning, he reached for her. "Katya, I love you."

She smiled into his face. "I'm glad," she whispered. "It's good, isn't it?"

He stood to hold her, hugging gently in the steaming pool. His hands softly traced the arch of her lower back. Fingertips lingered where fold met leg, then pulled her closer. He felt her stomach tense and flatten at his touch. His kiss was more urgent than soft.

He clung to her in the waist-deep water until she turned away. "I'm going to the fire," she whispered. "Close your eyes."

Alex squinted, his eyes almost shut, but he looked out through half-closed lashes as she drifted away from him. She passed once again in front of the lantern to become in an instant the etched vision that would taunt him for the rest of his life. He stood in the water breathing heavily, sweat dripping from his face, and realized that he did not know what to do next. At last he climbed from the warm pool to towel himself off and then wrapped the homespun cloth around his waist.

He found Katya kneeling by the fireplace on a mound of wolf pelts. A mix of shadow and fire-glow licked across her body in an ever-changing kaleidoscope of light. She patted the furry bed and Alex, face down, stretched out across the wide hearth. He noticed with surprise that she removed his towel, and without any comment or embarrassment began to massage his lower legs, cupping cool oil in the palm of her hand. The oil soon warmed in the reflection of the blaze, as Katya's hands now moved in long squeezing strokes gliding the length of his limbs. Perspiration dripped from her face to fall hot on his back. He could count each drop.

He felt her move up to massage his shoulders, sitting across him as one would straddle a horse. She poured more of the warm lotion down his back. Her thumbs pushed long firm strokes to his neck. "Your back is so warm," she said.

Alex tried not to think about her movements or her proximity. Holding his breath, he noticed how light she was. He felt his muscles relax, but inside he was like an armed catapult.

Katya moved again to massage Alex's shoulder and rolled him onto his side pulling his right arm across her knee. As she slid across his hip, the hot oil seemed to burn his leg. She rode across the crest of his pelvis and froze. Her grip clamped onto his arm.

Alex turned sideways to look up at her. She was holding her breath. Then he slowly rolled onto his back, and they were together. Neither one of them moved. The only sound was the tumbling creek outside and several sharp inhalations from Katya.

Alex remained motionless, inflamed by the sight of her. To prolong the rapture, he turned his head toward the wall only to see a giant silhouette of their ecstasy undulating to the dance of the wavering flames beside them. When Katya turned to look as well, Alex felt a deep shudder. This vibration was followed by his own hidden convulsions.

Katya collapsed onto his chest and lay for a time breathing heavily. Catching her breath, she looked up, smiling at him nose-to-nose. Alex returned her smile and soon they were laughing happily together without conversation; there was just the laughter between kisses.

Alex rolled her over toward the fire, and although she struggled playfully, Katya was amazed at how easily he overpowered her. He lay on his side, cradling her in one arm softly tracing graceful lines in the fresh oil he applied. Katya drifted in a helpless, trusting state. The warmed lubricant was massaged repeatedly, until she took on a receptive press of her own, and with a kiss she pulled him to her.

Throughout this long night the lovers called upon each other for attention with searching caresses and insistent kisses. The fire became no more than a glow. Alex fed the coals and carried Katya to the leather couch. They settled beneath a crush of fur in each other's arms. "I love you too," she whispered, just as they drifted into sleep.

For two days they stayed alone, reveling in the lodge's privacy. On the third day they led their horses down the path to the train.

"How are you?" Katya asked, watching Alex carefully as they walked hand in hand.

"Wonderful," he said with a questioning look. "As if I have been reborn. Why?"

"Did you know, you no longer slur your speech?"

"Stammer, you mean," he said. "Not for a while now. Strange, isn't it?"

Katya laughed and walked on happily. "You seemed a little pensive. Anything wrong?"

"Not really, I'm just trying to think of a way to get us out of here. That's all."

"Good," she said, but then added a little sadly, "Like Kiev, it was such a short time for us."

"Nonsense," Alex replied with a confident smile and a squeeze of her hand. "This is just the beginning. You'll see."

• • •

For the rest of that summer Katya and Alex lived on the train parked on an unused spur hidden from the main line by surrounding mountains. Alex ordered his men to disguise the spur with transplanted fir trees and loose earth to cover the track connecting them to the main line. This could be removed quickly enough by hand, but he supposed that the engine's snow scraper would clear the track in an emergency. Pavel tried as best he could to find reports of how the war was going, as Germany moved inexorably toward Moscow.

The fear of being found and captured bothered Alex less than the worry about how his relationship with Katya would affect the men. She slept in the Treasury's part of their caravan, while he remained in the Falcon's dormitory car. His time alone with Katya was rationed, but precious. They hiked in the mountains where they found a high meadow, and here they could make love and picnic and feed the birds. There was a clear lake where they swam, playing as if they lived on the other side of the world, away from the chaos that had overtaken Russia.

Alex found, to his relief, that the Falcons did not resent his obvious romance with Katya. They treated her with great respect, even to the extent of protecting the privacy of their time together. To see Alex's dream flounder would mean that their own hopes might also fail, or so he deduced. Katya became like a sister to men who had forgotten how it was to live near women. They reacted toward the married women of the Treasury in the same respectful way, and the Treasury children thrived on the constant attention they received from the Falcons.

Alex and Katya never went back to the hunting lodge together. Instead, Alex allowed his troopers two-day leaves to the mountain shelter. Here they bathed, rested and played cards. Some of them became friendly with the villagers and worked with them to improve the lodge.

One day when Alex hiked up the trail to check things over, he found four men kneeling on the roof, inspecting and adjusting each hand-split shake. "Hello, brother," one mumbled through a mouth full of nails.

Another crew labored in the nearby forest, cutting firewood for the stove. The sharp thunk of their axes gave an insistent cadence for sweating backs and muscular arms to follow. Two villagers, stripped to the waist, sawed fireplace logs for another Czech to stack against the wall in a long row built as high as a man could reach. The smell of pine sawdust filled the air, and the fine powder clung to their wet faces and eyebrows. Each man worked to leave his mark on the lovely retreat.

As September came to an end, the train dwellers watched, as might fascinated children, the gigantic, ragged chevrons of migrating birds. The sky was in the possession of flocks of geese and duck and heron calling out from one constantly wandering line to another, searching for leaders, or at least for some assurance as to the correctness of their direction.

The traffic made Alex uneasy. When he first woke each morning he would check the mountains for changes in the snowline. Silently, a white shroud gradually descended lower and lower over the shoulder of each tolerant peak. The blurred white line cut a cold horizon across the dark green forest and moved inexorably down toward the valley floor where the Treasury train sat poised, ready to run.

"We must not be trapped here," he reminded his officers.

• • •

Before the end of the month, the village spokesman came to Alex with a concern. His neighbors reported news of a Bolshevik build-up in Perm, one hundred and seventy kilometres to the northeast. This distance provided a safe enough buffer, but the villager reminded Alex that Nylga and Perm were equidistant from Ekaterinburg on separate tracks, and suggested that the Bolsheviks would surely attack Ekaterinburg from somewhere along the northern line.

"If Trotsky gets there first, you're here for the winter," he said, sniffing the crisp air and turning up his jacket collar. "It gets cold," he reminded them unnecessarily.

Alex turned to Pavel and Katya. "Call everyone in. We follow the birds. Let me know when you complete the head count, then uncover the track." He went to the supplies car, returning with a new rifle still covered with storage grease.

"Here you are, Comrade. A gift to thank you and your friends for your hospitality. I wish you good hunting."

Shortly after, with everyone in place, Alex climbed aboard the dark green train and steamed toward Ekaterinburg — and the tomb of Czar Nicholas Romanov.

• • •

On the cautious trip approaching Ekaterinburg, Alex overextended himself once again. Out on patrol, on long marches day after day ahead of the train, watching for trouble from the north, he knew that he should delegate to Pavel and Jan but would not. "They're only lieutenants. What we need for clarity is a colonel and two captains.

Late one afternoon Alex led a patrol through fresh snow on a ridge in the mountains above the railroad track. They were perhaps six kilometres from the train and had seen no signs of Bolshevik activity. Ten of them kept a steady pace. Even in sheepskin coats they felt the creeping chill of winter overpowering the waning sun at their backs, so they hurried through the pines down the steep mountain pass toward their train and hot food.

Alex did not feel well. His stomach hurt from cramps and he was annoyed by the need for frequent stops. Now he was forced to stop again. Sending the rest on their way with a promise to catch up, he gathered fallen leaves and crouched at the side of the trail. As he waited patiently, huddled in his coat, he thought of his father.

Alex remembered himself as a sinewy fifteen-year-old alone on the soccer field with his patient coach and companion. He would chase long through-passes past imaginary defenders; collect the ball in a speedy swerve to the goal before banging the ball home; then collect the ball again and jog back to the friendly smile, the approving slap on the shoulder, and the wise analysis for the next shot. A patient man, a great man, he remembered.

Alex did not know how long he spent in this reverie before coming to, suddenly aware of the cold. The sun had dropped behind the higher mountains to his left and the whole ridge had turned blue. The valley floor was already a deep purple. Frosty air turned breath into white mist. He hurried to dress himself to take after the patrol, aware now of how little light remained and of the danger of falling in the dark.

The safest place is between the rails, he decided, making his way carefully down the long slope out of the snow to the last hill of loose rock and dark trees. Stupid to fall behind, he thought, stumbling and sliding down the final few yards to a dirt road beside the tracks. He paused, putting down his weapon to blow warm air on his cold fingers. At that moment the darkness ignited and he was blinking into two headlights and a rifle barrel.

"Who is it, Comrade?" called a voice from behind the headlights of a truck, the outline of which was only just becoming visible to Alex.

"It's one of those Czech pigs," answered the indistinct form behind the rifle.

The two Red Guards spoke in Russian. "Careful. There may be more," the driver said.

Alex felt helpless when he saw the Bolshevik's frightened face in the shaft of light from the truck. The rifle was being jerked about by fear. It was a dangerous moment and there was no opening for Alex.

"Kill him," urged the driver. "Let's go."

Alex thought of Katya, feeling an ache in his throat. Dear God, not now. Not here, he thought. She'll never know . . . .

• • •

Katya ran down the railroad track to meet the patrol. "Where's Alex?" she demanded with an anxious frown for Pavel.

"He had to stop," Pavel said, looking a little worried himself as he peered back through the gathering darkness. "He'll catch up soon."

"No," Katya said flatly. "Go back and get him. It's too dangerous."

• • •

With the quivering rifle pointed at his face, Alex was about to charge his executioner when he heard: "No! Don't shoot him. You'll alert others. Strip him. I'll get water."

Alex slumped. Not an ice statue. I'll rush the gun, he determined.

The rifle gave a bruising jab to his ribs and withdrew quickly before Alex could react.

"Undress," the soldier ordered. Slowly Alex complied.

Again the rifle punched forward, knocking Alex off balance. "Hurry," demanded the hard voice. Alex disrobed. The ugly gun motioned him off the road and against the bank.

Shivering, Alex stood watching the driver throw his sheepskin coat, pants and boots into the truck. He did not know whether the trembling was caused by fear or by his nakedness and the heavy mountain air. He was forced to wait. There was no chance just now. The cold crept over his feet.

"No water," the driver called to his comrade with the rifle. "Everything's frozen. One shot will do just as well," he said as he kicked Alex's suit of underwear away with a curse, and climbed back into the truck. The foot soldier came forward. Alex readied himself.

As soon as the muzzle touches me, I move, he decided. But the man stopped short. "Turn around," he spat, and put Alex squarely in his sights.

Alex felt the adrenaline surge through his body. Instead of turning around, he flexed his knees slowly, slightly, like a cat ready to spring, and looked down the long black hole pointing through his eye.

A rifle shot split the frigid air and then rumbled echo upon echo across the narrow valley. The rifleman backed away in surprise, trying to place its origin. Another distant shot rang out, and although its reverberations mingled with the first, Alex calculated it to come from a kilometre or more down the track toward the Treasury train. My patrol! he concluded, becoming passive again, playing for time.

The Bolshevik ran for the truck as the asthmatic engine reluctantly coughed its way into action.

"Turn around," a voice barked. Alex numbly obeyed.

He'll do it now, Alex thought, waiting for some fractional signal to dart for the cover of darkness. He was silently hoping for one more shot from his patrol so that the Bolsheviks might look away for just one second. That was all he needed.

Alex tightened to brace himself against the thump of a bullet while he watched his shadow vividly outlined on the dirt bank in front of him. No escape there. He stiffened again when his shadow shrank as the truck backed away from him. With the grinding of gears, he understood. They'll swing the truck around. The rifleman will shoot from his seat on the passenger side, with his foot on the running board. There were no front doors. Alex knew he could dash for the darkness on his left, which was coming soon, but could he outrun a bullet? He watched his shadow grow and sway and stretch, then lean grotesquely.

Alex coiled and sprinted back into the light on his right. He raced for the driver's side, away from the rifle which could not follow him around the post holding the cab's roof and the windshield. The driver swore and tried to ram him, but with a mighty side-step Alex brushed past the mud guard and lunged across the graveled railroad bed, dropping to the ground in a ditch.

"Freeze slowly then, you dog!" the driver shouted as the truck bumped away.

Exhausted, Alex pulled himself to his knees. He had been wrenched that day from emotion to emotion and each different passion had seen its complete range of power. Now he was alone and reduced to a completely humble state. There was no pride, no dignity, no vanity. He never before felt closer to his Creator. He prayed.

The cold stiffened his body, driving what feeling and life remained into its center. Haggard and awkward, he searched in the growing intensity of a new moon to find his long underwear and heavy socks. With numbed fingers he pulled them on, then with stubborn inflexible movements he began the run toward the train and Katya.

Mercifully, the dirt road, although frozen to an unyielding firmness, was free from rock. Also, his undergarments soon trapped some precious body heat. His movement gradually became supple, and with a sob he acknowledged his accelerating heart rate and the gradual diffusion of warmed blood.

"I'll make it!" his voice rasped. I have to make it, he knew. I'm not going to lose her now. Careful, not too fast. No sweating. Steady pace. He slowed slightly. Is that my father speaking, or his memory, he asked himself now conscious of his steadier condition. "How far now?" he said through blue lips. "Pavel has vodka."

By the time Alex had run three kilometres, the patrol found him. Frozen perspiration encrusted his eyebrows and his breathing was hampered by plugs of ice in each nostril but he was still running well. The relief on their faces warmed his spirit, and he was able to accept their scolding. Pavel took off his fur cap and put it on Alex. Another gave him woolen gloves. A sheepskin coat was put around him and one trooper insisted Alex put on his trousers before hurrying him back to the train. Katya was running down the track toward them.

"Let's get out of here while there's still time," Alex said. "Russia's closing in."

CHAPTER 26

CHELYABINSK
OCTOBER 1918

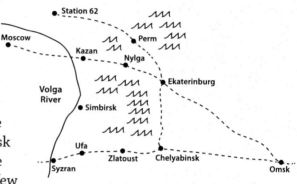

Alex thrust his head out of the engineer's window into a cold draft and squinted ahead to the railyard as Chelyabinsk rolled toward him. He felt good. In the last few weeks he had recognized a change. Certainly his old vigor had returned, and he had always been a determined person, but now he felt a new strength. It was difficult to define, not easily perceived by even his closest friends; and perhaps that was the key. To his usual tenacity was now added a touch of guile. It had occurred to him that although rules were important for large groups of people, it was important for individuals to bend these same rules to fit their needs — or hell would freeze over before those needs were tended to. Of course this could be just another rationalization for self-indulgence, he recognized, but it was also a practical skill he must be prepared to use if they were ever to escape.

To the Chelyabinsk stationmaster he flashed his 'special orders' from General Syrovy and requested an isolated spur for the train. This granted, he approved the sentry schedule set up by Pavel and Jan, noting and commending the easy cooperation between the two junior officers. He also noticed the shabby condition of every man's uniform, most of them threadbare. His own uniform was no better, and so he went once again to Supplies, looking for the sergeant who had so willingly clothed Colonel Lindal.

"Remember me?" Alex asked, smiling at his good fortune in finding the right man.

"Of course. I fitted a uniform for your American friend . . . he got me drunk for my effort. But it was no trouble at all, it was my job."

"Is he still here?"

The sergeant nodded. "At the Kurgan barracks."

"Good . . . any uniforms left?" Alex plucked at his worn jacket. "I've got a list of the ranks and sizes for two hundred eighteen men. What are my chances?"

"Anything you need . . . new uniforms from France."

"We're a special force. Do you have something distinctive?"

"Wait a moment," said the sergeant. Soon he returned with four different colored jackets: a dark blue, a lighter blue, an olive and a forest green — the color of the Treasury train.

"We'll take your green," Alex said, trying to appear nonchalant before attempting the request for which he had no authority whatsoever. "Tomorrow, four new lieutenants will be coming with Captains Pavel and Gemelka for fittings. You can measure me for a colonel's uniform right now," he added decisively.

"Of course, Colonel," the sergeant said, handing back the 'special orders.' "Right this way. Glad to be of help."

Later that evening, and wearing his new uniform, Alex entered a tavern called The Soldier's Bar. He looked around for Victor, finally spotting him at a back table talking to a laughing barmaid. Alex pulled a heavy chair away from the table. "Hello, Vic. Am I interrupting?"

Victor stood up. "Alex! Good to see you." He studied the new uniform for a moment and pretended to brush dust from the bronze insignia on the collar of the new jacket. "And congratulations on your promotion, old buddy." Vic beckoned to the waitress, pointing at Alex before raising his glass. "To your continued success!"

"Just a necessary field promotion," Alex said uncomfortably, looking around the dingy room. There was a pall of cigarette smoke rising past every dirty light fixture. "Something to keep the machinery moving."

"Well, you look a lot better in the new gear."

"Don't we all," Alex said, his hand sweeping around the room to include the rest of the men in the bar. "Look at all the new uniforms . . . and smoking tobacco instead of that peat moss or whatever it was. Where did all this stuff come from?"

Victor leaned forward, shifting his elbows onto the rough table. "The Western Allies. They think Moscow's ready for the kill. They want Lenin thrown out."

"I still can't believe we're attacking the people who were going to save us from Austria."

"You sound like a Red."

"I don't have to be a socialist to understand that the proletariat won't give up on Lenin so easily. You know damned well that Russians from the working class will never again tolerate going hungry while aristocrats feast. They will, now and forever, demand their share. That's why Lenin's hand is on the tiller."

The barmaid put down a pewter mug and a pitcher of dark beer in front of Alex.

"Different people now, Alex. Different game. Different rules."

"You're right," Alex said, "and I'm just finding them out. I'm not too bad a player when I know the rules."

"Of course. You learned from General Gaida, the master."

"General?" Alex laughed, shaking his head. "I don't believe it."

"Haven't you heard? A field promotion, like yours. He's at Ekaterinburg, in charge of the northern front. Tough job."

"But what happened at Baikal?"

He watched Victor fill his glass. "Have a drink. You should know the whole picture."

Alex enjoyed Victor's relaxed manner. Maybe it was his confidence. And perhaps because of their wealth . . . Americans had more of it than most.

In a private tone Victor continued, "This is going to be a Czech war from here on." He pulled his chair closer to Alex. "When they cleared out that tunnel, Gaida pushed on to Chita where he met the Czech troop from Vladivostok. What a sight that must have been! Nice, clean, rested men in their new French uniforms meet these grimy troops in their hand-me-down rags with the stain of five months' steady combat on them. Well, they party for a couple of days . . . the sick and injured get taken on to Vladivostok . . . but the other poor buggers . . . they get told they're all going back! I'll bet they wanted to hang Gaida."

Victor took a long drink.

"Where are they now?" Alex asked, mildly surprised that he felt no bitterness.

"Well, the French high command leaves Chita in the bloody hands of Semyonov and his Japanese friends — along with that unholy bastard Skipetrov . . . I want to meet that son-of-a-bitch again. Said he'd let me live — as a slave. I'll find him one day."

"Vic. Where are the Czech Legionnaires now?"

"Sorry. Sorry. They came to Omsk in September. Then by the northern line to Perm. Now they form the North Ural front under Gaida and have gone up north. They got as far as some place called Station Sixty-Two."

• • •

On the other side of the Urals and five hundred kilometres to the south from Station Sixty-Two, Alex stood waiting as Syrovy's train pulled into Chelyabinsk on the Trans-Siberian Railway's main line. He had to admit that he felt more secure here at Chelyabinsk, a town completely under Czech control, where Syrovy's troop-train shielded the Treasury train from the South Volga front. Also, he was looking forward to introducing Katya to the general. Now that his father was gone, there was no one else to formalize the simple pleasure of introducing the woman he loved to a family elder; Syrovy seemed to be the logical choice.

Victor, Alex recalled now, had not seemed very interested in Katya when he met her. He became uncharacteristically quiet, saying he had a lot to do, and excusing himself after he had shaken Alex's hand in a congratulatory way. Funny, Alex thought, he had actually been a bit nervous introducing Katya to Victor. With his good looks and experience, Vic was so sure of himself around women, but he hadn't seemed the slightest bit interested.

Syrovy looked tired as he came down the metal stairs of his train. His face showed the signs of fatigue and aging which could not be hidden. Alex was concerned, yet happy to see his mentor and comrade-in-arms once again.

"Brother Syrovy." Alex gave his friend a firm hand-clasp. "It's good to see you."

"Alex," Syrovy said, putting a friendly hand on his shoulder. "Considering what's been going on, I'm happy you can see me. I don't like giving anyone a second shot at me . . . they might get lucky . . . and I think this Workers' Army is getting better. Either that or we're growing lame."

"Well, limping or not, you're going to dine well tonight. I have two friends I want you to meet."

"Of course, Colonel, as you command," said Syrovy playfully. "By the way, who promoted you? Your friend Gaida?"

"In a sense, yes," replied Alex, lowering his eyes. "It was necessary." Then he added as an afterthought, "You've no idea how rank simplifies things."

"Simplifies things," Syrovy repeated with an explosive laugh. "How wonderful, there's some practicality at last, but still the touch of naiveté. Wonderful," he repeated, wiping the laughter from his one good eye with the back of his hand. "Just get the job done, Alex. If you lust after my position . . . you can have it without a tussle. Unless Gaida gets in the way; then you'll have an opponent. Let's go meet your friends."

Alex walked ahead of the general across the railyard to the station-house where Victor and Katya were waiting. The atmosphere was crackling with winter. Platform lights made every frozen splinter of moisture sparkle and flash as they were held suspended in the heavy air. Each breath released more diamond particles to spin out through space until the shadows were filled with miniature glistening stars. The light fall of new snow squeaked under winter boots crushing the dry powder along their path.

As they approached, Katya waved to them from the station entrance. Her cheeks were crimson; her eyes bright with life. She wore her black fur coat pushed up high at the neck to cover her ears. The warm air from her mouth had tipped the fur on its flared collar with needles of white. And from under a black mink cap, the blonde hair spilling out over her shoulders glistened with frost.

Alex could see that Syrovy was smitten by Katya at once, paying little attention to Colonel Lindal. Instead, he folded Katya's arm over his and led her to the Metropole Hotel while Alex and Victor followed.

A large and opulent dining room held thirty or more tables on different floor levels, separated from one another by white posts. Here, the dinner was tender veal, with a very sedate band playing quietly in a gazebo overlooking the polished dance floor. Katya seemed exhilarated in the midst of crisp linen and crystal, and could not stop smiling.

Later, Victor danced with Katya — a little self-consciously, Alex thought. Syrovy watched enchanted. At some length he asked, "What does she see in you?"

"I'm not sure," answered Alex truthfully. "But whatever it is, I'm glad it's there."

"What are your plans, then?"

"Ah, I'm not certain. I hope to stay with her until we figure a way out of this mess. As long as I'm in charge of the Treasury train I'll know where she is. Quite frankly, I couldn't guess what I could have done if Gaida hadn't sent me back from Baikal. Pure luck. But now I have to get us out."

Syrovy looked away from Alex thoughtfully. He watched Katya laugh while she danced, head back, eyes shining as she turned and leaned to the beat of a waltz. "If she'll marry you, there might be a chance," he said thinking out loud. "I can't give permission of course . . . but if you were already married, I'd have a reasonable excuse to evacuate her with us, if and when we do leave. So, think about that. And I do want you to stay with the train. It could be our trump card one day."

Before Alex could answer, a roll of the drums drew everyone's attention to the maître d'hotel who was standing before the musicians. "Ladies and gentlemen . . . your attention please," he began, pausing to wait for the click of cutlery on china plates to cease. "A wonderful moment! I have the singular pleasure to inform you all . . . that the official news bulletin predicts . . . at precisely eleven o'clock . . . tomorrow morning . . . Germany will sign a treaty of capitulation . . . bringing an end to the war in Europe!"

He was promptly drowned out by vigorous applause and excited conversation.

Katya came running back to the table to hug Alex as he and Syrovy stood to acknowledge her arrival.

"Oh, Alex, isn't this wonderful news? It's over at last."

"Waiter," Syrovy called. "A bottle of champagne, please." Turning to the others as they sat down, he asked, "And what shall we toast? Vladivostok and the voyage home by New Year? We'll be leaving soon, I should think."

"Perhaps, General, we should be satisfied with 'Vladivostok during 1919.' We could be here for a long time," was the sobering comment from Victor.

"Now what the hell is that supposed to mean? And how the hell do you know?" Syrovy asked, taking real notice of the American intelligence officer for the first time.

"It's my business to know these things, General."

"Then why tell me?" Syrovy asked in a menacing voice, put out that his good mood had been threatened.

Victor placed his hand on Alex's shoulder and said with some intensity, "This man saved my life from a Mongol bandit, I could fall in love with his lady, and they tell me you're not so bad. As a result, I don't want any of you walking around with bad information."

There was a moment of silence. Then Katya broke in cheerfully. "Well, that's straightforward enough. How do you think it will go, Victor?"

Syrovy gave a grudging smile and looked at Victor with new interest. "Yes, what's in store for us?"

"I think there are people who have big plans for you," he replied unhappily.

It was just then, as if by signal, that Alex saw an older man, perhaps fifty, in the uniform of a British colonel, approaching their table. He bowed to Katya before giving Syrovy a smart salute.

"General Syrovy of the Czech First Division, I presume?" he began. "Colonel John Ward, Middlesex Regiment, British army. I don't like to disturb you, sir, but I've been sent with a message, and wonder if I might have a moment?"

Colonel Ward spoke in Russian, which, although not without flaw, did reveal the accent of an aristocrat, Alex could tell. It was not difficult to predict his view regarding the monarchist cause. The English colonel arched his thick eyebrows like a trained actor. Alex watched Syrovy and Victor exchange a look.

"Please sit down, Colonel Ward," said Syrovy and, as a way of welcome, added: "We were just going to have a glass of champagne to celebrate the announcement of peace in Europe, and were groping for a suitable toast."

"Ah yes, of course. Wonderful news. And I would think especially good news for Czechoslovakians."

"Why do you say that?" Katya asked, and Alex noticed that her smile had gone.

"For two reasons, Mademoiselle," the English officer said in a confident tone. "The way is now open for the Czechs to assail Moscow without fear of German support for the Bolsheviki. Also, Czechoslovakians must be convinced, by now, that they've backed the right horse."

"Which horse is that, Colonel?" Katya asked.

"Why, the Western Allies most certainly. It's been a proper foul-up from the word go. First Czechoslovakia is forced into war on the side of the Teutonic powers. Then the Czech military rebels and shifts to Russia. As that monarchy faltered, Czechs had to choose once again — and they sided with Britain, France and the United States . . . And a very good choice it turned out to be," he finished, smiling broadly, "as witness our celebration tonight."

The waiter returned with champagne, opened the bottle with some ceremony and filled everyone's glass. Colonel Ward seized the moment. "General, if you would allow me, I believe I have an appropriate toast. Two days ago, up north in Ekaterinburg, I saw a most impressive ceremony. It was the presentation of Czechoslovakia's new flag which was to be paraded for the first time before her front line troops and the representatives of her allies. I felt that we were celebrating the birth of a nation. Therefore . . . in this company . . . may I propose a toast: To a free and independent Czechoslovakia!"

They all stood, touched glasses and while looking around the table of friends, solemnly repeated, "Czechoslovakia."

"Nicely put, Colonel Ward," Syrovy observed when all were seated again. "Now, what was the message you had for me?"

"It's more of a request, General. As you probably know, Admiral Alexander Kolchak has been touring the Ural-Volga front with General Gaida in the staff train, under the direction of the Omsk government."

"Is this the so-called Directory of Five Ministers appointed by the Western Allies to govern the present vacuum?" interrupted Syrovy.

"Yes, General, much the same thing you Czechs did with your Soldiers' Council when you were without a national government."

"And were these the same ministers who offered Rad Gaida the dictatorship of Siberia just two weeks ago — as he arrived in Ekaterinburg?" Alex asked.

"The very same," came the cool response. "But to be fair and not to dampen your natural and understandable democratic fervor, he did refuse the offer — and I might say, he expressed considerable surprise."

"Perhaps Gaida realized that Czechs will not follow a dictator," Alex countered.

The band struck up the lively Viennese waltz known as Artist's Life. Alex could see a frown on Katya's brow as she looked across the dance floor to the gazebo covered with silk flowers. She seemed to be studying the mural on the wall behind. It depicted meadows and gardens in the spring, things to remind patrons that there was something more to Siberia than searing cold.

The colonel softened his tone considerably without giving up his point. "Yes, perhaps, quite right, and he is a bit unpredictable. It is also understandable that the Czechs, with their new nationhood, should be completely wrapped up in the usual liberty, equality, fraternity . . . and all that. Perfectly natural. But General Gaida, like Caesar, did not accept. And Admiral Kolchak is not a dictator. He has been appointed Minister of War . . . and therefore wishes to meet with you . . . his chief of staff."

The maître d'hotel came to their table carrying a mahogany box of cigars and offered them around.

Syrovy took his time selecting one. "So now I'm his chief of staff, am I?"

"Why, of course. He's mine too. We're all in this together . . . as allies," Colonel Ward emphasized.

Alex saw Victor give Syrovy a sideways glance.

After a stiff silence Alex asked, "Could you tell us something about Admiral Kolchak?"

"Yes, by all means," the Englishman responded with enthusiasm. "He really is a very decent gentleman. Impeccable record: fine education, good family. His mother is Odessa nobility. He's forty years of age, twenty with the navy, disciplined, served with honor in the Sino-Russian debacle of 1904. The admiral is looked upon with great favor by the British royal family. They believe he can restore a monarchy in Russia. He's definitely the right sort."

"Do you think the Russian people will accept him?" Katya asked.

"Well, of course, it's not for me to say, Miss Kazakova," the colonel fairly purred, Alex thought. "But looking hard at his record, I'd say yes. Even the Bolsheviks respect him. Did you hear that during the revolution, he served with the Black Sea Fleet? There was a mutiny, and all the officers were killed save Kolchak. The mutineers demanded that he surrender his command symbolically by turning over the sword given him by the Czar. Do you know what he did?" The colonel stopped to look around the table. "He instructed them all to go to hell, and threw his sword over the side!" At this, the delighted colonel broke into loud laughter, punctuated by short and breathless observations. "They were flabbergasted . . . let him go . . . just the sort of chap we need."

When he had calmed himself, Katya persisted, "But what about the Russian people?"

"My dear Miss Kazakova, you've served the Czar. Surely I don't have to explain to you, that Russians have been ruled by royalty for a thousand years. For this wild land to be without a sovereign is as far-fetched as thinking of Great Britain without a monarchy. Absurd," he exclaimed with finality.

"Colonel Ward," Victor said in a low voice. "Isn't it true, what you mean to say, apart from all this monarchy fluff, is that the British would prefer a dictator to take command rather than endorse General Janin, who's in Vladivostok right now? After all, Janin's a 'Frenchie,' isn't he?"

"Hah, another revolutionary heard from," said Ward rising. "You Americans love candor, especially at the expense of Britain. I do not intend to dignify your suggestions with a comment."

Alex wondered how Victor would restore the mood and prepared to interrupt. But Victor continued smoothly, "Colonel Ward, I shouldn't be rude. But some people, and Americans are included, don't trust one-man rule."

Ward ignored Victor, asking instead: "General Syrovy, will you meet Admiral Kolchak and General Gaida tomorrow in their staff train at one o'clock?"

"Yes, I'll be there," Syrovy said, returning Ward's parting salute. He watched until Ward was out of earshot. "Alex, get your train out of here tomorrow. Go to Omsk and lie low. That train is a bargaining chip. The politicians are moving in."

"General, mind if I go along for the ride?" Victor asked.

"Please do, Colonel Lindal. I'm happy you're willing to help us clumsy Czechs in these messy political games," Syrovy said, standing and shaking Victor's hand.

"As clumsy as a circus tight-rope walker," Victor said, with a laugh.

Alex was relieved to see that they all laughed with him.

CHAPTER 27

TO OMSK
NOVEMBER 1918

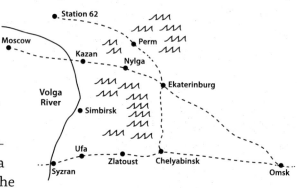

It was four in
the morning at
the Chelyabinsk
barracks when Victor
saluted the corporal
on duty before throw-
ing his suitcase onto a
horse-drawn sleigh. The
horse stamped its hooves impatiently, trying to break the metal
runners free from the creaking snow. In a few minutes the sleigh
pulled up to the sentries waiting by Alex's train. Victor climbed on
board without ceremony, and soon he felt the most valuable train in
history sliding away from the station-house to follow a long straight
track east across the steppe to Omsk, seat of government for the Interventionists: Great Britain, France, Canada and the United States.

When the Treasury train arrived in Omsk four hours later, Victor
left his dormitory car and walked down the track toward Alex's
administration car. He leaned forward into the biting wind. Wind-
whipped snow whirled all around him. He swung open the door and
lunged inside, his face stinging from the slap of warm kitchen air.

"It's colder than the whole of Minnesota out there," he announced,
while kicking the snow from his boots.

"Hey, Vic, glad you found us," Alex said. "Join us for breakfast. We
have to talk."

"Hello, Victor," Katya said, coming over from the stove. "Here you
are. Drink this."

"Thanks," he said, trying to avoid her electric eyes by drinking.
But he quickly stopped. "What's this?" he said, making a face.
"Cold water?"

"Victor, be patient," Katya scolded. "Hot water will crack
your teeth. Finish the cold water and you can have some tea. Are
you hungry?"

"Ravenous," Victor said.

As she passed the table, she smiled and kissed Alex's cheek. Victor watched quietly, realizing Alex had been correct back there on the ride out of Mongolia — her eyes were the color of that Navajo ring.

Victor felt a foolish wave of jealousy sweep over him. Then he turned away, silently rebuking himself for allowing his emotions to intrude on the love life of his friend.

"Vic, what have you found out?" Alex asked.

Victor sat down at the narrow table which took up the center of the railroad car. The stove was tucked away in the corner where the chimney disappeared through the roof.

He shook his head. "I've found one hell of a mess," he began. "Every time I ask myself how the Bolsheviks could possibly survive, the Whites and their intervening allies provide fresh hope for the Red Guard."

"What happens now?" Katya asked, setting down some cutlery.

He directed his answer to Alex. "Lenin and his Red forces are surrounded in the Moscow region. So don't you think the Whites would attack all at once with some coordinated effort? Oh no. The White Guard and their Cossack hired hands go in separated spurts from the south toward Kiev or north from Archangel toward Moscow — so they get beaten back by any concentrated effort from the local Bolshevik volunteers and the Red Guard. The Whites and their Western allies are far too coy."

Katya set down a bowl of steamed oats for each of them, alongside a pitcher of milk. There was brown sugar in a tin.

"What about the new man, Kolchak — Siberia's monarch. Will he make a difference?" she asked.

Victor shook his head. "I doubt it. The Siberian White Guard are less organized than all the rest of the White forces trying to oust Lenin. Kolchak is strictly from the old school. Monarchist to the core — plus, he has problems. General Boldyrev, the man in charge of the White army, wants Prime Minister Kerensky returned to power with a Republican Parliament — like Britain. Those two will never work in concert."

"Never mind the generals," Katya said. "The ordinary farmer, whom will he choose? Kerensky or Kolchak?"

"I really don't know. Either way, peasants lose the land. I don't see that happening. Do you?"

Katya shook her head. So did Alex.

"So . . . their hopes ride with Lenin and the Red Army, I would think," Victor said. "And apart from the peasantry, every Russian who can read knows that England and Japan are just two aggressive little islands craving oil and resources for their mills — and living space, in the case of Japan."

Victor unfolded a newspaper. "Now listen to what Lenin's telling them. Here in *Pravda*: 'November first. World revolution has begun. Nothing can stop the iron tread of revolution.' Compelling stuff — tell a lie often enough, and even the liar might believe it. There's more. Here's the most respected Russian journalist predicting that by spring all of Europe will be under Communism. And then there's the president of the Communist International telling us about how he is preparing to transfer his offices from Moscow to Paris. Beautiful! They're surrounded, and they pretend it's only a momentary condition. Isolated by capitalism, they continue with the aplomb of conquering heroes. Incredible! Alex, the local situation is hot. There may be some throats cut."

Alex remained calm. "Let's play the waiting game," he said. "See what the politicians do."

Victor nodded. "Fair enough. I'll keep my ears open. I'm stopping in at Petropavlovsk. Going to meet Admiral Kolchak with my commanding officer, General Bill Graves."

Walking away from Alex's railcar, Victor worried about his growing fascination with Katya. It's impossible, he told himself. She belongs to the man who saved my life, to the man who trusts me. Besides, she has shown absolutely no interest. "Shape up, for God's sake!" he called into the blustering wind.

He had enough problems already. If there were to be a clash between General Syrovy and Admiral Kolchak, the United States might be charged with interference in the affairs of Russia — or at least lack of cooperation with the Allies. When the fate of the Czech Legion was at stake, he couldn't afford to worry about matters of the heart. Just stay away from the lady and get these troops out of here to the Western Front!

The next day Victor met Admiral Kolchak in a private train where they waited with Colonel Ward for General Graves, the American commander, to arrive from the Allied headquarters in Omsk. It became apparent to Victor that Kolchak suspected that the Czechs would never support him in his quest to unite them behind the White cause and return Russia to a monarchy.

Colonel Ward began the conversation. "I'm sorry to say this, Admiral Kolchak, but I do not have complete confidence in the Czech Legion. They have a most enviable fighting record but is it only when fighting for themselves?"

"A good point, Colonel. I must agree." Admiral Kolchak said this solemnly while resting his hands on a heavy rosewood desk. Then he stood up, looking nervous, spinning the gold wedding ring on his left hand. The admiral had a large chin with a pronounced cleft. Dark eyebrows were perfectly attuned to the black sheen of hair brushed tightly back from a white expanse of forehead. The effect drew attention to his aloof, half-slanted eyes and the downwards arch of resolute lips.

"Why must we wait so long?" he complained, looking out of the windows at the bleak brown buildings of Petropavlovsk. The snow-covered prairie reached out like a begging hand toward the sun which hung all day perilously close to the horizon. Kolchak shivered. "Dear God, what a forlorn place. Why am I here?"

"Not so different from the sea really," Ward responded, watching the admiral with what Victor took to be concern. Perhaps it was a concern for Ward's own political position. Or was it Britain's desires? "You joined the navy at fifteen; surely there must have been a strong attraction for you."

"Yes, but there were always clear lines of command aboard ship. And I understand the sea."

"But Admiral, who knows Siberia better than you? Why, it was you and Baron Toll who charted the islands in the East Siberian Sea eighteen years ago, and what more desolate land exists on the face of the earth?"

"I was younger then," Kolchak explained.

"What is it like up there?" asked the awestruck colonel.

"Two years of hell," Kolchak spat. "It crippled me with rheumatism and pneumonia."

"And yet you returned. You went back to get the Baron in a rowboat — amazing."

"I'd given him my word," the admiral said solemnly. "He needed more time to look for his lost continent. He believed it was out there somewhere."

Victor had forgotten about that expedition and the disappearance of the explorers. He listened closely as Ward pressed the admiral to continue. "Did you find anything? Anything at all?"

"We came to the Baron's last camp in August 1903," Kolchak recalled, staring out the window as if he could see the vast sea of drift ice once again. "He had left me a note that said: 'Completely out of provisions. Heading due south.' Sadly, we never found a trace of them again."

Victor heard the whistle of the train from Omsk, and Colonel Ward reluctantly ended the conversation to go to the train as an escort for General Graves. A few minutes later Graves entered the carriage with a salute for Kolchak. "Sorry for the delay, Admiral," the American general said when the door closed. He then shook Victor's hand. "Colonel Lindal, good to see you again, and in one piece. Excellent."

Victor smiled his greeting as he held a chair for General Graves.

The admiral had turned to Colonel Ward. "Where is this damned fool Boldyrev?"

Ward looked startled. "Sir, he would like to see you on his train. He's heading back to the Ural front."

"Why his train? Why not mine?" the admiral snapped.

Ward seemed embarrassed. "Well, sir. He is the commander-in-chief of the White forces."

Admiral Kolchak sneered. "So be it." He turned to Victor and Graves. "I am afraid it is now your turn to wait. You may use this office. Take me to him, Colonel Ward."

When the door had closed behind Kolchak and Ward, Graves came over with a slap on Victor's shoulder. "Holy Hannah, you gave us a scare," the general said. "The two soldiers you sent back to Vladivostok gave me a full report. Said you were all in a bad way with that bandit."

Victor smiled at this show of friendship. "Yes, sir. I've got some unfinished business to fix one day — when I get the chance."

"Don't blame you. We've been getting a taste of it ourselves, even back in Vladivostok, far from the real trouble. Bandits shoot at our patrols — encouraged, we think, by the Japanese — and we can't do a thing about it or the Japanese will use it as an excuse to take control. Political crap. It's really galling to be forced to take a passive role while we're insulted: insulted by the Japanese, insulted by the press back home — they have me labeled as the biggest coward since

Benedict Arnold. They wonder what right we have to be in Russia, and why we came all this way to do nothing. And of course I can't say a thing, according to my orders. One day this could blow up right in my face — maybe yours, too. To Lenin we're considered spies . . . to Americans, cowards."

Victor was about to agree when Admiral Kolchak burst back through the door, followed by Colonel Ward. Flushed and enraged, Kolchak focused his glare on Ward.

"Boldyrev said I'm not to interfere," he sputtered. "That insipid republican says I'm not to have military responsibilities." He began wrenching at the buttons on his coat. "Then he had the nerve to tell me that the Czar — Boldyrev's Emperor, mind you — had already done enough harm to the armies of Russia with 'well-meaning ineptitude' without another amateur meddling about."

Kolchak threw his greatcoat into the corner, knocking over a coat-tree. "Amateur! I, who spent my life in military service . . . called an amateur!"

"Good Lord," Colonel Ward exclaimed. "Boldyrev's gone mad. Either that, or he refuses to play the game."

Victor felt uncomfortable. When Graves gave him a perplexed look indicating that he did not understand what was going on, Victor realized that Kolchak and Ward were speaking in Russian, so Graves was relying on him for translation. But this was not the time. He gave a reassuring nod and raised his hand slightly, hoping that Graves would be patient while the admiral continued his tirade. Kolchak paced up and down behind his desk as if it were impossible for him to forget this insult.

"I told him he must not speak of the Czar in that tone." The admiral wagged a finger at Ward. "He laughed at me! Then decreed I would be given an office, with two clerks, and that I should keep out of the way."

Kolchak slouched into the chair behind his desk. He seemed calmer now by forcing a control into his voice. "I told him I would continue east to the Omsk government and resign, rather than suffer that humiliation. And so I shall."

"Hold on, Admiral, I beg you," Ward said, quickly breaking in. "Don't let this silly fellow upset the larger scheme. You're still the one man who is able to rescue Russia from anarchy."

Victor watched uncomfortably along with General Graves.

"Thank you, Colonel, but I have no army. That idiot Boldyrev does, but doesn't know how to use it."

Ward changed his tone suddenly to ask, "Admiral Kolchak, if I could get you that army what would you do with it?"

Victor had been listening carefully, but felt his senses turn up to another level with the mention of an army. He looked at Graves, widening his eyes as a silent plea for patience. Graves shifted in his chair and looked out the window.

Admiral Kolchak sat up to ponder the question. He placed both hands down flat on the rosewood desk as if the question had focused his mind. "Well, I'd turn an army over to General Gaida, who is in Perm with his four regiments of Czechs. These men are the backbone of the entire front, and Gaida hungers for command. Gaida argues openly with Boldyrev. I heard him . . . demanding Siberian troops. I admire his spirit." But then the snap went out of the admiral's voice. He slumped with a sigh. "Unfortunately, that will not happen. I shall resign."

Victor held his breath, not wishing to attract attention to the fact that he was there listening to what really was, diplomatically, a privileged political conversation. Perhaps Ward did not remember that Victor understood Russian. Graves sat without moving, and Victor was relieved to hear Ward continue.

"Admiral Kolchak, when you went to see the British ambassador in Tokyo, is it true that you offered your services 'unconditionally and in whatever capacity' to His Majesty's government?"

"Yes I did . . . and I also volunteered to act as a private soldier, if so required."

"Most commendable, sir," said Ward, looking relieved. "That is the spirit which has thrilled the British royal family. You have the backing of Great Britain."

"I do?" asked Kolchak, who seemed to Victor to be genuinely flattered by this statement. "But why? I have no power."

"Let me read what Winston Churchill thinks about you." Colonel Ward unbuckled the leather straps to his attaché case and removed a letter.

"I would be interested in Churchill's opinion," Kolchak said — a little too eagerly, it seemed to Victor.

"Here we are. Winston Churchill is the war minister for the government in power, and he is in full support. Listen to what he says: 'My best wishes to Admiral Kolchak. The admiral is described as one who has more grit, pluck and honest patriotism than any Russian in Siberia. An honest man, with the courage of a lion.' Sir, you can't ignore that kind of encouragement," Ward said as he absentmindedly handed the letter to Victor, for what reason Victor could not guess, but he accepted it without question and read Churchill's words for himself; even the line that continued 'although he may not appear to have the wisdom of the serpent.'

When he had finished, Victor handed the letter to General Graves.

"Those words are very kind," the admiral admitted. "But words won't give me the power necessary to command a solution."

Colonel Ward smiled, looking very confident. "Admiral Kolchak, if you would issue the order to proceed to Omsk . . . perhaps you could leave that process to me, and to the Twenty-Fifth Battalion of the Middlesex Regiment."

Kolchak nodded his consent.

Good Lord, Victor thought. Great Britain is willing to give military support to the admiral. He's their man against Lenin all right.

Then the English colonel stood, turning to Victor and General Graves. "Gentlemen, perhaps we can continue this meeting in Omsk, in a day or two." It was a clear dismissal, and did not need translation for Graves, who had not even taken off his coat.

Victor climbed down the stairs. Graves followed, holding out his gloved hands in a gesture of bewilderment. "What the devil was that all about?"

"I would think some interesting stuff is developing, General. Perhaps we'll get to see some old-style British colonialism. We'll know soon enough . . . . God, it's cold."

. . .

"Alex, wake up. It's important," Victor said, shaking Alex's shoulder.

"Vic . . . what the hell . . . ?"

Katya propped herself up with one elbow on the pillow beside Alex, and Victor caught the smell of lavender. It must be from the freshly washed hair hanging loose over her bare shoulders, he concluded. His mouth went dry.

"Oh, sorry," Victor said quickly. He backed away from the bed not knowing how to act in the sight of this sensual, though natural pose.

He had assumed Katya would be in the Treasury section and he was surprised to find her here. He was moved . . . but what disturbed him most was the sudden flood of envy he felt, and how uncomfortable that made him feel. It was like a sharp pain. These are my friends, he told himself. They belong together. I know that. It's just . . . I never expected I'd feel this way about anyone . . . let alone . . . .

Katya had seen his look, he figured, because she turned her back and pulled the quilt over her bare shoulder.

"Victor, what's wrong?" Alex asked.

"Nothing much. It's seven o'clock. No one can move in Omsk. British machine guns at every intersection and in every damned government building." He walked away from the bed to busy himself by looking out the frosted window. He rubbed a clear circle in the ice with his glove.

Alex climbed out of his bunk and began to dress. "British! Why British troops? What are they after?"

"I would think we've just witnessed a little, bloodless palace coup," Victor said. "And the British, in that special way they have, are trying to influence the course of history. The monarchists are now in charge."

Katya listened nervously.

"What makes you think so?" Alex asked, pulling on his pants.

"There's no blood . . . at least not yet . . . there were only two pistol shots."

"I don't mean that . . . Why monarchists?"

"The Brits want the Czar's man, Admiral Kolchak, to be dictator of Siberia."

"There's evidence of this?" Alex asked, hurrying to put on his boots.

"Yeah, there is. The Republicans have all disappeared, looking for Kerensky supporters, and Admiral Kolchak wants to see you, with me, at nine o'clock."

Alex made a move for the car door at this announcement, but stopped when Victor asked: "Where you off to?"

"I want a report on the track ahead . . . ."

"What the hell for?"

Alex looked agitated. "To see if we have resistance. If so, how strong? And to see if we have the choice of running for it."

"What excuse could you offer for fighting off your British allies?"

Alex paused. "None really . . . this war . . . it's getting too damned complicated. Every time I think we're getting close to home, something caves in."

"You're screwed and don't forget it . . . this is big-time politics. Watch yourself."

He waited until Alex nodded his reluctant agreement. Alex went to stoke up the stove. "Breakfast?" he asked.

"No thanks. I want to stay on top of this," Victor said. "Besides, you have company."

"No, Katya will be off to her own quarters for breakfast with the Treasury staff. Wouldn't want any rumors. We're not married yet," Alex said with a straight face.

"You should fix that," Victor observed, even though his throat went tight at the thought.

An hour later Alex and Victor walked over roads packed hard with snow toward the Omsk Government Conference Hall. Made of granite bricks and mortar, and boasting four Ionic pillars, this was the most imposing building in the city.

Just before nine o'clock they entered the crowded main hall to sit with a subdued audience of military and government representatives. In the chilly air their breath looked like cigarette smoke. At a quarter past nine a side door opened, and Colonel Ward, followed by five military men, walked to the dais. The five men sat down and Ward went to the speaker's lectern. Ward looked over the full auditorium and cleared his throat.

"Ladies and Gentlemen, may I introduce the Directory of Five? Minister Vologodsky of Omsk," he said, and a civilian stood briefly before sitting again. Each man followed suit as Colonel Ward continued in a crisp voice: "General Otani of Japan; General Graves of the United States; General Knox of Great Britain; and General Janin of France."

There was polite applause as Ward paused. "Colonel Krasilnikov, of the Cossack White Guard, has been named as aide to the Directory. Colonel, will you invite Admiral Kolchak to the dais, please?"

"Sir," was the crisp reply, then everyone listened to Krasilnikov quick-march down the length of the long hall, his metal-tipped boots rapping sharply on the cold wooden floor.

Every head turned to the rear entrance as a tight-lipped Kolchak strode up the center aisle. The admiral wore an ankle-length greatcoat the color of dark blue ink. His cap was tucked under his left elbow. The only decoration on this vast expanse of blue was a white cross of St. George, presented by the Czar for valor, worn over the heart.

"I hadn't imagined he was so short," Alex whispered.

Victor did not respond. He was watching a good-looking woman in expensive, well-tailored clothes who had slipped into the hall behind Kolchak and was now quickly finding a chair in the back row. Her eyes were shielded by a full fur hat, but Victor was aware of her beauty, and he waited expectantly for the old familiar rush of desire and the delicious contentment in planning her conquest. When the feeling did not come, Victor felt instead a stab of self-recrimination. What had changed him? Katya? I have to stop thinking about her, he reminded himself and forced his attention back to the stage.

"Comrades and citizens," began the unsteady voice of Minister Vologodsky, "as pro tem chairman for the Directory of Five, I have two important tasks to perform." Before continuing, he looked over the audience as if expecting to be challenged. Hearing nothing, he read from a single page. "The first is to dissolve the Directory of Five on this eighteenth day of November, 1918, in the city of Omsk." He looked up once again. There was no sound. "Finally, I have the great honor to proclaim Admiral Alexander Vasilievitch Kolchak as The Supreme Governor of all Russia, and ask him now to assume the absolute power of this office."

At this announcement much of the audience stood with vigorous applause. Alex and Victor exchanged glances and then rose to clap their hands in polite accompaniment.

"Absolute power . . . it's hard to do better," Victor said, looking around at the woman in the last row. With bright red lips she was smiling broadly; her two gloved hands beat wildly against one another. Victor watched her almost sadly.

Then all at once everyone was singing. Colonel Krasilnikov, a belligerent-looking man with angry eyes, had launched into "God Save the Czar."

"They really believe Kolchak can bring back the dead," Victor said with a shrug.

"Or at least replace the dead," Alex replied.

As the tumult faded, a confident and business-like Kolchak directed everyone to be seated. His speech was short and to the point. "My fellow Siberians, and the Allies of Russia, there is nothing more to say other than: I accept." As the applause renewed, he waved it still. "This is my proclamation. I shall not travel on the road of reaction, or on the fatal road of party partisanship. I set as my main objectives: the creation of an efficient army; victory over Bolshevism; and the establishment of law and order. This, so that people may choose the form of government which it desires without obstruction, and realize the great ideas of liberty, which are now proclaimed throughout the world. I summon you citizens to unify for the defeat of Bolshevism, to labor, and to sacrifice."

"He sounds sincere," Alex said as the applause began once more.

"Who doesn't . . . when they speak of liberty?" Victor asked with a grin. "It's almost as if they believe it . . . especially after they give him 'absolute power.' This fellow frightens me."

Chairman Vologodsky, looking somewhat relieved, closed the meeting with an announcement. "His Excellency Admiral Kolchak thanks you for coming, and wishes the following people to stay for a brief interview: General Otani, of Imperial Japan; General Graves, of the United States of America; General Knox, of Great Britain; and Colonel Branda, of independent Czechoslovakia. Meeting adjourned."

Alex and Victor looked at each other in surprise. "General Graves is here, but how in hell does Kolchak know about you?" Victor asked.

"I'm not sure," Alex answered, thinking rapidly, "unless that other self-appointed dictator, Rad Gaida, has been telling tales out of school."

"Well, let me know what happens, old buddy. I'm going to check in with General Graves. He's probably wondering where I got to. See you later."

● ● ●

Alex sat for more than two hours alone in the main hall waiting for the Supreme Governor of Russia to see him. At last he was ushered into a chilly side-room. Bits of slushy snow, tracked in earlier from the outside, spotted the bare floor.

He was surprised by the polite greeting. The admiral rose up from behind his desk, looking more confident, Alex thought, than when he had first entered the great hall. The admiral's cap was on the desk. His shiny hair was brushed back, close to his scalp. His hooded eyes reminded Alex of a serpent.

"Colonel Branda, I apologize for the delay. Thank you for waiting. I have heard so much about the Falcon Regiment, and wanted to meet their commander as soon as possible. Please sit."

Alex saluted and said, "Thank you, sir. I beg your pardon. I'm not sure how to address you."

"Confidentially, neither am I," said Kolchak. "So why don't we keep it military? We're men who can understand those conventions . . . can't we, Colonel?"

"Yes, Admiral. Very well," said Alex sitting down.

"General Gaida has told me a great deal about you," the admiral began while striding around the desk looking very much in control. "You served under him in the Baikal region, did you not?"

"Yes, sir, although to be truthful, we Czechs viewed that period as serving with Brother Gaida."

"Of course," said the admiral quickly. "I understand. Very commendable attitude. The main concern, for my interest, is that you served Russia with gallantry and were even decorated by the Czar. You were never one to shirk your duty."

"Thank you, Admiral. I consider that a high compliment. However, you must realize that I now serve Czechoslovakia."

"Excellent, Colonel Branda." The admiral's cleft chin was raised in a proud way. "Quite correct."

"Czechoslovakia is one of our more useful allies," Kolchak continued, "and that is why I wanted you present during the ceremonies this morning. I also wanted to be certain that you recognized me as the commander-in-chief of allied forces in Russia."

There was an expectant tension in the icy room as Alex considered his next words carefully. A weak light filtered in from outside, where it was snowing. "Yes, sir, of course. My regiment will serve the wishes of the Allies with honor."

"Wonderful!" said Kolchak, relaxing his rigid posture. "General Gaida said you could be depended upon." The admiral began to twist the gold wedding band on his finger. "I will consider leaving you in charge of the Treasury train . . . but I must emphasize how important that bullion is to our success . . . ."

Alex felt a surge of elation, but just as quickly there was a clutch of fear. This proposal was double-edged — a snare. Kolchak, in a clever, hidden way, had introduced the threat of being separated from the train and Katya. Of course . . . this man could send me to the Ural front. How could I stay with Katya, if not with the train? Separated, we won't get out of the country. I might lose her again.

Alex shifted uncomfortably on the hard wooden chair. This train is my only hope; and that is my weakness, he concluded. He became aware of how closely he was being observed, as Kolchak continued.

". . . with this wealth we can submerge the Bolsheviks and drown them in debt. Is President Ordinov sympathetic to the monarchist view?"

Alex sat up, answering quickly, determined to play out his role. "Without a doubt, Admiral. But, I must tell you . . . I'm not sure I am."

"Your politics do not interest me, Colonel. You're a soldier, and you obey orders. That's enough for me. I understand there is also a young lady traveling with you."

"Miss Kazakova, sir. A Treasury accountant, and my fiancée."

"Are you planning on marrying soon?" the dictator asked, watching Alex closely.

"As soon as we're allowed to, Admiral," he said cautiously.

"Good! Then please let me arrange it. Would you let me do that, Colonel? Because I want to demonstrate something," he said. "I always keep my word."

Alex felt Kolchak watching carefully to see whether he had heard the hidden promise and understood its implications for mutual support.

"Thank you, Admiral," Alex said saluting. "We'd appreciate that very much. And I would like you to know something as well: I won't lie to you."

* * *

General Rad Gaida was in the depot office at Ekaterinburg Station thumping his fist impatiently against the wall above the telephone. He stopped to shout into the mouthpiece, "I don't care what he's doing, God damn you! Get General Syrovy to a telephone, or get a telephone to General Syrovy."

After several minutes Gaida sat down in a chair, leaning forward waiting for a response.

At last Syrovy was on the line with an angry voice. "Rad, what the hell are you up to? I told you to stay out of politics. That's one snake pit we avoid."

Gaida calmed down at this challenge, glad that he had something to confront besides isolation. "General Syrovy, what a pleasant surprise. How's the weather down there in the south? It hit forty below here this morning."

"Don't play games with me," Syrovy growled. "You've threatened the Omsk government against my express orders. What do you have to say about that?"

Gaida's temper was rising now. He had been up too late, too often. He felt taut, unable to let go. "What do I say? I'll tell you what I say. We're up here in Ekaterinburg freezing our asses off. We've had too much frostbite. Good men losing ears, noses, fingers, toes . . . why? Lack of supplies, that's why."

He paused to calm down. He knew that if his fighting troop turned on him, there would be no glory. No reward.

"Their boots leak. Packed with paper. Blankets pitifully thin. They've been fighting too long. My troops refuse to leave their dormitory cars. They know all too well that allied soldiers are swanking around Omsk charming barmaids. And by the way, what happened to 'allied assistance'?" he continued. "They've got five thousand British in Omsk, giving one damned band concert after another; there are nine thousand Americans we could use; and seventy thousand Japanese . . . seventy thousand for the love of Jesus . . . why the hell aren't they up here?"

"So what have you done?" Syrovy asked. His voice seemed weary.

Gaida decided to tell the truth. "I told them to send me a Siberian army or I'd march on Omsk."

"Good Lord," Syrovy muttered.

"You can appeal to the Lord all you like. I threatened to march, and it worked. A full division of Siberians is on its way to fight beside us. We're going to take Perm back from the Bolsheviks. You'll see. And then we move on Moscow itself."

It seemed to Gaida that Syrovy's voice had become icy and detached. "You will not initiate plans for battle without my approval as your commander-in-chief."

"That situation is not entirely correct anymore," was the defiant response.

"Meaning what?"

"It means," said Gaida, unable to hide the note of triumph in his voice, "that you and I have equal status now. I've been made commander-in-chief of the North Ural front and of the Siberian army. My battle plans need only the approval of the supreme commander, Admiral Kolchak."

Syrovy made no reply.

"Hello . . . hello . . . General Syrovy, are you still there?"

"Yes, I'm still here," came the stern answer. "You're the one who's moved away. Goodbye, Gaida. Good luck — you're going to need it." Then the line clicked dead.

Gaida listened to the steady buzz for a moment before placing the listening piece back on its cradle. "Hang up if you wish, Syrovy, but you'll never stop me!"

One week later, Gaida welcomed the remnants of the Czar's army — Cossacks mostly and Siberian conscripts — to join his four Czech regiments. In terrible weather conditions they consolidated their hold on Ekaterinburg. Next, Perm fell. And then they advanced through the Ural Mountains along the northern line toward Moscow to a place so desolate as to have no name other than Station Sixty-Two.

It was here that his fears were realized. His Czech regiments, watching the results of Kolchak's reign as dictator, rejected all directives from the admiral, and refused any orders from Gaida.

It was ironic. Gaida could cajole his men through dangerous assignments in damnable weather with cold known only in lands near sixty degrees north latitude, but he could not get them to cooperate with a dictator. The last straw to break the spirit of his men was a sign Kolchak ordered for public parks in Ekaterinburg and Perm: **Dogs and Soldiers Not Admitted.** Appalled, the Legionnaires would have nothing more to do with Admiral Kolchak. Then they turned their backs on Gaida as well.

• • •

"Alexander, it's me." Katya pounded on the frost-covered entrance to the railroad carriage. "Are you home?" she called. Her gloved fist made a series of padded thumps on the steel door until it opened outwards with a rush of stove-heated air.

"Come on in. Good to see you," Alex greeted her enthusiastically, gathering her in a bear hug and kissing her happily several times. "Your cheeks are cold. I'd better get you warm."

She tried to pull away. "I'm sorry, but no. I've been invited for lunch and mustn't be late. Will you have someone take me to town? How do I look?"

"Ravishable," he exclaimed, kissing her again.

"Alex, please. I must not stay here too long. People will talk."

"What do you think they'll say?" he laughed. "That we're in love?"

"They might say we should be married, and that is what lunch is all about."

Alex picked up the inter-car phone. "Bring a troika to the staff car please." He replaced the receiver, reaching for his sheepskin coat and fur cap. "If the luncheon's that important I'll take you myself. Where are we going?"

Katya smiled, happy to have his company. "Admiral Kolchak's house. Madame Timiryova is expecting me at twelve."

Alex arched an eyebrow. "My, my," he said. "Lunch with the admiral's mistress. What next?"

"Don't be gauche, Alex, please. She's a wonderful woman. Anna is his companion and keeps his house in order."

"Well, that is good to know. I'm certain her husband, the senior Russian naval officer for the Pacific fleet, will be relieved to hear that she's just keeping the admiral's house in order."

"You are wicked," she grinned, draping her arms around his neck. "But I'm too happy to care."

"Transport ready, Colonel Branda," came a voice from outside the door.

The runners skidded and squeaked over frozen ruts as the sled skimmed across sparkling fresh snow on the road into Omsk. Three energetic horses tossed their heads, snorting plumes of hot white steam into the sunlit arctic air. Katya leaned close to Alex under the bearskin cover, laughing aloud. She felt like a schoolgirl again.

"Faster, boys! Faster!" she called, and Alex obligingly snapped the long leather reins floating back from three gracefully surging sets of shoulders. The sled swung from side to side, until too soon they arrived at a street polished to glass by eight boys playing shinny. They wore knee-high boots and chased a wooden disc with carved wooden clubs.

Alex drove beyond their shouting game to disembark in front of a white plastered house that seemed diminutive for the official residence of the Supreme Ruler of Siberia. Omsk, however, was really nothing more than a dull little town in the middle of a vast and empty plain. This house, neat and freshly painted with purple and gold trim, was considered something of a mansion among its neighbors. The smoke from its chimney soared in a straight line high into a cloudless sky, while the music from a confident piano could be heard from within.

"Isn't it lovely?" Katya said enviously, squeezing his arm as they walked through a gate in the picket fence to the front door.

"Now, now," he joked. "Just remember, it's the middle of Siberian winter. If you're a robin looking for a nest, you're far too early."

The outside door was opened by two servants. One took their coats. The other gave them cold water in cut-glass tumblers.

"Madame Timiryova is at the piano," the servant said, returning the empty glasses to a silver tray.

"Her mother was a composer," Katya whispered as she led Alex through French doors into a room alive with music and the warmth of a crackling fire.

The woman rose from the piano; long black hair hanging straight down her back to the base of her spine. She stood tall with head and shoulders held perfectly still while she extended her hand. "Katherine Elenskaya, how fresh you look, and how nice of you to come. Is this gentleman the object of our discussion today?"

"Anna," a voice called from upstairs. "Don't stop playing!"

"Oh dear. Just a moment please," she said, gliding noiselessly into the hallway to call up the stairs, "Alexander Vasilievitch, we have guests. Would you like to meet them?"

"Yes." The answer was followed by a fit of coughing.

As she returned, Katya said, "Mrs. Timiryova, may I present another Alexander? Colonel Branda."

"Yes, of course," she said, offering her hand to Alex. "My Alexander is upstairs with a touch of pneumonia . . . and is very cranky . . . Would you like a short visit, Colonel?"

"Yes, certainly, Madame," Alex said. "I saw you at Admiral Kolchak's appointment as the Supreme Commander of Siberia."

"You must call him Admiral," she said, pointing to the ceiling and putting a finger to her lips. "But please call me Anna." Laughing, she led them up the stairs.

Kolchak looked up from his bed. The admiral wore a black satin robe, with blankets tucked up to his waist. "Mademoiselle Kazakova and Colonel Branda, come in. Not too close though," he warned. "I don't want to be responsible for you catching a cold — just when Mrs. Timiryova, my good friend of long standing, has convinced me it is time for your wedding. That is . . . if you'll still have him, Mademoiselle?"

"Yes, please, Your Excellency," Katya said, smiling at Alex as if they were standing before a priest at that very moment. "And we'd like to thank you for your assistance. You're very kind."

"That's fine, my dear. I always keep my word. Why don't you discuss things with Mrs. Timiryova? Settle the details. I'd like to talk to your young colonel."

"Thank you once again, Excellency. I hope you're better soon," Katya called back as she and her hostess returned to the fire downstairs.

Alex stood at the foot of Kolchak's bed. "Your bride-to-be calls me Excellency. Do you know what they call me within the ranks of the Czech Legions? A usurper of power. A dictator. What do you think of that?"

Alex felt uncomfortable but said anyway, "Admiral Kolchak, you always keep your word . . . Well, I tell the truth. It's the fair thing to do — and easier to remember. Do you want me to be candid? Or shall I try to make you feel better?"

"Give me the truth, always."

"Those words: usurper, dictator — it's difficult to argue. They're true by definition. And even though times have changed, ordinary people see you as bringing back the cruel days of serfdom under the Czar."

"It's not back to slavery. I'll bring in a constitutional monarchy. But citizens must know their place," the admiral said. He thumped his fist weakly into the bedcovers.

"Sir, two weeks ago, not one kilometre from here, you put down the railwaymen's revolt. Three hundred citizens of Omsk who did not know their place were killed."

"I was sick in bed at the time."

"Three days later, a hundred and sixty-six political prisoners in groups of ten were lined up against the wall in the alley behind the stockade and shot after their court-martial. Most were members of the Constituent Assembly."

"They were convicted of conspiracy. I gave some of them only a light sentence."

"But your man Krasilnikov dragged them from their cells, and his Cossacks cut them down."

"The Cossack colonel told me they were trying to escape," the admiral argued in a rising voice.

Alex's voice rose to match the admiral's. "The Cossack colonel will tell you that drinking wine from between two cupped breasts in a brothel is a cultural event!"

"You go too far," Kolchak warned with a scowl.

"Sir, do you want me to hold up a mirror, or only pretty pictures?" Alex asked. Then, as the admiral dissolved into another fit of coughing, he added: "I should go."

"No, wait. General Gaida has taken Perm. Have you heard? But now the Czechs won't fight. I have no support . . . only cowardice and greed."

"Their hearts may not be in the fighting anymore . . . but you'll find no treachery. They won't interfere with your policies . . . they'll just refuse to execute them."

The admiral sat up in his bed a little; he fingered a clean-shaven cheek. "I believe you, Colonel . . . so I'm going to pull the Czech divisions back from the front. Let them police the Trans-Siberian Railway as their service to the Western Allies. I'll replace them in the Urals with Siberians, conscripting every available body if I have to."

"I believe they'd fulfill that task diligently," Alex said firmly.

"You had better be correct," said the admiral, studying Alex with fever-bright eyes. "This trust I've placed on you puts you in a dangerous position."

Alex waited silently.

"If you betray this trust–" Kolchak began.

"I'm not much on betrayal," Alex interrupted. "I'm not politically ambitious — like other Czechs I just want to go home."

"On that we have agreement then, Colonel. Have a nice wedding."

"Thank you, Admiral. Get well soon." Alex saluted before going downstairs where Anna Timiryova called him from the piano room in a friendly way.

"Colonel, will you stay for lunch?"

"Thank you, Anna, you're very kind, but no. I'm going over to Allied Military Headquarters to see Colonel Lindal, and I should get the horses under shelter. What time shall I return for you, Katya?"

"I'm unsure. I could walk over," Katya said, looking at her hostess.

"Why not three o'clock?"

"Fine," said Alex. "Goodbye then. I'll let myself out."

. . .

"He seems very considerate," Anna said as the front doors closed.

"As much as can be expected," Katya agreed. "He's distracted by the war."

"Yes. So is my Alexander. But through it all, your Czech seems to put you first. That must be reassuring."

"Anna," Katya began cautiously. "It must be very difficult for someone . . . ?

"Someone in my scandalous position?" asked the smiling face.

"No. You're being too self-conscious. I was going to say . . . in our position. It's just so hard to know how much to expect. Alex is completely dedicated to his regiment."

"But Katya, he dotes on you. Surely you can tell."

"Yes," she agreed, walking around the piano, a troubled look on her face. "More and more, recently. I hope I'm not distracting him — pulling him in the wrong direction."

"He seems to know what he wants. Don't worry. He'd tell you. As would the admiral tell me. I could never be a diversion from his love affair with Russia. I'm merely a mild distraction from his troubles, while substituting for his wife."

"Where is his wife?" Katya asked in surprise.

"In Paris with the admiral's son. Didn't you know?"

"No! I've been in hiding with the Treasury train for a year and a half . . . A substitute? Not his first love? Doesn't that bother you? Why do you do it?"

Anna poured herself a cup of tea. "Why do I do it? I've asked myself that question before," she said with a sigh. "My husband is married to the sea. I was an afterthought, I suppose. Admiral Kolchak needs a companion. There is a chance he could become the emperor of Russia when all this is over. He might recall his wife to Leningrad of course . . . but even former companions of emperors are well treated. I could be very happy in a dacha near Odessa."

"I see . . . ." Katya said thoughtfully.

"Well now," Anna began. "Let's make at least one of us an honest woman. Do you have proper clothes?"

"Yes," responded Katya, brightening now. "There are four trunks. Clothes are the least of my problems."

"What is your reaction to this plan then? We can use the Omsk Cathedral. By the way . . . which faith do you two follow?"

"Russian Orthodox."

"Fine. The Cathedral is just right. We can have a balalaika ensemble if you like."

"It sounds wonderful."

"After the ceremony the admiral has asked me to arrange a dinner and dance at the New Siberian Hotel. The officers of the Middlesex Regiment will sing for us — they're such a delight at parties — and the Hampshires' band has volunteered a medley of martial airs. I like Tipperary and Colonel Bogey — the admiral's favorites."

"Anna," Katya replied. "It's too much to wish for. It's perfect."

"Well, my dear Katya, that's just the way it will be then: on Saturday, January eighth. Just after the religious holidays. Let's look over the invitation list."

. . .

At the same time, in town, Victor sat listening to Alex discuss the wedding. Most of the details were lost, but he heard one remark distinctly enough: "And so I'd really like you to stand up with me."

"Well, isn't that just great!" Victor replied with some bravado. "I'm really touched. To think you'd ask." He felt a rush of panic. I can't do it, he thought. I couldn't stand there watching. How can I decline without offending him? "Look, Alex, it's a great compliment, but Peter would be put out. Better to ask him."

"You're right of course, but he probably couldn't get here. He's still back on the Volga."

"OK. Then it would be Pavel or Jan. Someone from your past. Or Syrovy even."

"The general is giving the bride away," Alex said.

"You asked that old roué Syrovy to give away the best-looking woman in Russia? That takes nerve!" He laughed when he said this, but he was aware of the empty feeling deep in the center of his chest.

"Nerve is all I've got right now," Alex joked, "and I'm running out of that. Trying to do normal things with this insanity all around us. It worries me."

"Time is what you'd better worry about, old buddy. That's what's running out. Get this wedding over with — fast. I don't know how long Admiral Kolchak will be around. Things are really getting out of hand."

"What do you mean? His health?"

"Nothing so simple. It's the terrorism."

"Krasilnikov again?"

"Hell, yes. Every night some new 'suspect' is dropped through the ice. They won't be found for six months."

He saw Alex squeeze his fists. "I've got to get us out of here. Kolchak promised there would be an Assembly to help him govern."

Now Victor laughed. "What a joke! Last week in Irkutsk the local philosopher asked in public when the National Assembly would begin. And so 'in public,' the White officer hanged him from a water pipe. He swung there for three days, frozen solid, knocked around by passing trains. His family had to steal the body back to get it buried."

"Maybe this whole country's too big. It's impossible to control."

Victor considered that thought for a moment. "No, it's Kolchak's attitude. He sees cruelty as a tool. It's the only method he understands."

"Vic, I'm scared of what this maniac can do to us if something sets him off. He can't be stupid. He's an admiral, for God's sake. I had to bend the system to make colonel. He must do something right."

"Oh yeah? Like his diplomacy with the signs in Perm? 'Dogs and Soldiers Not Admitted to the Park.' What has he done correctly?"

Alex shook his head. "Krasilnikov is the loaded gun; Kolchak pulls the trigger."

"When you put all the parts together, you can see into the mind of an aristocrat. Look at his comments about the Czech Legion," Victor said, picking up the newspaper beside him on the table. 'Abandoning the front' and 'the sooner they are cleared out the better.' Every day in the Omsk papers there are the same types of insult to Americans; I've never seen General Graves so angry. Listen to this bit: 'The American troops, consisting of the off-scourings of the American army, and Jewish emigrants, with a corresponding commanding staff.' How do you like that? Disgraceful. There's more: 'I consider their removal from Russian territory necessary because their further presence will lead only to a final discrediting of America, as all these Americans are degenerates.'"

"The man's lost his grip," Alex said. "Perhaps he is mad."

"Don't be so sure," Victor said. "He's like the Czar — completely ignorant of the common man. And more dangerously, he believes he's the only one who can handle the Bolsheviks."

Alex paused before answering. "I was thinking he doesn't have the necessary energy . . . he looks tired . . . strained. But his mistake is more fundamental. He's trying to control the largest country on earth as if he's the captain of a pirate ship."

Victor agreed. "You probably don't want to hear this . . . but Kolchak and the Whites could be your only ticket out of here — especially if you want to keep Katya with you on a military train. She's a civilian; they won't let her go. If the Reds win, they could get very nasty with you — the man who stole their Treasury train. God only knows what they'll do with the Treasury staff. Get married while you can. Admiral Kolchak can't last."

Again Victor felt that empty feeling as he thought of Katya — inaccessible once married. Hell, he thought, she's inaccessible now, and you know it, and all the tossing and turning at night won't change that.

● ● ●

On the morning of Saturday January 8, 1919, Katya walked with Alex directly east toward the early morning sun and the front doors of Omsk Cathedral. She held her arm curled tightly around his, but relaxed her grip slightly as she looked up at the two tall oak doors. The thick wood, the iron straps and the heavy bolts looked capable of holding out the evil of the world. "It's cold," she said.

Alex was watching the reflection of the sun bounce from three golden domes. Each one was rounded like a Turk's hat, and each supported a golden cross on top. He pointed to the gathering haze in the sky beyond the largest cupola. "No, it's warming up," he replied absently. "It's going to snow."

He opened the door for her, and she noted its balance and the ease with which it swung wide as she stepped over the threshold into the anteroom. The high door closed behind them with a solid, echoing thump, and they stood in the empty vestibule separated from the main hall by four smaller doors made of leaded glass. "I'll keep this on," she said, shrugging inside her fur.

Alex hung his sheepskin coat on a wall peg and then straightened out his jacket. "I haven't taken communion for a long time," he admitted. "Too long."

Entering the main chamber of the cathedral, she walked softly beside him down the long red carpet toward the Ambo — the holy spot — under the domed center of the church. There was a strong smell of incense and occasionally a whiff of freshly baked communion bread from the kitchen below. At the statue of Christ they paused to cross themselves and to kiss the base beneath His feet.

A farmer in front of Katya was in full genuflection, touching his forehead to the floor in the traditional style. He looked as if he had worked hard all his life and Katya marveled at the display of devotion in such a harsh land. When the man crossed himself in the old way — starting at the top of his gray head, stooping to touch his toes, then the outside tip of his right shoulder before the left — she noticed that there were only two fingers remaining on the mangled hand.

She examined the priest standing just inside the sanctuary behind the icon screens and blessing the sacramental wine. In the doorway of the Iconostas with his back to the thirty or more people there for communion, he raised his hands to a painting of Christ, and his gold and purple robe stretched wide, accentuating the red Maltese cross in the center of his back. Candlelight sparkled in every fold when he sang his exhortations to the Lord, "Bless-and-keep-our-people."

The choir sang their answer, "and-their-spirit."

Katya listened to the soothing murmur of their deep voices, aware now of her own growing relaxation and the clarity of sound in the stillness. She felt the intimacy, and smiling contentedly took Alex's arm once again while he led her to empty chairs near the dome. A hymn was sung while two priests gave communion to those who came from their prayers to kneel on the lower step in front of the sanctuary.

Alex knelt to pray, placing his hands on the back of the empty chair in front. He seemed to stare up to the Iconostas, studying the faces of the holy saints on the eight screens that hid the sanctuary. Perhaps he was trying to gather his thoughts. Katya hoped he wasn't too nervous. He never seemed to be nervous at all.

"Are you all right?" she asked.

"Yes, I'm fine now," he said. "In here, the world and its problems are shut out." He paused as if preparing to tell her something. "I'm afraid," he admitted. "I'm so close to something I need. To lose it . . . " She felt him squeeze her hand.

Katya crossed herself before going to the sanctuary steps to kneel with hands beneath her chin. She watched the candles undulate in the still air, their yellow flames lustrous in the dim light. While she waited for the priest, she scanned the colored figures of the disciples sculpted in glass in the window over the altar, before looking away into the high shadowy corners of the ceiling. She felt an inner quiet; a comfortable stillness. It was a time for being alone, and she welcomed this.

A deep voice droned: "Take-this-bread-as-a-symbol-of-my-body-which-has-been-broken-for-you." She closed her eyes before opening her mouth to expose her tongue for the wafer. She held quite still until the bread melted. "Thank you, dear Jesus," she whispered.

When she looked back, she could see Alex at prayer, the shimmering amber lights bouncing from his hair. "Thank you for this wonderful man. Keep us safe . . . Thank you, Lord, for the time with my parents. Keep them well." She saw Alex place his hands on the back of the chair in front, pressing his face into the knuckles, his eyes tightly closed.

Katya looked up to study the figure of Jesus on the cross. Almost life-sized, the details absorbed her: the sagging body pulling at the black nails driven into each palm; the spike through crossed feet; shoulders slumped forward; and the sagging head crowned with thorns. Staring at the small board upon which Christ sat, she felt her pulse race. Tears welled up in her eyes until she squeezed them closed again. She knew what the board was for: Rest. Short relief. The victim was permitted to keep himself alive a little longer . . . as long as there was hope.

As she was returning to her chair she saw Alex staring at the statue, then he dropped his head onto clenched fists. She heard him whisper, "Give me strength to protect her. Give me strength to lead my friends to safety. Forgive my sins . . . killing that man. Killing Schumann was . . . was . . . ." It was a vivid moment. She could see his anguish, and now understood some of the pressures he had carried alone, hiding them from her. Why, if not to shield her?

She moved quickly to the empty seat beside him, taking his hand and squeezing it hard. "There are two of us now," she said, and was glad to see him smile again as he left for the sanctuary steps.

As he knelt for communion, Katya waited for the man she loved. Something up near the vaulted ceiling fluttered, catching her eye, and she turned to see a small bird flying to a beam high above a black iron stove at the back of the cathedral. Her eye moved from the stove back to the high perch again. Puzzled at how the bird got there, she searched the ceiling for others, but saw none. Was it injured, she wondered, or lost? Too slow to flee the cold?

Looking back at Alex she heard the priest murmur again: "The-precious-and-holy-blood-of-our-Lord-God-and-Savior-Jesus-Christ-are-given-to-the-servant-of-God-for-the-remission-of-sins-and-life-everlasting."

Her eyes widened as she turned back up to the bird caught by winter in a Siberian church. "We're like you," she whispered.

Alex left the step and walked back to his place beside her. She could tell by his expression that he could see the worry on her face. "What is it? What's wrong?" he whispered, sitting at her side and holding her arm.

"Nothing. Nothing . . . it's just . . . I'm so happy. I want this so much." She leaned her head on his chest for a moment. "Let's go now."

As they walked back down the center aisle, the bird flew across the length of the cathedral and Katya saw Alex smile. He opened the door to the vestibule where the old farmer was sweeping. As he closed the door behind them Alex said in a conversational way, "There's a lost bird in there."

The man nodded while he swept, his two good fingers hooked onto the broom. "Another of God's creatures stopping by," he explained unconcernedly.

Katya stepped out onto the front stairs through a small portal cut in the massive main door and held it open for Alex. He was buttoning his jacket, smiling again as he looked out at the occasional dots of snow which angled their flight onto the packed white road. He appeared to be feeling better, she was happy to see. "I hope the bird makes it," he said.

"So do I," Katya said, taking his arm. "Let's hurry to Anna's house. I must get ready."

Soon Katya stood in the living room while Anna checked the hem on the wedding dress yet again. Watching in the mirror, Katya flounced the body of the wide white skirt. "It's perfect," she laughed.

"Well, perfect enough," Anna said, standing up from her knees.

Katya adjusted the long white sleeves and the white spider-web of lace covering the back of each hand from the wrist. "My mother's wedding gown," she said softly. "We two are the only women ever to wear this beautiful dress."

Anna studied her face. "Your daughter will be the third."

"Yes," Katya said brightening. "Wouldn't that be wonderful? My mother would be so pleased. She loved tradition." She stopped, startled, as the tumbling bells of the cathedral rang out their invitation. "Oh, we must hurry."

"I'll call for the troika," Anna said, holding her palms up in a sign for slowing down.

Katya took two deep breaths.

As Katya's troika approached the cathedral, she could see Alex in his dress uniform waiting alone at the bottom of the stairs. She remembered the medal ceremony long ago at the Winter Palace in St. Petersburg. He had worn the same uniform then, and now she admired it once again, noting how tall and straight he looked. Then she noticed his gentle gaze, and felt a level of contentment she'd never experienced before.

Alex helped her down from the troika before waving his thanks to the driver. As they walked across the packed snow to the cathedral stairs, he held her arm and tried to brush away the few powdery flakes on the velvet plush of her sweeping burgundy cape. The cape had a cowl, with a cord sash tied at the waist. It almost completely hid the wide white dress beneath.

At the top of the stairs, he waited before opening the door. He held her shoulders. "I love you," he said, and kissed her softly.

"I know," she answered, reaching up to touch his cheek. "That's why I'm so happy — because I love you too."

As they entered the vestibule, the old man who had been sweeping earlier tinkled a bell. Alex helped Katya off with the cape and hung it on the peg beside his greatcoat while Katya adjusted a white lace cap held to her hair with a clasp of pearls.

From the side-door, a priest in floor-length white robes entered the vestibule and held the door open while the old man left. His robes were trimmed with gold which matched his peaked hat, and they rustled in crisp swishes as he approached, studying them through half-slanted eyes. "Children, I am Father Petr. I've been waiting for you. What is your wish?"

Alex stepped forward with Katya, his hand held lightly on her elbow. "Father, we are ready to marry."

"Have you both communicated your intentions to God?" the priest asked, his face serious, searching their eyes watchfully.

"Yes, Father Petr," Katya answered. "This morning."

"Are you in favor of this marriage, my child?"

"Yes, Father," she said.

The priest turned to Alex. "Before God, is there any impediment which should stand in the way of this marriage?"

"No, Father Petr. None."

He turned back to Katya as if to ask the same question.

"No, Father. None."

The priest's face became peaceful again as he sang with a full bass voice, "For-the-servant-of-God, Alexander, and-for-the-handmaiden-of-God, Katya, who-now-plight-each-other-their-troth-and-for-their-salvation, let-us-pray-to-the-Lord."

Down the staircase from the choir-loft above the ceiling of the vestibule came the answering chant of the choir, "Lord-have-mercy."

"That-they-may-be-granted-children-for-the-continuation-of-the-race, and-all-their-petitions-which-are-unto-salvation, let-us-pray-to-the-Lord."

"Lord-have-mercy."

"That-He-will-send-down-upon-them-perfect-and-peaceful-love-and-assistance. Let-us-pray-to-the-Lord."

"Lord-have-mercy."

Katya looked up into Alex's smile while the blessing was sung. When the chant finished, he handed two rings to the priest. The rings had belonged to Katya's parents, so Alex knew how much they meant to her. The priest blessed the bridal pair, making the sign of the cross with the ring over each of them. He repeated this gesture three times, saying "The-servant-of-God, Alexander, is-betrothed-to-the-handmaiden-of-God, Katherine, in-the-name-of-the-Father, and-of-the-Son, and-of-the-Holy-Spirit. Amen." He placed the rings on their open hand for the exchange.

Katya took a broad gold band and slipped it onto Alex's finger. She held his hand for a moment looking into his eyes, then raised his hand to her lips to kiss the ring.

Alex took a slimmer gold band, placing it on Katya's finger. He kissed her on the cheek before turning back to the Holy Father.

"Your friends are waiting for you inside," the priest said with a smile. Then he turned, and still chanting his prayers for their betrothal, led them into the cathedral's great hall. His incense lamp swung before him, the chain rattling with each cast, sending puffs of sweet-smelling smoke billowing into the air above the congregation.

Katya was suddenly embarrassed by the attention of the crowd, and looked above the stove searching for the bird.

From the choir-loft, a bell-like falsetto bounced above a buzz of rumbling bass notes as the couple walked slowly to the center of the church. The voices were rich, and the warm sound rolled up into the dome only to spill back down on them like drafts of summer air.

The church was full. It seemed that the entire Falcon Regiment was there, standing proudly as Alex walked by in their country's boldly colored uniform: blood-red jacket and royal-blue trousers with their broad white stripe. Katya could see Anna Timiryova standing beside Admiral Kolchak. Their eyes met, and Anna gave her a satisfied smile and a slight, almost imperceptible nod by simply raising her chin. There was Victor standing over by a side door — not looking that happy, she thought. She had noticed his veiled reactions to her — and had been thankful that they were veiled from Alex. They were good friends, bonded by Victor's rescue from God only knows what. Victor was loyal and principled; he would get over this.

The bishop, in robes of scarlet and gold, stood off by himself near the south side of the sanctuary. Alex stopped with the priest in the center of the church to bow to the bishop, who dropped his head in acknowledgement.

Almost completely surrounded by onlookers, Alex and Katya stood at the center of the church under the dome, as the priest began to sing. "For-the-servants-of-God, Alexander-and-Katherine, who-are-now-being-united-to-each-other-in-the-community-of-marriage, and-for-their-salvation, let-us-pray-to-the-Lord."

"Lord-have-mercy," answered the assembly.

The sonorous interchange echoed through the church. He loves me, Katya thought as she listened to the singing. She watched the priest turn toward the altar and she looked once again deep into the eyes of her husband for life.

". . . . for-by-Thee-is-the-husband-joined-unto-the-wife. Unite-them-in-one-mind; wed-them-into-one-flesh, granting-to-them-the-fruit-of-body-and-the-procreation-of-fair-children . . ."

Katya glanced at the peaceful faces watching the crowning ceremony. She could feel their happiness and felt a new confidence. His friends like me, she realized. Two younger priests held golden crowns over Katya and Alex. She glanced over to the side door. Victor stood without expression.

"The-handmaiden-of-God,Katherine,is-crowned-unto-the-servant-of-God, Alexander, in-the-name-of-the-Father, and-of-the-Son, and-of-the-Holy-Spirit . . ."

Katya watched the bird fly from a perch high above the altar and soar in a graceful dive over the audience. Others saw the bird and smiled at his acrobatic display. The voice of the priest became a pleasant drone. How shall we get out, she asked herself. How long do we have together? My husband is a soldier. Unobtrusively she reached over and held his hand as the congregation sang the old song "Many Years" for them.

"May-God-remember-our-beloved-Alexander-and-Katherine-in-their-new-life.Remember-too,the-young-men-who-are-armed-to-protect-the-Christian-Orthodox-Church. God-be-with-you-all." He raised a small hand-held cross while the congregation sang The Lord's Prayer. "Our Father who art in Heaven. Hallowed be Thy name, Thy Kingdom come . . . ."

• • •

Victor slipped out the side door noiselessly, out onto the snowy street. He could take no more of the conflict he felt inside. He was being torn apart by the strict code he was determined to follow in honoring his friend's trust, and the intense pull to Katya that he must suppress. This wasn't the lust that was oh so familiar; that's what frightened him. He wanted to be near her. If that was love, it would also be a dangerous and impossible reality. He would walk in the bracing air, to think this through again.

As he came to the corner he could see a patrol of horses moving away from him. It looked as if they were escorting prisoners toward the train yard and he hurried after them to get a closer look.

When he turned at the end of the street he saw a small crowd of villagers standing watching while nine prisoners were positioned to sit backwards on a row of nine horses. There were sounds of stifled moans and whimpering. Krasilnikov was in command.

After nooses were slung around their necks, Krasilnikov chopped the air with his hand. His men jerked the bridles they held, and the horses lurched forward. Nine men dangled on lines of twitching rope.

The formation they made in front of the wailing crowd was very much like the line of icons in the cathedral, it seemed to Victor. He watched horrified as Krasilnikov's men remounted. He ducked back around the corner and ran for the church. He could still run at least, but more — he knew what he had to do. He had to protect his new friends. He would shepherd them out of this madness.

• • •

Katya and Alex followed the bishop and Father Petr to the office in the vestibule and signed the cathedral's register. "Thank you, Master. Thank you, Father. What a wonderful day," Katya said happily.

Alex led her to the front door and helped her with her cape. As they came through the doorway they were met by an honor guard who stood with cavalry sabers sheathed at their sides. As Katya and Alex paused on the top step, she heard Pavel bark a command. At once the sabers leaped from their casings with a ringing sound to be placed in the salute position with the blade in front of each soldier's face. A pause for the next command, and the swords were thrust upwards, their blade-tips touching to form an archway. Laughing, she hurried beside Alex down this tunnel toward a troika and the applause of their friends.

Katya took Alex's hand with a laugh and stepped up from the iron stair into the troika. But just as Alex was about to climb in beside her, she spotted Krasilnikov on a black horse in front of a squad of Cossacks, and the lighthearted feeling drained away. He was not their friend. She watched him trot silently down the snowy street and catch Kolchak's eye to give a solemn nod. Victor stood at the edge of the crowd watching her. She hoped Victor would always be their good friend, although she believed he had once wanted more. He must have realized that anything of that nature was now impossible.

• • •

At the hotel that evening, Katya could see that each dinner guest looked genuinely happy for them. Spectators applauded the newlyweds as they danced alone on the giant ballroom floor — Alex in Czechoslovakia's dress-uniform, proudly worn, and she in her mother's lace wedding gown. Every tight turn she made flared the wide hem in a whirling full-circle.

"Katya, this is so wonderful. I hope my father can see you." Alex was smiling, but she could see that his eyes were sad. He held her gloved hand high as they danced to the music of the Middlesex Regiment's band.

"And I wish that you could have met my father. You would get along so well. Mother too . . . ." She looked away. "I'll always remember this waltz," Katya said. "Perhaps they can play a bit longer. I have a feeling . . . this might be our last dance in my homeland."

"Beauty, it's just the beginning for us," he said, kissing her cheek. "Someday we'll dance at weddings for our children. You'll see."

"I'll look forward to that. Let's enjoy Russia for a little while longer and then I can turn away. I'd rather be with you."

His powerful shoulders hunched over until he could kiss her lips, a gesture causing much applause from the onlookers who rapped their glasses with spoons until the air vibrated with ringing crystal. Alex dipped and spun her away to the gay music. No one but Katya noticed that his eyes were filled with tears.

● ● ●

In the darkness of the next morning it was business as usual for Alex. Syrovy arrived from Ufa to supervise the Czech withdrawal from the front and went straight to Alex's staff car without the formality of as much as a knock, catching him by surprise with Katya at the breakfast table.

"Married, are you?" Syrovy said, shucking off his coat. "And by the decree of His Excellency Admiral Kolchak. Well, there's nothing to do but give you my full blessing." He seized Katya and kissed her with mock-savage gusto. "I hope you don't mind me dropping in for breakfast. I've one devil of a lot of business, and we have to see Kolchak — soon."

"An incredible romantic, the general," Alex observed. "Sorry, Katya . . . will you call the kitchen for more food?"

"Of course, dear husband, I've had you to myself for all of twelve hours now. Besides, General Syrovy is as good as family."

"Better," Syrovy shouted after her. "I never stay too long." Turning to Alex he said, "I've still got forty trains to distribute along the line. Almost seventy thousand men. A little different from our original fifteen hundred mutineers."

"Are you taking my train with you?"

"I'll try," the general said with a shrug, "but I'm not confident. Let's ask Kolchak."

Kolchak stood at the head of a long table in the committee room of the Admiral's Command staff car. Of all the various railroad conference cars where Alex had attended meetings, this was certainly the most ornate. The table alone, made of richly colored rosewood, was furnished in obvious deference to Kolchak's power. Unlike the Spartan military atmosphere of Syrovy's car, this room was designed to serve the ruler of Siberia, and perhaps one day the new czar of Russia. There was the mighty golden eagle, symbol of the old kingdom, perched on the admiral's desk. Kolchak stood beneath a portrait of the sad-eyed Czar Nicholas; certainly this portrait would never be taken down — not like the empty dark stain above the dais in the Omsk Conference Hall.

At the table just in front of Kolchak, Colonel Ward waited with General Syrovy. Alex sat down beside Victor, who, since General Graves had returned to Vladivostok, was now representing the United States of America at these strategy sessions.

"General Syrovy," Admiral Kolchak said imperiously to open their meeting. "You will assign sections of track to your troops in order to maintain the stability of our supply system. The trains must be protected. This is your only job, and should not be too difficult for Czech heroes, should it?"

Alex cringed inwardly. It was difficult to understand why the admiral thought it necessary to be rude to Syrovy.

"As you order, Admiral," Syrovy replied, apparently ignoring the remark. "There might be some trouble from the citizenry." Syrovy gestured to the window. Outside they could see the remains of eight suspected Bolshevik sympathizers swinging stiffly from permanent gallows. "Scenes like this could be part of the reason."

"Those traitors damaged the track. Now don't complain about discipline like that! It makes your task easier," Kolchak said, swiveling his chair back to the table.

"Admiral, that form of discipline is turning the townspeople against everything that smacks of White authority. The end result is raw fear."

Alex watched Kolchak carefully. The dictator had the face of an adder. Unblinking eyes surveyed the Czech general without expression. "I want them to fear me. It demands respect."

"Respect!" Alex interrupted. "Sir, how can anyone respect White Guard discipline? Burning homes of citizens merely suspected of sympathizing with the enemy. Did you know, Admiral, about the priest in Novosibirsk who was turned into an ice-statue in front of his horrified parishioners? He was stripped naked at thirty-five degrees below zero, sir, and repeatedly doused with water. Bucket after bucket tossed over his blue body until he was encased in a thick coffin of transparent ice. Is that the kind of discipline you want?"

There was a crackling silence. Then, before Kolchak could reply, Victor broke in. "Our observations show that fear fosters hatred, not respect, Admiral. Surely as a mariner, you would agree that the methods used by press gangs a century ago proved useless. Bludgeoning men is not—"

"That's enough, all of you! Simply follow my orders. You're as bad as that English general, Knox. Always fretting about 'proper training for recruits.' He wants three months. Claims if we don't begin soon, we won't have a spring offensive. Ha! How conservative. Three weeks are all recruits need. By March we'll launch a one thousand kilometre front driving into the heart of Muscovy."

"Good Lord, Admiral, don't be precipitous, I beg you," exclaimed Ward. "General Knox is an expert. He is appalled at the condition your recruits are in. They tie sacks together for outer garments. Where are the supplies that British Parliament has lavished on this campaign? This is the problem to solve."

"What are you saying?" Kolchak demanded.

"He's trying to tell you, sir, that the supplies Great Britain shipped six months ago have not yet reached the front," Syrovy replied.

Knowing Syrovy as he did, Alex guessed that he was trying to deflect the admiral's rage from Ward. "Your new combat troops at the front wrap their shoes with bark. Where are their winter boots?" Alex hoped Syrovy wouldn't push too hard.

Now Victor spoke: "The Omsk supply center doesn't help your decisions by hiding reports of these thefts from you. Here's a sample list."

Victor handed over the memorandum. "Admiral, this paper is six months old. To date, the blankets, clothing and boots are still missing."

SUPPLIES REQUISITION – OMSK:

Items remitted 09-30-1918

100,000 sets - Personal equipment (soap, razor, brush) .... received.
6,000 sets - Sam Browne belts .... received.
400,000 sets - Blankets .... to follow.
100,000 sets - Clothing .... to follow.
100,000 pair - Winter Boots .... to follow.

Kolchak skimmed the paper. "To follow . . . There we are again," he shouted. "Thievery and treachery on every side. Where is the leak?"

Colonel Ward spoke first. "We'd better find it. General Knox reports that 50 to 70 percent of the conscripted recruits from Omsk have deserted because there's no winter gear."

Syrovy picked up the theme: "Then these deserters make up raiding parties, associated with neither the Reds nor the Whites. They come together for protection and steal the equipment they need." Alex could see the effect this information was having on Kolchak. The man was showing the strain.

"If I may, Admiral," said Victor, raising a hand for attention. "General Graves, who just spent the last five months with the American Expeditionary Forces around Vladivostok, told me the key factor to your problem is Ataman Semyonov and his partner Igor Skipetrov. Both these bandits are hired by our Japanese 'allies' who would like nothing more than chaos in Siberia for the simple reason that Japan wants control of the Maritime Territory."

The admiral was strangely quiet and seemed to sag slightly. "I met Semyonov once. He refused to discuss issues with me. I was dismissed within an hour. He did not seem interested in Russia."

"He's a bloodthirsty bastard!" Victor exclaimed.

Alex saw everyone turn in surprise at this outbreak of passion.

"Semyonov kills for plunder. He's not as bad as Skipetrov! That murderous son-of-a-bitch kills for pleasure. He dragged me in my bare feet behind his horse."

Alex listened to Victor's rapid breathing. It was, in fact, the only sound as they grimly waited for him to regain control.

Kolchak certainly seemed taken aback by this sudden display of emotion. "Where are his headquarters?" He spoke to the others, but Victor continued: "The wall of Genghis Khan. South from Chita and parallel to the Manchurian-Siberian border. They loot your trains, selling supplies behind the wall. Semyonov and Skipetrov are supposedly fighting Bolsheviks . . . what they actually do is terrorize the region . . . and the Japanese pay them! These two commit every crime conceived by demented minds — and they get away with it." Victor gave a wry laugh. "When he marched us away from the train robbery, Skipetrov chose to amuse his men. He threw a bomb into a schoolhouse — in session. His mob went into hysterics mimicking the screams of children . . . a scene like that is not easy to forget."

The room was now deadly quiet. As they recovered from Victor's revelations, Kolchak muttered, as if to himself: "Heavenly Father, give me guidance. How can I pull this mad jumble together?"

Alex wanted to put an end to the dangerous tack the meeting had taken. He did not want to lose the possibility of persuading Kolchak to a more cooperative tactic. But Syrovy was his leader, so he waited for the general to speak.

"A beginning might be your disapproval for the forms of discipline used by your White officers," Syrovy volunteered. "By accepting their excesses, you make the same mistakes as the Czar."

Admiral Kolchak turned on him with a cold stare. "Do your job as directed, General. Protect the Trans-Siberian Railroad, but do not meddle! The only mistake the Czar made was listening to soft-hearted imbeciles."

Shaking his head in disbelief, Alex stared down at the table.

CHAPTER 28
SIBERIA
SPRING 1919

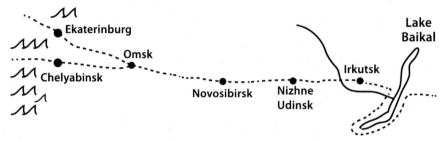

Victor sat beside a pile of newspapers in the railroad car Katya shared with Alex. Katya was preparing lunch and Victor was determined not to watch her as she kneaded dough for their bread — nor even think about her — so he concentrated on the news.

He was disturbed enough after his final briefing with General Graves, who was as frustrated a commanding officer as Victor had ever seen. The American general had been given an impossible assignment in Siberia. "They've tied my right hand behind my back," he had complained to Victor in private just before he left for Vladivostok. "Not only is America in Russia's Soviet Republic illegally, but the politicians won't let us operate in a proper military fashion. The Japs know it. The Bolsheviks know it. They scoff, at our expense. If push comes to shove we're right behind the eight ball." The general had removed his glasses to pace the floor like a man practicing a speech for Congress. "The United States military must never be put in an untenable situation like this again."

Victor wondered whether the political mess could get any worse. He stole a look at Katya bending over to feed the tins of dough into the oven.

"Alex, listen to this," Victor called. "I can't believe the naiveté of the international press. They think it's all over. They're telling the world Kolchak has won." He read out loud from the newspapers: "'Tide of Victory in Russia.' Here in the *London Times* they quote Kolchak. 'I have given orders for the launching of an offensive, the final objective for which will be Moscow.' And from Paris . . . 'Within two weeks Kolchak will take Moscow and remove the Soviet

Government.' What incredible fantasy. The Siberians are strung out from Perm, south down the Volga to Ufa. Almost any concentration of force will break them."

"We'll get some first-hand news later today," Alex said. "Peter Kechek's coming in from Ufa. He's always the last one out."

"General Peter Kechek," Katya reminded them as she cut up mutton and dropped it into a boiling pot.

Victor kept sorting through his collection of newspapers. "I'm looking for at least one reporter who expresses a note of caution . . . Aha, the *Manchester Guardian* seems to be thinking critically . . .

"'March 28, 1919: Churchill is speculating on the impending collapse of the Bolsheviks. The speculation may quite possibly be just, though a few past speculations of Mr. Churchill's have not been too happy. Is a Kolchak government likely to endure and give Russia stability? It is easier for it, just now, to win power, than to maintain it.'

"And what about this last bit on Kolchak . . . ." Victor turned the page to keep reading.

"'There will be pressure to outbid the Red Terror with White Terror. If he yields to the pressure, he will alienate the masses; if he resists, he will find ranged against him the émigrés. We would conclude, therefore, that a Kolchak regime has very little promise of enduring.'

"And that about sums it up," Victor said.

Katya watched, her face worried. She finished slicing the last potato and wiped her hands on an apron splattered with flour. "Will there ever be stability in this sad land?"

"Certainly," Alex said with conviction. "But only when Russians decide." He walked over to the table and punched a forefinger at the stack of newspapers. "Not the *Manchester Guardian*, not British Parliament, nor the *New York Times*–"

He was interrupted by a tapping on the window pane in the door at the end of the car. It was Pavel and Peter. The train from Ufa had arrived and there stood Peter in his combat clothes — tired and dirty, but smiling. "God, it smells good in here! Anything to eat?"

"Come in. Come in," Alex called enthusiastically. "Brother Pavel, where did you find this fine general? Peter, meet Madame Branda . . . Katya, meet the man who put us together."

Victor saw that Katya was quick to wipe her hands on the apron. She brushed a few strands of golden hair from her forehead back behind her ear, and smiled that smile that made anyone in its glow feel special. For a moment Victor felt a flash of resentment that this benefaction should be for Kechek alone.

"General Kechek," she said, "I've been so grateful for your help." There was a slight hesitation before she held out her hand. "Thank you, forever."

Victor could see her sincerity, and he watched Peter blush in reaction to it. Perhaps it's not just me, he thought. She affects all men this way.

"My dear lady," Peter said haltingly. "There is no need, Alex arranged everything — he always does. I'm only his rubber stamp."

Alex laughed at this remark, and hugged his friend with one arm around the shoulders, pointing to three rows of ribbons on Peter's chest. "Victor, look at these decorations. You sense immediately that Petya is just your average rubber stamp."

Victor shook hands with Peter with a feeling of pleasure. He had heard a lot about Peter — good things. The man was completely dependable. In fact, General Graves was of the opinion that the whole Czech exodus swung on Peter's ability as commander of the rearguard. Peter and his men had been in this role for two years now. What an impressive group. Of course, they all were. Look at the Falcons as a striking force, and still together as a fighting unit — held together by what? Victor thought about that . . . What indeed, if not the determination of men like Alex and Syrovy. Remarkable they were, and he felt proud to be in their company.

● ● ●

Alex waited until Victor sat down at the table with Peter. Katya took the bread out of the oven, holding the pan with the hem of her apron. He wanted to join them, but saw that Pavel had lingered by the doorway. "Brother Pavel, stay for some lunch. Listen to what Peter has to say. We have mutton and potato soup with fresh baked bread."

"I can't," Pavel said, lowering his voice. "We've got trouble."

Alex stepped outside with him into the enclosed vestibule. "What's happened?"

Pavel's face was drawn and serious. "The men are really angry. They hear rumors about Hungary getting ready to invade, and they want to get back home to help. They won't tolerate anything more from Kolchak."

"All right. I understand," Alex said, placing a hand on Pavel's shoulder. "Tell them that I will see Admiral Kolchak today. We'll meet the Falcons immediately after."

"Good," Pavel said, looking relieved and brightening up a bit. "I'll tell them."

Alex stepped back into the warmth of his carriage to join the others at the table. Katya brought him a bowl of peppery stew, while Peter and Victor dipped warm bread into theirs. Peter groaned, his mouth full. "Alex, this life is too good for you — you don't deserve it."

Alex laughed. "You're quite right, of course. But eat quickly. We have to visit Admiral Kolchak. Then I'd like you and Victor to talk to the Falcons."

"Sure. What's concerning the Falcons?"

"Well, you have to report to Kolchak anyway . . . but the men want to know what's going on. What the situation looks like from your point of view. At least they'd like to hear about a timetable to Vladivostok."

"Sounds all right to me," Peter agreed. "There's not much left of the front; certainly there's no conviction out there. Only bad signs . . . neglect, disobedience."

Peter glanced toward Katya who was folding towels she took from a drying rack beside the stove. Her cheeks were pink; her face content and happy. Perhaps he need not disturb her with ugly scenes . . . but they should know the facts.

"Not long ago we stopped near a hospital train on a siding. No one was around. Our patrol crept up not knowing what to expect. They found all the patients in their bunks, quite blue, frozen stiff. The medical staff? Gone. That's the way you find everything now . . . frozen to death or gone." He tilted his bowl to get the last spoonful of mutton broth. "The only adhesive at the front is the remains of winter. So just what is keeping us from heading full speed to Vladivostok?"

Alex ladled more soup from the pot on the stove. "Victor will tell you — he's here with the Americans to get us out," and Victor nodded as Alex sat down. "Admiral Kolchak thinks we should turn on the Bolsheviks, and depose Lenin. This is the obstacle of the moment. And of course, this train," Alex admitted. "Admiral Kolchak is not going to let the Treasury out of his control."

Peter nodded solemnly. There was no doubting that remark. He smiled when Katya gave him some more soup.

Later that day Alex ushered Peter and Victor into Admiral Kolchak's office where Peter could make his report. After a lengthy discussion, the admiral gave his orders: "General Kechek, you and your men are to be responsible for the track between Chelyabinsk and Omsk. Colonel Branda will remain in Omsk. The Czech Legion will complete their journey to Vladivostok only when we take Moscow. That shouldn't be too long." The admiral said this with some satisfaction, his eyes darting from face to face. "British and Canadian troops are planning a thrust to Moscow from Archangel, in order to link up with your own General Gaida."

Victor looked uncomfortable. "A commendable plan, Admiral. Do you have assurances that the British forces will launch such an attack?"

Kolchak glared at him, but before he could respond Alex broke in. "Sir, I read that an English Member of Parliament received great applause last week when he said that all of Russia was not worth the bones of one British grenadier."

"Words," spat Kolchak. "Words from a dilettante, safe in London. Let me tell you what's happening with real men on the line, like Lieutenant Dyer, a young Canadian officer in Archangel. He has recruited a regiment of Bolshevik prisoners and has them in training as we speak. It is initiative like Dyer's that will swing the war our way."

There was nothing more that anyone could say; Kolchak's view of the front seemed far from that of Peter's. Alex leaned over their empty table in an awkward silence. Kolchak shivered before turning up his collar and continuing. "If things go the way I plan, we Siberians can win this unnecessary civil war on our own. The Allies want too much. They say I must join the League of Nations — as well as settling Russia's international debts! I'm to organize free elections. And on top of all this, and I quote" — he picked up a letter — "'Countenance no attempt to revive special privileges of any class or order, or to reintroduce the regime which the revolution has destroyed.'" Kolchak sneered. "Idiots. The revolution didn't destroy the regime! What do they think I am?"

When the meeting concluded, Alex walked with Peter and Victor through muddy streets toward the center of town. They lowered their heads against the spring rain and wind, troubled, each alone with his thoughts.

Inside the town auditorium, Alex introduced General Kechek from the platform. Then Peter assured the attentive faces packed into the hall that he, with the Sixth Regiment, would escort the Falcons all the way from Omsk to Vladivostok. "None of our brothers will be sacrificed," he concluded to loud cheers.

Colonel Lindal also won grateful applause by speaking in Czech, later receiving a wild ovation with his summary: "You're not out of trouble yet, but I can tell you this. The American contingent has been instructed by Major-General William Graves to hold the port of Vladivostok for the purpose of getting every Czech soldier out of here safely. General Graves assures me that they'll stay until hell freezes over — if they have to. They won't abandon you. And I believe him!"

Alex, who was last to speak, tried to be succinct. "Brothers, we've endured because of the trust and commitment we've given each other. We survive because of discipline. Don't get distracted now — stay together. I'll keep you informed. You'll get the truth from us and that's my promise to every man here."

Alex watched as his regiment paraded back to their railroad home that dark afternoon. They had taken on a new presence, he believed. It seemed that the men stood a bit straighter, somehow taller, as they marched back through the streets of Omsk. He recognized the old determined precision, and they had become again of one mind; an impregnable unit. Townspeople on the side of the road stopped to watch. Recognizing the regiment's unquestioned vigor, they began to applaud. Perhaps they felt hope in the face of their worries about what would happen next.

• • •

In the white plastered house, Admiral Kolchak picked up a lunch-time glass of sherry poured by Anna Timiryova, and with a shaking hand brought it hurriedly to his lips. Two thirds of the sweet liquor was drained before he held out the glass to set it back down. Instead, it slipped — perhaps a droplet under his thumb, he thought — and smashed down on a tea saucer. Pieces of crystal scattered across the table top. The sherry stained the white linen tablecloth.

"Oh dear!" Anna cried, startled by the noise. "Never mind, Alexander Vasilievitch. I'll get it cleaned up." And she rang a silver bell for service.

"Something's wrong," Kolchak said in a worried voice. "That's the third time . . . ."

"Not to bother, dear Alexander. You have so much to think about."

"You're right, Anna, and very kind," he added. "I don't know what I'd do without you." He sighed, then summoned his resolve. "But you must leave, you realize."

"Dearest Alexander, no–" she began, but was silenced by his hand.

"There is no argument. I want you to return to Vladivostok as soon as possible. I don't want you to see me deteriorate."

"But . . ."

"We can talk about it later. I have to see General Gaida now. He's back from the front . . . with some crisis, I predict."

●　●　●

Gaida marched briskly into Kolchak's extravagant office. He felt the tension pulling at his neck as he glanced up at the portrait of the Czar posing in a Cossack uniform. He shook his head. Did the Czar know that Cossacks were still fighting for a dead image that most likely would never be replaced? Especially not if stupid bastards like Kolchak were to represent him.

Gaida's lips pulled tightly over his mouth. He had determined to stay in control while presenting his case. He could think of no other alternative but to present an ultimatum to a man he knew would not listen — especially to a Czech not of aristocratic blood. But his desperate situation presented no other solution, and he deeply resented that. He wanted to succeed but could not. Gaida felt his frustration rise again.

As he stopped in front of the wide rosewood desk to salute, he knew that his eyes must have widened in reaction to the admiral's ashen complexion. The amount of decay astonished Gaida. Nevertheless, he gathered himself to begin his argument, while Kolchak seemed to stare with equal astonishment. Perhaps it was his appearance; admittedly, his kit was not up to standard. Life was different on the North Ural front.

He looked at the shelves full of registry books. The dark wood made the room all the gloomier. There was no chair for him. So that was it. Stand like a schoolboy and wait for directions. To hell with that. "I've just come from Omsk military headquarters to inquire about missing supplies, munitions, troops," he said. "Do you know what I found?"

Gaida tried to modulate his voice, although even at the beginning of the meeting he could hear his own irritation. "Fifty-two censors. Bloody censors," he repeated. "All able-bodied officers, wielding rubber stamps. When I told them they were needed at the front, they melted away like slush in the gutter. They've got new uniforms and polished boots to read letters, while we're in rags, without proper armament, wondering where the bloody Bolsheviks — who are blockaded, for Christ's sake — get their weapons!"

"Don't resort to blasphemy," the admiral snapped. "Kindly address your commander-in-chief with a proper tone."

"When he deserves it!" Gaida snarled defiantly, feeling his cheeks grow hot with anger. "Our battle is on a teeter-board. Arrest those pirates you call Cossacks. Get fresh troops and munitions to the front immediately, or suffer the consequences. You must–"

"Stop!" Kolchak bellowed, picking up a crystal inkwell and raising it above his shoulder. Ink ran down his wrist staining the cuff of his white shirt. "You're not giving me orders! I'll replace you with Dieterichs!" he shouted, and then threw the bottle. It shattered off the top of the desk, the pieces rattling across the floor toward the shelves on the far wall. His body slumped with the effort.

Both men, red in the face and breathing heavily, glared at each other across the black puddle. "Dieterichs has the wisdom to lead men," Kolchak sneered.

"Ha!" Gaida laughed, picking up a pen and piece of paper. He dipped the pen into the mess at the corner of the desk and scrawled his resignation. "Let him try, while his leader rides this table like a toy boat."

He strode across the room to the door, pausing to look back. Kolchak stared at him with hate-filled eyes. Gaida waited for a moment then slammed the door shut on the admiral, on Omsk and, he had no doubt, on his military career.

Gaida left the Omsk Government Conference Hall immediately, walking quickly through the dusty streets to General Janin's office near the railroad station. He needed one of the new Czechoslovakian passports and clearance on the rail-line to the Pacific. He hoped Kolchak would be slow to react, and was pleasantly surprised that it was not until the next morning that Colonel Ward, on orders from the admiral, approached Gaida's armored train loaded with his personal troop from the Ural campaign.

Ward looked up at the steaming train before he said: "The admiral hopes you are not planning to abscond with this train. It's the property of the Allied Military Command. Nor are you to leave with any foot-soldiers."

Gaida grinned. There were six manned machine-gun stations on two armored cars, and men, bitter men, lean from short rations, looking down at the English colonel. Eyes hardened by months of combat watched, unblinking. An unshaven man sat behind a machine gun, his finger caressing the brass trigger. No one spoke. The engine wheezed, ready for effort, and Ward backed away slowly.

"I can't imagine who might stop me," Gaida mused out loud. "Such a risk is not recommended for you, Colonel." He grasped the handrail to swing onto the stair. "You wouldn't finish the reach for your holster. Besides, I have a message for your sailor friend. Tell him Anna Timiryova waves goodbye . . . She's coming with me."

. . .

Victor had predicted the effect of Gaida's private revolt. It was as if General Gaida's departure left a hole in Omsk. Almost immediately, thousands of refugees rushed to fill it. A city of less than two hundred thousand occupants soon struggled with more than a half million. Spare beds were non-existent. Toilets built above the permafrost on a flat prairie were strained far beyond capacity, and drinking water became fouled.

Victor paced the gravel road near Alex's train, which Alex had arranged to be as far from town as possible. Alex always wheedled his way to the far end of the storage yard, and always arranged a fast emergency way out. They rarely strayed from their home between the rails any more. "Alex, doesn't Kolchak realize that a lot of these so-called refugees are in fact Bolshevik spies? I tell you they're after your Treasury train. They're watching us."

"And what the hell can I do about it?" Alex said. "You heard President Masaryk's orders: no interference, no incidents. Running off with the White's chief source of economic power could be considered an incident. We're to see that our European allies, and that includes you, get out of here safely."

"Oh, so now you're rescuing me again," Victor joked. "Well, I'll tell you, pal. It's General Bill Graves and the good old Yanks who'll hold the back gate open for all of us. Let's not be tardy."

"I'm ready. My boys laid two kilometres of private track out the back end of the yard in case we have to leave in a hurry. It scoots us out through those trees over there, out onto the main track. We don't even have to wait our turn."

"But what are you going to do with two hundred tonnes of bullion? The Reds will never let you out of the country with it."

"I know," said Alex with a shrug. "No incidents. We'll turn it over, to whomever I'm told . . . when the time comes."

"Well, speaking of incidents . . . I've just heard the latest on Gaida. He got as far as the Onon River . . . a hundred miles or so east of Chita. Finds the railroad bridge blown up. Twisted steel. Blasted to hell. They don't know who is out to get him: Kolchak and Semyonov, or just the Bolsheviks. Anyway, his engineers figure it'll take two years to fix. Well . . . he puts his troops to building big wooden boxes. They're floated out, and filled with rocks . . . so all of a sudden, he's got firm supports for the railroad in two weeks."

"And a good turn for the rest of us."

"Hell, yes. But typical Gaida — while he's held up, he starts nosing around looking for carts for his rocks, and he finds the remains of a couple of thousand bodies . . . Every male over fifteen taken from the village . . . and the survivors claim it was the Bolsheviks. Well, Gaida takes photographs, so now every newspaper in the world is whipping up the public."

"Will it do the Whites any good?" Alex asked.

"I doubt it," Victor said. "When Zlatoust and Ekaterinburg fell, the British gave up all thoughts of a northern offensive. They're ready to pull the pin — much to the horror of the Russians in Archangel who helped the British. One White officer marched in to General Ironside's office, removed the Distinguished Service Order from his blouse and threw it on the desk. He then gave Ironside an earful about trust, and marched out again. You know," Victor said as an aside, "I've heard that English officers were really upset by the inconveniences of the war. They expected 'the Russian Expedition' to be a jolly good outing with lots of fish and game, that sort of thing."

Alex shook his head. "What about Dyer, the Canadian, with his regiment of Bolshevik prisoners of war?"

"Dead as hell," Victor said. "Another innocent betrayed. His new troop revolted and went back to their comrades. The British were upset and Churchill gave instructions: 'Don't do anything that will require a relief column because it won't be coming.' So General Ironside decides to leave . . . and the whole lot are following suit. Especially the miners and railwaymen. They threatened a general strike if the troops weren't withdrawn immediately."

Victor watched the worried look spread across Alex's face. "The French left last week. When the British go, do you realize the position we'll be in?"

Victor nodded. "Yeah. Something like, just you and the Falcons, Peter's bunch and Syrovy's Sixth Regiment in Omsk. No Czechs for five hundred miles until Novosibirsk. You'll be easy pickings."

"When the British leave, we'll be surrounded by people who hate us — Red and White," Alex observed. "Krasilnikov held a big, fancy banquet for Peter's men last week. He tried to get them to join the White Guard against Lenin and the Reds. Became quite nasty when refused. I'm going to try to persuade Admiral Kolchak to withdraw. Coming?"

"Good thinking," Victor said jumping up. "I'm right behind you."

• • •

In his railroad car, a gaunt Kolchak stood up from behind the rosewood desk to greet them. Surprisingly, he was in good humor.

"Gentlemen, have you heard the latest reports? General Dieterichs has made great successes. He's chasing them back into the mountains," Kolchak said.

"Remarkable news, Admiral," Victor said. "What was the turning point?"

"Our army moved close enough to Omsk for Supplies Division to truck equipment from our warehouses. The Siberians are now properly clothed, well fed and armed. You were right about Krasilnikov. He's a thief, as well as a drunkard . . . and a libertine. Now the Allies can leave — we won't shed a tear. They've done so little, they might as well go home."

A surge of outrage moved Victor toward debate but he quickly changed his mind, deciding to hold his tongue. What good would it do? The man simply will not listen.

But he heard Alex try. "Admiral," he began, "I was thinking it might be wise if we took the Treasury train east, closer to Novosibirsk, closer to Czech protection."

"Nonsense," said Kolchak, looking suspiciously at them both. "There's no need. We have them on the run."

CHAPTER 29

OMSK TO NIZHNE UDINSK
AUTUMN 1919

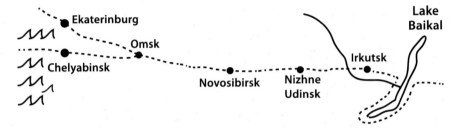

Alex waited with Victor outside Admiral Kolchak's administration car watching flocks of birds flying away from winter and once again filling the endless Siberian sky with cries of warning. It had been a summer of excruciating tension, and now, as if following the birds, the Red Guard swept toward them out of the western foothills and across the steppes toward Omsk.

The Falcon Regiment knew that the great open plains offered no natural barrier to the Bolshevik advance; neither was there a way to prevent the possibility of them surrounding the Treasury train, because now the Red Guards were within a rifle shot of the gates to Omsk. Alex had been worrying about their predicament all day.

"Enough of this. Come on with me, Vic." He turned and bounded up the stairway to Kolchak's office door. As they burst in, the Ruler of All Siberia half stood with a startled look. Admiral Kolchak seemed a haunted man. He slumped back down behind the rosewood desk, his normally hooded eyes now sunken and staring. Puffy skin hung in gray folds under each socket. "What is it now?" he demanded.

"Admiral, for God's sake," Alex said insistently. "They'll be in the city by dark. Do you want to lose everything? We have to leave right away."

"You seem very certain of that, Colonel Branda," Kolchak said, tracing with his finger a black knot on the amber desktop.

"Yes, Admiral, I am. We're the last. General Kechek can't hold them much longer."

"Colonel Lindal, do you agree?" Kolchak asked, trying to hide his trembling left hand.

"That is correct, sir. Nightfall will finish us."

"Very well," the admiral sighed reluctantly. With considerable effort he pushed himself up with both hands on the desk. Gone was the look of the adder. "Give these as my orders," he said, and Alex exchanged a relieved glance with Victor.

Kolchak placed an open hand on his chest. "My train will go first . . . followed by Colonel Branda and the Treasury train. Then the train for the Siberian Guard."

Kolchak paused, waiting for a response, so Alex nodded.

"My staff and possessions will follow. The Czechs under General Kechek will remain as our rearguard." He sat down again, leaving Alex and Victor waiting.

After several seconds he looked up at them. His eyebrows arched in aggravation. "So," he snapped, "have the track cleared for our passage. We should be in Novosibirsk in two days. I'll set up headquarters there."

* * *

From their siding in Omsk, Katya carried a pail of garbage from the kitchen-car, crunching through the first fall of snow toward the pit they used as a dump. Apart from the uncertainty of war, she was content enough with her life on the train — although she certainly looked forward to the day when they could leave. Things were under control here, with the tight security. Everything was controlled: the sentries, the watchfulness, the tension. Even their love was controlled. She accepted Alexander's aversion to the hazards of conceiving babies during a war, and she knew he did not need distractions of that magnitude, so she contained their lovemaking within the rhythm of her body and he followed her lead. But she longed for the day when they could be alone and uninhibited.

As she emptied the bucket of food scraps, a movement from behind a tree caught her eye. She watched nervously. "Who's there?" she called. There was no answer, but she could see the vapor from someone's breath, and she could hear rapid breathing. "Who's there?" she called again, and this time she heard the faint sound of a child crying. She rounded a tree to find a young boy hiding there.

He was perhaps eight years old; his face pale and thin. When Katya approached, he scurried into thick brush, trying to hide.

Katya advanced cautiously, following the sound of stifled crying. She peered into a darkened bower where she could see the boy holding his mitten over the mouth of a young girl not more than four years of age. Her eyes were full of terror and she leaned against the frozen corpse of an old woman.

● ● ●

"Katya, Katya, where are you?" Alex called. "We've finally talked some sense into Kolchak. We're leaving . . . and not a moment too soon." He stopped, staring at Katya who held her finger to her lips.

"Don't say anything," she said in a determined tone. "I'm looking after this."

Alex looked behind her on the bed where a little girl was asleep while a boy, lying beside her, watched with wide eyes.

She gave Alex time to take in the situation before she spoke: "Their parents are gone. Their grandmother died days ago. They've been living on frozen cabbage stalks from the garbage dump."

"Katya," Alex began, looking distressed. "We can't rescue civilians. We have over seventy thousand soldiers to move out."

"These two aren't civilians. They're abandoned children."

Alex studied the determined face of his bride and then looked again at the children in her bed. "My father would have made you a great champion," he said absently. "Did I tell you we're leaving?"

She smiled, tucking a warm blanket around the children. "The sooner the better. Would you like some lunch?"

"I've been talking to Peter," Alex said, taking a seat. "He's ready. Have you and your Treasury colleagues finished checking our . . . shall we say, cargo?"

"Counted and re-sealed. It took us two days," she said, looking through a window-slit as their railcar began to move.

"Tell me again how much this train carries. I never really knew."

Katya looked at him for a moment before responding. "I took an oath before the Czar . . . but he's gone. Kerensky, too. You're in command of the train now. So I can tell you . . . we're carrying in excess of one billion 551 million rubles in precious metals." She paused as Alex shook his head.

He saw her look over again at the two sleeping children. "There are 1,678 leather bags of gold coin, paper money and gems without settings. These are worth 500 million rubles. The platinum is another fortune by itself of just over 100 million. Then there are, in round numbers, 30 million in ingots of silver. We also carry boxes of the Royal Family's jewelry, the value for which is incalculable, of course . . . now that the Czar and Czarina are gone." Katya crossed herself before continuing.

"Finally, we have in our care 5,153 cases of bullion ingots. One brick is worth, by weight, 20,480 rubles each. The total for the gold is 651 million rubles."

Alex whistled softly. "There's too much to steal."

"Nevertheless," Katya said, "there are those who will try."

"Hmm . . . yes, and not too long from now, I'd guess. You know, I can't tell who really owns it anymore."

"Neither can I," Katya said frowning. "But we both know where it belongs."

"Of course," he replied quickly. "It should stay in Russia." And Katya felt herself relax at this reassurance.

* * *

While Kolchak's seven trains clicked their way to Novosibirsk, Rad Gaida met with fifteen young White officers in Vladivostok. They sat in a banquet room of the city's most elegant restaurant — which by European standards Gaida found to be quite sparse, if not drab. The floor was bare; the paint on the walls had faded. Gaida understood how Siberia had come to symbolize everything that was isolated, because that is how he felt, here in this bleak, cold land beside the Sea of Japan. The rocky hills surrounding the city had been stripped of trees and were now covered with army tents and latrines. In the center of town, the squat buildings dedicated to the shipping industry crowded around the harbor which flourished only when free from ice. Rather than this far-flung sea port, Gaida longed for the luxury of old St. Petersburg or Prague.

He had worn his cavalry uniform to the dinner and carried a swagger-stick with a general's insignia. The young officers were enthusiastic to see the sash of combat medals he had slung across his chest. This might be the last time I wear them, he thought when preparing for this meeting, but now they were imploring him to resume his former rank. At the opening of the business section of the meeting, they promised to vote him in as head of a White government to replace that of Kolchak's. He was flattered by their hero worship and had been pleasantly surprised to find that he had become an international figure. It might be interesting to take over from the admiral.

"The people of the entire Maritime Territory will flock to your leadership," a fresh-cheeked officer announced. Gaida involuntarily stroked a hand over his own changing face, noting that the young man must have taken holiday time from his university studies in order to play soldier. General Rozanov, the local White commander, had closed theatres, gambling houses and schools so that "youth could fight for freedom."

"The Cossack Rozanov is a degenerate," the young man continued. "The Czarist bullies are all alike . . . butchers with sword and whip. They feed on fear. Rozanov's cavalry has been a murderous plague, and people are frantic for relief. The partisans will swarm to your command!"

Gaida was very much aware of the keen faces crowding around the table to watch him consider their offer. He was tired physically, and yet exhilarated by the invitation. He recognized a familiar pattern beginning once again. How many times can I reach for the glory? How much strength have I left? In the end he did not bother to examine answers, he was too tired, and chose only to dwell on the excitement of this new challenge.

His thoughts wandered like a rough hand over memories of the milk-white body of Anna Timiryova, once Kolchak's prized possession. Gaida recalled her penchant for men of power and prominence. But now he frowned, setting his jaw as he remembered that she was at this very moment with her husband, not four kilometres away. He reached for a glass of mineral water while silently reassuring himself: Anna will survive. She'll outlive us all. Women who can separate their emotions from physical love always do. They are the real masters, with lasting power over men.

With a sudden move he banged the heavy glass on the table and said, "Gentlemen, we are about to depose a dictatorship. We'll begin with Rozanov's headquarters, tonight." The young men cheered.

. . .

For that night and the next two days, Gaida watched from a barricaded warehouse as White Russian fought White Russian in a confused battle from street corner to street corner within the center of Vladivostok. An informant reported that Japan's General Otani stood on the highest hill overlooking the city: "Keep me informed concerning the Americans," was all he had asked.

It was obvious to Gaida that Japan hoped that Rozanov, the man on their payroll, would eventually persevere. Gaida concluded that any interference would mean a counter by the Americans. And then the game would be on. No longer would greedy spectators be allowed to stand by and watch, waiting for the spoils from someone else's hardship.

Gaida also knew that the American general, William Graves, was no doubt on the roof of some other high building, watching the progress of the battle through binoculars as rain turned to sleet. He would calculate the movement of muzzle flashes, analyzing the skirmishes into which he refused to be drawn. "Damn fools," he'd say. "The rebels are trapped like rats down there in the railyard." Maybe, as an American, he would favor the rebels over aggressive Japan, but Gaida knew the American would merely fret a bit before handing the binoculars back to an officer at his side, and say something like: "We're here to keep the railroad open, not to choose sides. Keep your eye on the Japanese. Let me know immediately if they make a move. Remain on full alert." That was the way it would be, Gaida knew.

Gaida's uprising was forced into gradual retreat. They pulled together until the core of Gaida's rebels were contained within the railroad station. Gaida was in the waiting-room shouting at one of his once-keen young officers while a dozen of his comrades fired their rifles out through broken windows. The youth had lost his cap, and his face dripped with sweat. His white uniform was disheveled and smudged with burns. Stains from under his arms turned the white cloth yellow as the damp circles spread out toward the colored ribbons stitched over his chest.

"When are the Czechs coming to help us?" Gaida called above the noise.

"I don't know, General," the young man said, looking with horror at the distorted and gray faces of two friends on the floor. They lay in the clutter, dead hours before, with open mouths caked with dried blood. Their glazed eyes stared fixedly into space.

"What do you mean, you don't know?" Gaida shouted through the commotion. He pulled the shaking fellow to face him. "I sent you to get help yesterday afternoon. That's fourteen hours ago, for Christ's sake. Where are they?"

"The Czechs are on an island . . . in the middle of the harbor," he stumbled. "All the boats have been taken away . . . They can't get off."

Gaida sagged. "The bloody Japanese. I'll never–" Just then the gunfire outside increased to a frenzy and a ball of fire plowed through his hair, knocking him down.

When Gaida awoke, soaked in his own blood, he struggled to rise on one elbow. The noise had stopped. There was little light. He winced, heaving himself to a sitting position, groaning as he rolled over on all fours, preparing to stand. "Don't let me die on this goddamned railroad," he said to no one.

But then he heard a match being struck, and watched it illuminate the unsmiling face of General Syrovy as a cigarette was lit. The flame spun across the room before disappearing. The dark shadow said, "We can arrange a more suitable place. Get up. You're coming with me."

• • •

In the haze of early morning, General Syrovy strode into a guarded room at Rozanov's headquarters. There were temporary bars set in place to separate the jail from the outer office where a sentry stood watchfully.

Syrovy looked down at Gaida slouched in an uncomfortable wooden chair, and shook his head in disbelief. "Rad, you're obsessed with power. You are utterly corrupted by arrogance." He pulled a table away from Gaida, and sat on it.

"No more," Gaida said. "I'm whipped."

"Well, I'm not sure if that's true, but you look it." Syrovy put his knee-high cavalry boot on an empty chair — the only other piece of furniture in the room. "You've had one hell of a war. Let me see . . . first there were Austrians and Germans. Then the Bolsheviks. You deserted the Czechs, then Kolchak. And now you attack the Whites. What's left?"

"When will I be . . .?" Gaida asked, sounding contrite for the first time in Syrovy's memory.

"Any minute now," Syrovy answered, waiting for any explanations or excuses. There were none, so he added: "If I had my way."

Gaida looked up dully.

"It seems they believe they're paying a debt by giving you back to us. This is the Whites' way of thanking Czechoslovakia for our efforts in the counter-revolution. You're quite the bloody prize."

"What will happen?" Gaida asked, an astonished look on his face.

"You leave Russia within twenty-four hours, if . . . you promise never to return, on pain of death. Is that understood?"

Gaida was stunned into silence, no doubt relieved that he had escaped the firing squad. Syrovy hoped that he was not scheming again and searching for avenues of escape. "Yes, I agree, of course," Gaida said in a hollow voice. "But how? I have nothing. Perhaps Anna could . . . ."

"No. No more schemes, Mr. Gaida," Syrovy interjected bluntly. "As a private citizen in a war zone, you will do as you're told. You'll be taken aboard the British destroyer *Suffolk*. This satisfies the out-of-Russia ruling. You'll be confined to quarters on board until we can transport you out of here. There'll be no more of your antics."

He watched Gaida carefully. "I won't be a problem," he heard the disgraced general say. "That's a promise. I'm finished." Gaida said this while hanging his head, but Syrovy was skeptical. I know you too well, he thought. Gaida is probably searching frantically for a way out. No doubt playing for time to think.

"Good," Syrovy said, "because I have more important things. I'm going to Novosibirsk and get our boys out of there."

"You're going back?" Gaida asked incredulously as they walked to a waiting car. "Into that wreckage?" he continued. "It'll collapse around your ears. The weather has changed. You should stay near the ocean before the ice locks us in."

"You never did learn anything from Alex, did you? About loyalty, I mean. You couldn't see beyond your own interests. No, Mr. Gaida . . . . I'm going back for my friends. Alex would. Just like he always said: we're getting out of here together."

• • •

The Treasury train was stalled in Novosibirsk, and Alex knew this was no longer a safe place for a headquarters. Refugees clogged every road begging for rides and food. Bolshevik sympathizers, knowing that the Red Guard was not far off, became increasingly bold. Local partisans murdered refugees for pocket watches, and Alex knew that if the nature of their train's cargo were to be discovered, he could not hold back rioting mobs. The Red Guard also knew the need for security, he guessed, but they were also determined that the gold must not get past Irkutsk.

Alex had waited three days in the Novosibirsk station-house for a telephone call from General Syrovy. When the ringing bell shattered the silence, he snapped up the receiver. Katya watched with eyes wide.

"Yes," he answered.

"Alex? Syrovy. How are things with you?"

"Not great, General, we're just sitting here waiting for instructions. Are you coming?"

"I'm not so sure. I'm still in Irkutsk with General Janin. The situation here is highly volatile. Kolchak's representatives have been thrown out, and Semyonov is lurking about like a rabid dog waiting to pounce. It's probably best that I stay here. We're playing leap-frog with trains again. If my train ran against the flow, it would only obstruct, and not help anything. Truth is, old coq, you're on your own."

"We're coming out then," Alex said. "There's no control here. The trouble is . . . ." Alex stopped for a moment. "How secure is this telephone line?"

"Still in our hands," assured Syrovy.

"Good. The real trouble now is that Kolchak's guards are slipping away. They could spread the word about the Treasury. What happens to this train . . . eventually?"

"No one knows? General Janin doesn't. What's Kolchak's plan?"

"That's just it. He doesn't seem to have one. He talks vaguely about taking the bullion to Japan. But Colonel Lindal assures me the Americans in Vladivostok would never permit that to happen."

"He won't get past us in Irkutsk. I tell you what . . . I'll have more troops waiting for you at Nizhne Udinsk; about halfway here. Meanwhile, General Janin and I will try like hell to arrange some political solution. You're under the gun."

"Right again," Alex agreed.

"How's Katya? Do you want to send her out ahead of you?"

"Yes I do, but she won't listen." Alex paused to kiss Katya's fingertips. Smiling now, he said, "She says we mustn't be separated ... ever again."

The line went quiet for a few seconds before Syrovy began again. "All right," he said. "Pull the pin. And remember Masaryk's orders: no interference, no misadventure and no sacrifice! We're waiting for you."

• • •

Alex watched winter reclaim the frozen steppes of central Siberia as he rode from Novosibirsk in the Command train. The Treasury train was right behind. Traveling east by day from 6:00 a.m. to 6:00 p.m. they made good time and were halfway to Irkutsk, the Baikal District capital, when the train squealed to a stop at Nizhne Udinsk, still four hundred kilometres short of Lake Baikal.

"I command you to drive on to Irkutsk!" Kolchak shouted. His temper seemed to be rising with each bump of the skidding train.

Alex looked out the window to see several hundred villagers standing in the snow, waiting. "We can't, Admiral," Alex said as patiently as he could. "No doubt there's an armored train blocking our path. It might be the Red Guard, or it might be the local citizenry. They probably want our Treasury train to remain here. It's time to negotiate a settlement, I would think."

The admiral looked wildly around his darkened car. "Get us out of this place, or I shall relieve you of your command!"

Alex tried to remain above this threat, hoping his face did not signal the depth of his vulnerability. He could see that Kolchak watched him carefully. "Why don't I reconnoiter our situation?"

The admiral fell back in his chair weakly. "Bring me a telephone. I want to speak to your commanding officer."

"I'll have an extension brought from the station-house for you. I'd better speak to whomever is in charge of that armored train."

Alex put on his sheepskin coat before stepping out into the chill of winter. He must stay with the Treasury train and Katya. The admiral was just desperate enough to try to fight his way through a blockade with his Siberian Guards. He took a deep breath and immediately felt the sting of frosty air. Bright snow squeaked under his boots as he walked over to Pavel. "Morning. Sentries in place?"

"All ready, Brother. The men tell me there's constant nattering from the villagers. They want us to desert . . . and join the Bolsheviks."

"Tell the men to keep tight ranks. Watch out for their partner . . . If they do, we might get out of here. Don't let anyone close to the train. The Reds remember our fighting skills. They'll be respectful."

Squinting against dazzling reflections, Alex walked down the snowy track toward a company of Czechs he recognized as men sent by Syrovy. He smiled gratefully. They stood in parade formation, and although in bulky sheepskin coats and fur caps, their formation was sharp. They were unified and prepared for anything. Their posture showed that — tall, straight and athletic. Alex felt more and more confident as he studied each serious face because he could see that their appearance had an effect on the ragged crowd of villagers looking on in respectful silence.

The sturdy-looking officer in charge stood at attention as Alex approached. "Major, many thanks for the welcoming committee," Alex said. "What orders do you have for me?"

"No orders, Colonel . . . only suggestions. Apparently you're in a bit of a mess and pretty much on your own. Any direction from France changes daily . . . then they're contradicted. Your guess is better than anyone's."

"Good Lord," exclaimed Alex, standing close to the major and speaking in a low voice so as not to let the onlookers see his concern. "Do you realize how much I know? Nothing! And I know more than anyone else."

The major grinned. "That's the way I remember you . . . a joke in spite of everything. Just another big game, isn't it? No one can predict how the ball will bounce."

Alex turned away with a smile. "What am I laughing at?" He looked at the severe faces across the ranks, and thought he saw them relax as his smile grew. Turning back to the major, he asked loudly, "Were you there, when General Gaida predicted that this would be one hell of a trip?"

Now the major was laughing. "I certainly was. And he's right." Alex could see the troops smiling with them.

"Well, then, none of you has anything to complain about. Can't say you weren't warned." He laughed with the men while the Red Guard in front of the armored train watched them soberly.

"Have you anything for me besides this fine body of men?" Alex asked, strolling away from the formation.

The major walked beside him. "Of course, Colonel. I've several horses." Then he added quietly, "And the suggestion, that if you're a good salesman, you might be able to persuade Admiral Kolchak to do everyone a favor by disappearing."

"Hmmm," Alex replied. "If that's all there is, I could give it a try. See you soon." Then with a wave to the troops he called, "Good luck, brothers."

● ● ●

Kolchak heard Alex knock and quickly hung up the telephone. He had tried to bully General Syrovy into letting his train continue — to no avail.

"The Allied command will strip you of your rank for this insubordination," Kolchak threatened. "I shall see to that!"

"Sorry, Admiral," was the stoic response from Syrovy. "The Allies now find you an embarrassment. They've directed Czech forces to withdraw peacefully, and to maintain order as we leave. Those who formally ask for our protection will receive it."

His head ached. "Why would they abandon me . . . now?"

There was no sympathy in Syrovy's tone. "No doubt because of past atrocities, where villages are ravaged in the name of discipline. Or perhaps because of the murdering savages you–"

It was at this point that Alex knocked, and Kolchak clicked off the receiver.

"Come in, Colonel Branda," the admiral called, noticing that for some reason he was having a little trouble controlling his breath. "What have you learned?"

He did not like the determined look on Alex's face. "It's the end of the line, Admiral."

Kolchak felt a needle-like stab of pain in his stomach. "There must be a way out."

"May I show you the map, Admiral?" Alex asked politely enough. Upon receiving a curt nod, he spread one out on the desk before him. Kolchak's nerves were tightening by the moment as he listened to Alex outline a possible escape route. "I have myself gone through the mountain passes from Sludyanka to Troitskavask down to Muktui," this confident young Czech said. "It's an easy ride," he concluded, as if he were talking to a physically fit sailor of twenty years ago. "And from there you could follow the trade routes through China to Harbin or to Peking."

Kolchak looked up at the optimistic face. Those eyes, as black as the hair, could hide signs of a plot to deceive him. Once he had seen innocence in these eyes. Now he thought there could be cunning. "There are many questions to be considered," countered Kolchak. "I am a mariner, not a cavalryman . . . but I'll think it through. In the interim, I formally request the protection of Czech forces."

"We'll do our best. Did you talk to General Syrovy?" Alex asked.

"No. Not yet," he lied. "Leave me now. I'll try later."

"All right, Admiral, goodbye."

As soon as Alex had closed the door, Kolchak sat upright. He grabbed the telephone and ordered a line to Kultuk. Within minutes he was speaking to Ataman Semyonov, known to the Baikal population as the 'Ogre of Chita'. At length they weighed the possibility of taking the gold reserves by camel train through Mongolia, but rejected the idea. Kolchak hurriedly gave his concluding message: "Ataman Semyonov, don't forget that the Czechs are to be regarded as my prisoners; do not let them escape. I don't care if you have to destroy the railroad . . . don't let them leave the Baikal region."

"It is possible to explode the tunnels," Semyonov suggested.

"If you must. I leave that to your discretion," responded Kolchak grandly. "For your loyal service I place you in command of the entire region."

"Including the city of Irkutsk?"

"Yes, the city is yours," confirmed the admiral.

"A Christmas gift?"

"I don't understand."

Semyonov sounded puzzled. "It is Christmas Eve. Christians give strange presents on this occasion, do they not?"

Kolchak gave no response. Christmas Eve? He was confused. Where had it all gone?

There was nothing but the crackle of static on the line until the Mongol said: "It will be as you wish, Excellency." Kolchak, deep in thought, cradled the telephone.

● ● ●

On another line, minutes later, another conversation began when Alex snatched up the ringing telephone. "Hello," he said quickly.

"Brother Branda . . . Syrovy here. You can ignore all requests from Kolchak from now on. He is not to be trusted . . . We just listened to him prove it."

"What's he up to now?"

"He's given Semyonov free rein, and tipped him off about the Treasury. Be ready for him. We are."

"All right, General . . . . Merry Christmas."

● ● ●

Later, Alex hiked through falling snow to his train and a supper table with Katya and the two children. He held up a cup of mulled wine to give them the same wish. "Katya, Paul, Olga . . . Merry Christmas to us all." He saw the children's faces, excited, but content in the security of a family group again. Katya was radiant.

The children ate dinner happily, interrupting with joyous questions and frequent observations about the packages under the small tree Katya had decorated. When one of the gifts would no longer stay quiet, Katya declared that it was now time for presents.

There was a kitten which little Olga could not stop hugging. And Paul studied every item in the kit Alex had brought him from supplies. Comb, brush, nail-clippers, scissors, soap, file — all in their own olive green pouch as precious items that now represented everything Paul owned.

Alex told them the Czech story of the good King Wenceslas. Then they sang the old song together. He saw the children's faces change; they seemed peaceful at last.

With the two orphans asleep, Alex said sadly, "I have no gift for you, Beauty."

She kissed his cheek. "There'll be time enough for gifts someday. Soon perhaps. Come to bed."

Alex was awake early because he worried about the defenses that Kolchak had forced him to use in re-arranging the cars. From a military viewpoint it was really nothing more than a static line of railway cars three kilometres long and open to the taiga along the southern perimeter. There were two curves in the track, so that the full length of the seven trains was never completely in view. It would be impossible to defend any concerted attack against trains that Kolchak had arranged in order of political importance.

Admiral Kolchak's two cars were in front, with the Treasury cars right behind. The next few cars housed the Siberians, and after that, Alex's cars for the Falcons. The last car was for Peter's rearguard. They were strung out, and vulnerable. And now, because of this unscheduled stop, this poor positioning must be corrected quickly, Alex knew.

The temperature had dropped, this bright clear morning. The sun reflected off the snow, hurting his eyes as he hurried to confer with the others. Alex arranged with Peter's Sixth Regiment to deploy patrols a few kilometres down the track to the west, watching for Bolshevik bands and deflecting refugees north to the Great Moscow Road. Peter was to protect the western-most trains. The remainder of the Siberian Guard held the center, and the Falcon Regiment covered Admiral Kolchak's two trains as well as the Treasury at the eastern extreme. This is where the main obstacle stood — the Bolshevik's armored railcar, head-on to the front of the admiral's. In the crisp air a red flag hung limp on the front of the engine.

Major Kadlec walked across the empty storage yard, and Alex waved him over. "I think we have a few days before Semyonov could possibly reach us from Kultuk. Peter's having trouble redirecting refugees around us . . . . Why not arrange the trains side by side, because then we can encircle the whole yard with our defenses in a tighter area. We're too spread out just now."

"Good idea," the major agreed. "I'll back into position along-side you."

It was during this maneuvering they were attacked. Alex heard the first shots which seemed to be concentrated on Major Kadlec's train in a line of fire from the east. He quickly shifted the Falcons to the eastern edge of the railyard, laying down an answering barrage to the attackers positioned in the forest on both sides of the track. After the first few volleys, Alex spotted two men in the focus of his binoculars — Mongol bandits. How did they get here so fast from Kultuk?

Alex whirled around looking back down the tracks. A riderless horse galloped into the open railyard from around a slight curve near the center of the caravan, just where Kolchak's staff train met the last car of the Treasury.

"A diversion!" he shouted. "Jan, stay here. Pavel, come with me. Bring a squad."

Running hard, Alex came to the middle of the Treasury train where the bullion was stored. No Siberian Guards to be seen. What the hell? Had they deserted? He scrambled under the car to the forest side, his squad of Falcons right behind.

The door of a bullion car had been broached. There were horse tracks in the fresh snow, and they led away from the train south, into the taiga.

"They can't have gone far," Alex called. "Come on!"

He counted eight Falcons as they fanned out through the slender pines, following the trail briskly and straining for any sound penetrating the smother of snow on the stiff green needles. At the bottom of a long hill perhaps five hundred metres from the bullion car, Alex raised his hand in a silent command to stop. From up ahead came muffled gun fire. There were two or three more shots heard in answer, then a few more, then nothing.

Alex waved his men forward again, and the squad moved farther down the wooded slope. After two hundred metres or so he came to a clearing at the bottom of the hill. A horse was down, lying on its side, pinned to the ground by a case of bullion skewed at a crazy angle. Its legs thrashed wildly as three Mongols tried to whip the frantic beast into a standing position.

On the red-stained snow behind the helpless horse lay the bodies of two White Russian officers.

Alex stepped into the clearing, calling out to the Mongolians, "Yield!" The Mongolians drew their weapons, but died before they could take aim.

"Pavel. Scout ahead. Release that animal. We'll need him."

Two Legionnaires untied the straps on the heavy crate, which allowed the horse to scramble to its feet trembling and stamping with fear. A trooper held the bridle, stroking the jerking head. Another brushed away snow from the horse's hairy side with a Mongol's fur cap. Others checked the immediate area. Alex searched the two Siberian officers, taking their identification wallets from the inside pouch of their coats.

He stood as the scouts returned. "Alex, they've gone. The forest opens up just ahead. They've been joined by a lot of horses. We need more men."

"No, we don't. The orders are clear: no heroics, no sacrifices. Russians stole Russian gold and we've rescued one chest — that's enough for today. What else is there?" he asked, while sliding the identification wallets into the deep pockets of his sheepskin coat.

"Only this leather bag, Colonel."

Alex set it on the snow, kneeling to examine the contents. The bag had been slashed open with a knife and was virtually empty. He reached in, pulling out all that remained: a thick stack of new banknotes in 5,000-ruble denominations, and a handful of cut diamonds the size of garden peas. On the back of the fat bundle of rubles was a picture of the Summer Palace. Alex turned it over to find the doleful gaze of Czar Nicholas Romanov. Some of the patrol pulled back. One man crossed himself.

Alex dropped the banknotes into the leather bag. "Well, that's all we can do," he said, picking up the diamonds.

"Wait, brother. Didn't we find this fair and square?" a trooper asked with some hesitation. Looking at the diamonds hungrily, he picked one up and said, "Don't think it'd be stealing if we kept one each. I could open a little bake shop with this."

Alex looked past the scarred countenance mutilated by the frost of four Russian winters and tried to read the dreams behind the man's bright eyes. He looked at the others, and saw faces of once youthful friends now full of hope again. He then felt his own twinge of avarice from the years of scraping by — years of doing without. If there were a diamond for each, he could buy a house for Katya. He set his jaw. "Sorry, men," he said briskly. "We have our job to do."

"I suppose," Jan suggested, "that these could strictly be called the right of salvage. Even Kolchak, the old sailor, would recognize all this as the flotsam and jetsam of war." He raised his eyebrows slightly, waiting for Alex's response.

Alex could see the others waiting too, but he just shook his head. "Gentlemen, let's quit daydreaming and get back to work." He dropped the diamonds into the pouch and handed it to Pavel.

"No one would know, if we took just one each," Jan persisted, though gently.

"Not 'til you tried to spend it," Alex said, straightening out the horse's harness. "Then they'd hang the lot of us."

He smiled when he saw that his men immediately turned to begin what had now become a salvage job. With considerable effort, they reloaded the bullion crate onto the pony's back to lead it slowly up the hill through the trees toward the train.

"I can't understand how Semyonov managed to get here from Kultuk so quickly," Pavel said, as they trudged back through the taiga.

Alex shook his head with a shrug. "Maybe it wasn't Semyonov. Anyway, let's get this load back to the accountants. Let them sort out the mess."

• • •

In the Treasury train, Katya heard footsteps coming down the corridor toward the children's playroom. Expecting Victor or Alex, she pulled open the door. Instead, she was startled to find herself confronted by two strangers. She fought to slam the door but the two men leaned hard to heave it open, forcing her back, her shoes slipping on the carpet.

Olga began to whimper as one man closed the door behind them and dropped his winter coat over the rocking horse.

"You are most fortunate," he crooned, walking toward Katya. "My name is Igor Skipetrov, the greatest lover in all Mongolia."

Katya pulled Olga back to shield her. She could feel the child hugging her knees from behind, trying to hide. Then the Mongol reached out, and with a swift tug he tore Katya's blouse and sweater from shoulder to waist.

"Better," he said, while his companion watched excitedly.

Katya raked her nails down his face, leaving four tracks of blood on each cheek. "Pig!" she shouted.

Skipetrov swore, raising a fist. She held up her hand to block the blow but his hand clubbed her across the forehead. As she reeled across the floor, she heard Olga scream and caught a glimpse of Paul bolting out the far door. Had they seen him? The toys and posters on the wall became blurred. Katya recovered her senses while she was being dragged face down across a table, held at the wrists by Skipetrov's accomplice. He stretched her arms to the table's edge, pulling her face level with his bright eyes.

"Not in front of the child," she pleaded, suddenly weak with fear. "Let me go," she begged, trying to pull away. But Skipetrov had secured her around the waist from behind. Katya could feel him. She could smell him. She heard his rapid breathing. With her mind reeling, she felt as if she might faint, but then she saw Olga peeking around the corner of the desk. She could see the terror in the child's eyes and this allowed her to focus for an instant so that she regained some control of her mind at least. Then Katya suddenly remembered her ballet mistress saying: "You're a strong young woman" — and fear was instantly replaced by rage.

"No!" Katya bellowed, as the skirt was thrown up over her waist and her underclothing wrenched from her hips.

"Never!" She howled this promise so intensely that the Mongol facing her tightened his grip while his chieftain fumbled with the buttons on his trousers.

Katya lashed her right leg back in a wide sweep. She felt her heel crunch into the side of Skipetrov's head, knocking him to the ground. He sat beside the table cursing, holding his torn ear. Blood rushed out between his fingers. When he saw the blood on his palm, his face twisted hatefully and he rose shakily to his feet. Then Katya heard the door open.

Victor stepped into the room, his pistol drawn and ready. Without a word he sighted down the barrel at the man holding Katya's wrists. The Mongol looked up astounded, releasing her just before the roar from the pistol caught him full in the face. Katya swept Olga from the floor and ran out the far door which was held open by Paul.

"Skipetrov, you filthy bastard, get up! Do you recognize me?"

"No, comrade," Skipetrov said, searching Victor's features with a brutish stare.

He wiped his bloodied hand on his shirt and then reached up, gently feeling the torn ear. "Perhaps when I dress myself for a little dignity, I can–"

Victor discharged a blast from the pistol, splintering bone in the left shoulder. The bandit fell back to the floor, his face contorted with pain.

"Dignity is a word that will never grace your name," Victor said, barely in control. "I'll tell you who I am, you son of a bitch. You sold me, and laughed. Said you'd kill everything I loved. I now return the favor." Victor sent another shot crashing through the main joint of the right shoulder. "You'll never swing a sword again."

Skipetrov cursed as he lay writhing on the floor. He screamed when Victor held the gun against the side of his knee. "You'll never ride a horse." Victor spoke as if reciting a list, and fired again.

Katya came back into the room with a pistol in her hand. Victor could see horror in her eyes when she understood what he was doing. But he had no intention of stopping.

"You'll never look at another woman either," Victor said through clenched teeth, shoving the barrel of the gun between the helpless man's legs.

"Victor, stop!" Katya cried. "Enough!" She pulled him back by the arm pleading. "Please," he heard her sob.

Victor could feel his own heavy breathing now. His unblinking eyes watched Skipetrov in agony on the floor. To a Russian, revenge was the sweetest emotion, and from the way he felt now, they were right. Perhaps this was enough. He took several deep breaths. With one last look at Skipetrov's agony, he holstered his pistol.

He turned to Katya, her hand clenched over her mouth and her eyes wide with fright and spilling tears.

"Katya, are you OK?" he asked, searching her face. He gathered her into his arms, closing his eyes. "Dear God," he whispered. "Katya, I...I..."

Victor stopped when he heard running down the carriage hallway. Alex raced through the open door with Pavel behind him, their guns drawn.

"Katya!" Alex called fearfully, "What happened?" as he scanned the room and the two Mongols on the floor.

Victor felt her pull from his embrace. She hurried over to Alex who began to rock her in a bear hug, crooning soothingly into her ear. "Katya, Katya. You're safe. You're safe now," he whispered quietly.

Katya was crying, and pulled a hand across her cheek. "I'll be fine," she said in an unsteady voice. "Just give me a moment." She straightened up, although Victor could see that she still trembled. "I must calm the children," she said. "They're terrified."

As she went over to Paul and Olga cowering behind the desk in the far corner of the car, Alex searched Victor's face. "You all right?" he asked.

Victor nodded between rapid breaths. "I don't know where these two bastards came from. It was terrible. Terrible." His heart wouldn't stop pounding.

He watched Alex walk over to Katya who was standing with her arms around the children. Alex took off his sheepskin coat. "Pavel will take you to our car. I won't be long. Here, put this on."

Alex hung it over her shoulders. Then he kissed her cheek tenderly before she left with the children. Her eyes filled with tears again as she passed by. "Thank you, Victor," she said. "Thank you."

When she had gone Alex turned to Victor. "Vic, how can I ever thank you?" He grasped Victor's hand in both of his. "I am forever in your debt."

Victor saw Alex gaze deep into his face. This must look suspicious, he thought. My eyes must show the fear of what might have been, and that my conscience is ripping me apart. He closed his eyes, trying to hold in the pain. He loved Katya and had been in the act of confessing it when Alex rushed in. Had Alex heard?

Victor heard his own rasping voice: "The boy . . . he came and got me . . . or I don't know . . ." he stopped, holding Alex by the elbows. "I don't know what I'd have done, if . . . if . . ." He shook his head slowly from side to side.

He watched Alex go over to the cupboard for some vodka, which he hurriedly splashed into two teacups.

Skipetrov groaned, unable to move, but Alex gave him only a glance before turning back to Victor. "I'll never forget this, Vic. Now, I owe you."

Victor drank quickly and the burning down his throat seemed to brace him. "You got me out of a hell-hole," he said, pausing to drink again. "I can never balance the books." He looked up at the sound of a rifle exchange down the track.

Victor could feel his pulse begin to slow down as Alex studied him. "Yes you can," Alex said with some intensity. "It's simple. Promise me you'll look after Katya if anything happens to me."

It was quiet again outside. Victor looked at his friend in disbelief. "But . . ."

"Promise me!"

"Of course I will, but . . ." He sat down with his face in his hands. "Oh, Jesus . . ."

He could feel Alex patting him on the back while he sobbed.

"Thanks, Vic. I need to know she'd be all right." Alex's voice was calm, as if he had all the facts needed for his decision. "I would want to be certain she was with someone who cares."

Then Alex bent over and picked up Skipetrov in a fireman's carry, ignoring the Mongol's cry of pain and the blood staining his coat. "Drag that snake outside, will you?" Alex asked, jerking his head in the direction of the corpse. "We'll send them both back to their friends."

Victor tossed down the last of his vodka before grabbing the dead bandit's collar to drag him down the corridor and into the railyard. He pulled him through the fresh snow leaving a smear of blood in his wake.

Two Falcons threw his body, stomach down, over the saddle of his horse. They tied his wrists and ankles under the horse's belly.

Skipetrov groaned as he was similarly slung and tied. Victor then led the two horses to the head of the train where nothing more than sporadic rearguard rifle fire indicated the withdrawal of the Mongols. With a shout and a slap on the rump, Victor sent the two mounts cantering away.

Months later Victor learned, from bandits taken prisoner by the American Siberian contingent, that Skipetrov's men intercepted their chief and the body of his companion. Skipetrov had then traveled twenty pain-wracked kilometres before the group met with Kolchak's Siberian deserters and the stolen gold. Here, a wild celebration began. Someone had shot a bear. A huge pit was dug and a massive fire lit. Over a wide bed of glowing coals the meat sizzled on a thick iron rod.

When Skipetrov, in a croaking voice, pleaded for vodka, they poured tea down his throat. They laughed when he choked, ridiculing his helpless condition. As the drunken din grew louder, and the weakening Skipetrov complained of being cold, a scoffing comrade jumped up and kicked him down a slight grade toward the pit. On his back he slipped slowly over the last few feet of snow, looking wild-eyed at the flames. They jeered as his useless limbs clumsily tried to arrest his slide. Then a barbaric howl went up as their chief rolled over the edge of the deep pit, falling face-first into the glowing orange coals.

Living in an animal-like society, they discarded Skipetrov like a broken tool. Victor linked the date of receiving this information with the end of his nightmares.

• • •

Katya walked silently with Pavel to her quarters. A little chilly now, as shock took control, she pushed her shaking hands deep into the jacket's woolen pockets so that Pavel would not notice. "I want to rest. I've left the children with Mrs. Ordinov."

She held herself together as she bade him farewell and entered the car. From the sheepskin coat she automatically removed the identification purses Alex had retrieved from the dead Siberians, and she placed these two leather wallets in the drawer of Alex's desk reserved for official documents. Katya hung the heavy coat in its place on the wall. Then she lay down on their bed and tried to control the gagging and retching.

• • •

When Skipetrov's horse galloped away into the taiga, Alex hurried to Admiral Kolchak's command car. With him he took the Bolshevik representative for Nizhne Udinsk. "Admiral, may I present Comrade Shalapin, chairman of the local soviet?"

"No, you may not," Kolchak snapped. "I will countenance no Bolshevik."

Alex watched the anger flash cross Shalapin's face. The Bolshevik looked around the room, glaring at the rich furnishings, the brass fixtures and the portrait of Czar Nicholas, but he said nothing. With a quick movement he merely slapped a formal document against Alex's arm. Reading quickly, Alex realized there was no need for argument; the chase was over. The Bolshevik's demeanor told the whole story.

Alex felt a calmness come over his mind. He had lurched from one crisis to another during the past few weeks. Now the tension in his neck and shoulders had drained away somehow, and what remained was a new clarity to his situation. There was no more need for hiding.

"You should listen, Admiral. They are attempting to do this properly . . . with negotiation, rather than a major assault . . . and the loss of more lives."

The Bolshevik spoke to Alex in an even voice. "There's no rush. We're prepared to allow the Czechs to complete their duty . . . which is to transport the Treasury gold, and the admiral, to the city of Irkutsk where this train will be turned over to the government there. It is expected that foreigners will then leave with all haste."

Alex placed the document on the desk in front of the glowering Admiral Kolchak. He guessed that Kolchak was frantically thinking of a way out. The admiral, no doubt, believed that the remnants of his

Omsk government still held control. Even if they were overthrown, he probably believed that Semyonov and the Wild Division could still find a way to rescue him. Whatever scheme Kolchak had in mind, Alex was determined to have none of it. He watched the dictator glance across the page and then, putting on a conciliatory air, ask, "And if we refuse Lenin's demand?"

"We will turn this area into a wasteland before you turn one wheel further," the Bolshevik replied firmly.

"Admiral, I believe we should operate with the brutal facts in full view," Alex added. "You have no bargaining position. This is not Lenin's demand . . . It is the demand of the people from this region. You will sign this agreement here and now, or we will not be allowed to move. We'll get no coal, no water. The rails will be sabotaged. The fight will be unyielding. I'm halfway to Vladivostok harbor with my regiment . . . I'm not ending our journey here. You sign, or I'll sign for you."

"I have formally requested the protection of the Czech Legion and expect no less," Kolchak countered. "You are relieved of your command — immediately."

Alex shook his head, then turned to the commissar. "I will accept responsibility for the safe conduct of the Treasury train to Irkutsk . . . as well as Admiral Kolchak. When do you want us to begin?"

The Bolshevik looked relieved and sat down without invitation. There was a long silence until Kolchak spoke out, "How does the agreement read?"

"It promises that you surrender the gold reserves at Irkutsk . . . and that I surrender you," Alex stated flatly. He felt another release of pressure as he said this.

"But that's sure death!" Kolchak protested.

"Maybe not," Alex said. "No doubt, you've become part of the New Bolshevik history, to be preserved. It's likely that they'll keep you safe — not comfortable, but safe. There is no option other than to sign. The cold truth is, Admiral, you've had your day."

CHAPTER 30

IRKUTSK
JANUARY 1920

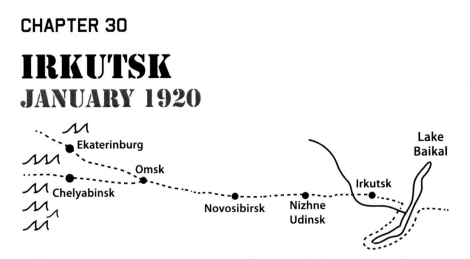

Sitting in an easy chair before a crackling fire, Syrovy swirled cognac in a warmed snifter. He had visited the house rented by the commander-in-chief of the Western Allies representatives expecting nothing more than a recitation of policy, but he had been pleasantly surprised by General Maurice Janin. The French general admitted that he had no power whatsoever, but he seemed genuinely sensitive to the Czech predicament, and wanted to help Syrovy get his troops out.

These French know how to live, Syrovy thought to himself, looking across a bold Persian rug of red and blue. The French general sat back, lounging in a leather chair. He brushed a drooping white moustache with the back of a smallish hand.

"General Janin," Syrovy began. "I am forced to play a card . . . Can you help me?"

"Probably not, mon general," replied the commander of the Combined Allied Military Forces in Siberia. "But you know I would like to. What is your problem?"

"Kolchak's henchman, that brute Semyonov . . . I'm going to bring him down."

Janin raised an eyebrow without comment, but Syrovy was grateful to see that the French leader did give an understanding nod.

"Semyonov has taken thirty-one citizens of Irkutsk to Lake Baikal. Claims he'll kill them all unless Admiral Kolchak is released — and we won't do that. I understand that the Japanese are on their way here to back up the blackmail. But here's the sticky part — Semyonov has his train between us and the tunnels. He says no one gets out. Is he ruthless enough to goad us into fighting for Kolchak? I believe so. Is he determined enough to blow the tunnels? I'm not sure."

Janin looked into his cognac. "From what I have heard, he is capable of both. So what is it you propose, mon ami?"

"I'm going after him. I believe him to be a coward, just like any back-alley thug."

"The Allies cannot join you in such a misadventure," Janin said with considerable feeling. He was a small man, but his determination was strong enough. "An international war could develop right here — a second world war, one short year after the first."

"I'll secure the tunnels and then chase him off and no more," Syrovy promised. "I want you to prevent a war. Just keep yourself between the city and Kolchak's forces, to keep the Japanese out of this."

"To that I can agree," Janin said. He raised his brandy snifter in salute.

The next day Syrovy boarded his armored train and set off for Baikal Station just as Alex and Gaida had done eighteen months before. It seemed so long ago, he thought, but the identical strategy might work again to prevent Semyonov from dynamiting the tunnels. In winter, however, these Legionnaires had to labor over snowy mountains through darkness broken only by the eerie smear of color from the northern lights.

Syrovy sent his strongest troops in tireless flanking sweeps to surround Baikal Station and Semyonov's train. Syrovy rode at a walking pace on the deck of an armored car, sliding ominously between the lines of infantry, who by now were well aware of the importance of their mission. Four-man crews on machine guns waited in sandbag nests, one in front and the other two controlling each side. The gunner was in charge. While one man would feed the belts carefully into the machine to avoid jamming, another would guide the emptied belt out of the way. The fourth would prepare the next belt for loading. Smooth and efficient, the deadly machines were ready.

Syrovy stood at the back of the ore car beside the light cannon bolted to the metal deck. He shivered in the wind. With the headlight extinguished, he peered down the tracks and could barely make out the figure of Major Kadlec at the side of the roadbed. Kadlec wore a hooded white smock over his sheepskin coat, but Syrovy saw him wave, signaling that Baikal Station was surrounded. The snare was ready.

Syrovy called back to the engineer, "Give me everything you've got," and the engine thundered down the track toward Baikal, machine guns blazing. The attack was swift, furious and final.

An hour later in the glare of the single headlight, his men assembled almost fifteen hundred Mongols. They stood on the railroad bed, their hands on top of their fur caps.

Syrovy jumped down from the armored car to search the ranks for Semyonov. He studied each sullen face. He caught Kadlec's stare and the shake of the major's head. The bandit chieftain had not been found.

Syrovy beckoned Kadlec over and then grasped one of the prisoners by the elbow. The Mongol looked up fearfully and tried to pull back, no doubt terrified by the stern look from a general with a black leather eye-patch.

The barrel-chested Kadlec quickly grabbed the other elbow and forcibly dragged the terrified man away from the rest. Syrovy stepped in front of the Mongol, drew his pistol and held the barrel between the man's eyes. "Ataman Semyonov," he growled.

He could see the prisoner's knees sag, but Kadlec held him up. "Semyonov," he said again, and pulled back the hammer.

The Mongol pointed to the dock, frantically gesturing out to where the river widened. Syrovy could see the lights of a steamer heading toward the lake. He felt a burning rage; they had come so close.

"Hostages," Syrovy barked. The prisoner thrust his finger out to the steamer two or three more times. Syrovy felt cheated. What would he say to the families in Irkutsk?

Shortly after, Syrovy stood on the deck of his armored train with the Mongol prisoners following in behind. At Irkutsk, his men paraded the bandits down the icy main street in front of silent onlookers who cast hateful looks as they huddled under the wide stone building entrances on each side of the road. There was little satisfaction for anyone without the return of the hostages, he knew.

This gnawing feeling of outrage became worse over the next few days when it became known that Semyonov had clubbed his victims to death on the decks of the steamer and dumped the bludgeoned bodies into the tainted lake like so many table-scraps. Most of the bloated corpses were drawn downstream by the current, then snagged on the bank as the river turned its way toward Irkutsk. The families were horrified, and so, instead of relieving the tension, Syrovy found that he had inadvertently inflamed the citizenry, who had been assured by Admiral Kolchak himself that the hostage-taking was merely a gesture, promising that no harm would come of it.

Now Syrovy faced an outraged city where hate crackled through every conversation. They could not wait until they got their hands on Kolchak. Syrovy knew that the Treasury train was scheduled to arrive on January 13th and hoped that Alex would be ready for anything. A riot was one possibility.

Syrovy could not rest. The arrogance of the bandit leader grated like a raw sore. He could not stop thinking about the appalling crimes this brute seemed to get away with. Semyonov had kidnapped and then murdered ordinary citizens in a remote region. These were people who not only struggled constantly and mightily against nature, but also had to deal with butchers who somehow attracted followers just as unscrupulous as themselves. Perhaps from their ranks would spawn more such leaders. Good Lord, what a thought. He put his elbows on his knees and massaged his forehead. How could he end this outrage? And it certainly was an outrage. It must be stopped.

The next morning was very cold; from a cloudless sky the sun gave no comfort at all. It seemed to be nothing more than a light that made the creaking snow more painful to the eye.

Syrovy sat on his horse in Semjonovsky Square in the center of the city. It was in this same square, he recalled, where Feodor Dostoevsky had been read the death sentence for criticizing government censorship. As Dostoevsky stood in the second rank, next to face the executioner, he had been offered a cross to kiss, but just as he was about to be called forward a reprieve came from Nicholas I. Why His Imperial Majesty had granted Dostoevsky imprisonment in the city's fortress instead of the firing squad was not difficult to understand. Nicholas wanted to improve his reputation, which was at that time described by people as being cold and without feeling. Syrovy gave a low grunt at the thought that this gesture would soften that image. Nicholas was teasing his prisoner in a cruel way, and now what would Syrovy do? Must he join forces with a Red Guard just as cruel?

Wearing a long fur coat and fur hat, Syrovy stationed himself at the head of the assembled Mongol prisoners. He could feel some warmth from his horse and gripped tighter with the inside of his legs as he moved down the main street to the north woods.

He looked back to see the Irkutsk constabulary riding at the sides of the marching prisoners. One hundred metres up ahead of him rode a squad of stern-looking soldiers from the Red Guard. They preceded him through the city streets to a trail leading into the forest on the northern edge of Irkutsk. He rode this quiet trail in the soothing green shadow of the taiga until they came out into the blinding glare of an open snowy field which covered a long frozen lake.

The Red patrol stopped and waited a few metres off to the side of the trail. Syrovy could not read their thoughts through the hard-eyed stares as he nudged his horse over to them offering a salute. The officer in command seemed reluctant to even nod.

Syrovy motioned the Mongols to follow after the Red officer who led the way across the open field of dazzling white. He felt numb realizing that he was going to cooperate with men like that.

Syrovy sat listening to his horse snorting steam as the Mongols shuffled by in the loose snow. The constabulary stopped along the sides of the trail. The Mongol bandits kept marching, closely followed by three soldiers of the Red patrol who moved in behind with pistols drawn.

Syrovy and the mounted Irkutsk constabulary waiting beside him watched the fifteen hundred Mongol captives march after the one lone officer of the Red Guard. When the officer raised his hand, the parade stopped. Then he and his three comrades cantered their horses back to the edge of the forest where Syrovy waited. The flying hooves kicked up powdery snow, and steamy breath blew from the beasts' flaring nostrils. The Red patrol leader exchanged a look with Syrovy just before he nodded to a comrade.

This man slid down from his mount and went over behind a tree to pull aside a tarpaulin covering some equipment, including a battery-driven plunger.

Syrovy raised his chin, looking to the low hills above the frozen lake where the Mongols stood resting. Gathered together like vermin, he thought, and he relieved the strain on his eye by staring into the green forest. He could not, however, shake a feeling with which he was quite unfamiliar. Oh, he knew what it was well enough. It was shame. What saddened him was that he had never felt it before this day.

Syrovy heard a series of six muffled explosions. He listened as the rumbling echoed and tumbled among the low hills, until his ears rang in a frozen silence. There were shouts, but he tried not to listen by keeping his eye hard on a distant tree. A scream forced him to bring his gaze down on a man clinging to a small raft of ice. While he watched, a wave boiled up and turned the raft over. Then it was quiet again.

The white field was now filled with nothing more than black water and floating ice; there was not a trace of the fifteen hundred prisoners. He wondered if they had known it would end like this.

The captain of the Red Guard gave Syrovy a cold stare as he reined his horse away down the path toward Irkutsk.

• • •

Alex stepped down from the train at Irkutsk Station carrying the strain of two disturbing problems. The first was the necessity of turning over the Treasury train to proper authorities as quickly as possible before some nasty incident embroiled them in a fight he knew would be to the death. The chase had taken almost two years, and with emotions at the flashpoint, he knew he must surrender the treasure at once. If Kolchak and Ordinov would cooperate, he and Katya might get out of this mess alive. This was no place to fight a battle. They surely would lose, because the Treasury was essential to Bolshevik success and Lenin would stop at nothing to reclaim the train.

The second problem was that Alex had only just discovered that, unwittingly, he had come into possession of some of this treasure. While at his desk that morning, he opened the identification wallets taken from the corpses of the Siberian guards. In each was a stack of mint-fresh 5,000 ruble notes, obviously stolen. Their presence would be impossible to explain to Soviet officials, or to Katya — especially Katya. Would anyone believe he had not stolen them? Even his men, who had asked in vain to keep the eight diamonds from the slashed leather bag, would be hard to convince.

Alex pondered this situation as he stepped onto the platform. He was met by a bristling government official who saluted while announcing, "My name is Colonel Holidiloff. I'm here to take over." He had a red moustache with beard trimmed short, and when he spoke, he looked beyond Alex, as if uninterested in the Czechs or their purpose. Without waiting for a response, he signaled a platoon of fifty or more men to surround the train. As they began the move into position they were met by twenty Falcon sentries who dropped suddenly to one knee and released the safety catches on their rifles with a forbidding metallic click.

"Squad halt! About face!" Alex called loudly, relieved to see that Bolsheviks, too, obeyed a military voice. "Falcons! At ease!" Then turning to the open-mouthed city soldier, who apparently was far from battle-experienced, said, "Colonel Holidiloff, my compliments to you and your men. We are anxious for your help . . . My men are tired. Looking after this train for six months has made them a bit jumpy. Perhaps you and I should work out a schedule satisfactory to your government. We wouldn't want an unfortunate incident between professional soldiers, would we? Especially when we're working toward the same objective."

"No, certainly not, but I have my orders," said the flustered colonel.

"Yes, of course. And our superiors honor both of us by expecting that we will work together without difficulty. Correct? So, let us review these orders," Alex said in a kindly tone, gesturing with his hand up the iron stairs to his staff car.

"Brother Pavel," he continued. "Stay here with your platoon so that nobody bothers our comrades. They have a job to do, and we're going to help them."

Inside the staff car, Alex spoke first. "I welcome your help, Colonel. It's a great relief to us . . . sharing guard duties for this important transfer. I'm sure you agree that the procedure must be done carefully, without error."

"That was my intention, of course," said the Soviet colonel, who seemed somewhat more relaxed as he glanced around Alex's office which also served as home for Katya and the children. Unmade beds and clothes drying on a line cluttered the far end of the car.

"What's our first step?" Alex asked.

"Well, I suppose we should set up a schedule for the sentries."

"Then we shall," Alex smiled. "A shared responsibility . . . so that when this sorry task is over . . . our duty done, no one can say that we did not cooperate. Is that acceptable?"

"Perfectly," agreed Holidiloff.

Alex brought vodka to the table. "When would you like to make the transfers?"

Alex expected that Colonel Holidiloff would be warmed by the importance of the task, and by Alex's compliance, and perhaps he was correct, because the Soviet colonel assumed a more nonchalant air. He unbuttoned his coat and said rather expansively, "I think we should begin with the gold. Bank examiners will be here soon. Your accountants should be ready. As soon as ledgers are balanced, the official papers can be signed and then the train returns to Moscow. The admiral will be moved to the fortress at first light tomorrow."

"Agreed," said Alex quietly. He sipped his vodka before asking in an offhand way, "What happens to the Treasury staff?"

"I don't know," Holidiloff said. He seemed a bit surprised. "It wasn't considered."

"Some of them have dedicated their entire adult life to their sworn duty. Most wish to continue their service, I would think."

"Admirable," the colonel said. "Can they be trusted?"

"Completely. They're like monks. Non-political."

Holidiloff nodded as if satisfied, and this encouraged Alex to continue. "Why don't you set them to work? You can visit your superiors and find out what happens to them?"

"Good idea," Holidiloff said. "You're making this sensitive task much easier."

"I want it completed smoothly, as do you," Alex smiled. "We'll work together to make this a success. You could go down in history, you know. Shall we begin?"

In the heavy night air they walked together across the railroad bridge and beyond to the frozen streets of Irkutsk. The concrete fortress appeared as austere as a building could be. The only indication of life was a blurry glow of light through one of the high windows, completely covered by several inches of ice.

Alex turned off to Syrovy's headquarters alone. Everything bristled with splinters of hoarfrost — the rails, telephone wires, even the walls of those homes facing the wind.

One hour later Alex left Generals Syrovy and Janin. He now had full legal authorization to proceed. He met Colonel Holidiloff on the Angara River Bridge with Syrovy's admonition at the front edge of his mind: "Remember, Alex . . . caution. Tonight you're a juggler with some very sharp knives in the air."

The colonel from the Irkutsk Soviet had changed. Perhaps the vodka had worn off, for it seemed to Alex that a certain edge had returned to his voice.

More likely his superiors wanted to make sure that it was their man who was in charge and he acted the part. Alex determined to maintain a cooperative stance.

"Any accountants wishing to serve the new government in Moscow will be welcomed and respected," Holidiloff announced, turning his shoulder into the wind.

"A wise decision," Alex said. "They are, after all, dependable public servants. I'll take responsibility for anyone wishing to leave."

"Those who depart the Treasury leave everything behind. That train and its contents belong to Russia's Soviet Republic."

"Of course," Alex said agreeably. "Except, I suppose, for personal effects . . . toilet articles, private correspondence, clothes . . . that sort of thing."

"Only what they can carry in a single grip," snapped Holidiloff. "Everything will be searched."

Alex tried to appear calm but his mind raced. How could he get rid of the stolen currency in his desk drawer? He must not be caught with it in his possession. "As you wish, Colonel . . . and I'll back you on that."

"Might there be a problem?" the colonel asked, softened again by Alex's acquiescence.

"Nothing significant, surely . . . There are women and children who may have formed attachments to," he shrugged, "shall we say, bric-a-brac? My wife, for example, will be coming on General Kechek's train with me, and she has several trunks for clothes."

"Only what she can carry in a single bag," repeated Holidiloff warily. "We are talking about property of the Soviet Union."

"You have my word . . . By the way, why don't we stop by the railroad car that I call my office? I can clean out my desk and transfer to the Czech train right now. It will give you a headquarters through the next few cold days while things are formalized."

"A generous thought, Colonel Branda, if it wouldn't be too much trouble."

"Not at all," Alex said, trying to remain calm as he thought of the stolen rubles. "Just a few regimental papers in the desk . . . your desk. It won't take long."

Under the casual scrutiny of Holidiloff, Alex found his leather attaché case, unbuckled two straps and began filling it from the top of the desk. He gave an unsolicited accounting of the contents in a droning monotone: "My best pen — leave the ink for you; sentry roster; duty roster." He began opening drawers while he continued a dull litany: "Regimental register; casualty records; identification wallets of the deceased." His hand did not pause as he transferred the wallets of the two Siberians who had robbed the Treasury. His voice did not miss a beat as he thought of the banknotes within. "Sad business. The arms registry; and lastly, our bank records. There, that should do it. It's all yours, Colonel, with my best wishes. If there's anything I've forgotten . . . you can send it over, can't you?" Alex asked this while opening the door.

"Yes, certainly," said Holidiloff. "What about this rifle?"

"Ah, very good of you, I'd probably have to pay a levy if I didn't turn one in at Vladivostok. And there's my old foot locker. I'll have a couple of men bring it along, if that's all right?"

"No trouble," the Russian said, summoning two of his squad. "I'll just check the contents."

"Pavel," Alex called to his friend outside. "Would you mind taking my rifle to General Kechek's train? Tell Peter that I'll need quarters for me, my wife and Colonel Lindal. Here, you can take this as well," he said, carelessly tossing his attaché case on top of the foot locker. "Make sure that gets done, won't you?" he asked, putting a hand on Pavel's shoulder.

He saw Pavel look into his eyes for a split second with that tacit communication which special friends share. "I'll take care of it personally," he said, and Alex immediately breathed easier.

"Shall we move on now, Colonel?" Alex suggested innocently as he walked down the stairs to the snowy ground.

Alex walked with Colonel Holidiloff down the length of the Treasury train until they came to President Ordinov's carriage. Pavel, with the two Soviet guards who carried Alex's foot locker, continued on to the last car where they were challenged by Holidiloff's sentries.

"It's all right, comrades," Holidiloff called before climbing the stairs to the Treasury office. "I've cleared those items, let them pass." Alex watched his foot locker and the attaché case holding the banknotes being taken aboard Kechek's car. Then, with a sigh of relief, he followed Holidiloff up the stairs of Ordinov's lounge car.

Just inside, Alex caught up to Holidiloff who was talking to Katya. "Ah, Colonel, may I present my wife, Katherine Elenskaya Branda."

"We've just met," he said before turning again to Katya. "I understand you'll be leaving with your new husband."

"Yes, I shall," Katya replied with a wide smile. Her eyes shone with anticipation. "And the children." She pointed into the car where Olga and Paul were playing on the floor with other children. Little Olga watched the others at their game.

"You have children?" Holidiloff asked curiously.

"Well, yes. We've adopted them," Katya said matter-of-factly. When she noticed Holidiloff's silence, she suddenly became nervous. "Their grandmother was dead. They were starving. Back at Nizhne Udinsk." She looked fearfully at Alex, no doubt sensing she had said the wrong thing.

"We'll take care of them, Colonel," Alex said.

"That's not possible, I'm afraid," Holidiloff said, looking determined but not happy with the situation.

Katya was horrified. "They're orphaned! They have no one but us." She spoke frantically to Holidiloff who would not look her in the face. She seized his arm. "These two little ones have peered over the edge into hell. They're afraid of shadows . . . I . . . we, love them."

"Enough, Madame." Holidiloff pulled his arm away angrily. "How do you know they're orphaned? We have hundreds of inquiries for lost children — every day. This is their homeland. They will stay here! Everything that belongs to the new Union of Soviet Republics will remain." And with that he hurried on into Ordinov's conference car.

Katya came over to Alex with watery eyes. "Do something," she whispered forlornly.

Alex hugged her, holding his emotions tight. He was silent for a long while before speaking. "If you come across a fawn, lost in the woods . . . do you take it home? Or do you swallow hard, and leave it where it belongs?" He felt Katya sag against him. "You saved them. The war's over. What if someone is searching for them?"

He watched as Katya stood tall to wipe her eyes. Her face had that determined look. "I'll think this through," she said, and took the children out.

Alex closed the door behind her, then joined Holidiloff by Ordinov's desk. "This is a new situation. She needs time."

Holidiloff watched him soberly, without argument, and merely turned to Ordinov to ask: "President Ordinov, have you considered the wishes of your staff?"

"I can assure you, Colonel, that we have discussed the situation at great length," Ordinov said in his formal style. "Mrs. Branda will travel with her husband, but the remainder of us will stay with the exchequer — which is, after all, our life's work."

"Most commendable, Comrade. How is the tally progressing?"

"Everything is being scrupulously examined with the bank officials. Every seal has to be broken, the contents counted and the seals reset. The books and signatures will have to be balanced to record the theft by Admiral Kolchak's personal guard."

"Theft!" exclaimed Holidiloff. "What theft?" he asked, standing up aggressively.

"Back in Nizhne Udinsk," Ordinov said with great assurance. "There was a Mongol raid held in concert with the Siberian Guard at the behest of Admiral Kolchak."

"How do you know all this?" demanded the colonel, now highly agitated, a condition that made Alex uneasy as well, having spent so much time trying to make the Soviet colonel satisfied, even unconcerned — anything but belligerent.

"Because they overpowered my staff and held us captive while they stole thirteen cases of bullion, including five sacks of banknotes and platinum. We'll know exactly how much by tomorrow . . . then the examiners can sign the registry."

"Any Czechs involved?" Colonel Holidiloff asked, glaring at Alex.

"Certainly not!" said Ordinov, startled. "Why, Colonel Branda was most heroic; he and a small patrol showed courage enough to chase Mongols from the Wild Division. They caught some of the stragglers, recapturing one case and one leather pouch."

"Any gold missing?"

"Emphatically not! You can see for yourself that the seal is still intact. These men are above reproach."

Holidiloff glanced over at the Irkutsk bank manager who sent back a curt nod.

"Please, Mr. Ordinov. It's all right," Alex said in a reassuring way. "Colonel Holidiloff is doing a difficult job in a straightforward and professional manner. The inquiry he has just completed was a military necessity." Alex spoke in a positive tone, hoping that anyone listening would unconsciously accept his word "completed." He was relieved to note that no one challenged him.

"Forgive me, Colonel Branda," offered Holidiloff. "I'm glad you understand."

Alex raised his hand in a silent gesture of protest for the unnecessary apology, while thanking God that he had not allowed his men to keep the diamonds.

"And please excuse me, Colonel Holidiloff," said Ordinov. "We are all under pressure . . . put upon us by this unfortunate situation, whereby a man without the proper experience seized control of operations beyond his abilities, winding up as no more than a common thief. If you will permit us, we shall return to our labors."

Side by side Alex walked with Holidiloff back along the track toward Irkutsk. Both men were deep in thought, not speaking until the Soviet colonel stopped at Kolchak's car. "I want to say . . . it's a difficult thing about the children . . ."

"It is, Colonel. I appreciate your concern."

"They are Russian treasures, after all . . . like the jewels, I think."

Alex nodded sadly. "I know," he said, feeling a strange emptiness. He always knew the children would have to stay. It was just that Katya . . . and young Paul . . . . "It's getting late," he said, his voice cracking. "I'd best check my men for the transfer."

Holidiloff looked embarrassed, Alex thought, and he gave the Bolshevik colonel a wan smile. "We'll have to hook some cars onto General Kechek's train. Shall I meet you here at nine tomorrow for the formal relocation?"

"Very well, Colonel Branda. It's been a pleasure working with you. And congratulations on recapturing that case of bullion . . . you've proven your reliability by protecting Soviet property — if not your loyalty to our government. It won't be forgotten. The currency we don't worry about. That will be worthless as soon as we've secured the Treasury gold . . . then we print our own. Of course that is why the gold is so vital. Until tomorrow," he said, touching the brim of his cap.

"Goodnight, Colonel," Alex said with a salute, relieved to hear the paper money would soon be without value. But he still worried about Katya, and hurried back to their car where he found her packing kit bags for the children.

She was kneeling on the floor, Paul and Olga by her side. Alex could see the pain in those blue eyes. She was trying so hard to be cheerful. Katya looked up at Alex with a side glance and then continued packing with quick movements as if her emotions teetered on the edge of a cliff.

"You each have some food for emergencies, and some nice warm clothes from the other children. You may take one favorite toy." Her voice wavered. "Which one?"

Olga hugged her kitten.

Paul picked up the field-kit Alex had given him.

"All right," Katya said, fastening a strap to close the pack. "Now, this is what will happen. We'll all have supper. Then we'll have a good night's sleep, in the big bed, together. Tomorrow morning a nice lady will take you back to your village where you'll be safe, and they will find your family. I have spoken to her, and she has promised me that will happen."

The children smiled when she squeezed them to her.

Alex blew them a kiss. "I'll be right back," he said quietly.

On his way down the outside stair, he met Peter. "Petya. Good. Come on with me. We have a message to deliver." He then led the way to the door of the Dictator for All Siberia.

"Enter," Kolchak answered in a weak voice, standing sickly pale in the shadows. "Who is it? Oh, Colonel Branda. General Kechek. Any news?"

"Yes, Admiral. Would you like to sit down? . . . We can talk," Alex suggested.

"No, I shall stand," said Kolchak beginning to pace. "I feel like a prisoner running out of time and space. Is there any good news?"

"News, Admiral. But none of it good," Alex said.

Kolchak stopped pacing. "I demand to see General Syrovy or General Janin."

"I'm afraid it's too late for that."

Kolchak flinched as if he had been slapped. "What do you mean? Too late at night?"

"No. The fact is . . . your rule is over," Alex said quietly. "You'll be transferred to the Irkutsk Soviet tomorrow at first light. Please be ready."

"Ready? How does one get ready for the end?" Kolchak pulled back the gauze-like curtain covering the window and blew his breath to melt the frost. He rubbed the warmed spot in circles with his sleeve. He then bent low to look at the sky. It appeared as if he had not slept in days. "I hear a cello. Just a single droning note. One monotonous hum. I should do the job myself — and rob them of the satisfaction."

"They've paid dearly enough for their prize," Alex said quietly. He stood beside the rosewood desk wishing he had something better to offer. The silence was intense.

Peter appeared to grow exceedingly uncomfortable with the way the conversation was turning, and injected a new thought. "There are rumors, sir, that the Japanese are prepared to intercede on your behalf."

The admiral turned his head very slowly like someone who had run out of options. "Do you offer false hope, General?" Kolchak asked.

"No, sir, it's true. They have steam up. They're on full alert."

"Hah," Kolchak grunted quietly as he turned back to the window. "The Japanese . . . This is the farthest into Siberia they've penetrated, yet still they do nothing. It will be interesting to guess how far they are willing to go. I can't see a confrontation. They prefer to buy what they need." He began to pace again.

"What do you think of my chances, Colonel Branda? You wouldn't start lying to me at this point would you?"

"No, Admiral. No lies . . . . I think the Moscow Soviet will want you alive — in prison, of course, but alive. For at least a year, I'd guess. It's difficult to predict the actions of the Irkutsk government, though."

"Why is that?"

"Because of the thirty-one hostages. And because of the fact, Admiral Kolchak, that you are hated throughout Siberia."

The haunted man looked disturbed by this thought, and began to stalk the length of the car. "Well, what about the Allies? They were all here. But what did they do? Nothing correctly. Munitions, money, supplies, plans, troops . . . All here, but not put into effect. Result? Failure." He paused to look out the window at the clusters of guards wrapped in wool and fur, shuffling from one foot to the other in front of the little fires burning up and down the track.

Alex could see the admiral's hands shaking. It would be a long cold night for the man who once held so much power. It must be terrible to contemplate what might have been, and not be able to reverse one's own history.

Kolchak continued talking as he paced. "The Allies won't attack the Bolsheviks they hate, because they don't want the Bolsheviks to know about this hatred. But they know," Kolchak snorted. "They know." He stood nodding his head as if he had discovered something. "Oh, well, if I must go . . . perhaps this is as good a place as any. To spend my last days in the fortress wherein Dostoevsky was captive is some small honor. Some vile little cell, I suppose. It is comforting to know that my good friend Anna Timiryova has asked to join me."

Kolchak picked up a framed photograph from the cabinet. He studied the picture, and a softer expression relaxed his face. "I was married in Irkutsk, did you know? So I may as well die there." He abruptly looked up as if waking from a dream. "Gentlemen, you can leave now. I want to write some letters to my wife and to my son. Good night."

"Good night, Admiral," Peter mumbled.

Alex shook his hand. "Every wedding anniversary, Katya and I will remember you . . . and Anna . . . and your hospitality. Good-bye, Admiral."

The next morning, a sharp wind drove splinters of snow hard at Alex's squinting eyes. He watched carefully as Katya helped the children down the steep steps of the train. Her face was a tight mask; her jaw clenched firmly while she walked slowly between the two children alongside the train toward an elderly woman who stood beside a waiting truck.

Alex followed, carrying their kit bags, and watched Katya kneel in the snow to hug each child with a kiss. Her eyes closed hard, but when the creases between her eyebrows wrinkled, a tear squeezed out and started down her cheek.

Alex lifted Olga and Paul up to the woman on the truck's deck, watching until they were seated, then he stood beside Katya, who remained on her knees even as the truck drove away. She watched the children waving and she waved back holding the other hand over her mouth as if to stifle a cry.

Pulling Katya to her feet, he held her gently for a time. She lay against his chest, her arms holding him as if there was nothing else left for her to cling to. She opened her brimming eyes and he could see the pain. Tears had frozen on the collar of her fur coat. Alex led her back across the railyard where he left her with Peter and then knocked on Kolchak's door.

The admiral, in a peaked cap and full-length blue coat — so vividly dark against the snow — emerged from his carriage carrying an attaché case. He glanced around with eyes raw and troubled before walking trance-like over to the waiting staff car.

When he recognized Katya standing near Peter and Victor, he gave them a slight nod then continued to walk stiffly past the sentries toward the open door of the car.

The admiral gave Alex one last look. "Don't worry about me," he said quietly. "Russia without the Czar is like a day without the sun — lifeless, and lonely."

Alex felt his scalp tingle with the strain of the moment. He saluted, and then watched as the admiral ducked into the back seat.

Colonel Holidiloff closed the door with an expression of relief. It was only then that his face relaxed in a satisfied way, and he removed his glove to shake hands with Alex as the car drove away.

"Congratulations, Colonel Branda . . . without incident . . . as we had hoped."

"Thank you, Colonel . . . you made a nasty job a little easier. The admiral had too much power for his own good." Alex was surprised to find himself thinking about Gaida at a time like this. I wonder where he is? Will he ever find his place, Alex wondered. Turning to Holidiloff he asked, "What happens now?"

Holidiloff walked away from the others, pulling Alex along and speaking in a confidential tone. "I would guess that he lasts two . . . maybe three weeks. Enough for a hearing."

"And then?"

"Firing squad."

As he tugged on his glove, Holidiloff spoke with a bemused smile: "You are aware, of course, that there are only two live rounds and ten blank cartridges for the firing squad . . . so that no sharpshooter really knows . . . and is, therefore, without guilt or remorse. Do you want to hear something odd?" he added with a chuckle.

Alex did not like the smug tone in the colonel's voice. The matter was over. To revel in this sort of conquest put a bad taste in his mouth. "What might that be, Colonel?"

"The firing squad's already been chosen . . . all volunteers . . . and every man requested a charged bullet." Holidiloff looked ready to burst into laughter and raised the glove to his face to hide a smile.

Alex clamped his lips tight. "Well, Colonel, it was interesting to share this piece of history with you. We shall probably never meet again."

With an exchange of salutes Holidiloff and Alex stepped apart; the Czech responsibility complete. Holidiloff got into the car and drove away. Alex took Katya's arm and walked her back to the Treasury train for her appointment with Ordinov. Now everything came down to a simple question: would they really be allowed to leave?

• • •

"My dear Katherine," President Ordinov began sadly, "how we shall miss you."

Mrs. Ordinov was crying. "Where will you go?" she asked in a way that frightened Katya. "How will we know where you are? This is all so confusing. Trains have been rumbling by all night. Did you hear them, Katherine?"

Katya was emotional as well, but somehow felt stronger when she heard Mrs. Ordinov speak. The Treasury is all this poor woman knows, she realized. She doesn't want a large world. She doesn't want uncertainty. Katya took the woman's hand. "Dear Madame Ordinov. I shall miss our afternoon teas . . . I'll write as soon as we're settled."

"If the Bolsheviks will even allow us conveniences like the post," Mrs. Ordinov protested. She reached into a black velvet bag. "I have a small gift for you . . . my cameo brooch. The one you like."

Katya could feel her emotions rise to a tight knot in her throat. She kissed the older woman on both cheeks. "Thank you. Thank you so much," she said.

Mrs. Ordinov began to cry against an embroidered handkerchief, moving away and leaving Katya standing alone in front of President Ordinov's desk.

He cleared his throat while he scanned a ledger. "Katherine, the new Socialist government has given me permission to pay you for almost five years of service. I find this a genuine bonus, because many accounts are under bureaucratic scrutiny and that could last for months. Even more surprising is the fact that they will honor your father's bequest. I believe this is allowed because of pressure from the world's banking community — and this is most fortuitous."

He stood up unexpectedly to apologize. "I am so sorry for leaving you standing." He indicated an hourglass-shaped chair with burgundy velvet upholstery. "Please sit down. I don't know where my mind has gone. Perhaps it is crumbling — like most other things from my time."

Removing spectacles from a case, Ordinov paused before putting them on. He looked at Katya sadly, and with a bitterness she was not used to said: "There is a new way in Russia, you know. Everyone is equal; all property is shared, and so there is no need for one to be polite or to rise above commonality."

When they were both seated Ordinov began again. "Now to business. The old currency will soon be useless, and I don't think it wise to use foreign notes . . . They might not be honored, you see . . . so I propose to pay you in gold coin."

Ordinov looked away but quickly gathered himself. "The Czar had a specially crafted twenty-five ruble coin made as gifts for special friends. Will that be satisfactory?"

She watched him tap a finger on the stack of slender white boxes. "What a lovely idea. Thank you," Katya said. "You know . . . I've never needed money before. What is my balance?"

Ordinov looked at her through oval glasses. "A little over 1,200 rubles in wages, plus another 20,000 from your father."

They were like long chocolate boxes, and she opened one carefully, finding a neat row of gold coins set on edge; each in its own niche. She took out one of the glittering new twenty-five ruble pieces, holding it up to shine in the light. The visage of Czar Nicholas was etched on one side; a Russian eagle on the other. "Beautiful," she murmured, turning the one-inch coin in her fingers. She hesitated, then put it back in the box and snapped the lid. She could not shake the feeling that the money was not hers, or at least not deserved, when so many had been held in a form of slavery to support her life in court. Even her father's legacy might be tainted, but at least she could call this her own. As for the rest, she would think about how best it might be used. "These will be fine," she said. "Goodbye, Mr. Ordinov," she said extending her hand. "It has been an honor."

President Ordinov moved around the desk to stand in front of her. He bowed and kissed Katya's hand.

When he stepped away, Mrs. Ordinov hurried up again and grasped Katya by the elbows, burying her head into Katya's shoulder. Then Katya walked down the line of the sad and worried faces of her Treasury companions with kisses and tearful embraces. She realized that it was likely she would never see them again, but she also knew that she must control her emotions, for everyone's sake. Even Rovskoy bowed graciously.

With Alex, Katya left for her new quarters on Syrovy's train. She was bitter at being allowed only one small suitcase even though she saw the Bolsheviks' point about the re-distribution of national wealth. She knew all too well that she had lived on the luxurious side of an unfair society; so she turned her back on the trunks of gowns and memories, walking away, no longer feeling guilty. Katya held her head high; happy that she had at least managed to keep her mother's wedding dress through the simple expedient of wearing it. They would not confiscate this dress. It was intended for her daughter one day.

Two Falcon Legionnaires walked just behind her, one carrying the small valise with her personal belongings, the other carrying her boxes of coins. Katya paced a measured step, remembering the way Grand Duchess Marie had walked at the Winter Palace in old St. Petersburg, and she smiled inwardly when the sentries came to attention as she strode by. Over the wedding gown she wore mink cut well below the knee, and from under a matching hat, her hair was a splash of yellow against the black fur.

"Well, Katya," Victor said grandly, walking just behind her and right beside Alex. She turned to see him smile. "This moment, at this place, would appear to be the official end of Imperial Russia . . . and, I suppose, the end of the privileged class."

"I agree," Alex said, looking at Katya with what she took to be considerable pride. "An historic moment. And here walks the last aristocrat to leave Siberia, looking every inch the part."

She smiled at this thought. I wish Papa were here.

CHAPTER 31

VLADIVOSTOK
SPRING 1920

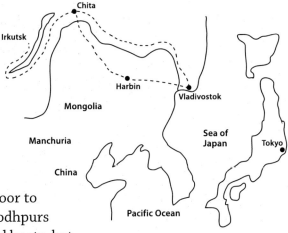

Katya walked up the frozen road in the Irkutsk marshalling yard as quickly as she could on the treacherous ice. She could see General Syrovy waiting on the platform outside the door to his carriage. He wore jodhpurs and beautifully polished boots, but above a broad belt he had only a fresh shirt. With a shaven head, he must be perishing in this cursed Siberian cold, she thought. He also appeared anxious. "General, you had best get inside quickly before you freeze," she said in a gentle way.

Syrovy beamed, and reached down to help her up the slippery iron stairs. "Katya, you look wonderful," he said with his usual conviction.

He kissed the hand she offered, and she felt better immediately. Syrovy liked to play the part of a lecher, but she knew that it was an act — just a tease from a friend.

She followed him into the conference room, with Victor and Alex right behind. Two Legionnaires took their luggage through the far door to their new quarters on Syrovy's train. "You are very kind, General, but I don't feel so wonderful. We had to leave my two babies behind; I've just lost my career; my luggage has been confiscated; and on top of this, I must leave Russia. I don't think I can bear it."

"Well my dear, first of all . . . let's save our skins. Then, during the last leg of our trip, you'll have enough time to think, and to plan where you're going."

"When do we leave?" she asked, taking off her fur to hang on a wall hook. She could feel the blood coming back to her face. Her fingers tingled in the warm air.

Alex and Victor took off their heavy coats and then poured tea for everyone.

Syrovy went to the window to look out onto the marshalling yard which was almost empty now. "See that train pulling away? We follow in perhaps five minutes. Then it's just us and the rearguard. So we mustn't linger. The Red Guard will be right behind."

"What about the French and the Japanese?"

"The French left last night. The Japanese disappeared early this morning. I suppose they decided Kolchak wasn't worth the risk."

"So we're on the last train out," Katya said. "I hope there's no more trouble."

"That's right, the last five cars are for Peter's rearguard. They'll pick up every sentry and any stragglers. By the way, Colonel Lindal . . . glad you're still with us. Now, let's all get some rest. It's been a tense few weeks."

"I for one would like to be well clear of the city before I rest," Katya said. "Lenin might change his mind again."

"You can relax," Syrovy replied with a fatherly pat on her arm. "I have machine guns stationed on the roof of every car. Personally, I believe Irkutsk will be happy to see the last of us. Aha! Here we go now," he said as the train jerked into motion.

She felt a snap of couplings protesting the first skidding surge forward by the driving wheels, but she knew that when the wheels found their grip, it would be full speed ahead to Baikal Station.

"Semyonov might be somewhere around the tunnels again, I suppose," Alex said.

"If he is, he won't get near them," Syrovy answered firmly. "I've got a Czech guard standing on every railroad tie from here through tunnel thirty-nine."

Katya laughed, and that was exactly what Syrovy and Alex wanted to hear, she suspected. She knew he exaggerated, but she also knew he had taken some important precautions, and that if she were settled then everyone else would be more comfortable. So she reached out to touch his arm, saying, "Thank you, dear General Syrovy. I feel much better now."

As she sat with Alex and Victor sipping tea, Victor mentioned news of the worldwide outbreak of influenza. "It's devastating," he said soberly. "As many killed by the 'flu as by war. We've been isolated. Lucky," he added, and they all thought about that.

Each of them had much to think about, Katya reasoned. They rested in long stretches with scarcely a word amongst them at times, dozing, or staring out of the window. For herself, Katya listened to the hypnotic click of rail-joints and swayed with the motion of their carriage. She watched the mountains and the telegraph poles flitting by. In bed, Alex would hold her, and they would let the train rock them to sleep.

• • •

During these days on the train, heading east to Vladivostok at last, Victor felt a strange sort of emptiness. The two people he loved were soon to be moving out of his life. There were moments of panic trying to think of some way to remain in their company.

There was news from General Graves — which he shared privately with Syrovy so as not to upset the others. Semyonov had captured eight hundred Bolsheviks and threatened to sacrifice them in groups — some by rifle, some by strangulation, the rest by poison or fire — unless Kolchak was released. Syrovy refused to get involved, being convinced that the matter was completely a Bolshevik problem, not his. However, he did keep his sentries on full alert.

Graves had also told him that Stanford University had been chosen to represent the United States in rugby for the 1920 Olympic Games to be held in Antwerp that summer. He sighed. So Lefty and the boys had made it without him. Maybe, he mused, they could complete the miracle by winning the gold medal. And maybe, just maybe, if things go right, he could join them in Paris four years from now. Wouldn't that be something?

• • •

Katya was thoughtful too. She had been living on trains for too long. Through the images of childhood, her heart spoke to her of a home. The trouble was, she could no longer think of Kiev as home, because she was convinced that living under the new Communism would be as intolerable as would be a return to the old days. Lenin promised a new social order and had even banned the death penalty — although she noticed that they had still managed to execute Admiral Kolchak. It came as Alex and Victor had predicted: by firing squad in Irkutsk.

She supposed that even in the new order there was at least some small sense of redemption through revenge, and privately she doubted that things would ever really change in this massive land that crept by her window so slowly.

But now, she knew, it was time for a new life. They were both young and strong. Alex could teach. They would start over again. She needed a home.

● ● ●

Alex stretched out in the rocking car, his feet on the empty seat across from him. As he watched the taiga roll gently across the hills, he hoped to see the ocean soon. Once in Vladivostok, though, he knew he would have to face parting from his lifelong friends, and with this knowledge he felt a peculiar mixture of sadness and elation. It was almost over. He was actually getting them out, as he had promised his father, and he felt so relieved because the two hundred conscripted classmates he led from Charles University were still virtually intact. Not by anything he had done, really; it was just discipline, the discipline drummed into them as athletes by his father. That, and the physical prowess which made them different from other young men. Victor had confirmed this observation for him by pointing out the fact that the Falcons had suffered fewer casualties than any other regiment — from either side — during the long war. That in itself was an accomplishment, considering almost six years of sometimes brutal fighting. Perhaps now they could all return to their lives in Prague; what a joy to be part of that. If only his father could have met Katya.

There had been a surprise when Syrovy offered to promote him to general if he remained with the army of new Czechoslovakia. But Alex knew the military was not for him. "War is the ultimate arrogance," he had once said, and he still believed it. Besides, he now knew the answer to Syrovy's challenge to name the one thing that isn't horseshit: something real and lasting, not a sham. It's me, he had realized somewhere back along the long hard trail. I'm the one thing I really know. Another person never understands completely . . . not even good friends.

"My dear Alex, congratulations," had been Syrovy's soft response. "The philosopher has returned. Please reconsider my offer of a military career. You'll find that decisions are so much easier coming from that foundation."

"Thanks again, but no. I'm going to start a new life with Katya. I feel as if I have to hurry to Prague before anything else can go wrong."

"When do you want to leave?"

"The sooner the better. How much money do I have?" Alex asked, thinking about practical things from another world for the first time in a long while. "I'm going to need a passport."

"All in good time . . . But before you go, we'll have one last dinner."

Alex smiled. "Of course. With all the originals . . . a final banquet. What a night that will be."

Three days later, Alex woke in his berth aware that the train had slowed to a crawl. An unfamiliar cry of sea-birds alerted him, and in a scramble, he hurried to the Dutch-door to pull the top half open. A slap of salty air filled his lungs. Gulls dipped in a spanking breeze and bounced sharply with each sudden buffet of wind above the sea. Dark blue water was spattered with white capped waves. "Katya, we made it!"

That afternoon General Syrovy presented Alex and Katya with their new Czechoslovakian passports. "I've had your bank account prepared. Just a minute, I'll get the adjutant in here." He called through an open door, "Lieutenant, what's the state of Colonel Branda's account?"

The officer came in to sit at an empty desk, opening his ledger beside a cash box on the table. "Colonel Branda began service in February 1915 as a lieutenant . . . one ruble per day for . . . twenty-six months equals . . . 780 rubles. Plus, field-allowance-in-action . . . comes to 1,280 rubles. Then as captain . . . three rubles a day . . . for twenty-one months comes to 1,890 rubles . . . no field allowance granted by France — the war being technically over — total 3,170 rubles. At this point, General, it's not clear when Brother Branda became a colonel."

"I can tell you that," Syrovy interjected quickly. "It was when he came back to Omsk with his regiment from Baikal. That was, um, October 1918 . . . wasn't it?"

Alex gave Syrovy a self-conscious smile while nodding slowly.

"Very well. I'll vouch for that," Syrovy said grandly.

"Well, then," the lieutenant continued, "four rubles per day for fifteen months and no battle allowance is . . . another 1,800 rubles, for a grand total of 4,970 rubles. You would like this in what currency, please?"

"Czech crowns please," Katya said. "We're going to Prague."

The paymaster opened his metal cash-box and removed two stacks of bills. He broke the paper seal, and with a rubber cap over his forefinger rapidly counted out the new bills. "Here you are then . . . exactly 2,085 koruna."

Syrovy dismissed the lieutenant. "Not much for six years, but the Austrians won't pay you and neither will the Soviets."

"It's a start," Alex said, fitting the bills into his wallet.

"What now?" asked Syrovy.

"We have to go to Harbin. Not that anyone looks forward to another train trip. Victor closes the American office there, and Katya wants to visit . . . maybe find some of her old friends with news of Grand Duchess Marie. It's not too far. West-northwest into Manchuria. Only five hundred kilometres or so. Victor has the paperwork."

Syrovy looked interested. "Harbin. Perfect . . . I have a proposition for you. Go to Harbin. I'll pay the fare for you both — if you'll just do me a small favor."

"What small favor?" Katya asked suspiciously. "No more fighting."

"Certainly not, my dear. Well, it's just . . . If you could simply escort a Mr. Rad Gaida out of Russia," Syrovy said cautiously.

"Gaida . . . out of Russia . . . with us!" Katya said, disbelieving.

"Where is he?" Alex asked.

"On a British ship. They want him off, and the Japanese want to hang him. So he should get out, fast. The military prison in Harbin will hold him for the Allied Command to deal with. He'd be under your authority. Mr. Gaida no longer holds military rank."

"I don't want anything to do with him!" Alex stated emphatically.

"Just out of the country . . . as a favor to me," pleaded Syrovy. "The troops will get upset if they find out he's here. He'll be no trouble . . . To sweeten the pot, I'll put you in a first-class compartment."

Katya brightened. "Be tolerant, Alexander. You were once friends and fellow sufferers," she reminded him. "And we're on our way to Harbin anyway."

"Some of us suffered a little more than necessary because of him," Alex remembered. "Throw in a cabin on the first ship out of Vladivostok for home?"

"Agreed," Syrovy said. "Just get him off my hands."

"All right, General, just for you . . . not to mention the first-class transport."

• • •

A stinging rain slanted in from the sea. The wind was sharp. Katya paused for a moment to look across the bleak hills before continuing down the station platform toward the carriage secured by Syrovy. "My last glimpse of Russia might be from the back door," she complained. "But if someone knows what happened to Marie, it will be worth the trip."

"Harbin is more like old Petersburg than Leningrad is today," Victor said. "The city is choked with monarchist émigrés waiting and praying for the time they can return."

"What are their chances?" Alex asked.

"Slim and none, according to our sources. The Whites still hold part of Ukraine, but it's only a matter of time. Two days ago Deniken turned over his command. He's burnt out . . . disillusioned. Great Britain dropped him, so he has left everything to General Wrangel. He's the Whites' new man, and he's talking about a massive summer offensive."

Alex shook his head. "Wrangel is forced to attack, and has to do it with people sick of fighting, sick of suffering and sick of him. All Lenin has to do is wait. He promises relief from war. Wrangel offers more agony. There isn't even a royal family in exile to rally round. The people will follow Lenin. They even call the old city Leningrad."

"Cold, practical politics," Victor agreed. "Say, where's your traveling companion?"

"Don't know," Alex said, handing the carriage tickets to Katya. "Why don't you find our compartment, Katya? Vic and I'll go back to the station and see where he is."

• • •

When Katya entered the compartment, a British officer got to his feet. Following at a slower pace and with a disarming smile, Gaida stood, pulled by handcuffs on the officer's wrist. "Hello, Katherine. Don't be upset by the shackles," he said in Russian. "Alex no doubt will be more civilized than this idiot — who can't even speak the language, by the way."

"Don't be too certain of Alexander's civility," she answered coldly, scanning his poorly tailored gray business suit. "What are you doing in our compartment?"

"Why, I just assumed . . ." he said with a vague shrug.

Gaida looked off balance as the officer took the cuff from his own arm and locked Gaida's wrists together. He looked miserable, and Katya realized that it was the first time she had ever seen him this way. Perhaps he was unsettled because of his civilian dress. Perhaps he was embarrassed by the handcuffs. Feeling a bit sorry for him, she gave a half-hearted smile.

Unexpectedly the British officer stepped out into the narrow corridor — out of politeness, she supposed.

Gaida immediately sat down beside her. "Katherine, we haven't much time," he said urgently. "Listen to me. I want you to come with me. You know I'm still mad about you. Let me take you where you belong."

Katya was incredulous. "To prison, you mean?"

She watched him laugh, dragging out the word "Never." It was the old Gaida again. He was irrepressible. "I mean that we belong with Harbin's new society. It's now the center of Russia; that is, until we take Moscow and Petersburg this summer. I'll put you back with the people who understand you, who are the same as you. Come to Harbin with me, life will be just as it used to be."

Katya stared at him. He believes it, she thought. She could see it in his eyes. She thought of the glory days in St. Petersburg. The balls, the ballet, Grand Duchess Marie, but she also remembered people living in the back streets and the hate.

She recovered to say, "There has been no way for you to know that I am married to Alex, your former comrade."

Gaida looked startled, she thought, but a smirk came over his face soon enough. "I was going to rescue you from that fate," he said. "Idealists will forever break the spirit of those nearest to them."

Katya was appalled at his disrespect, but before she could answer, Alex arrived at the door with Victor. "Gaida, how the hell did you get in here?"

The British officer looked in from the corridor. Speaking English, he said: "I'm waiting for Colonel Branda."

Victor pointed, and heatedly said, "This is Colonel Branda. You were to meet us on the platform." He watched the young officer blush. "But you were bamboozled by your prisoner, weren't you? Take him to compartment six in the next car," he said in a voice only slightly less scolding, while holding the door open for Gaida.

Alex took off his pistol before following. "Vic, keep this for me will you? I'm afraid I might shoot the bastard. Stay with Katya . . . until I can turn him over?" He leaned down to kiss her cheek. "I'll be back soon. I promise."

Katya waved as he slid the door closed. "I didn't get to answer Rad," she said to no one but herself.

Victor watched her with a puzzled look, not knowing what she meant.

"He wanted me to leave Alex, and run away to Harbin."

Victor looked startled for a moment. A frown creased his forehead beneath the nut-brown hair, and he became intensely serious. "Katya, if ever you were to . . . ."

Katya put a finger to her mouth, shaking her head. "Victor. Shh. You and I are too deep in friendship for that. Gaida is only an acquaintance. Can't you tell? He always calls me Katherine."

● ● ●

Alex watched Gaida massage his wrists after the British officer had removed the handcuffs before leaving the train. "Brother Branda," Gaida began sarcastically. "I was so happy to hear that an old comrade would accompany me from this accursed place."

The train began to roll slowly forward. Vladivostok Station slid by on Alex's right. Gaida sat across from him in the empty compartment, stroking his soft brown moustache. He still looked lean and fit with a compact gymnast's figure. "Will you ever change?" Alex asked, shaking his head. "I'm not accompanying you, I'm escorting you. This is a deportation order. You're being thrown out of Russia, as persona non grata."

"Quite true and you're doing it so well. Just a hint of a smile, I like that. Oh, I've changed, I can tell you. No more of the old shenanigans."

"Good to hear," Alex said casually, glancing out the window as the train rattled around the hills away from the city, heading inland to the west. "We've walked a long hard road together; it's time to settle down. You have to think about what you're going to do in military prison, and after."

"What I'm going to do?" Gaida laughed. "I'm going to Harbin. Haven't you heard? General Wrangel is in command now, and the whole town is waiting for his summer offensive . . . I'll wait with them. What a place. It's like a smaller St. Petersburg from the halcyon days."

Alex watched the energetic Gaida in disbelief. "Rad, I can't read you. Two minutes after saying how you've changed, you're ready to break the deportation order when the train isn't even out of the country yet. You could be quite mad."

"Well, if you'd been cooped up on a British warship for four months you might be deranged too . . . But don't worry, I won't enter Russia until invited by Wrangel."

Alex gave a short laugh out of surprise. "Until invited . . . You're irrepressible."

"And why not?" Gaida enthused. "What an opportunity! Say, why not join me? I'll make you a general. Between the two of us, we could take Moscow by September. What do you say to that?"

Alex was laughing hard now, although still shaking his head. "As soon as I resign from the army, everyone wants to make me a general. Not a chance. There's far too much of the fascist in your heart. You're going to get yourself strung up. Me? . . . I'm going to settle down."

"To what?" Gaida scoffed. "The humdrum? The dull? And with what?" he sneered. "Look at what they gave me!" he said, throwing down a roll of white notes on the opposite seat. "Six years of struggle for 11,000 rubles!"

"Eleven thousand?" Alex exclaimed in astonishment, reaching for the roll. "More than twice what I got."

"Well, don't forget. I was a general."

"How could I forget?" Alex said, opening up one of the bills. "Say, these aren't rubles. They're ten pound notes."

"That's another thing. They paid me off in pounds sterling, saying I was technically on British soil. I want rubles."

"No, you don't, Rad. Rubles aren't worth much these days."

Gaida laughed. "That's all you know. Harbin is a Czarist town. They won't even look at pounds sterling."

"When Lenin takes complete control, the Czar's ruble won't be worth a damn. You'd better–"

"That's what I'll always remember about you, Branda . . . your inevitable gullibility. 'When Lenin takes complete control.' Never! You mean when Wrangel runs him off. The ruble won't lose its real value . . . except in the eyes of simple-minded fools."

Alex watched his confident adversary with a calmness built from experience. He took his time to study the former general. This man will never change. He has learned nothing. "Would you like to buy some rubles, then?" Alex asked casually.

"Why . . . yes. Yes, certainly," Gaida seemed to stumble a bit. "How many do you have?"

Alex reached for his inside pocket, pulling out the neat packet of one hundred crisp banknotes he had found in the identification wallets of the dead Siberian officers.

"Five hundred thousand," he said, tossing them on the seat beside Gaida's English banknotes. Alex rubbed his hand over the whiskers outlining the hard line of his jaw.

As if completely disinterested in Gaida's reaction, he then rubbed the scar on his lip with a finger.

"A packet of 500 thousand rubles! Where did you get these?" asked the astonished Gaida. He stared at the stack of 5,000 ruble notes until his expression took a slight change, and then he straightened up, ready to answer his own question. He turned on Alex with a smirk. "I know where these came from."

"Of course you do. I knew you'd figure it out. Admiral Kolchak . . . for services rendered . . . . How much are you willing to buy?"

Rattled now, Gaida gave him a puzzled frown. "Well, I don't know. I've only got the English pound notes. That's all," said Gaida, sounding unsure.

"Too bad, then," Alex said, taking back the rubles.

"Wait." Gaida nervously licked his lips. "Kolchak gave me some Treasury platinum." He said this in a low voice while extracting four pale wafers from the inside pocket of his jacket. He placed them on the seat beside the sterling banknotes, saying: "They will hang me if I'm caught with these."

"All right, then, Rad. Here's a proposal. You take my pay-out, and I'll take yours. Call it a wager. To be decided by who wins the war: the Whites with Wrangel, or the Reds under Lenin. My half million rubles to your English pounds and platinum. What do you say to that?" The train began to slow down.

Gaida snatched up the rubles triumphantly. "Whites!" he shouted. "What a pathetic businessman you are!"

"Just a simple schoolmaster," Alex said agreeably, while pocketing the Bank of England certificates and the platinum wafers. "Now . . . do you think we ought to salute or something? Here's the border. You are now leaving Russia, forever."

Gaida looked out the window onto the dry landscape and the shacks housing the border guards. "Not me," he said with a laugh and a slap to his wallet. "I'll be back, in style."

"Style you never lacked, Rad," Alex said, getting up. "You're on your own now. You have your papers for customs. I'm sure I'll be reading about you . . . Goodbye."

Gaida stood up, his face ignited by the excitement. "You're leaving me? But why? What about the police?"

"You'll find a way around them, like everything else you do," Alex said without feeling, and was pleasantly surprised at his lack of attachment to what was Gaida's problem and not his. "My job was to get you out of Russia. You're out. Now stay out!"

Gaida sat back down, staring hard at the floor as if looking back in time. "You always said you'd get us out . . . I guess you have. Now you'll be leaving with Katherine, I suppose?"

Alex stopped at the door to the corridor. He could feel his fist clenching, but relaxed it immediately. "That's correct, Rad," he said. "And there's just one more thing. Keep out of my life."

Alex walked down the side aisle of the first-class carriage back to the compartment where Katya and Victor waited for him. They both looked up in surprise, watching expectantly while he sat down with a satisfied sigh and began to make himself comfortable.

"Where's Gaida?" Victor asked.

Alex met their stares with an innocent look. "Out of Russia, as agreed."

"But where is he now?" Katya persisted.

"Escaped," Alex offered. He watched Katya's shocked look change to a knowing smile. Then she reached over and squeezed his hand.

She turned to Victor who had a worried look. "Alexander would never forsake an old friend."

Their train arrived in Harbin by mid-morning and Alex walked down the aisle leading the way for Katya and Victor. As they stepped out onto the platform, he was surprised to find a band waiting in front of a considerable crowd. It soon became obvious that the townspeople were waiting for Gaida, because as he stepped from his compartment, the band struck up and the well-dressed crowd began applauding enthusiastically. Gaida flashed a triumphant smile, sending at the same time a knowing look toward Alex. Then he was swept away by the grand exiles of Harbin.

● ● ●

Two days later, Katya was happy to return to Vladivostok with Alex and Victor. Victor had completed the business of closing the American Expeditionary Forces' office in Harbin. Alex had helped her gather the only information she really needed, which was that Grand Duchess Marie was thought to be in Paris. She was alive and safe — as they all hoped to be soon. In fact, the exiles in Harbin were more afraid of the influenza epidemic said to be sweeping Western Europe and North America than the distant threat of Lenin. Surely he would be crushed soon enough, and perhaps the remoteness of Siberia and Mongolia would continue to protect them from the devastating epidemic.

When the night of the banquet for the Falcon Regiment arrived, Katya was certain that she had no right being there, feeling extremely self-conscious as Alex insisted that she sit between himself and Victor. The Russian Island Hotel had festooned a hall with flags and banners across the high beams that supported the peaked roof. Here she sat down with the Legionnaires for their last regimental dinner. As far as she could tell, no one seemed the slightest bit concerned about her presence, so she sat quietly and watched.

Two hundred and eighteen comrades sang the brave songs, seemingly determined to savor every heroic image and stirring note. Later, when the food had been devoured and the wine decanters emptied, liqueurs and cigars were passed around. Alex, in his last act as their colonel, stood ringing his empty wine glass with a fork until the persistent, sharp note commanded everyone's attention. The great audience settled down expectantly.

"Dear friends . . . my dearest friends, I now present our first general, Brother Syrovy, and our second general, Brother Kechek. As you might have suspected, Brother Syrovy wishes to speak . . . while Brother Kechek does not." Alex sat down to loud laughter.

As Syrovy stood waiting, the laughter and whistles turned into a prolonged ovation, an action that seemed to unsettle him at first, but by the time he thanked Alex for the introduction, he had recovered fully and turned to smile at his audience.

Then in a strong voice, he began: "Faithful comrades . . . Katya, our one sister," he paused for the warm applause. "Colonel Lindal, our one guest, greetings, and farewell." He waited long enough for the cheering to end. "We sit here tonight, together, perhaps for the last time . . . at least with these numbers . . . and we sit here together, as testimony to Czech stubbornness." Laughter swelled into table thumping, but the guffaws soon died away as Syrovy, serious again, continued. "We, the original mutineers, the last of the Czar's Czechoslovak Rifle Corps, and the now famous Falcon Regiment, have performed a remarkable adventure. We first escaped the Austrians to stand with the Russia of Czar Nicholas — until it crumbled. We next escaped the Germans and then the Bolsheviks by traversing Siberia's marshes, pushing trains, choking on mosquitoes, fighting running battles. And then, just to prove it was no accident . . . we went back and did it again . . . only this time, we did it in winter!" Now, there were howls of laughter lasting long enough for Syrovy to drain a glass while he watched his audience with his one twinkling eye.

"What we did has never been done before . . . and I dare say will never be done again." More applause and shouted comments. "You held duty as your foremost goal, performing so well under such terrible conditions, that you made 'a-job-well-done' . . . all the more remarkable. What I want to warn you about . . . is that there will be many people who will not believe you, when you try to tell your story. You will be hurt to find that some don't care. And worse . . . there will be many voices who will find fault with what you've accomplished and how you performed it. The only satisfaction you really have is that here, in this hall tonight . . . we know the truth; and, as members of the Falcon Regiment, we will have this bond for as long as we live. For that, and for that alone, I am proud and grateful to have served with you."

Katya found herself crying. She looked up self-consciously to see that, at table after table, there were men who cried without shame or embarrassment. She realized that it was nothing more than a release — for it certainly had nothing to do with courage. The hand-clapping rolled around the beamed ceiling like thunder, until Syrovy insisted on calling them to silence once again.

"One last toast, dear brothers." The hall stood while their general began. "We the survivors celebrate the memory of our beloved comrades who did not complete the journey . . . Here are but a few names . . . you all have your own . . . And we call the roll one more time: Lieutenant Skorinsky — tortured at Barabinsk; Colonel Svec — by his own hand in Ekaterinburg; Lieutenant Marek — in an ambush at Seberta where Major Zotov saved the day; Sergeant Pollak — in the Baikal tunnels; and Colonel Usakov — as a personal sacrifice for all of us at Rosalskaya. For them, I remember the old poem.

Rest soldier, rest! Thy warfare o'er,
Dream of battled fields no more;
Sleep the sleep that knows not breaking,
Morn of toil, nor night of waking.

"In their memory, let us salute the Falcons — Czechoslovakia's first army."

"The Falcons!" roared the crowd as one voice before they drank. And Katya shouted out too: "The Falcons!"

As the assemblage sat in thoughtful silence, she saw that Alex remained standing in a call for their attention. "Brothers, I'm leaving you tomorrow; leaving the friends of my youth. But before I go, I must tell you, we've been through some extraordinary times. War, the final insanity, is really just a desperate substitute for reason. The only good from it is what it brings out in people, and we've seen that. You watched out for one another and accomplished the impossible.

"I doubt we'll receive any official recognition for sharing these years. Neither does my wife, Katya. She has, therefore, taken it upon herself to provide you with a memento of your sacrifice, and our time together. There's one for each of us — a special medallion for a special force. Please keep it in memory of our odyssey, and of our love for you. God bless!"

Katya got up to walk the aisles between tables, and with Alex's help offered the long white boxes she had received from President Ordinov as wages for her years with the Treasury. She saw each trooper gratefully select a mint-fresh, twenty-five ruble gold-piece as his medal, and smile with satisfaction as he inspected this special coin. Victor was especially moved, she thought, when she presented him with the last one.

When she had finished, Alex stacked the empty containers on a side table before sitting down again; he did not at first notice that she remained standing before them all, waiting quietly. She waited until the great hall fell into a sudden hush. Two hundred puzzled faces followed her nervous preparations, until finally her trembling voice broke the silence. But so quietly did she speak, that some men held their breath, straining to hear.

"Gentlemen," she began, "you are my husband's dearest friends. He thinks so much of you. Now I feel as if I'm stealing him away. I . . . I just want to say, that I didn't get to meet each and every one of you, but I sense that I know you all very well. When I was frightened, you protected me. If I needed help, you gave it, even though I was with you for only a few months, and that is what I shall never forget. I always felt . . . I always knew . . . that I was in the company of heroes."

She listened to her heels tap out the length of the table stride by stride as she walked slowly to her chair in the electric hush. She was sure now that she had overstepped her bounds because the audience sat utterly still. Syrovy appeared shaken, but recovered when Katya arrived back at her place. Alex, with a proud smile, held her chair.

It was Syrovy who woke them up, calling in a loud voice, "Three cheers for officers who care for their men . . . and women who think for themselves." Shouts and cheers rang throughout a standing ovation which brought back her smile and the blood to her cheeks; and as she stood in front of the shouting men, the prolonged applause washed away any remaining doubts.

• • •

On the dock the next afternoon, Alex stood near the gangplank slanting up to the deck of the SS *Soleftea*, a Swedish vessel, whose deckhands scrubbed her white-work with long-handled brushes. Alex fidgeted self-consciously in the new blue business suit Victor had arranged for him in Harbin. He and Katya would be the last to board. Unlike larger Red Cross troop-carriers at anchor in the harbor, the *Soleftea* was a mid-sized freighter with room for only eight passengers. Alex's inside pocket held their tickets for one of the state-rooms — and they were bound for Marseilles in fifteen minutes. Katya stood beside him as their friends watched soberly.

"Well . . . have a good life, Brother Branda . . . I will miss you," Syrovy admitted.

Alex turned to Kechek. "Peter . . . Brother Syrovy is getting emotional. Please remind him that I'll write you both from Prague . . . August . . . September at the latest."

Peter embraced his friend, lifting Alex off the ground with a laugh. "Find me a wife when you get home; I helped you after all."

"Peter . . . I can be of service in that department," Katya said. "We pass through France on the way to Prague, and Grand Duchess Marie now lives in Paris." Katya's eyes sparkled. "She got out through Romania. I'm sure she'll have someone in mind for a hero."

Syrovy and Peter were laughing now.

"You'll love Prague, and Prague will love you," Syrovy said, kissing Katya's cheek. "See you there soon."

"I hope so," she said.

"Of course you will," Alex said, saluting his two friends. "Hurry home, Petya . . . we'll find some grass and kick the ball around. But for now, as my American friend says, so long."

"What does that mean precisely?" Syrovy asked.

"It means . . . not goodbye."

"I like it," Syrovy grinned. "To both of you, I say: so long."

• • •

From the broad balcony of the American Headquarters chosen by General Graves expressly for its commanding view of the harbor, Victor watched Alex and Katya depart Vladivostok. He knew that he would have been welcome down there at the ship, but chose instead to say his goodbyes at the banquet the night before. Perhaps it was because he was afraid that he might embarrass everyone by breaking down — he was close to that when Katya gave him the special gold coin the night before. Not only was it thoughtful of Katya but it was also like an invitation to membership in an exclusive club — and he was honored even to be considered.

More than this, though, he had woken this morning with an empty feeling that he couldn't shake. He swept the dock with the telescope, turning the focus knob carefully until the laughing faces of his

Czech friends came clear. He twirled another knob and Katya filled the circle. Those eyes, that smile, when would he see them again?

When she had kissed his cheek last night, he thought that he would disgrace himself by weeping. But then Alex had taken his hand in a strong grasp and reminded him, "You said you were going to help us and you did. Make certain that you keep in touch, and that you thank General Graves. He made sure we got out."

Alex had grabbed him again. He felt the strong arms squeeze. "Somehow you must find us when you come to Europe and your birthplace."

I'll leave it like that, Victor thought to himself. There must be some way of getting to Europe. Maybe the Olympics in Paris with the Stanford rugby team; Lefty Rogers had said it would happen. That would do.

"Hey, Vic, let's get going," General Graves called from the spacious office that opened onto the balcony with a view of the harbor and part of the city to the north. Victor returned through the double-paned French doors and sat across the table from the general. There was a glass of orange squash at his place.

"Did you see all those ships out there?" Graves asked. "We'll be the busiest harbor in the world during the next few weeks, getting all these folks out of here. Some by Panama. Some by Suez." The general poured himself a Coca-Cola.

"When do we leave?" Victor asked.

Graves paused, thoughtfully taking a drink before answering. Standing up, he walked to the harbor side of the large square room, took another pull on the Coke and looked back at Victor. "What did you notice out there?"

Victor walked over to join him. "Japanese gun positions," he said. "Every road to and from the port is covered."

Graves stepped out through the French doors onto the balcony still bright from the mid-day sun. "All communication systems are in Japanese hands," he said, handing Victor an oversize set of binoculars. "Take a look at what they have aimed at us."

Victor went to the northwest side of the office and scanned the peak of the next hill which was as high again as the American position in relation to the harbor. On at least a dozen high vantage points across the southern slope of Vladivostok, he could see light artillery on wheels.

He followed Graves inside and sat down again at the table. "General Otani has been watching ships take Czech troops away for weeks now. General Dieterichs took his bunch off to Harbin to stay in touch with the Whites. My point is that I'm scheduled to pull out in a few days, and when that happens, the Japanese will have full control."

The general looked up expectantly, but Victor did not know what to say. "What do they want?" he finally asked.

Graves reached across to the map at the center of the table and pointed to the peninsula of land containing Vladivostok. He moved his finger across the water to the southwest. "Korea! That's what they're after."

He got up and walked over to the west side windows. "Come here," he said, pointing to the mountains just across the water. "Hell, we can watch the Japanese build-up from here, and I'm not supposed to do anything about it. Meanwhile, the community of Korean workers in the city has been terrorized. Three hundred Koreans have been killed for no other purpose than the intimidation of what Japan considers to be an inferior race."

Victor followed Graves back to the table, wondering what was coming.

"Vic," the general began slowly, "I'd like you to go back to Harbin and set up shop. That place is humming. General Wrangel, General Dieterichs and General Gaida are there now, and they're not just playing bridge."

So that's it, he thought. This damned war is going to drag on forever. But then again, what the hell, he had nothing better to do. "Whatever you need, General," he said, and was glad to see a smile of relief on Graves' face. "You know," he added cautiously, "when this is over I thought I might go back to Stanford again. Perhaps you could give me a recommendation?"

"That's a sure thing, Vic. Just let me know," Graves said, getting up.

Victor stood too. "And what are your plans, sir?"

"Well, I'm not sure what influence I have left in Washington. The press has given me a real going-over, accusing me of cowardice, inefficiency and anything else they could dream up. But I'm going to try my damnedest to convince the War Department of a thing or two." Graves pursed his lips in a thoughtful frown as if rehearsing his argument. "The United States Army must never again be sent into a domestic dispute without full capability for success, and the support of the people. I hope I can convince them of that. I sure hope we've learned something . . . Guess the future will tell."

Victor stopped at the door to shake Graves' hand. "One thing, sir. You got the Czechs out. Nearly seventy-two thousand of them. They can't easily forget that."

"Thanks, Vic. I hope they have a few kind words . . . but you and I both know that we didn't do a damned thing about Lenin. Could you ever have imagined that one sour little Bolshevik could take control of the largest country in the world by outfoxing the Western Allies? Wrangel and Gaida are going to need an awful lot of luck."

CHAPTER 32

PRAGUE
JUNE 1920

Alex felt a new sensation of comfort as he watched Katya finish her unpacking. They really were leaving the nightmare behind. Somehow they had made it out and she looked radiant. Her energy had returned, with the smile.

"Alex," she said with enthusiasm. "This is a wonderful state-room. I've never been on a large boat before. Have you?"

"In Czechoslovakia?" He turned out the light before climbing into bed where he lay on his side watching her face in the moonlight. There was a cream-colored moon and a soft breeze through the porthole.

"I know exactly what I want in Prague," she declared with a quiet confidence.

"What's that?"

"My own restaurant. We have enough, I think — what with the platinum to add to Rad's English pounds. I wasn't sure about the platinum at first . . . but how could you possibly have returned it from Mongolia? It would never have reached the Treasury. So, let's buy a restaurant. We'll make a fortune."

"Hmm," he muttered cautiously. "What kind of restaurant?"

"Russian, of course. Rich, luxurious, expensive haute cuisine. Vodka, wines, caviar . . . the best . . . and music. Right in the center of town. What shall we call it?"

"Do you remember Kiev? The Balalaika was a special place."

She kissed his cheek. "Perfect," she said.

He smiled to himself, content with the simple fact that she was happy again. They lay in bed listening to the ocean and feeling the surge of the waves.

"Alex, why aren't you asleep?"

"I was just thinking how much I miss the click of train tracks," he whispered.

"Oh no!" she laughed. "Well, I don't. I don't care if I never hear those damned rails again. I'm happy for the change, and this, our honeymoon at last."

• • •

On a hill overlooking the river, Alex and Katya walked through an ancient cemetery not far from Prague Castle. Alex searched through the jumble of gravestones looking every so often at the map given to him by the caretaker.

When he found his father's place, he was surprised to see that the granite marking-stone was larger than most of its neighbors. There was a solid-looking half-pyramid made out of chipped granite. At eye level there was a heavy iron plaque. It was obvious that someone, or some committee, had put a lot of care into this remembrance.

He stood in his dark blue business suit with a bouquet of flowers in his hand. Katya wore her yellow summer dress and held his arm tightly while he translated the inscription for her.

ANTON BRANDA
1870 – 1915

A TRUE PATRIOT AND PRESIDENT
OF THE FALCON ATHLETIC ASSOCIATION

REMEMBERED BY HIS FRIENDS
AND HIS BELOVED SON

Alex saw tears glide over Katya's cheeks while she listened to him read the tribute. He was moved too, but not to tears. He had cried long ago. It was normal, he thought, to expect to stay in control, but he was surprised to find himself smiling. It was a smile of pride — even though it quivered a bit near the edges.

He watched Katya arrange his flowers in the metal canister in front of the granite stone. She crossed herself, and he followed her lead. He noted that they both seemed to recover composure after a silent prayer.

When he was ready, he took from his jacket a package picked up that morning during a visit to the barracks where his father had been executed. He had no interest in viewing the executioner's wall, but he did want to collect his father's property. All that remained now was a gold pocket watch, in a box bound with string.

Alex unwrapped the box and swung the timepiece from its thin gold chain, letting it spin in the sunlight like a gleaming planet on its own orbit. Hesitating, he fingered the clasp on the side of the cover before finally snapping it open. He studied the picture on the inside of the shell, all the while shaking his head in wonderment. Turning the watch, he showed Katya the picture of a young woman holding her baby. "There I am with my mother," he said. "I knew you reminded me of someone."

• • •

Katya, in her middle years, stepped carefully across the cobblestones as she made her way toward the eastern entrance of the Charles Bridge where four solemn men stood in front of a public notice-board. There was a frown on her face as she moved slowly forward, and when two men walked away shaking their heads, she slipped into a space close enough to read the terse message tacked to the board:

SEPTEMBER 30, 1938. AT 12:00 P.M. GREENWICH TIME, PRIME MINISTER NEVILLE CHAMBERLAIN AND CHANCELLOR ADOLPH HITLER SIGNED THE MUNICH AGREEMENT, ALONG WITH FRENCH PREMIER, EDOUARD DALADIER. THE AGREEMENT RETURNS 11,000 SQUARE MILES OF CZECHOSLOVAKIAN TERRITORY TO THE NATIONAL SOCIALIST REPUBLIC OF GERMANY.

CHAMBERLAIN STATED IN PARLIAMENT THAT: "HOWEVER MUCH WE MAY SYMPATHIZE WITH A SMALL NATION CONFRONTED BY A BIG AND POWERFUL NEIGHBOR, WE CANNOT . . . INVOLVE THE WHOLE OF THE BRITISH EMPIRE IN A WAR SIMPLY ON HER ACCOUNT.

Katya put a fist up to her mouth and turned back toward the curving street leading from Charles University's history department — to see Alex, in a professor's gown, grimly hurrying toward the bridge. She fell in beside him as they passed under the arched entrance.

He looked at her hard. "Sell the cafe. Things are going to get bad. We have to be ready for it."

Her face grew white and drawn but she tried to sound hopeful. "Victor phoned from the American Embassy . . . He wants to help." A gathering crowd looked up as Alex and Katya came out onto the bridge under thirty-one life-sized statues set solidly on sturdy stone foundations. "Are you going to speak?" she asked.

"You know I have to," was the cryptic reply as he pressed on toward the statue of Jan Nepomuk.

"Be careful."

Katya watched as Alex put his hand on the stone railing and vaulted up onto the base of the statue where his head was just level with the bronzed feet of Saint John. The expectant crowd pushed closer. A breeze ruffled his graying hair, and fallen leaves, the color of his tweed jacket, swirled on the cobblestones. She looked away down the east embankment toward the National Theatre where there was the faint sound of a brass band playing a strident marching song. In the distance, stark Nazi flags could be seen thrust high on pikes. A shiver ran the length of her spine.

Alex called for attention with both arms outstretched to the gathering of students who crowded the wide road below him. His gaze searched the park across the river to the west bank, where he had walked with his father years before and where a youthful Peter Kechek had met him every morning before class. In his mind, Alex could still see his handsome friend running across the lawn to meet them, his Viking hair bouncing with each long stride. He had named his only child after his friend, and now the memory was so clear that his voice broke as he shouted above the sound of the band.

"We were like you," he called. "We wanted the same things . . . They made us slaves. Never again! The pact signed yesterday in

Munich is an abomination. You must resist. Hitler and Chamberlain lie to the world!"

Alex glanced over to the far side of the bridge where Katya stood listening. In those sad eyes he could see her fear. She wanted him to stop, he knew, but he could also see the approaching flags down the east embankment behind her. Black silk flew on the wind with a blood red circle in each center — all designed to highlight the broken white cross. He saw more of them coming now. Row after row of black flags rippled in the chilly air so that the twisted swastikas danced like angry claws hovering over the spectators who watched with growing apprehension.

Jerking his attention back to the gathered students, the professor shouted earnestly. "You will be tested. Meet force with force. And remember your history. Ask what these men would do." Alex gestured to the dark statues looking down on them all. "Here stands Saint John who died so that you and I could speak our minds. At the stake, Jan Hus shouted for liberty as he choked on the flames. This bridge is where your history resides. Remember your heroes! You stand before them!"

Two stern men in black leather coats appeared under the arch of the town-side tower and began pushing through the crowd on the bridge. Alex recognized an arrogance in the way they elbowed a path for themselves. It was as if they believed this right-of-way had been ordained for them, and they kept their expressionless eyes on him as if expecting him to run.

Alex could tell that Katya saw them too because she tried to work toward him through the throng of thoughtful young faces. But being smaller, her passage was difficult. "Excuse me. I must get by. Please let me through," he heard her anxious voice.

Alex studied the men for a moment, calculated their rate of progress, and began to speak even more urgently as they came closer. "Your country needs patriots. You are the ones who will win back freedom. Seize the chance to serve your country!"

The two men in black leather coats broke through the front edge of the crowd near the balustrade upon which Alex stood shouting his message: "Remember your history! Freedom! Freedom is your prize!"

The first man to reach him pulled a metal rod from a sheath sown inside the forearm of his leather coat. With a studied movement he swung a blow at Alex's knee.

Alex jumped from the ledge, dodging the blow. He shoved the man aside just as the other smashed a metal rod down onto his shoulder. There was a loud crack as the collarbone snapped. Alex fell to the road in agony. The pain came in waves and he tried to concentrate on controlling his vision as it blurred in and out of focus. He was disappointed to see that the students merely looked on — shocked, he supposed, by the unexpected violence. Others turned away.

Then some hope — a few students surged forward when the smaller of the two men continued the attack even as Alex sagged again onto the cobbled stones. Just as the man raised his bludgeon for a final strike, Alex saw Katya hurl herself out of the crowd to grab the upraised arm. She shouted while fighting to hang on. "Get up, Alex. Get up! He'll kill you."

Alex struggled to his knees then heaved himself onto his feet, holding the damaged left arm across his chest by the elbow. His teeth were clenched to hold in the pain, but he kept his eyes wide with determination.

The first man flung Katya away from him, losing his hat in the struggle. Sweat shone through the bristles of close-cropped hair. He planted his legs wide apart poised for the attack as Alex turned away, but it was his partner who struck first. A metal rod was swung viciously from behind — a terrible blow to the back of Alex's head.

There was an ugly, soft sound and Alex collapsed onto the cobblestones. Katya ran over to his crumpled body — hoping for some sign that he would be all right . . . some movement . . . anything.

Katya's scream froze everyone in their place.

It was then she heard a voice back in the crowd calling. "Let me through! Clear a path!"

Katya turned toward the voice. "Victor. We're here. Hurry!"

Victor was dressed impressively in a tan overcoat and chocolate brown homburg, but it was his bearing that was most prominent; he was all business. At his shoulder followed the serious face of a young Marine.

Victor glared at the two men in black leather coats. "I represent the United States Government and carry visas for this couple. As they are under my custody, I will thank you to leave them alone."

The two assailants stood a little less aggressively, although neither backed away. The smaller man seemed to be calculating the odds of winning a serious scrap until his partner gave an almost imperceptible motion of his head, and he slipped the metal club into its sheath. They both stared hard at this new threat. "You must think you're quite the white knight," the small man said to Victor.

His partner laughed. "Watching over the world . . . we'll see. There's plenty of time," he sneered. "Get them the hell out of Prague if you know what's good for trouble-makers." Then he turned to the students. "Remember your history," he said mockingly, and spat on the road. "You belong to Germany and always will."

Victor looked at Alex then gestured to the Marine. He took Katya's arm and with a curt nod, walked back toward the western gate. The Marine picked up Alex's limp body and followed through the silent crowd, their faces creased with anger. Katya looked back, her eyes flooding with tears. "Will he be all right?"

Victor hurried on, his face pinched with pain. "It doesn't look good. We'll get him to hospital right away."

Katya stumbled, clinging fearfully to Victor's arm. "Dear God . . . I'm three weeks pregnant . . . I haven't told him yet. He worries about bringing babies into a war zone."

● ● ●

Two days later a sombre crowd poured out of Saint Catherine's Church to the sound of muffled bells. The assembly marched toward Charles Bridge down the ancient, twisting street now lined with rows of sad faces. Katya walked as if in a daze while holding tightly onto the hand of her fourteen-year-old son. Victor walked on the other side of the boy, hand in hand, while occasional calls from the watching throng called out in short, angry fragments.

"Nazi bastards!"

"We'll get them, Alex."

Victor studied young Peter's face carefully at these outbursts, and could see hate in the boy's dark eyes. "I'll be with them," the boy said under his breath.

Victor leaned in close. "You have to prepare," Victor said forcefully. "I'll help. Your father was a soldier . . . I promised him once that I'd look after you and your mother, if anything ever happened."

Peter looked up. "Dad will lie in state in Old Town Square under the statue of Jan Hus. When he's buried, my friends and I will begin what has to be done."

Katya looked anxiously at Victor.

"Begin what?" Victor asked, his voice a low growl. "Shooting elephants with pea shooters? That's all you have . . . pea shooters. Come to America . . . finish school . . . I'll get you into West Point. Learn how to do things that bring results."

Peter frowned but stared hard at Victor. He turned to his mother who nodded firmly.

"West Point . . ." Peter looked ahead toward the funeral bier. "Yes . . . that might be good. West Point," he said, standing taller. "I think Dad would agree."

Katya squeezed Peter's hand.

EPILOGUE
SAN FRANCISCO
AUTUMN 1988

Fifty years later, on the patio of her grandmother's penthouse high atop Russian Hill in San Francisco, Natasha jumped up to greet a man coming out onto the deck. He had wiry gray hair and dark eyes. "Uncle Peter," she called happily.

"Ah, Natasha." He laughed, scooping her up off the deck in a bear hug. When he put her down he went quickly to Katya's chair and took her hand.

"Mother," he said, kissing her fingers. "You're a beautiful sight. You belong in a setting like this."

Katya smiled. "Just like your father . . . Alex always had the right thing to say . . . Where's your uniform?

"In mothballs. Don't need that anymore. It's California-casual from here on."

Irena came over. "Colonel Peter Branda, US Army, retired. It has a nice ring, big brother."

"Hi, Irena. Gimme a squeeze. Anything to drink?"

She threw her arm around his shoulder. "Step right this way, big boy. Any soldier who serves in three wars gets free drinks around here. We have some special wine . . . Say, how many guys did the Second World War, then Korea, then Vietnam?"

"There are a few," Peter said while strolling to the bar with his sister. He stopped with a smile as a tall man in a black jacket under a full head of white hair came out of the kitchen with a wave and walked straight to Katya.

"Victor!" she said. "Perfect. Now we're all here. Irena, will you give everybody a glass of wine please?"

Katya stood up to kiss his lips, then looked into his eyes. She caressed his cheek with her hand and kissed him again. "Vic," she whispered, her lips still on his cheek, "I've told them everything. They know you're not Irena's father."

Victor stepped back and looked across to Irena who studied him closely. Natasha was staring as well, with her brow wrinkled in doubt.

Victor chose his words carefully. "I had to get Peter and Katya out of Europe. There were too many regulations . . . and paperwork of course. It was simpler if we married. Then we let everyone — including you two — assume the rest. What the hell, I wanted the role anyway. So I accepted it without a second thought."

He shrugged in a what-can-be-done gesture. "So, Irena . . . not precisely my daughter . . . and Natasha . . . not exactly my granddaughter . . . but still my favorite two kids." He opened his arms wide.

Natasha rushed into his embrace. "I love you, Grandad."

"And I'm lucky enough to love you," Victor said, quietly stroking her long hair. "Very lucky."

Irena came over and put her head on his shoulder. "All those years, Papa . . . all those years. You made me feel as if Mama and I were the center of your world. You did it well. Thank you," she said with a kiss to his cheek.

He stepped back blinking flooded eyes before taking a camera from his jacket pocket. "All right you young people . . . put on those necklaces . . . I'm going to take a picture."

Natasha, Irena and Peter each lifted a gold chain over their head and held the Czar's coin sparkling in the mid-day sun. Smiling and laughing, they gathered behind Katya's chair, and stood against the railing with San Francisco Bay in the background.

Katya contentedly raised her glass — and the others followed her lead. Then she blew a kiss toward the camera saying, "To you, Alex . . . from all of us with love."

COOKIES AND TEA WITH KERENSKY
SEPTEMBER 1968

I often think how lucky I was to have met Alexander Kerensky, the last democratically elected prime minister of Russia. In late September 1968, I was a history teacher at Templeton High School in the east end of Vancouver, a district informally called Little Italy, and a place where it was fun just being there. For a teacher, the trick was to expand students' minds beyond the east end. They understood their community, but it was very difficult to get them to consider something larger — like Russia.

Mr. Waites the gentlemanly principal often pushed me to "take a field trip" but I resisted until one morning in the staff room when I saw an announcement of a lecture by Kerensky presenting his new book: *Russia and History's Turning Point*. I ran to the principal's office and knocked. Mr. Waites looked up puzzled. "Yes?" he said politely.

"I want to take our five top history students on a field trip. It's important."

"Wonderful," he enthused. "When?"

"Today at noon."

The principal hesitated, torn between his desire to push me toward modern education practice and his determination to uphold correct procedure.

"This happens only once," I said while he chewed his lip. "UBC today. 12:30."

"All right. All right," he sighed. "Leave their names with Ms. Ross. She'll cover your classes." I hurried down the hall and grabbed Phillip Brascia. "I'm taking you out of school for the rest of the day. Get Mike. Sophia. Dominic and Claudio. Meet me at my car. Ten minutes."

I ran to the audiovisual services room and checked out a two-reel tape recorder, extra bulbs and an extension cord, and put them in the trunk of my 1948 four-door Dodge Ram just as the kids arrived.

Two jumped in the front without questioning what was really going on. The others threw my lacrosse gear into the trunk with the AV equipment, and climbed in the back seat. We were four blocks away before Claudio asked, "Hey, where we goin' anyhow?"

"UBC for a great lecture. You'll love it."

I sped across town as fast as I could, for two reasons: I wanted good seats in the lecture hall, and I did not want my students abandoning ship as we sailed deeper into the unknown west-side of the city. They were nervous just at the thought of visiting the university twenty miles from home turf. Sophia protested, "This is definitely unfair. I'm not dressed right. This trip is uncool."

I parked in the delivery zone behind Buchanan Hall and pressed the kids into carrying our taping equipment into the main amphitheatre. "Follow me," I hissed. "Don't say anything." They were trapped. "Make way, please," I called loudly. "Audio-vis." The crowd separated to let us through.

Down the steep aisle of the theatre, students sat shoulder to shoulder munching sandwiches and balancing coffee mugs. "Excuse us, please. Audio-vis." My kids were in shock, but they followed me down and down . . . down to the small flat floor at the bottom, flanked on three sides by high curving banks of seats crammed with university students. The high schoolers' shock had turned to terror by now, but they dumbly obeyed when I ordered, "Set it up here." Then, as instructed, they sat on the floor with their backs leaning against the wall, looking up at 350 bemused UBC students watching them. Sophia's face was crimson. I thought she might faint. Or die.

Fortunately, before anyone could bolt, the sound of applause filtered in from the outer hallway high above us, then spilled down over the packed rows as the hand-clapping swelled to announce the arrival of our esteemed visitor from a Russia which had perished fifty years earlier. The students who crowded the aisle somehow squeezed over once again, and we watched a balding professor descend, wearing an open tweed jacket over a sweater-vest designed to hide a tummy that had never suffered through a Russian winter. He led a slower-moving, older man down to the microphone. The clapping was polite but unanimous, and it continued until the older gentleman was seated.

The professor, whom I took to be head of the History Department, looked pleased with the proceedings. He took his time, in a gentle sort of way, as if watching over some national treasure. The audience picked up on this spirit, and with quiet respect waited as the elderly man approached the lectern. None of us knew what to expect. I glanced at my kids and found them as transfixed as the rest of the audience — we were being introduced not just to a head of state but to a link to those mysterious and terrifying "ten days which shook the world"; to the last elected prime minister of what was today the most feared country on earth, a fear that had been ensured by the Cold War, McCarthyism, the Cuban missile crisis and a hundred Hollywood spy films.

Alexander Kerensky stood calmly at the microphone, examining the audience and their motley dress. He stood tall in a suit tailored to his lean form so that not a wrinkle showed. It was light-gray, and from the breast pocket peeked an electric-blue silk handkerchief. His tie was the same bright color, and he stood proudly under a full head of kinky, white hair.

"Ladies and gentlemen of the faculty, and my dear friends . . . the students," he began in a sincere voice. His charming accent rumbled out over the hushed crowd. It was soft, not overpowering enough to distract . . . but there were enough Slavic notes to remind us of his birthplace as he carefully began to describe the social and political elements that laid the foundation for the Czar's downfall. Over the next hour, he told of Nicholas II answering the pleas from France and Britain to open an eastern front in order to relieve the pressure of the swift German and Austrian advances toward Paris. He told of titanic battles like Tannenberg, where 92,000 poorly equipped peasants were captured as the Czar's army was ensnared by their Prussian foe. He took us onto the battlefield, describing how three soldiers would chase a fourth comrade who carried their only rifle. When he fell — dead or wounded — one of the others would pick up the gun and carry on. "They picked up the rifle, not the man," he emphasized.

Bitterly, he recounted the lack of supplies for the troops — no boots, little food, few blankets, the absence of reliable transportation — where whole trains would be lost by their turncoat crews; and the infiltration of the army by "saboteurs and traitors!" He shouted these labels like curses, and there were flecks of saliva at the corners of his mouth.

Kerensky gripped the lectern with both hands now. Intensity fired his eloquence. He perspired freely and shouted out his vision for retaking his homeland from the Bolsheviki and the socialist hordes. And by God, we were ready to sign up. We'd march into Leningrad and give the citizens back St. Petersburg . . .

But then an insistent bell forced us all to return to 1968 . . . and Kerensky slumped from his exertion. He looked up gratefully as the crowd in the amphitheatre stood to applaud this man who had stepped out of their history books on that sunny autumn afternoon.

And then the students — his "dear friends" — slipped out of the auditorium and off to class. My kids packed up our equipment while I watched, wondering whether I would have a chance to thank this man for sharing the ghosts of his past. I silently calculated Kerensky's age at eighty-seven and was surprised: he was so committed; so convincing; so passionate.

The department head, whose tweed jacket was just like mine, thanked Kerensky once again, looked around the empty hall, then spoke to me in a collegial way, "Will you be able to take His Excellency back to the Faculty Club? I have a class."

"Of course," I replied quickly. "Not a problem."

Kerensky took my arm as we climbed the steep aisle up to the exit. The kids came behind carrying the equipment, and were un-characteristically attentive as we made our way out the back of Buchanan to the delivery zone. I gave Claudio a gesture with my head and he hurried to take the parking ticket from the windshield before opening the door on the passenger side and holding it politely for our fragile guest. With the AV equipment stowed, five teenagers climbed into the back seat without complaint.

As we drove slowly to the nearby Faculty Club, Kerensky perked up enough to look over his shoulder, inviting the kids to introduce themselves. It was like taking a famous grandfather for a Sunday drive. The kids were perfect, and I couldn't believe it when he asked them in for cookies and tea. He wanted to talk to them about school.

A little later, when Kerensky excused himself to retire to his guest-room at the Faculty Club for a nap, I drove the kids back to Little Italy. They seemed different somehow. Quieter, of course . . . but something else . . . Could it be, thoughtful? I hoped so, but I had thoughts of my own now. Kerensky had grasped my elbow as we left, inviting me back for dinner, and I wondered if my only suit had been pressed recently. But I didn't worry about it that much. I was going. No matter what.

That evening, Kerensky sat waiting for me at a corner table. He looked relaxed in a dark tailored suit, the soft glow of candlelight gracing his rested face. He was happy to answer my questions. I showed him Russian currency from his time in power, and he pored over each bill pointing out its highlights: the name of a Treasury Minister who had no idea where the Treasury was, or whether it was still in Menshevik hands; the etching of a steam train, which like all the others was probably never on time; war bonds, purchased by anxious aristocrats, still containing the picture of the sad-eyed Czar. I thought Kerensky might cry.

"They shot him like a dog in the basement at Ekaterinburg. With his family. All of them gone. And the other Romanovs . . . at Alapayevsk . . . thrown down an abandoned mine shaft. Terrible."

We ate quietly for a while. "Only Grand Duchess Marie made it out," he began again. "She was a nurse at the front . . . treating the common soldier, not the officers. She had recently married, and had new papers for 'Citizeness Marie Putiatin'. She got out through Romania and I met her later in Paris . . . Barely made it myself."

I had enough courage now to ask about his last-minute escape from Petrograd just before the capture of the Winter Palace, and he painted a wild scene in the capital that earth-shaking night. "Mobs were everywhere . . . some looking for me. I had not enough time to burn my papers. It was all over for me . . . but Mr. Davis, from the US Embassy, he sent me a limousine with a chauffeur and I lay on the back floor . . . not like a president, but like a cringing coward with a car-rug thrown over me." He shook his head at the memory. "There were two American flags snapping in the wind as we drove to the west searching for the Cossacks. They were very little flags on the front fenders, but I think they saved me."

Kerensky ranged through his favorite topics again, in no particular order. His fervor rose and fell with his energy until at length, the wine, or the lateness of the hour, or his eighty-seven years took over, and the meeting between the peasant school teacher from Vancouver and the last elected prime minister of Russia was done. He died two years later in New York, where he was an historical consultant. I hoped that Kerensky knew somehow that, seventy years after the events he had regaled us with that afternoon, Bolshevism had failed, Leningrad was gone, and St. Petersburg had been reborn.

POSTSCRIPT

After the armistice for World War I, hundreds of thousands of men and women struggled home to begin again. Here is what happened to a few of them.

ANNA TIMIRYOVA

Anna Timiryova was a Russian poetess, the daughter of composer Vasily Safonov. At age nineteen she married Sergey Timiryov, a naval officer and friend of Admiral Alexander Kolchak.

By 1917 Anna was openly Kolchak's mistress. Upon Kolchak's arrest and imprisonment in Irkutsk, she requested that she be allowed to join him — the man she loved — in prison. "Arrest me. I cannot live without him." Her request was granted by the Communist government, and she was imprisoned in Irkutsk until October 1920, when Kolchak was executed.

Anna then requested that she be allowed to rejoin her first husband in Harbin, but was refused and punished further with a series of six charges over several years of "having connections with foreigners and former White officers" and of "concealment of the past."

She spent the next forty-eight years in and out of work camps until Khrushchev granted her freedom when she reached seventy years of age. She died in Moscow in 1975.

KERENSKY

Alexander Kerensky was the last prime minister of monarchical Russia before the October Revolution. He narrowly escaped capture as the Winter Palace was taken and the whole Czarist organization collapsed.

Kerensky fled Petrograd to live in Paris and London before moving to New York and then to Stanford University as Professor Emeritus. He worked with the Hoover Collection of Russian memorabilia.

He died in New York in June of 1970 and was finally buried in London at Putney Vale's non-denominational cemetery because neither Russia nor the Orthodox Church would have him.

LENIN

Following the Red and White Civil War, Vladimir Lenin became premier of the Soviet Union.

Born in Simbirsk, he attended a boys secondary school whose headmaster, ironically, was Alexander Kerensky's father. After the execution of his brother in 1887, Lenin studied leftist revolutionary politics while at Kazan University and became a lawyer as well as a radical politician.

Arrested for sedition, he was exiled to Siberia for three years, after which time he fled to western Europe until he was smuggled back to Petrograd in time to orchestrate the October Revolution in 1917.

After leading the Russian Social Democratic Labor Party, he became chairman of the Communist Party of the Soviet Union, which some say acted as a "single-party dictatorship."

Lenin died from a stroke on January 21, 1924 at age fifty-three. He is considered to be one of the most influential figures of the twentieth century.

SYROVY

Jan Syrovy was Czechoslovakia's first general, and after leading his 'Lost Legion' home via Vladivostok by ship around the Cape of Good Hope he became chief of staff for the Czech army. In this position he helped develop the Czechoslovak Air Force and moved military materiel away from Nazi Germany.

As the Munich Agreement was signed, Syrovy was appointed prime minister and minister of national defence. He warned his Czech countrymen in 1938 that "We stand alone."

Following World War II, the Communist government charged Syrovy with "collaboration" and sentenced him to twenty years in prison under severe conditions. He was released in 1960, with no pension, and was forbidden to work. He was allowed to take a job only as a night watchman, his sole means of support until his death in 1970.

KECHEK

Peter Stanislav Kechek (Czech spelling Cecek) maintained his rank as major general in the new Czech Republic's army before leaving to study at L'Ecole de guerre in France until 1923. He was then named commander of the Fifth Infantry Division.

He died in 1930 at the age of forty-three, following surgery as a result of lingering wounds from World War I.

GAIDA

Following the end of World War I and his misadventure in an attempted coup against the White forces in Vladivostok under General Rozanov, General Rad Gaida joined Generals Deniken and Wrangel to battle unsuccessfully against Lenin.

There were further attempts at political action but all was swept aside when Germany reclaimed Czechoslovakia in 1938. Gaida moved to Spain to fight on the side of fascism, thus losing all credibility with many Czechs, including President Tomas Masaryk.

During World War II, Gaida helped escaping army officers and hid the underground activities of his son. Gaida was investigated by the Gestapo but avoided imprisonment until May 12,1945 when the NKVD, Russia's secret police, arrested him. He was charged with the "propagation of Fascism and Nazism," then jailed under conditions harsh enough that he lost his eyesight. Sentenced to two years, he was released early, but died penniless and forgotten a short time later.

GRAVES

Major General William Graves suffered vicious and unwarranted criticism from the American press, fed by complaints from the Western Allies, for his refusal to interfere in Russia's Civil War.

The French, British and Japanese forces certainly had ambitions beyond protecting the citizenry during a bitter civil war. The Americans were there in smaller numbers and were dedicated to guarding the Trans-Siberian Railroad to guarantee the safe passage of troops — particularly more than 72,000 Czech Legionnaires. Despite savage incidents from Japanese, Bolshevik and Cossack forces, they stood their ground and completed their job successfully.

The American president was challenged by critics at the Paris Peace Conference who labeled General Graves "an obstinate, difficult and unacceptable commander because he wouldn't deviate."

President Wilson responded with a smile and an observation: "I suppose it is the same old story. Men often get the reputation of being stubborn merely because they are everlastingly right."

More recently, Columbia University historian Benson Bobrick, on the subject of Graves in Siberia, has concluded that: "In the whole sad debacle, he may have been the only honorable man there."

William Graves was a Texan born in Mount Calm to a Baptist minister father. He died at age seventy-five on February 20, 1940 and became a West Point model exemplifying the characteristics and actions that become an apolitical soldier-diplomat.

SEMYONOV

Ataman Semyonov was born a Cossack in the Lake Baikal region. He joined the Imperial Russian army in 1908, and at the end of World War I he supported Admiral Kolchak during the Red and White Civil War.

He displayed an alarming capacity for cruelty and savagery which did not escape the notice of General William Graves. At the end of civil war hostilities, Semyonov sailed to Vancouver from Tokyo and then entered the United States as a celebrity. General Graves quickly informed the War Department of Semyonov's true character as a psychotic murderer, and the Cossack chieftain was immediately deported.

General Wrangel, Commander of the White Guard, described Semyonov in part as: "An exemplary soldier, especially courageous when under the eye of his superiors. He knew how to make himself popular with Cossacks and officers alike, but he had his weaknesses in a love of intrigue and indifference to the means by which he achieved his ends. Though capable and ingenious, he was uneducated, so that his outlook was narrow. I have never been able to understand how he came to play a leading role."

Semyonov had a pragmatic pact with Kolchak who "arranged" a grand theft of thirteen cases of bullion and five leather sacks of platinum and banknotes from the Treasury Train under Kolchak's command at Nizhne Udinsk. The bullion and platinum were never recovered.

The final note was struck when the Soviet Army captured Semyonov in Manchuria and sentenced him to death by hanging on August 29, 1946. This execution marked the end of an era.

GRAND DUCHESS MARIE OF RUSSIA

Through her loyalty to Russia and the common Russian citizen, Grand Duchess Marie escaped Lenin's relentless extermination of the Romanov family.

Lenin wanted no trace left that could act as a symbol for the Czar's memory, around which opposition could rally, but he could not find Marie. She was a nurse on the front lines, and when she married Prince Sergei Putiatin, one of the palace guards, she carried credentials that read "Citizeness Marie Putiatin."

The escape with her husband at Orsha, near Ukraine's border, was made possible by a German officer recovering from his wounds. Then a Canadian, Colonel Harold Boyle, arranged a private train in Odessa bound for Budapest and safe haven from her cousin Queen Marie of Romania.

Marie next went to Paris and London, opening fashion and perfume businesses financed by her jewels smuggled out of Russia.

She lived in San Francisco's Russian Hill district until the United States officially recognized the Soviet Union as a member of the United Nations. In denunciation of this act, Marie left for Argentina.

Marie died in Germany while visiting her brother in 1958, and the world lost the final link with the last Czar of Russia.

Two things have altered not,
since first the world began.
The beauty of this wild green earth
and the bravery of man.

Cameron Wilson
1889–1918

Dr. Ted Hunt is a third generation Vancouverite whose grandfathers came to Canada from Britain for the Gold Rush of 1898. He earned degrees in History and Kinesiology at the University of BC, where he captained the Thunderbird rugby team, and became an honoured member of the BC Sports Hall of Fame for his days with the BC Lions, the Vancouver Burrards and the Canadian National Ski Team.

At the University of Washington, he studied for an advanced degree in History and was fortunate enough to interview Alexander Kerensky, Dr. Lister Rogers and Czech President Vaclav Havel.

Returning to BC with his wife Helen and daughter Shelley, Ted was a high school teacher and administrator before becoming a published author specializing in dramatized history. He has also written two books about golf: *Ben Hogan's Magical Device* and *Ben Hogan's Short Game Simplified*, both published by Skyhorse Publishing in New York.

Ted and Helen live in Vancouver, near their daughter, her husband and their son Wesley.

The author can be contacted with comments or questions and to arrange speaking engagements at **tedhunt@shaw.ca**

His website is **www.tedhunt.org**